GENDER AND PARENTHOOD

GENDER AND PARENTHOOD

BIOLOGICAL AND SOCIAL SCIENTIFIC PERSPECTIVES

Edited by
W. Bradford Wilcox and Kathleen Kovner Kline

COLUMBIA UNIVERSITY PRESS   NEW YORK

COLUMBIA UNIVERSITY PRESS
Publishers Since 1893
New York Chichester, West Sussex
cup.columbia.edu
Copyright © 2013 Columbia University Press

Library of Congress Cataloging-in-Publication Data
Gender and parenthood : biological and social scientific perspectives / edited by
W. Bradford Wilcox and Kathleen Kovner Kline.
    pages cm
Includes bibliographical references and index.
ISBN 978-0-231-16068-1 (hbk. : alk. paper)—
ISBN 978-0-231-16069-8 (pbk. : alk. paper)—ISBN 978-0-231-53097-2 (ebk.)
1. Parenthood. 2. Sex role. 3. Parent and child. 4. Husband and wife. I. Wilcox,
William Bradford, 1970–. II. Kline, Kathleen Kovner.

HQ755.8.G463 2013
306.874—dc23

2012039624

CONTENTS

ACKNOWLEDGMENTS

THE EDITORS WISH TO ACKNOWLEDGE the generous financial support of the Administration for Children and Family Services at the U.S. Department of Health and Human Services that funded the project "Gendered Parenting and Its Implications for Child Well-being and Couple Relationships" (grant no. 90XP0196/01), which led to this book. This book is based on a conference that was held at the University of Virginia in the fall of 2008 and that was sponsored by the Institute for American Values in New York City. We are also grateful to David Blankenhorn, Skip Burzumato, David Lapp, Elizabeth Marquardt, and Charity Navarrete for their practical help and substantive advice in moving this book forward. Finally, Sam Richardson played an invaluable role in editing the manuscript.

GENDER AND PARENTHOOD

INTRODUCTION

W. Bradford Wilcox and Kathleen Kovner Kline

"BABIES CHANGE EVERYTHING." It is a refrain often heard by anyone contemplating becoming a parent. From sleep disruption to loss of free time, from financial worries to discipline conundrums, couples are frequently warned that after a baby life will never be the same again. Yet despite how much parenthood can feel like a leap into the unknown, millions of us continue to make that leap, every year. Some of us long for a warm bundle to hold against our chests, a smiling gaze to rivet us, a silly toddler to chase and buy toys for and make a fuss over at the holidays. Others imagine someone to throw a ball with, to tussle with on the floor, to teach life lessons, or pass on a bit of our legacy into the future. We know, all too well, what an impact we parents will have on our children. But what is less well known is how our children will change *us*, as mothers and fathers—even at the biological level.

Today, natural scientists and social scientists are learning a great deal about how babies change their parents and how mothers and fathers are changed in both similar and different ways. Animal studies of pair-bonding mammals are yielding fascinating insights into how fathers as well as mothers experience changes at the biochemical level, beginning even before the offspring is born. Meanwhile, social scientists are learning how parental investments in areas such as money, time, discipline, and play are both similar and different for fathers and mothers. It turns out that, for men and for women, parenthood changes both our bodies and our lives. Parenthood quite literally changes us from the inside out.

Why is this the moment to share and reflect on these findings? It is perhaps now more confusing and more daunting than ever to be a parent. In recent decades, profound changes have upended accepted notions of mothering and fathering, providing new opportunities but also often leaving new mothers and fathers feeling as though they must figure out how to do their parenting jobs largely on their own.

Over the second half of the twentieth century, the United States saw widespread changes in women's labor force participation, in the time that fathers and mothers devote to their children, and in public attitudes toward the public and private roles of men and women.[1] In an effort to get more schooling, get established in a job, and find the right partner, many young men and women in the United States are taking more time to get married and to have their first child. Men and women are marrying on average about five years later than they did in 1970. The age at which a woman has her first child rose from about twenty-one in 1970 to twenty-five in 2006.[2] Later childbearing is especially true for college-educated women. Their average age at the birth of their first child is more than thirty.

Parenthood has also become a more intense and expensive experience. Today's parents devote more time and money to the parenting enterprise than did earlier generations. In the United States, it is estimated that residential mothers and fathers now spend 50 percent more time with their children than they did in 1975. According to 2008 figures from the U.S. Department of Agriculture, the average family spends $221,190 on each child, up from $183,509 in 1960.[3] At the same time, as parenthood is starting later, people are having smaller families, and people are living longer, the intense experience of being a parent of children in the home now covers a smaller portion of the adult life course than it once did.

Parenthood can also be more isolating than it used to be. Recent increases in out-of-wedlock childbearing, cohabitation, and divorce make men and women much more likely to bear or rear children outside of marriage and to raise them alone. The retreat from marriage has been especially common among Americans without a college degree. One study found that more than 42 percent of children of less-educated women spend some time outside of a stable, married family in their first fourteen years of life, compared to just 19 percent of children born to college-educated women.[4] While most single parents have less help with the demanding tasks of child-rearing, even married parents today have less help from extended family and their community than did parents in previous eras.

These changes in parenthood have made some aspects of the contemporary transition to parenthood especially daunting. For many of us, there is no longer a shared script when it comes to marriage, work and family, and home life. The sacrifices that come with parenthood can be mystifying for adults who may have spent a decade or more living outside of a family and have grown accustomed to an adult-centered lifestyle. Some couples feel that the arrival of a baby turns a marriage upside down. They discover that nothing stresses even a good relationship like the round-the-clock needs of a fussy infant.[5] Yet despite the challenges, parenthood remains one of the most transformative and meaningful events in our lives. Our children ground us and enliven us. They give us joy and satisfactions that we cannot imagine having lived without.

This book grows out of an academic conference on gender and parenthood involving seventeen scholars from the natural and social sciences at the University of Virginia in the fall of 2008. It seeks to provide scholars, journalists, policymakers, civic and religious leaders, and the public with a more well-rounded portrait of parenthood in America.

We edited this book because we believe that men and women will be intrigued by new evidence about the biological and social changes that parenthood brings about. We also suspect that learning about these findings will help make the transition to parenthood a happier one for men, women, and couples. Recent research suggests that parents can find the tests of parenthood more enjoyable when they find meaning in them and when they realize they are not alone.[6] We aim to help men and women better navigate the critical transition to parenthood by giving them a richer portrait of the changes, challenges, and opportunities that parenthood presents.

NATURAL AND SOCIAL SCIENTIFIC PERSPECTIVES ON GENDER AND PARENTHOOD

The volume begins by examining the evolutionary and biological underpinnings of parenthood before moving on to consider, from a social scientific perspective, how parenthood is and is not gendered, both in the United States and around the globe. What makes many of us want to be parents? Even if we are hesitant about parenthood, what aspects of our biology help us step up to the plate when the occasion arises? What happens to our brains and bodies when women become mothers and men become fathers? Are the stakes the same for each sex, or are they different? Why, across history and cultures, are women typically more involved in childcare? Why are some fathers very involved in their children's lives and others not at all? Finally, how do mothers and fathers approach parenthood in similar ways, and how do they approach parenthood in different ways, both in the United States and in non-Western cultures?

We are familiar with the most visible and dramatic ways in which pregnancy changes a woman's body—from increases in appetite to swelling abdomens. But today, science is probing ever more deeply into the mothering experience. From studies of mammals and of human mothers, researchers are learning just how profoundly motherhood changes women from the inside out. One surprising insight from this research that emerges in the chapter by psychologists Kelly G. Lambert and Catherine L. Franssen is that for humans and other mammals, the most critical reproductive organ just might be the brain.

In their chapter "The Dynamic Nature of the Parental Brain," Lambert and Franssen note that for mammalian mothers, caring for their babies requires focused attention and an increased awareness of the environment. Mothers must guard their young against predators and other threats. They must also feed them, which makes finding food sources and maintaining food stores a constant challenge. To successfully raise their young, mammalian moms require the cognitive capacity not only to solve problems but to solve multiple problems at the same time—what some now refer to as "multitasking."

To learn more about how motherhood builds the brains of female mammals, Lambert and her colleagues developed a series of maze experiments with rodents. These tests compared the cognitive abilities of rodents who had been mothers at least twice—some call them "multi-moms"—with first-time mothers and with females who had never had a litter. Her research showed that the mother rats learned more efficiently and retained their knowledge longer. These multitasking mothers had to prioritize tasks, tune out distractions, solve problems, make decisions, and change strategies when required. In one study in which the rats had to use their memories as well as their social awareness in a competition to find food, the multi-moms bested the competition 60 percent of the time, compared to 33 percent of the time for first-time moms and just 7 percent for the never-moms. The multi-moms triumphed too in studies of physical agility, balance, coordination, and strength.

Lambert and Franssen caution that it is difficult to say whether the brain boost seen in mother rats is mostly a product of the nurturing experience, or the biochemicals stimulated by the experience, or both. Whatever the exact causes, this research suggests that motherhood may boost the cognitive capacity of women in important and surprising ways, and with implications for their intellectual performance both in and outside the home.

Until recently, we might not have had reason to think that men experience much in the way of biological changes when they become fathers.

But researchers are now finding that in mammalian species in which both fathers and mothers care for their young, fathers too encounter physiological changes. Fathers also are changed quite literally from the inside out.

The male hormone that people are most familiar with is testosterone. A growing body of work suggests that men typically experience a drop in testosterone after becoming fathers, especially if they are living with the mother of their offspring. But the chapter by Charles T. Snowdon, a psychologist and zoologist, indicates that mammalian fathers who cooperatively parent with the mother of their children experience far more than just a drop in testosterone.

In his chapter "Family Life and Infant Care," Snowdon notes that for mammalian fathers at least two processes seem to be at work during and after the birth of their offspring. Some biological changes seen in fathers seem to come from exposure to the mother of their offspring. But others seem to come from the active experience of caring for their offspring. Specifically, it now appears that first-time fathers begin experiencing hormonal changes *before* the birth of their offspring. Researchers speculate that these changes occur perhaps in reaction to scents emitted from the expecting partners and from affectionate interaction with the partner herself. For example, marmoset fathers showed increased prolactin, cortisol, estrogen, and testosterone during the course of their mate's pregnancy. Marmoset fathers even gained weight during the pregnancy, apparently in preparation for the energy demands that helping to care for the new infant would require.

But the bulk of the biological changes seen in fathers appear to come after the birth, from their experience of actively caring for their young. In his studies of tamarin and marmoset males, Snowdon found that experienced fathers, like mothers, demonstrate enhanced boldness, food-finding abilities, and problem-solving. When presented with a needy pup, males with caregiving experience showed the greatest activation of the problem-solving and memory centers of the brain. He also found that marmoset males who were fathers were less likely to show interest in unfamiliar, ovulating female marmosets than males who were not fathers.

When Snowdon and his colleagues went deeper, they discovered that the prefrontal cortex of experienced marmoset fathers shows both changes in cell structure and an increase in the neuroreceptors for vasopressin. This hormone, along with oxytocin and prolactin, is associated with affiliation. Thus, at the biological level, involved fatherhood seems also to improve male mammals' cognitive capacity, and to focus mammalian dads on their responsibilities to their young, even making them less distracted by available

females ambling by. It will be interesting to see if future research can repli-
cate these results among human beings.

We are learning more and more about the biology of parenthood and its
behavioral expression in nonhuman mammals. But what about humans?

For insights, we can turn to the fields of evolutionary psychology and
cross-cultural anthropology. One of the primary tenets of evolutionary
theory is that the species that survive are the ones that are able to adapt
to their environment. Evolutionary success is not based on whether you
survive—rather, success is measured by whether you are able to produce
offspring who survive, reproduce, and carry your genes into future generations. Survival of one's offspring is in the interest of both the mother and
the father, but their interests are not identical, as psychologists David F.
Bjorklund and Ashley C. Jordan note in their chapter "Human Parenting
from an Evolutionary Perspective."

Drawing on the parental investment theory of biologist Robert Trivers,
they suggest that over time males and females develop different psychologies related to their distinctive investments in mating and parenting, with
men oriented more toward succeeding in mating and women oriented more
toward succeeding in parenting. Because fathers are oriented more toward
mating, women are more likely to demand "love and commitment, dependability, and emotional stability" before engaging in sexual relations with a
man; by doing so they build on men's interest in mating to ensure "that they
and their offspring will continue receiving resources necessary for survival."

Bjorklund and Jordan's chapter also suggests that men and women's
distinctive biological endowments and psychological orientations, which
evolved over time in connection with their distinctive reproductive strategies,
also translate into different strengths when it comes to parenting. Fathers, for
instance, can translate their orientation toward "aggression, power, and dominance" into the protection of their daughters and—as a consequence—girls
who grow up with their fathers are more likely to delay sexual activity and
childbearing. Mothers, in turn, can translate their superior ability "to regulate [their] emotions" to establish a strong attachment with their children; in
turn, this attachment provides their children with a secure emotional base
for navigating the emotional and social challenges of life.

Bjorklund and Jordan are also careful to point out that particular sociocultural conditions are more likely to favor higher levels of paternal *and*
maternal investment. For instance, men are more likely to invest in one
mate and in one set of children when they have a high degree of paternity
certainty, when a culture demands monogamy of them, and when their

paternal investment increases the likelihood of their offspring's survival. Judging by their work, some aspects of contemporary social life favor high parental investments, while others do not.

Psychologist Marc H. Bornstein also stresses the importance of thinking carefully about how biology and the social environment both coproduce the experience of parenthood for men and women, as well as the development of gender identities among boys and girls; but he stresses the importance of social environment more than do Bjorklund and Jordan. Thus, even though behavioral gender differences result "from genetically, anatomically, or hormonally influenced predispositions" these differences are also shaped by the social environment in which the child develops.

In other words, socialization, not just biology, also matters in the development of gendered identities for boys and girls, mothers and fathers. Studies show, for instance, that adults are more likely to treat the same infant differently, depending on whether they think they are interacting with a boy or a girl. "Boys are described as *big* and *strong* and are *bounced* and *handled* more physically than girls who are described as *pretty* and *sweet* and are handled more *gently*." This kind of treatment, in turn, reinforces the development of distinctively gendered identities among males and females over the life course.

Nevertheless, even though different societies treat gender in quite varied ways, what is a virtual human universal is that women tend to invest more in parenting—especially of infants and toddlers—than men. In Bornstein's words, "in almost all species and regions of the world, across a wide diversity of subsistence activities and social ideologies, observational studies indicate more maternal than paternal investment." At the same time, as Western forms of schooling and popular culture become more influential in societies around the world, gender differences in parenting are in many societies becoming less salient. Thus, one of the questions Bornstein's chapter leaves the reader with is this: How do global shifts toward more egalitarian gender roles interact with "genetically, anatomically, or hormonally influenced predispositions" that tend to push males and females in somewhat different directions as parents?

In his chapter "Gender Differences and Similarities in Parental Behavior," psychologist Ross D. Parke takes up a related question: How do mothers and fathers parent in similar and different fashions in today's world? Focusing largely on studies from the United States, Parke concludes that there are many similarities in the ways in which mothers and fathers approach parenting—and for a range of social, cultural, *and* biological reasons. He points out that both mothers and fathers can provide children with the attention, affection, discipline, and socialization they require to thrive. And in many contemporary families, both mothers and fathers supply their children with the ingredients they need to thrive.

Take the care of infants—an arena of parenting that has traditionally been dominated by mothers. Parke and his colleagues have conducted studies that found that "mothers and fathers showed patterns of striking similarity" when it came to interacting with their newborns; "they touched, looked [at], vocalized, rocked and kissed their newborns equally" in this research. Parke also found that fathers can be as responsive to infants' behaviors and verbal cues as mothers. After assessing his own research and the larger body of literature on this topic, Parke concludes that "both men and women seem to be equally competent caregivers and exhibit high degrees of similarity as caregivers."[7]

At the same time, Parke also acknowledges that, even in relatively egalitarian societies such as the United States, parenting remains gendered in important respects. Mothers are markedly more engaged, more available, and more responsible for their children than are fathers in countries such as Australia, France, Japan, and the United States. The style of parenthood is also gendered. With infants and toddlers, for instance, fathers' "hallmark style of interaction is physical play that is characterized by arousal, excitement, and unpredictability" whereas mothers are more likely to attend to infants and toddlers' needs for feeding, diapering, and emotional security.

And while Parke stresses the social and cultural factors that are implicated in these gender differences, he also thinks that biology helps to explain these differences. Here, he believes that research on primates is instructive: "Biological factors cannot be ignored in light of the fact that male monkeys show the same rough-and-tumble physical style of play as American human fathers and infant male monkeys tend to respond more positively to bids for rough-and-tumble play than females." In general, then, Parke paints a complex portrait of contemporary parenthood that suggests many areas of overlap between fathers and mothers, some areas of difference, and a range of biosocial reasons that help to account for the similarities and differences we now find among today's mothers and fathers.

As organic systems of care, we know that families are not static organizations. They evolve and change over time in the ways in which they care for their members. Ayelet Talmi, in her chapter "Gender and Parenting Across the Family Life Cycle," describes the ways in which mothers and fathers respond to changing developmental needs of children and other household members, demographic forces, historical trends, and economic circumstances.

Incorporating a brief look at economic and demographic perspectives, Talmi proceeds to a closer examination of the family life course as it moves from couple formation, the transition to parenthood, the care of young and school-aged children, through meeting the needs of adolescents, the launching of young adults, to the later stages of retirement, caring for elders, and establishing reciprocal relationships of care and support with adult children. She notes that at each stage, factors internal to the family, such as the birth of a new child, or the developmental needs of a particular age, work in tandem with external factors such as employment options, or historical events to "drive renegotiation of roles and responsibilities and alter expectations regarding partner contributions."

At each stage, mothers and fathers consider child-rearing needs, partner suitability to provide certain types of care, partner preferences, and economic realities as they decide how to divide domestic and paid labor. Gender similarities and differences appear more or less prominent at different family life stages. In addition to married heterosexual parents, Talmi considers how these issues are managed by single parents, same-sex parents, and parents who remarry. Talmi argues that the dynamic needs of the family, its internal constellation, and its external context shape the way in which parents orchestrate the care of its members throughout the family life course.

IMPLICATIONS FOR CHILDREN, COUPLES, AND FAMILIES

The second half of this volume takes up the significance of gender and parenthood for children, couples, and families. We consider questions such as the following: What aspects of parental care are essential to the welfare of children? Do gender differences matter to the successful development of children? How do women wish to combine work and family life in today's society? How does parenthood affect relationship quality among contemporary couples? And, what lessons can single parents learn from the literature on gender and parenthood? Once again, our contributors address these questions with an eye on both nature and nurture, and with an appreciation for the ways in which mothers and fathers experience parenthood in both similar and different ways.

In their chapter "Essential Elements of the Caretaking Crucible," psychiatrists Kathleen Kovner Kline and Brian Stafford reflect on the crucial role the biological and social environments that encapsulate babies play in fostering optimal early childhood development. Starting with the development of the fetus in utero, Kline and Stafford note that the "structural development of the brain is completed largely before birth" and point out that fetal mental development is closely tied to biological factors (such as maternal nutrition) and social factors (social support) that mothers experience during pregnancy. They then go on to outline the ways in which a young child's optimal neurological and emotional development depends on the child successfully attaching to at least one caregiver and being raised in a social environment minimizing such risks as single parenthood, low maternal education, and stressful life events. Throughout their chapter, they are careful to specify the ways in which biological and social factors interact, for better and worse, to influence the development of children both in utero and in the outside world.

Overall, then, Kline and Stafford argue that the "caretaking crucible" that surrounds a baby before and after birth can greatly affect the child's intellectual, emotional, and behavioral development, and for both biological and social reasons. They also acknowledge that their chapter focuses more on mothers both because "mothers have a biologically more intimate relationship with their offspring" and also because research on early attachment has focused more on mothers. Nevertheless, they think that fathers play an important role in the lives of young children, insofar as they make a genetic contribution to their children, they extend physical and emotional support to children and their mothers, and engage the "extended familial, social, institutional, and cultural systems that promote optimal child development." Thus, one take-away message from Kline and Stafford is that even though mothers and fathers make distinct contributions to young children, they both play important roles in establishing the proper "caretaking crucible" for the bearing and rearing of young children.

Psychologist Rob Palkovitz extends the focus of this section beyond early childhood in his chapter "Gendered Parenting's Implications for Children's Well-Being." His chapter offers conclusions that parallel many of those found in Parke's chapter, in large part because both scholars believe that mothers and fathers both bring many similar talents to the parenting enterprise, even as they typically retain some distinctive gendered orientations to that same enterprise. Specifically, Palkovitz argues that the most fundamental factors associated with good parenting—such as "positive affective climate, behavioral style, and relational synchrony"—are often found in both mothers and fathers; moreover, in his view these factors are more important than the distinctive factors associated with gendered parenting in fostering optimal child development outcomes.

Nevertheless, Palkovitz also concludes that children benefit from the distinctively maternal and paternal styles that mothers and fathers typically offer to their children. For instance, the literature suggests that fathers "play a particularly important role in stimulating children's openness to the world in exciting, surprising, destabilizing, and encouraging them to take risks and to stand up for themselves." He also notes that fathers play a key role in protecting the sexual and reproductive welfare of their daughters, insofar as "paternal absence has been cited by multiple scholars as the single greatest risk factor in teen pregnancy for girls."

Most provocatively, Palkovitz reports that there is some evidence that parents who exhibit traditional (father exhibits primarily masculine traits, mother exhibits primarily feminine traits) or androgynous (both parents exhibit masculine and feminine traits) parenting styles have children who are better adjusted than parents who exhibit nontraditional traits (where parents primarily exhibit the personality traits of the opposite sex). He concludes that parents should take into account these findings, while also understanding that their own needs for fulfillment and family justice are important. Thus, from Palkovitz's perspective, while parents should be aware of the ways in which children benefit from being exposed to traditionally sex-typed parenting styles, they also need to be attentive to the importance of creating a family context that is attractive and appealing to the parents as well.

In his chapter "Do Fathers Uniquely Matter for Adolescent Well-Being?" sociologist David J. Eggebeen also takes up the relative contributions of mothers and fathers to the welfare of adolescents and young adults. He analyzed data from the National Longitudinal Study of Adolescent Health (Add Health), a nationally-representative, longitudinal survey of more than 15,000 young persons in the United States, to determine the ways in which fathers offer contributions to their children that are additive, redundant, or unique in comparison to the contributions of mothers. He looked at a range of parental predictors—from parents' education to parent-child closeness—and their links to depression and delinquency among teenagers in the second wave of Add Health, as well as at depression, antisocial activity, and civic engagement among young adults in the third wave of Add Health. An estimated sixty potential relationships between these parental measures and these adolescent/young adult outcomes were explored in his chapter.

Eggebeen found that 42 percent of the relationships between parental inputs and children's outcomes were significant and additive. That is, in these cases *both* mothers and fathers appeared to make similar contributions in reducing the odds that their adolescents and young adults experienced depression and antisocial behavior, or in increasing the odds that their children were civicly engaged later in life. In another 12 percent of the cases, the parental contributions were redundant. That is, children appeared to benefit from the involvement, support, or education of at least one of their parents but the contributions of the second parent did not improve the child's outcomes as a teenager or young adult. Thus, in 54 percent of the associations between parental inputs and child outcomes, the contribution of one or both parents mattered for the welfare of the children in a way that does not seem to have been distinctively gendered. Accordingly, his study does provide some support for the notion that both mothers and fathers make important contributions to their children in ways that can often be similar.

But Eggebeen also found that 22 percent of the relationships between parental inputs and adolescents' outcomes were unique and statistically significant. (He found that 24 percent of the relationships between inputs and outcomes were not statistically significant.) This means that for slightly more than one-fifth of the outcomes, young persons benefited from the input of their father or mother, but not both. In particular, "fathers appear to especially make unique contributions to the well-being of their children through their human capital while mothers make unique contributions through their availability and closeness to their children." He concludes by suggesting that his research demonstrates that young persons living in intact families can benefit from the parental investments of both their mother and their father but "significant questions remain." In his view, what is not clear is if these patterns of gendered patterns of parental influence extend to cohabiting families, same-sex families, and other nontraditional families. More research is required to determine if fathers and mothers make contributions that are also additive, redundant, or unique in these nontraditional families that are similar or different from the types of parental contributions that are made in the intact, married families Eggebeen examined in his chapter.

Sociologists W. Bradford Wilcox and Jeffrey Dew explore the impact of gender on the division of parenting labor, family-work strategies, and marital quality among married couples with children in the contemporary United States. In their chapter "No One Best Way: Work-Family Strategies, the Gendered Division of Parenting, and the Contemporary Marriages of Mothers and Fathers," they argue that a broadly neotraditional set of arrangements now characterizes the lives of most married mothers and fathers in the United States. They are "neo" in the sense that fathers are doing much more childcare now than they did forty years ago; most mothers work, and most married parents endorse egalitarian gender role attitudes. But they are also "traditional" in the sense that mothers still do markedly more childcare than fathers, most mothers do not work full-time, and most married mothers indicate that they would prefer to work part-time or stay at home.

Take, for instance, the time that parents devote to their children. Mothers continue to take the lead when it comes to the amount of time parents invest in their children. In spite of dramatic increases in maternal labor force participation since the 1960s, mothers are investing more hours in parenting than did mothers a generation or two ago, and they continue to outpace fathers. Wilcox and Dew point out that the total time that mothers in married-couple families spent in the presence of their children rose 17 percent from 330 minutes in 1975 to 387 minutes in 2003. The total time that fathers spent in the presence of their children rose 240 percent from 73 minutes in 1976 to 248 minutes in 2003. The time that mothers devoted to one-on-one interaction with their children, or primary time, increased 17 percent from 81 minutes in 1975 to 95 minutes in 2003. Likewise, fathers' primary time tripled from 14 minutes in 1976 to 42 minutes in 2003. These trends illustrate the increasingly intense character of parenting in contemporary America, and the fact that parental investments of time in children continue to be gendered.

When it comes to work-family arrangements, Wilcox and Dew find that the vast majority of married couples with children have fathers who work full-time—91 percent in fact. By contrast, only 44 percent of married mothers worked full-time. Even more telling, only 18 percent of married mothers wished to work full-time. A plurality (46 percent) wished to work part-time, and 36 percent wished to be at home full-time. Finally, in examining the link between these patterns and the marital quality of contemporary women, they find that married mothers are happiest in their marriages when their work-family preferences are realized in practice.

Wilcox and Dew conclude by noting that no one ideal or pattern of behavior captures the organization of contemporary parents' work and family lives; nevertheless, "most parents—including most mothers—do not wish to pursue an egalitarian work-family strategy where both parents work full-time." In their view, this neotraditional "reality is often ignored by elite academics, journalists, and policymakers," something they hope to remedy in their chapter on gender, work, family, and marriage among contemporary U.S. couples.

Psychiatrist Scott Haltzman tackles similar themes in his chapter "The Effect of Gender-Based Parental Influences on Raising Children: The Impact on Couples' Relationships." He points out that the dramatic investments that fathers and mothers make in their children as they respond to what some scholars call the "parental emergency"—that is, a child's need for nurture, food, protection, socialization, and discipline—have important implications for their own marriage. The first is that women shift much of their relational attention away from their husband and their work, and toward their child(ren), whereas men tend to maintain their commitment to their work, in part because they see providership as a way of supporting their family. The second is that both parents typically take somewhat different approaches to parenthood, and often along gendered lines.

The divergent ways in which husbands and wives handle the transition to parenthood, and the parenting enterprise itself, can pose a real challenge to the quality of their married life. "Because a woman is less likely to identify herself with her job, and more likely to see her prime identity as wife or mother, she may feel a husband's commitment to his workplace as abandonment," notes Haltzman. Nevertheless, he maintains that couples need to work through these challenges, in large part because "research indicates the profound benefit of a child being raised with both parents."

How can this be done? First, he points out that the research indicates that couples who realize that the challenges they face adjusting to parenthood are common ones do better. Second, couples do better when they receive support from friends and family, for instance, with babysitting help that allows them to maintain time for couple-centered activities. Finally, Haltzman believes that efforts to educate couples about gender differences in parenting will be helpful in providing husbands and wives with a new appreciation of the unique contributions that they both make to the welfare of their children. Or, in Haltzman's words, "efforts should be made to educate society at large, and parents in particular, that gender differences in parents are real, and, rather than be extinguished or ignored, they should be embraced."

Of course, more and more children are growing up in homes without both of their parents; for instance, one recent study found that 25 percent of U.S. children in 2009 were living in a single-parent home.[8] In their chapter "Single Mothers Raising Children Without Fathers: Implications for Rearing Children with Male-Positive Attitudes," family scholars William Doherty and Shonda Craft point out that single-parent homes tend to be headed by mothers, that nonresidential fathers often lose regular contact with their children, and that, as a consequence, children often lose out on the benefits of being exposed to a positive, consistent male role model. Moreover, this deficit can lead children to develop negative attitudes about fathers and men, especially if mothers express critical comments about the children's own fathers and men more generally.

In light of these realities, Doherty and Craft counsel single mothers to take three steps to help them provide their children with male positive attitudes. First, they encourage single mothers whenever possible to speak positively to their children about their fathers. Second, they advise single mothers to do what they can to encourage their children's fathers to maintain a consistent, authoritative presence in their children's lives. Finally, they urge single mothers to identify and involve positive male role models for their children, especially when nonresidential fathers are not playing a constructive role in the lives of their children.

How is this to be done? Doherty and Craft conclude by suggesting that single mothers "seek out positive relationships with men at a faith community, at work, or in other venues. It is important to show children long–term, positive relationships with men that are not sexual and that do not end in breakups. And it is important to have boys involved with men they can emulate, particularly if their father is not in their lives." They also acknowledge that any effort to promote male positive attitudes in communities marked by high levels of fatherlessness and male irresponsibility must also include an acknowledgment of men's failures. Still, because they wish to break the patterns of male irresponsibility and gender distrust that are endemic in some communities, Doherty and Craft contend that it is essential that community leaders, policymakers, and practitioners initiate a dialogue with single mothers in these communities about how to "raise children who value and trust men."

Clearly, this introduction suggests that readers will encounter areas of agreement along with contrasting, sometimes conflicting viewpoints among the book's authors. These occasionally jarring differences in assumptions, claims, and tone reflect the varied patterns of analysis and viewpoints that emerge not only from different academic disciplines, but also from the personal perspectives of the authors themselves. Readers will also notice that while we have attempted to provide some exploration of the diversity of patterns of family life through history and across cultures, this discussion is by no means comprehensive. The reader must be ever cognizant of the varied ways mothers and fathers have balanced their need for economic and physical survival with their efforts to create and nurture the next generation in a particular cultural milieu. The history of gender and parenthood is a work in process, and readers should put the references, examples, and statistics cited in this book's chapters into their historical and cultural contexts, and carefully consider their relevance to the current era, particularly acknowledging the family workforce changes that have emerged in the United States in the wake of "Great Recession."

Overall, then, this book brings together a large body of natural and social scientific evidence that shows the manifold ways in which parenthood is a transformative event—biologically, socially, and psychologically—for both women *and* men. Moreover, the chapters found herein also indicate that mothers *and* fathers both play important roles in the biological, social, and emotional welfare of their children. In some respects, their roles are similar and at times even redundant, especially in relatively egalitarian societies such as the United States. But in other respects, the roles they play are unique, and in ways that suggest biology has a hand in the unique contributions that mothers and fathers play in the lives of their children. Moving forward, and given the dramatic shifts in family life and childbearing around the globe, it will be interesting to see how children and adults are affected, if at all, by the following social facts: more children are growing up apart from one of their biological parents and more adults are moving through the adult life course without having fathered or mothered a child.

NOTES

1. Hakim 2000; Bradbury and Katz 2005; Bianchi et al. 2007.
2. Matthews and Hamilton 2009.
3. Lino and Carlson 2009. These figures are adjusted in 2008 dollars.
4. Wilcox 2010.
5. Whitehead and Popenoe 2008.
6. Cowan et al. 1985; Dew and Wilcox 2011.
7. Parke 1996:10.
8. Wilcox 2010.

REFERENCES

Bianchi, Suzanne M., John P. Robinson, and Melissa A. Milkie. 2007. *Changing Rhythms of American Family Life*. New York: Russell Sage Foundation.

Bradbury, Katharine and Jane Katz. 2005. "Women's Rise: A Work in Progress." *Regional Review* 14:58–67.

Cowan, C. P., P. A. Cowan, G. Heming, E. Garrett, W. S. Coysh, H. Curtis-Boles, and A. J. Boles III. 1985. "Transitions to Parenthood: His, Hers, and Theirs." *Journal of Family Issues* 6(4):451–481.

Dew, Jeffrey and W. Bradford Wilcox. 2011. "If Momma Ain't Happy: Explaining Declines in Marital Satisfaction Among New Mothers." *Journal of Marriage and Family* 73(1):1–12.

Hakim, Catherine. 2000. *Work-Lifestyle Choices in the 21st Century: Preference Theory*. New York: Oxford University.

Lino, Mark and Andrea Carlson. 2009. "Expenditures on Children by Families, 2008." U.S. Department of Agriculture, Center for Nutrition Policy and Promotion. Miscellaneous Publication No. 1528–2008. Accessed April 1, 2010, www.cnpp. usda.gov/Publications/CRC/crc2008.pdf.

Matthews, T. J. and Brady E. Hamilton. 2009. "Delayed Childbearing: More Women Are Having Their First Child Later in Life." *NCHS Data Brief* 21. Hyattsville, MD: National Center for Health Statistics.

Parke, R. D. 1996. *Fatherhood*. Cambridge, MA: Harvard University.

Whitehead, Barbara Dafoe and David Popenoe. 2008. *The State of Our Unions*. New Brunswick, NJ: National Marriage Project, Rutgers University.

Wilcox, W. Bradford. 2010. "When Marriage Disappears: The Retreat from Marriage in Middle America." *The State of Our Unions*. Charlottesville, VA: National Marriage Project.

PART ONE

HOW AND WHY IS PARENTHOOD GENDERED?

1

THE DYNAMIC NATURE OF THE PARENTAL BRAIN

Kelly G. Lambert and Catherine L. Franssen

DURING THE BUILDUP to the 2008 presidential election, Beau Biden, son of Democratic vice-presidential candidate Joe Biden, gave a heartfelt introductory speech at the Democratic National Convention. He relayed how after the tragic death of his mother and sister in an automobile accident in 1972, his father, a newly elected senator, had refrained from his duties, stating, "Delaware can get another senator, but my boys can't get another father." Once Biden had resumed his work, he commuted to Washington every day (four hours round-trip) so that he could see his children every night.[1] The GOP similarly touted their vice presidential candidate's parental qualities; Sarah Palin was repeatedly introduced as a "mother of five." Soon after the announcement of Palin's being chosen to join the McCain ticket, she wrote the following brief note to her Alaskan constituents: "It is the honor of my life to represent you as your Governor, and over the next two months I will continue to do so. As the mother of five, I know how to multitask, and I will continue to promote the path of reform that we set out on together in the state of Alaska."[2]

These scenarios provide interesting observations about our nation's perceptions of parenting roles and their benefits to personal development. Palin's case reinforces the perception that being a mother enhances cognitive abilities such as multitasking. On the other hand, fatherhood is rarely touted as relevant experience for executive leadership roles; indeed, Biden's choice of paternal connection over career aspirations is powerful specifically because it is perceived as rather unique.

Of course, political and cultural perceptions of parenting change with the times. So let us consider more empirical evidence here. Are our national perceptions of gender-dependent styles of parenting (as discussed in other chapters in this book) accurate biologically? How does the experience of parenting influence the brains of mothers and fathers?

The complexity of our culture presents challenges in determining the fundamental similarities and differences in parental males and females, especially when investigating specific neurobiological effects. In response to these challenges, our lab has utilized rodent models to explore the neurobiological alterations that accompany parental responses. These models have provided fascinating clues about how pregnancy, lactation, and parental nurturing drastically alter the female brain and behavior. To understand more about the paternal response, we have studied a unique rodent that is monogamous and biparental, the California deer mouse (*Peromyscus californicus*). And this research program has revealed interesting data related to the potential impact of paternal experience on mammalian neurobiological responses. Before turning to our findings, however, let us set an appropriate evolutionary context as we consider the impact of parental responses on the subsequent emergence of the mammalian brain.

EVOLUTIONARY SIGNIFICANCE OF PARENTAL RESPONSES

According to Paul MacLean, one of the most accomplished neuroscientists of the twentieth century, parental responses—specifically, maternal responses—significantly guided the evolution of the mammalian brain. In fact, he suggests that the three behaviors that separated mammals from nonmammalian vertebrates all centered around maternal care, characterized by nursing, audiovocal communications (important for maintaining contact between mother and offspring), and play behavior (MacLean 1998). His book *The Triune Brain in Evolution* includes an entire chapter on a brain circuit (the thalamocingulate circuit) that he identifies as maintaining family-related functions (MacLean 1990). Further, he notes that the separation of the mother from her offspring could have fatal consequences and that the separation cry of the offspring, possibly representing the first case of mammalian vocalization, enabled the mother to locate the young mammal before it came to harm. According to MacLean, vocalizations provided a valuable dimension to social contact and led to the development of the complex social brain now observed in mammals, especially humans (MacLean 1990, 1998; Lambert 2003).

In an article entitled "Women: A More Balanced Brain," MacLean emphasizes the role of maternal responses in the evolution of the mammalian

FIGURE 1.1 An interpretation of MacLean's "triune brain," emphasizing the reptilian brain (hindbrain), the paleomammalian brain (limbic system), and the more recently evolved neo-mammalian brain (neocortex). Because Paul MacLean wrote extensively about the maternal-infant relationship, the brain is depicted in a maternal squirrel monkey, a species frequently used in his neuroethological research.

Source: Artwork by Jacqueline Berry; design by Kelly Lambert.

brain: "For more than 180 million years, the female has played the central role in mammalian evolution" (MacLean 1996:422). He argues that mothers directed the human species toward right-hand dominance as they held their offspring near their hearts so that the rhythmic beating would calm the baby. This response required the mothers to rely on their right hands to manipulate their environmental surroundings. Thus, holding or carrying the infant on the left side likely influenced the functional and anatomical expansion of the right hemisphere in women. This neuroanatomical expansion may have further contributed to a more *balanced* brain in the female. In fact, neuroimaging research has indicated increased *inter*hemispheric activity in women compared to men, who exhibited enhanced *intra*hemispheric activity (Azare et al. 1995). As observed in figure 1.1, as vertebrates evolved from reptiles, which exhibited few maternal responses beyond laying eggs, to mammals such as squirrel monkeys, which engage in the metabolically expensive behavior of carrying their offspring almost continuously for months, the brain changed accordingly (MacLean 1990, 1998). Having another animal to care for likely required the brain to evolve from the reflexive responses of reptiles to the more complex emotional responses of ancient mammals and finally to the focused attention, enhanced vigilance, multitasking, and enhanced problem-solving skills observed in mammalian mothers today. Consequently, it appears that the maternal hand (or paw) has indeed rocked the evolutionary cradle, leading to the emergence of the most advanced brains, those of mammals. It has been suggested, however, that prior to the evolution of the mammalian brain, post-hatching parental responses were present in certain dinosaur species. And today, such parental responses are observed in some reptiles, such as crocodiles, as well as in avian species (Tullberg, Ah-King, and Temrin 2002; Meng et al. 2004). Noted anthropologist Sarah Hrdy describes several aspects of the maternal response that have been conserved throughout the process of evolution:

> A mother's body merges into synchrony with her baby's needs, and the baby's well-being becomes her pressing concern. Parts of these responses are incredibly old. Prolactin, the same hormone that coordinates maternal responses to infant demands for milk, was already orchestrating metamorphoses in amphibians and controlling water balance in the tissues of bony freshwater fish millions of years before any mammal existed. Every aspect of our neurochemistry and emotions has a rich and convoluted history, bearing witness to multiple long-running legacies that we share with earthworms, amphibians, small mammals, and other primates. . . . Many of the emotions we feel today, many of our autonomic responses, first evolved in environments inhabited by ancient ancestors. Many of these conditions no longer pertain or have long since disappeared, yet . . . their legacy remains relevant to what we are
>
> (Hrdy 2000:10)

THE MATERNAL MAMMALIAN BRAIN

About fifteen years ago, Craig Kinsley (of the University of Richmond) and I (KGL) became intrigued by the potential effect of pregnancy and motherhood on the female brain. Studies had reported that even short-term exposure to estrogen in rodents augmented a part of the brain known for its involvement in learning and memory, especially spatial memory

FIGURE 1.2 A rat grooms her offspring, a behavior critical for the health of the young pup.
Source: Photo by Doug Berlin – Randolph-Macon College Behavioral Neuroscience Laboratory.

(Woolley and McEwen 1992, 1993).[3] Past research had focused on the roles of brain areas known to be involved in traditional maternal responses[4] (Numan and Stolzenberg 2008), but new indications that a brain area not typically associated with maternal behavior was influenced by alterations in reproductive hormones were intriguing. Soon we began to realize that the area of the brain involved in spatial memory, the hippocampus, could indeed be central to a female's success as a mother. Spatial memory appears to be especially important for maternal success when we consider the metabolically expensive lactation response, which is maintained in maternal rodents by up to three times more food-caching responses than nonmaternal rodents exhibit (Calhoun 1963). Accordingly, we hypothesized that, in addition to the traditional maternal responses of crouching, nursing, retrieving, and licking/grooming (see figure 1.2), other responses such as heightened vigilance/boldness and enhanced foraging responses were necessary to successfully raise the female's offspring, a significant genetic investment.

Initially, we investigated the effect of maternal experience on foraging ability by conducting a spatial-memory task in a dry-land maze. A dry-land maze consists of a circular arena with eight little cups (wells) equally spaced along the perimeter. The floor of the arena is covered with the rats' usual bedding, so nothing novel is present to distract the rat from its task of discovering—and subsequently remembering—which one well contains the food (bait). We tested three groups of Long Evans rats: first-time (primiparous) moms about two weeks postpartum, never-pregnant (nulliparous) females that had had no exposure to another female's pups, and nulliparous females that had been exposed to pups for the equivalent of two weeks (and so were pup-sensitized). In a second experiment, we tested two groups of Sprague Dawley rats—moms that had had two pregnancies (multiparous) and nulliparous females—in a radial-arm maze. A radial-arm maze is shaped somewhat like an asterisk, with eight dead-ended tunnels radiating out from the center starting point. One path ends in the desired food, and a rat must use spatial cues in order to remember which path has already been checked and found empty before discovering the baited one.

In both experiments, the maternal animals exhibited enhanced spatial memory; interestingly, in the dry-land maze, even the pup-sensitized non-mothers (that is, the foster moms) demonstrated increased spatial ability (Kinsley et al. 1999).

Because lactating females have altered metabolic rates and energy demands—and this could potentially affect their behavioral responses—we focused subsequent studies on the more long-term effects of reproductive experience. Nulliparous, primiparous, and multiparous Sprague Dawley females were tested in the dry-land maze at the ages of six, twelve, eighteen, and twenty-four months. Results suggested that primiparous and multiparous females learned the tasks more efficiently, showing less decline than the virgin rats as they got older. The brains of the rats were then assessed for deposits of a protein associated with Alzheimer's disease in humans (amyloid precursor protein). The multiparous animals had fewer deposits of the protein in their hippocampus than did their virgin and primiparous counterparts (Gatewood et al. 2005).

In a similar study, nulliparous, primiparous, and multiparous Long Evans rats were assessed in the dry-land maze at four-month intervals from the ages of five to twenty-two months. No learning-acquisition differences were observed in this study; the probe trials, however, told a different story. In these probe trials, conducted one week after the final test trials, no food is placed in the previously baited food well. In this way, we assess the animal's longer-term memory by removing any sensory cues that may have been influential in earlier phases of training and testing. At five and thirteen months of age, the parous (primiparous and multiparous) animals exhibited an advantage in these longer-term memory tests.

In a final adaptation of the dry-land-maze assessment, triads of thirteen-month-old weight-matched females from each of the reproductive groups were placed in the maze at one time to compete for the food at the baited well. The multiparous animals retrieved the reward in 60 percent of the trials, whereas the primiparous females were victorious in 33 percent of the trials and the nulliparous females in only 7 percent of the trials. In this competitive task, the females had to engage in multitasking—as they processed the novel fact that they were not alone in the search and accessed earlier memories of the baited well's location—while experiencing the elevated stress of competition for this valued resource (Love et al. 2005).

In a second phase of the aforementioned longitudinal study (Love et al. 2005), emotional resilience, or boldness, was also assessed by exposing the animals to the elevated-plus maze at four-month intervals. In this behavioral assessment, rats can choose between safe covered platforms or the open arms of an elevated maze. Traditionally, animals spending more time in the covered arms are considered more timid, anxious, or stressed; animals spending more time in the open arms are viewed as bold and uninhibited. Focusing on the percentage of time spent in the open arms, significant differences were observed at ten, fourteen, eighteen, and twenty-two months of age. At each of these ages, the animals with maternal experience spent more time out in the open than did the nulliparous animals. When exposed to a novel stimulus (that is, an object they had never seen before) at twenty months of age, the multiparous animals spent more time exploring the object than did the nulliparous rats, once again confirming an enhanced boldness—and perhaps a more efficient stress responsiveness—in the maternal animals. These results supported earlier research in our laboratory indicating that animals with maternal experience responded to being exposed to a novel open field with less activation in the areas of the brain known for their involvement in fear and stress (Wartella et al. 2003).[5]

Further explorations of the brains of maternal animals confirmed that the hippocampus was modified through the reproductive experience. In 2006, we reported augmentation of this area of the brain in late-pregnant and lactating rats (Kinsley et al. 2006).[6] We have also found increased numbers of astrocytes, a type of cell that provides physiological support to the brain, in the hippocampi of late-pregnant, lactating, and hormone-treated females. These astrocytes were more structurally complex in the animals with reproductive experience (Gifford et al. 2003). These findings are in agreement with other reports of reproduction-induced alterations in areas of the brain not typically thought to be involved in maternal responses (Salmaso and

Woodside 2006, 2008).[7] Although there are many potential explanations for this plethora of neurobiological modifications we see in the hippocampus, we can perhaps thank an enriched environment. Having pups is an experience of increased sensory stimulation—auditory, visual, tactile, gustatory, and olfactory—all presented against the physiological backdrop of the altered hormonal milieu that accompanies pregnancy and lactation.

Focusing on maternal-related modifications in neurochemistry, Tomizawa and his Japanese colleagues have proposed that the hormone oxytocin may be the neurobiological fuel for the adaptive learning changes that accompany motherhood. Working with mice, these researchers found direct relationships between increased oxytocin levels and improved spatial-learning abilities.[8] These researchers also reported that a proposed physiological mechanism of learning known as long-term potentiation was enhanced in the animals with increased levels of oxytocin (Tomizawa et al. 2003).

In addition to studying laboratory rats, we wanted to investigate wild rats, which face a drastically different set of contingencies and exigencies in the real world. So we analyzed the brains of wild-caught pregnant, lactating, and nonmaternal (at the time of capture) rats. Although our investigative tools were limited in these animals, our analysis[9] revealed a trend for the pregnant rats to have fewer microglia (cells involved in immune-type defensive functions because they constantly scan brain tissue for pathogens or other threats) in the hippocampus than do the lactating rats. This suggests heightened activity of these cells once the pups are delivered. Additionally, the cell body size of neurons in the basolateral nucleus of the amygdala (a brain area involved in fear and aggression) were larger in the pregnant and lactating rats than in their nonreproductive counterparts (Lambert et al. 2005).

The research described here provides evidence that the maternal brain is altered in ways that make the female rodent a more successful provider for her offspring. A few questions remain, however, about the generalization of these results. First is the consideration of human data suggesting that the pregnant brain is compromised in several ways. Indeed, approximately 75 percent of pregnant women complain of short-term memory loss as well as other compromised cognitive abilities such as forgetfulness, lack of concentration, and disorientation (Pawluski and Galea 2008). Also, Buckwalter and his colleagues report that pregnant women had below-normal verbal memory but that scores increased to a normal range following childbirth (Buckwalter et al. 1999). More recently, Henry and Rendell report that pregnant women demonstrated slight deficits in executive functioning (for instance, complex decision making, planning, and judging), and these effects lasted for up to one year postpartum (Henry and Rendell 2007). Brain images suggest that the pregnant brain shrinks approximately 4 percent during pregnancy but returns to a normal volume following pregnancy (Oatridge et al. 2002). Liisa Galea and her colleagues found that the hippocampus volume was also smaller in pregnant rats than in nulliparous females (Galea et al. 2000). In a recent interview explaining these data, Galea commented that pregnancy and the early postpartum period may be considered a "down time" for the brain: "Given that hormone levels rise to at least 1,000 times their normal levels during the third trimester, then plunge around birth, it is not surprising that some things get muddled in that hormonal soup" (De Angelis 2008:30). Galea's interesting research focusing on spatial learning and the production of new nerve cells (neurogenesis) during the various stages of reproduction also leads to persisting questions about the exact nature of the plasticity of the pregnant and lactating brain. Her research, along with that of others, suggests that whereas spatial learning is enhanced postpartum in rodents, it is compromised during pregnancy. Further, lower rates of new cell production were observed in postpartum primiparous and multiparous animals compared to their virgin counterparts (Pawluski and Galea 2008; Pawluski et al. 2009). Thus the intense energy demands needed for the development of a fetus may require a downsizing of the anatomical and functional efforts of the brain before the appearance of the offspring; however, it is likely that after giving birth, the behaviors necessary for the facilitated survival of the offspring come online once again in a prevalent and long-lasting manner to ensure the offspring's survival.

WORKING MOMS AND THE NEUROECONOMICS OF MOTHERHOOD

Neuroeconomics is a relatively new discipline that investigates aspects of the decision-making process by exploring the adaptive integration—the balancing of costs and benefits—of relevant sensory and motor-response systems (Lambert and Kinsley 2008). The new or veteran mother, for instance, is constantly faced with a series of cost-benefit calculations between what is best for her and what is best for her offspring. These calculations result in maternity-induced neurobiological changes. The most successful maternal female makes the most adaptive decisions and responds to her dynamic environment in the most efficient manner (as depicted in figure 1.3).

FIGURE 1.3 Every mother balances trade-offs between work necessary to provide sustenance for her offspring and nurturing responses necessary to raise emotionally and physically healthy children.

Source: Photograph from Hrdy 2000:47; photographer unknown.

A successful maternal rodent is not terribly different. She must take into consideration her own fitness as well as that of ten or so pups all representing aspects of her genetic code. Making the situation even more challenging, the female rodent is often pregnant (and hungry) while she is nursing (and so feeding offspring). The context of neuroeconomics, then, provides an interesting foray into new ways of interpreting the plastic maternal brain.

Intrigued by our previous findings that maternal animals foraged more efficiently and, in the midst of stress, responded in a more toned-down, less metabolically expensive manner, we designed additional studies to assess cognitive and physical responses. Initially, we focused on cognitive decision making and the importance of the mother's focused attention on the key elements of a task related to successful responding. Specifically, using Long Evans rats, we assessed nulliparous, primiparous, and multiparous animals in the attention set–shifting paradigm. In this task, rats learned to associate specific odors with small terra-cotta pots containing pieces of sweet cereal (Froot Loops) that were buried in some type of bedding. To make the task more challenging, we presented distracting cues such as different types of odors and different bedding materials. These distractions required the rat to focus solely on the salient cue to determine the most likely source of food. But as the name of this task suggests, the salient cue shifts throughout the assessment. In the intradimensional shift, the animal learns to respond to a new odor while ignoring other distracting cues; in the more challenging extradimensional shift, rats previously rewarded for paying attention to odor have to learn to ignore this once-valuable cue and direct their attention to a new salient cue, such as type of filler material in the pots. Essentially, rats in this task have to constantly monitor the cues leading to the greatest "payoffs" in the form of high-incentive food treats. Interestingly, the multiparous animals in this study responded to the appropriate cues in the test trials of the various phases close to 100 percent of the time. In contrast, the nulliparous animals exhibited an accuracy rate of about 50 percent. The primiparous animals performed better than the nulliparous but were not as impressive as the multiparous animals (Higgins et al. 2007; Lambert and Kinsley 2008).

In another assessment of the economy of the maternal animal's responses, we focused on the demanding physical terrains rodent moms have to navigate to forage for their offspring; we designed a series of tests to assess physical agility, motor learning, and strength. Using nulliparous, primiparous, and multiparous animals once again, rats were exposed to a wire-hang test, a series of increasingly challenging surfaces on a wooden dowel rod that they were required to traverse, and a rope-climbing training protocol. In the wire-hang test, designed to assess strength, the multiparous animals persisted much longer (twenty-three seconds compared to twelve seconds for the primiparous animals and fourteen seconds for the nulliparous animals). In the rod-traversal tasks, designed to assess motor agility and balance, the multiparous animals excelled in the challenging smooth-rod task, crossing the rod in a third of the time required by the primiparous animals and less than 20 percent of the time required by nulliparous animals (see figure 1.4). These trends persisted in the rope-climb test, designed to assess motor learning; specifically, 75 percent of the multiparous animals exhibited a full body climb (lifting the entire body off the platform to obtain the reward), compared to 13 percent of the primiparous and 37 percent of the nulliparous animals (Lambert et al. 2008; Lambert and Kinsley 2008).

Finally, in the same group of animals described earlier, we decided to look at a more ecologically relevant assessment of working efficiently for resources by exposing each animal to an open field containing a cricket, a natural prey species for the rat. In this task, the nulliparous rats took four

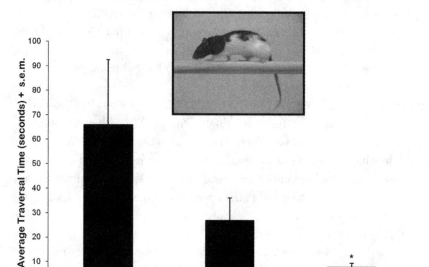

FIGURE 1.4 Female rats with various degrees of maternal experience were assessed for their ability to traverse a smooth wooden dowel rod approximately five weeks following relevant pup exposure; the multiparous animals traversed the rod faster than did their primiparous and virgin counterparts (* = significantly different from virgins; $p = < .05$).

times longer to catch their cricket than did the multiparous rats, with the primiparous animals taking approximately twice the time exhibited by the multiparous animals (Lambert and Kinsley 2008). This foraging task required focused attention (to process sensory information) and efficient response execution (to process motor information) in a novel and open environmental terrain that forced the animal to assess the costs and benefits of responding versus retreating. The task provided further evidence that the decision-making process is altered in adaptive ways in the maternal animal.

THE PATERNAL MAMMALIAN BRAIN

Considering parental responses in most of the world's 5,400 mammalian species, fathers generally engage in remarkably little parenting beyond behaviors important in the mating process (Hrdy 2008). Indeed, only about 10 percent of mammals display paternal responses (Kleiman and Malcolm 1981). Interestingly, Sarah Hrdy has suggested that, across human cultures, more variation in paternal behaviors is present than observed in all of the remaining 275 species of primates combined. Generally, hunter-gatherer cultures engage in higher rates of male care than do herding, horticultural, or even post-industrial societies. Even within foraging societies, however, the diversity of parental care is apparent—from the lowest care levels observed in the South African !Kung to the more frequent paternal care observed in the Central African Aka pygmies who reportedly hold their infants 22 percent of the time (Kleiman and Malcolm 1981; Hewlett 1991a, 1991b). Focusing on fathers in the United States, most recent data suggest that fathers hold their infants an average of fifty minutes per day (Sayer, Bianchip, and Robinson 2003).

It is important to understand the variation in paternal care before embarking on a neurobiological investigation on the response. The variability across and within species is recognized as an important aspect of paternal responses. (Ironically, the consistency of maternal responses across mammalian species makes it difficult to discern some of the more delineating mechanisms related to enhanced nurturing of offspring.) In our laboratory, we have focused on the California deer mouse (*Peromyscus californicus*) due to its being monogamous and biparental; essentially, these male mice engage in all of the parental behaviors the mother engages in with the exception of giving birth and lactating. In order to learn more about the underlying neurobiological mechanisms responsible for these paternal responses, we compare their brains with those of their non-biparental genetic cousins, the common deer mouse (*Peromyscus maniculatus*). Our initial explorations confirmed that the California deer mice with paternal experience exhibited enhanced foraging and exploratory/boldness behaviors in a similar fashion as that observed in maternal rats (Kinsley and Lambert 2008).

The degree of nurturing responsiveness is emphasized in the male California deer mouse when a male is exposed to an alien pup (not its offspring); in this situation, most males retrieve the foster pup, groom it, and crouch over it in a position similar to that of the lactating female—especially if the male has had previous experience with pups (see figure 1.5). In pursuit of relevant neurobiological mechanisms of this paternal response, we investigated the involvement of two neuropeptides, vasopressin and oxytocin, which are known to be involved in social interactions, especially those related to reproduction (Roberts et al. 1998). After exposing the male mice to an alien pup for a mere ten minutes a day for four days, we observed more evidence of vasopressin in the brains of the pup-exposed mice than in

FIGURE 1.5 A male California deer mouse with prior paternal experience demonstrates various nurturing responses upon his initial exposure to this alien, or foster, pup.

Source: Photos by Stephanie Karsner – Randolph-Macon College Behavioral Neuroscience Laboratory.

those of mice never exposed to pups. We also observed greater evidence of vasopressin and oxytocin in the California deer mice than in the common deer mice with comparable pup exposure (Everette et al. 2006).[10]

To investigate the male deer mouse's motivation to approach a pup that was restrained in an enclosed container, we exposed male California deer mice and male common deer mice with varying paternal experience to this parenting challenge. We then assessed the activation of problem-solving portions of their brains. Interestingly, males with parenting experience from both species exhibited more extensive neural activity than did the mice that had never previously seen a pup (Everette et al. 2007).[11]

Most recently, we assessed the brain plasticity of paternal deer mice— California and common deer mice—with varying paternal experience. We looked at the brains of males with families, virgin males exposed to pups, and virgin males with no pup exposure. Our preliminary results for the California deer mice suggest that the full paternal male brains were more plastic than those of the virgin males with no pup exposure (Franssen et al. 2009).

CONCLUSIONS

Our research suggests that maternal experience modifies the brain in adaptive ways to increase the likelihood that the offspring, a significant genetic investment, will survive. Further, some of these modifications appear to be long-lasting in some cases, potentially benefitting the animal in non-reproductive challenges, such as enhanced learning abilities throughout the animal's life or neuroprotection against aging-related neural decline.

From an evolutionary perspective, observations that the maternal response in mammals led to the emergence of a brain more in tune with affiliative social responses introduces the opportunity to use the parental response as a means of investigating positive social responses and accompanying neurobiological alterations.

Aspects of the modifications reported in the maternal brain and related behaviors have also been observed in paternal animals. Although a vast diversity of paternal responses exists across mammalian species, valuable models such as the *P. californicus* species allow neurobiologists to investigate specific aspects of the parental response in a systematic manner. Alloparenting, the provision of parental care to other animals' offspring, is observed across various mammalian species, including primates and rodents, and may provide additional relevant clues about the neurobiology of nurturing responses (Hrdy 2009). Indeed, the identification of neurobiological mechanisms contributing to an animal's "choice" to direct valuable energy toward the care of another animal, as observed in parental and alloparental cases, may reveal the evolutionary roots of cognitive abilities most often associated with humans, including the demonstration of empathic responses or the possession of a social conscience (Churchland 2008).

The consideration of a political candidate's unique family circumstances, as described at the beginning of this chapter, provides a vivid reminder of the evolutionary seeds of social conscience. These seeds, as evidenced by the animals, were most likely planted in the mammalian maternal brain and extend to other types of caregiving, such as alloparenting and fatherhood.

DISCLAIMER

A portion of this material is based upon work supported by the National Science Foundation under grant #0723341. Any opinions, findings, and conclusions or recommendations expressed in this material are those of the authors and do not necessarily reflect the views of the National Science Foundation.

NOTES

1. The Associated Press, "Transcript: Beau Biden" (August 27, 2008), http://www.politico.com/news/stories/0808/12913.html. Accessed September 18, 2008.
2. The Office of Alaska Governor Sarah Palin, "Governor Palin Releases Statement to Alaskans about VP Nomination" (August 29, 2008), http://www.gov.state.ak.us/news.php?id=1439. Accessed September 18, 2008.

3. The estrogen exposure had increased dendritic spines in the CA1 area of the hippocampus.

4. Such as the medial preoptic area of the rostral hypothalamus and the ventral region of the bed nucleus of the stria terminalis.

5. Fos-immunoreactivity was measured in the amygdala and the CA3 area of the hippocampus, known for fear and stress, respectively.

6. The rats exhibited increased numbers of CA1 dendritic spines.

7. Such as the cingulate cortex.

8. Specifically, oxytocin antagonists led to compromised spatial functioning, whereas animals infused with oxytocin exhibited enhanced spatial learning.

9. We used a cresyl violet analysis.

10. "Evidence of vasopressin" following pup exposure was measured by vasopressin-immunoreactive cell bodies and fibers in the paraventricular nucleus of the hypothalamus. "Greater evidence of vasopressin and oxytocin" in the *P. californicus* was measured by amounts of vasopressin- and oxytocin-immunoreactive tissue.

11. Amounts of c-fos (an immediate early gene that expresses fos protein when activated) were measured in the prefrontal cortex and hippocampus. Males with parenting experience exhibited more c-fos *immunoreactivity.*

REFERENCES

Azare, N. P., K. D. Pettigrew, P. Pietrini, D. G. Murphy, B. Horwitz and M. B. Schapiro. 1995. "Sex Differences in Patterns of Hemispheric Cerebral Metabolism: A Multiple Regression Discrimination Analysis of Position Emission Tomographic Data." *International Journal of Neuroscience* 81:1–20.

Buckwalter, J. G., F. Z. Stanczyk, C. A. McCleary, B. W. Bluestein, D. K. Buckwalter. K. P. Rankin, L. Chang, and T. M. Goodwin. 1999. "Pregnancy, the Postpartum, and Steroid Hormones: Effects on Cognition and Mood." *Progress in Brain Research* 133:303–319.

Calhoun, J. B. 1963. "The Ecology and Sociology of the Norway Rat." Bethesda, MD: US Department of Health, Education, and Welfare.

Churchland, P. 2008. "The Impact of Neuroscience on Philosophy." *Neuron* 60:409–411.

De Angelis, T. 2008. "Priming for a New Role." *Monitor on Psychology* 39:28–31.

Everette, A., D. Fleming, T. Higgins, K. Tu, M. Bardi, C. H. Kinsley, and K. G. Lambert. 2007. "Paternal Experience Enhances Behavioral and Neurobiological Responsivity Associated with Affiliative and Nurturing Responses." *International Society for Neuroscience Abstracts.*

Everette, A., K. Tu, R. Contino, B. Rima, J. Major, A. F. Conway, C. H. Kinsley, and K. G. Lambert. 2006. "Plasticity of Paternal Responsiveness in Two Peromyscus Species." *International Society for Neuroscience Abstracts.*

Franssen, C. L., S. Karsner, E. Tu, M. Hyer, and K. Lambert. 2009. "Neuroplasticity Following Paternal Experience in Two Congeneric Species." Talk given at the Society for Integrative and Comparative Biology. Annual Meeting, Boston, January 3–7, 2009.

Galea, L. A., B. Ormerod, S. Sampath, X. Kostaras, D. Wilkie, and M. Phelps. 2000. "Spatial Working Memory and Hippocampal Size Across Pregnancy in Rats." *Hormones and Behavior* 37:86–95.

Gatewood, J. D., M. D. Morgan, M. Eaton, I. M. McNamara, L. F. Stevens, H. A. Macbeth, E. A. A. Meyers, L. M. Lomas. F. J. Kozub, K. G. Lambert, and C. H. Kinsley. 2005. "Motherhood Mitigates Aging-Related Decrements in Learning and Memory." *Brain Research Bulletin* 66:91–98.

Gifford, G., S. Miller, P. Quadros, K. G. Lambert, and C. H. Kinsley. 2003. "Alterations in Glial Cells (Astrocytes) May Accompany Changes in Reproductive Conditions in the Female Rat." *Society for Neuroscience Abstracts.*

Henry, J. D. and P. G. Rendell. 2007. "A Review of the Impact of Pregnancy on Memory Function." *Journal of Clinical Experimental Neuropsychology* 29:793–803.

Hewlett. B. 1991a. "Demography and Childcare in Preindustrial Societies." *Journal of Anthropological Research* 467:1–37.

Hewlett, B. 1991b. *Intimate Fathers: The Nature and Context of Aka Pygmy Paternal Infant Care.* Ann Arbor, MI: University of Michigan Press.

Higgins, T., A. Everette, D. Fleming, L. Christon, C. H. Kinsley, and K. G. Lambert. 2007. "Maternal Experience Enhances Neurobiological and Behavioral Responses in an Attention Set-Shifting Paradigm." *International Behavioral Neuroscience Society Abstracts.*

Hrdy, S. B. 2000. *Mother Nature: Maternal Instincts and How They Shape the Human Species.* New York: Ballantine.

Hrdy, S. B. 2008. "Cooperative Breeding and the Paradox of Facultative Fathering." In *Neurobiology of the Parental Brain,* ed. Robert S. Bridges, 407–416. Burlington, MA: Academic.

Hrdy, S. B. 2009. *Mothers and Others: The Evolutionary Origins of Mutual Understanding.* Cambridge, MA: Belknap.

Kinsley, C. H. and K. G. Lambert. 2008. "Reproduction-Induced Neuroplasticity: Natural Behavioural and Neuronal Alterations Associated with the Production and Care of Offspring." *Journal of Neuroendocrinology* 20:515–525.

Kinsley, C. H., L. Madonia, G. W. Gifford, K. Tureski, G. R. Griffin, C. Lowry, J. Williams, J. Collins, H. McLearie, and K. G. Lambert. 1999. "Motherhood Improves Learning and Memory." *Nature* 402:137–138.

Kinsley, C. H., R. Trainer, G. Stafisso-Sandoz, P. Quadros, L. K. Marcus, C. Hearon, E. A. Meyer, N. Hester, M. Morgan, F. J. Kozub, and K. G. Lambert. 2006. "Motherhood and the Hormones of Pregnancy Modify Concentrations of Hippocampal Neuronal Dendritic Spines." *Hormones and Behavior* 49:131–142.

Kleiman, D. G. and J. R. Malcolm. 1981. "The Evolution of Male Parental Investment." In *Parental Care in Mammals*. ed. D. Gubernick and P. H. Klopfer. 347–381. New York: Plenum.

Lambert, Kelly. 2003. "The Life and Career of Paul MacLean: A Journey Toward Neurobiological and Social Harmony." *Physiology and Behavior* 79:343–349.

Lambert, K. G., T. Higgins, A. Everette, D. Fleming, L. Christon, M. Bardi, C. Chan, A. Baranova, L. Felicio, C. H. Kinsley, and C. L. Franssen. 2008. "Maternal Experience Enhances Motor Abilities and May Potentially Alter Cerebellar Spine Number and Morphology in Long-Evans Rats." *Society for Neuroscience Abstracts*.

Lambert, K. G. and C. H. Kinsley. 2008. "The Neuroeconomics of Motherhood: The Costs and Benefits of Maternal Investment." In *Neurobiology of the Parental Brain*, ed. Robert S. Bridges. 479–492. Burlington, MA: Academic.

Lambert, K. G., G. Love, L. Stevens, S. L. Klein, A. F. Conway, and C. H. Kinsley. 2005. "Nissl Analyses Indicate Maternal-Induced Hippocampal and Amygdalar Neuronal/Glia Plasticity in Wild-Caught Norway Rats." *Society for Neuroscience Abstracts*.

Love, G., N. Torrey, I. McNamara, M. Morgan, N. W. Hester, E. R. Glasper, A. C. DeVries, C. H. Kinsley, and K. G. Lambert. 2005. "Motherhood Mitigates Aging-Related Decrements in Learning and Memory." *Behavioral Neuroscience* 119:1084–1096.

MacLean, Paul. 1990. *The Triune Brain in Evolution*. New York: Academic.

MacLean, Paul. 1996. "Women: A More Balanced Brain." *Zygon* 31:421–439.

MacLean, Paul D. "Paul D. MacLean," in Larry Squire, ed., *The History of Neuroscience in Autobiography*. New York: Academic Press, 1998, 246–275.

Meng, Q., J. Liu, D. J. Varricchio, T. Huang, and C. Gao. 2004. "Palaeontology: Parental Care in an Ornithischian Dinosaur." *Nature* 431:145–146.

Numan, M. and D. Stolzenberg. 2008. "Hypothalamic Interaction with the Mesolimbic Dopamine System and the Regulation of Maternal Responsiveness." In *Neurobiology of the Parental Brain*, ed. Robert S. Bridges. 3–22. Burlington, MA: Academic.

Oatridge, A., A. Holdcroft, N. Saeed, J. V. Hajnal, B. K. Puri, L. Fusi, and G. M. Bidder. 2002. "Change in Brain Size During and After Pregnancy: Study in Healthy Women and Women with Preeclampsia." *American Journal of Neuroradiology* 23:19–26.

Pawluski, J. L., S. Brummelte, C. K. Barha, J. M. Crozier, and L. A. M. Galea. 2009. "Effects of Steroid Hormones on Neurogenesis in the Hippocampus of the Adult Female Rodent During the Estrous Cycle, Pregnancy, Lactation and Aging." *Frontiers in Neuroendocrinology* 30(3):343–357.

Pawluski, J. L. and L. A. Galea. 2008. "The Role of Reproductive Experience on Hippocampal Unction and Plasticity." In *Neurobiology of the Parental Brain*, ed. Robert S. Bridges. 493–508. Burlington, MA: Academic.

Roberts, R. L., A. K. Miller, S. E. Taymans, and C. S. Carter. 1998. "Role of Social and Endocrine Factors in Alloparental Behavior of Prairie Voles (*Microtus ochogaster*)." *Canadian Journal of Zoology* 76:1862–1868.

Salmaso, N. and B. Woodside. 2006. "Upregulation of Astrocytic Basic Fibroblast Growth Factor in the Cingulated Cortex of Lactating Rats: Time Course and Role of Sucking Stimulation." *Hormones and Behavior* 50:448–453.

Salmaso, N. and B. Woodside. 2008. "Fluctuations in Astrocytic Basic Fibroblast Growth Factor in the Cingulated Cortex of Cycling, Ovariectomized and Postpartum Animals." *Neuroscience* 154:932–939.

Sayer, L. C., S. M. Bianchip, and J. P. Robinson. 2003. "Are Parents Investing Less in Children?" *American Journal of Sociology* 110:1–43.

Tomizawa, K., N. Iga, Y. Lu, A. Moriwaki, M. Matsushita, S. Li, O. Miyamoto, T. Itano, and H. Matsui. 2003. "Oxytocin Improves Long-Lasting Spatial Memory During Motherhood Through MAP Kinase Cascade." *Nature Neuroscience* 6:384–390.

Tullberg, B. S., M. Ah-King, and H. Temrin. 2002. "Phylogenetic Reconstruction of Parental-Care Systems in the Ancestors of Birds." *Philosophical Transactions of the Royal Society of London* (Series B, Biological Sciences):357, 251–257.

Wartella, J., E. Amory, A. H. Macbeth, I. McNamara, I. Stevens, K. G. Lambert, and C. H. Kinsley. 2003. "Single or Multiple Reproductive Experiences Attenuate Neurobehavioral Stress and Fear Responses in the Female Rat." *Physiology and Behavior* 79:373–381.

Woolley, C. S. and B. S. McEwen. 1992. "Estradiol Mediates Fluctuation in Hippocampal Synapse Density During the Estrous Cycle in the Adult." *Journal of Neuroscience* 12:2549–554.

Woolley, C. S. and B. S. McEwen. 1993. "Roles of Estradiol and Progesterone in the Regulation of Hippocampal Dendritic Spine Density During the Estrous Cycle in the Rat." *Journal of Comparative Neurology* 336:293–306.

2

FAMILY LIFE AND INFANT CARE

Lessons from Cooperatively Breeding Primates

Charles T. Snowdon

FOR THE PAST THIRTY YEARS, I have been interested in the reproductive and parental behavior of a group of small primates from South America known as marmosets and tamarins. These monkeys differ from almost all other nonhuman primates in the necessity of multiple caretakers for successful infant care. A cooperative infant care system requires several features: a strong relationship (or pair bond) between the mother and father, the recruitment and keeping of additional helpers (typically older siblings of infants but also unrelated individuals), and close coordination of the behavior of multiple group members in order to provide adequate care for infants. I will discuss each of these points in more detail including data collected from both in the wild and in captivity, and I will discuss some of the hormonal relationships that we know are important in regulating these behaviors. My colleagues and I have studied two species, the common marmoset (*Callithrix jacchus*) and the cotton-top tamarin (*Saguinus oedipus*). First, I will provide some information on the natural history of these animals, and then discuss why I think these animal models are critical for understanding human families.

NATURAL HISTORY OF MARMOSETS AND TAMARINS

Marmosets and tamarins are found throughout Central and South America from Panama through southern Brazil. They are small, weighing from 300 to 700 g as adults, and they live in groups of five to eight individuals in the wild. They live entirely in trees and eat a variety of foods—from exudates extracted from trees to fruits to insects and small animals, such as lizards.

In many species, there are two birth seasons a year with females typically giving birth to twins that weigh approximately 20 percent of the mother's weight at birth. In our captive colony of cotton-top tamarins, mothers have a postpartum ovulation within two to four weeks after birth and frequently become pregnant on the first ovulation. Thus, mothers may be simultaneously nursing one set of heavy infants while already pregnant with the next set.[1] The monkeys do not build nests and may travel from 1.5 to 2.5 km a day in search of food while needing to carry the twin infants.[2] It is difficult to imagine the mother being able to carry the infants through the trees while she forages for food to support lactation and her new pregnancy without some sort of assistance. Indeed, two field studies have found that infant survival is much greater when there are multiple adult male helpers available.[3] Much to our surprise, when we looked at data from our captive cotton-top tamarin colony, we found a similar result: We did not see 100 percent infant survival in families that had fewer than five helpers — mother, father, and three others.[4] This was true despite the fact that our captive animals had an abundant food supply, temperature was carefully regulated, travel distances were much smaller, and there were no predators.

We and others have found that even in captivity a father will lose up to 10 percent of his body weight during the period of infant carrying, but that with increasing numbers of helpers involved in infant care, the weight loss of any one individual is reduced linearly.[5] Even for captive tamarins, there is a high cost to infant care, and the costs are reduced and infant survival increased when multiple caregivers are involved. We suspect that one source of weight loss relates to thermoregulation since infants are frequently carried on the back directly over the interscapular brown fat pads that are metabolized for heat production. Thus, helpers serve as "radiators" for infants until they can thermoregulate on their own. Nonmaternal caregivers do not only carry infants throughout the day, but they also provide vigilance against predators[6] and search for food, which they announce to others with vocalizations used only in feeding contexts.[7] As infants reach weaning age, the helpers play an important role by offering solid food to infants through active and passive food transfers; we have found that the earlier food transfer behavior begins, the sooner the infant has acquired the skills to forage for itself.[8]

Thus, the presence of multiple helpers or alloparents in marmosets and tamarins allows a faster rate of reproduction with greater infant survival. Helpers play multiple roles of carrying infants, providing heat for thermoregulation, protecting against predation, and locating food resources. These behaviors raise many provocative questions: We have been told by evolutionary psychologists that it is to the male's advantage to desert his mate and seek other breeding opportunities as soon as the mate is pregnant; so why and how do these monkeys form close, long-lasting relationships? What do the helpers gain by looking after the offspring of someone else? Would they not be better off finding their own mates and reproducing on their own? What keeps helpers from breeding within the family—since we rarely see more than one pregnant female in a group? What are the consequences to infants of growing up in a cooperative care system as opposed to being cared for by a single mother? Before moving to these questions, I will make a brief digression to consider why those concerned with human parental behavior should be interested in results from monkeys.

THE VALUE OF ANIMAL MODELS

Animal models are frequently used in biomedical and comparative psychological research. The value of a model is the ability to study animals under controlled environmental conditions where we know the entire social and experiential history of the individuals. We can carry out experiments with greater control over more variables than is possible with humans. In addition, human culture represents a significant artifact in understanding what "natural" behavior might be. With humans, we can never disentangle the effects of cultural practices or religious beliefs from how humans behave. With animals, we can assume that religion and culture do not control behavior, allowing us a better understanding of which mechanisms are significant in reproductive success.

At the same time, we must recognize the limitations of animal models. Humans are cooperative breeders since the long gestation and long duration of postnatal care that human infants require are more than one parent can handle alone without significant economic (indirect) or direct caretaking.[9] Marmosets and tamarins are also cooperative breeders, but the reasons (as listed here) are very different. Whereas humans reproduce slowly with many hunter-gatherer populations reproducing once every four to five years, marmosets and tamarins can in the wild give birth to twins up to twice a year. But despite this important difference, I think there are some potentially important parallels that can be drawn between cooperatively breeding monkeys and human families.

DEVELOPMENT AND MAINTENANCE OF PAIR BONDS

Evolutionary biologists and psychologists have argued that there is a fundamental asymmetry between male and female mammals. Females have a relatively long gestation period and postpartum lactation is essential. Males on the other hand are simply sperm donors and, in addition, can never be certain of paternity—whereas all mothers are certain of their maternity. The consequences of this asymmetry are major. Females should be cautious and choosy about mates; males should seek as many mates as possible and make no commitment to any one female after ensuring that a female has become pregnant. Thus, males should guard mates closely at fertile periods and should exhibit jealousy, but be indiscriminant in mate choice; whereas females should be careful in mate selection and perhaps require evidence of either good genes or a potential for parental care before agreeing to mate. In many species, males are much larger than females and have special coloration (silverback male gorillas) or evolved weapons (antlers in deer) that can be used as weapons or as ways to impress females or both. Females, in contrast, are small and usually without any adornment.

So goes the conventional wisdom. But what happens if infant survival is dependent upon male investment? The conventional wisdom no longer works. When male parental care is critical for infant survival, not only do females need to make careful choices about mates, but males need to be careful as well. Furthermore, because males can never be completely certain of paternity of an infant, if a male is involved in infant care, he must have a high probability that the infants he is caring for are his own. Trust in a mate becomes important. In species with both parents needed for infant success, males and females should be similar in size and (1) neither sex having any special features to indicate competitive skills or good genes, or (2) both sexes showing special features. For example, in tamarins and marmosets, females have specialized scent glands maturing at puberty that attract and communicate reproductive status to males; and the secondary sex characteristics of human females—breasts and broad hips—are seen nowhere else among mammals.

Courtship plays an important role in evaluation of potential mates and many species that form long-term pair bonds engage in extensive courtship behavior. Often courtship leads to physiological changes. Thus, in monogamous prairie voles, females do not begin to ovulate until they have selected a mate.[10] In voles, sexual activity in new pairs is virtually continuous for up to two days at the beginning of courtship and also produces the neuropeptide, oxytocin, which acts on the brain to cement a pair bond.[11] In male voles, a related peptide, arginine vasopressin, is increased during mating and helps cement the male commitment to a particular female.

Grooming or stroking the hair or fur of another animal can also induce hormonal changes in both oxytocin and in endogenous opioids, both of which produce feelings of well-being and serve as mechanisms of social rewards.[12]

If a young, sexually inexperienced female tamarin is placed with her father or brother away from her mother, she will not ovulate. However, as soon as she is placed in an enclosure adjacent to a novel male, she will ovulate before there is any direct contact.[13] Unlike voles, in female tamarins the mere sight or smell of a novel male is enough to start ovulation.

However, similar to voles and the experiences of many new human couples sexual activity is quite high at the start of a new relationship. Based on observational sampling of newly formed pairs, we calculate that they may have sexual contact as often as once an hour during the early stages of pair formation.[14] Also as with human couples, sexual activity decreases with time, but based on our observations we still see long-term pairs mating on average once a day. What might be the reason for such high rates of sexual activity?

One theory about the behavior of socially monogamous animals is that females should conceal when they ovulate. As a result, males never know when the female is ovulating and so must stay close to her and mate with her for a long period in order to ensure conception.[15] As a consequence, the male cannot leave to find another mate and thus will invest his time with only one female and will care for their infants. Basically, females are tricking males into staying around for infant care. But is this really the case?

Several years ago, my long-term collaborator, Toni Ziegler, and I had a friendly argument. She noted that more than 85 percent of ovulations that she had detected using urinary hormonal samples resulted in pregnancy. Surely, she said, such a high rate of conception is possible only if there is some cue about ovulation. I disagreed, saying that the same success could be achieved simply by having sex each day. She designed a clever bioassay presenting the odors of a novel female to pairs were the female was already pregnant. She tested pairs each day throughout the donor female's ovulatory cycle. There were no changes in rates of attraction to the mark or sniffing it as a function of the donor's cycle, but males had erections more often on days when the donor female was ovulating and the pregnant female mated with her mate more frequently on days when the donor female was ovulating.[16] There was no concealed ovulation, at least from the point of view of male and female tamarins, although ovulation was concealed to us scientists prior to this study.

This returns us to the observation of nearly daily sexual activity in pairs. If males can detect when their mate is ovulating, why do they have sex so often? We suspected that non-conceptive sex might actually play a role in maintaining relationships and in restoring the relationship when challenged. We found that not only were males aroused and pregnant females sexually receptive to the odors of novel, ovulating females, but females also solicited sex more often in the presence of odors from any unfamiliar reproductive female, whether ovulating or not.[17] We also found increased rates of sexual activity during reunions when mates had been separated for brief periods.[18] And when marmoset pairs lost their infants, they increased rates of sexual activity. All of these are consistent with the hypothesis that non-conceptive sex may be important in restoring a relationship after a threat.

We find that grooming is a very frequent behavior between mated marmosets and tamarins. In a study of wild common marmosets in Brazil, Cristina Lazaro-Perea and colleagues[19] found that pairs groomed each other about 21 percent of their activity cycle, the greatest proportion of grooming reported for any primate. Interestingly, males groomed females significantly more often than they were groomed by their mates. We found similar results in captive tamarins where in every single family fathers groomed mothers more than the reverse.[20] We also found that males appeared to be more upset during separation and that they, rather than the female, initiated grooming and sexual contact on reunion.[21] As noted earlier, male mammals can never be certain of paternity and so one might expect males to be more anxious than females about maintaining a good relationship.

In prairie voles, the hormone oxytocin is stimulated presumably during sexual contact in the early hours of pair formation and seems to reinforce a pair bond between a female and particular male. In a closely related species where voles mate promiscuously, there is no change in or effect of oxytocin. We noticed that there was great variation in the amount of time spent in pair activities among our cotton-top tamarins, which led us to ask whether there would be any within-species variation in oxytocin levels and whether these levels would reflect relationship quality. We studied fourteen pairs of tamarins where one animal in each pair had been sterilized for colony management purposes. We did not want pregnancy or presence of nursing infants to confound the results. We observed the behavior of each pair nearly daily across an entire ovulatory cycle and collected daily urine samples that we subsequently analyzed for oxytocin levels.[22]

We found a tenfold variation in the amount of social behavior between pairs as well as a similar tenfold variation in urinary oxytocin levels. Unlike voles, both male and female tamarins had detectable levels of oxytocin and there was a close correlation between the male and female in each pair. Furthermore, there was a close correlation between our rankings of the affiliation between each pair and oxytocin, with pairs with high affiliation having higher oxytocin levels than pairs with less affiliation. We then asked whether the same affiliative behaviors were equally responsible for male and female oxytocin levels. In a multiple regression analysis, we found that female oxytocin levels can be predicted by the amount of grooming and physical contact they receive whereas male oxytocin levels are predicted by the amount of sex they have. If oxytocin plays an important role in maintaining pair bonds in marmosets and tamarins, then the combination of high rates of grooming, especially by males, and the high levels of non-conceptive sex are valuable for both sexes to be maximally affected.

HOW MALES ARE CHANGED BY FATHERHOOD

Is behavior indicating affiliation sufficient to maintain a pair bond? In studies of common marmosets, males appear to behave in a way typical of the caricature of male mammals described earlier. In the presence of his mate, a male will be aggressive toward a novel female, but in the absence of his mate a male will often court a novel female.[23] We have developed a method to do functional magnetic resonance imaging (fMRI) in male marmosets and have found that males showed immediate activation of the parts of the brain that are involved in sexual arousal (medial preoptic area and anterior hypothalamus) when presented with the odors of a novel, ovulating female.[24] Given this response, we became interested in how odors affected males in different reproductive states. The males in our imaging study were either virgins or males housed with a female who was on contraception. We tested single males, males in nonreproductive pairs, and fathers with the odors of a novel ovulating female versus a control odor for ten minutes. Males showed a great interest in the novel female odors and had shorter latencies to inspect the odor and higher erection rates. We also took a blood sample thirty minutes after the first exposure to the odors. Single males and males in nonreproducing pairs had significantly increased testosterone levels compared with control stimuli. However, fathers showed no hormonal response to novel female odors.[25] Recently, we have found that fathers, but not other males, show a decrease in testosterone levels twenty minutes after smelling the odors of an infant.[26]

We have been interested in hormonal changes relating to infant care. Several studies on marmosets have shown that males carrying infants have higher levels of the hormone prolactin than males not carrying infants.[27] We measured prolactin levels in father cotton-top tamarins, and as expected, found high levels in fathers while they were caring for infants.[28] However, we also found that prolactin levels just before the birth of infants were as high as after infant birth. When we measured hormones in fathers through-out the pregnancy of their mates, we found many hormonal changes with increases in cortisol, estrogens, and testosterone as well as prolactin occur-ring during the last half of pregnancy;[29] we also found males increased body weight during pregnancy.[30] In addition, there were differences between first-time fathers and experienced fathers with experienced fathers undergo-ing the cascade of hormonal changes earlier in pregnancy than first-time fathers. When a female becomes pregnant, many hormonal changes occur to prepare her body for pregnancy and infant care. It appears that marmoset and tamarin fathers undergo a "sympathetic pregnancy" along with their mates; but how do fathers know that their mates are pregnant?

COMMUNICATION BETWEEN FETUS AND FATHER IN PREGNANCY

We have already seen how olfactory signals can communicate a female's ovulatory status to a male. Can similar signals communicate pregnancy? We have examined the temporal relationship between hormones excreted by the mother and the changes in hormones in males to identify possible correlations. Early in pregnancy, females produce increased levels of chori-onic gonadotropin (the hormone measured in urinary pregnancy test kits) and progesterone, but these changes occur much earlier than any changes in male physiology. Halfway through pregnancy the adrenal gland of the fetus becomes active and secretes high levels of glucocorticoids. High levels of these hormones, typically associated with stress, are potentially damaging to the mother and so the hormones are excreted by the mother and are easily detected in the mother's urine. Within a week of the excretion of these glucocorticoids, every single experienced father showed a significant increase in corticosterone (one of the glucocorticoids) and subsequently three fathers started through the hormonal changes we see in males in late pregnancy. Interestingly, the immediate reaction by fathers to changes in excreted glucocorticoids was not consistent in first-time fathers that showed hormonal changes only in the last month of pregnancy.[31] We hypothesized that the fetal adrenal gland produced the signal that initiated changes in fathers' hormones effectively preparing fathers for infant care. We further hypothesized that experienced fathers had learned the cues associated with pregnancy but first-time fathers had not.

However, there is a confound in the design of the study, since all experienced fathers had recently been caring for newborn infants during the early pregnancy of their mate, whereas first-time fathers did not. In another study, we paired experienced fathers with first-time mothers, so that there would be no prior infants present. All of these experienced fathers exhibited hormonal changes within a week of the excretion of glucocorticoids from the mother, showing that this hormonal response is not due to the presence of infants from the previous birth.[32] How do first-time fathers prepare for the birth of infants since they do have elevated prolactin levels before infants are born? We found an increase in affiliation behavior—grooming and huddling in the last month before infants were born. Since these behaviors can affect hormonal levels in the recipient, it is likely that this increase in affiliation (not seen in experienced parents) substitutes for the lack of an earlier response to hormonal changes.

However, first-time parents are much less successful in rearing infants than experienced parents. There is a much higher infant mortality rate with first-time parents. Part of this may be due to the fact that the more helpers there are in the family in addition to the parents, the greater infant survival will be. But part can also be the hormonal environment and behavioral skills of first-time parents. We have shown that with successive pregnancies, fathers have increasing levels of prolactin.[33] We have also observed in the wild that first-time mothers will carry infants more than 90 percent of the time in the first few weeks after infants are born. It seems that only with increasing experience will mothers relinquish care of their infants to others. In order for biparental or cooperative infant care to develop, mothers must be willing to let other group members look after their infants.

HOW PARENTS REWARD HELPERS AND PREVENT THEM FROM BREEDING

Helpers are extremely interested in new infants and from the very first day of birth, other group members will compete with each other to carry infants.

This can lead to increased levels of aggression among family members.[34] Despite the excitement of other family members for infants, the continued presence of adult helpers creates a biological conundrum. Individuals will have greater reproductive success if they breed on their own, so why should helpers set aside their own potential for reproduction? If they are related to the infants as full siblings, then they will gain as much reproductive success as if they were to breed themselves. But often in the wild, helpers are not full siblings and may even be unrelated. What can parents do to secure the services of helpers and prevent them from breeding?

We, and many others, have found that daughters in tamarin families never ovulate while living with their parents. To date, we have taken near daily hormonal samples from thirty-one daughters over many months and have never observed a single daughter ovulating. We see occasional spikes of hormones but these are never organized into the cycles typical of ovulation.[35] We know that females can reach puberty by the age of sixteen to eighteen months but we have studied females living in family groups for as long as forty-eight months without any signs of ovulation.[36] Yet as soon as we remove a female from her family group and pair her with a novel male, she will immediately ovulate and may become pregnant. (The record is eight days from family group to pregnancy.) When we transfer scents of the mother to the cage housing her daughter and her new mate, the daughter does not ovulate until after we stop scent transfers.[37] The suppression of fertility in daughters is not due to stress. When we examined cortisol levels in females, those that were reproductively suppressed had low baseline levels of cortisol no different from other family members.[38] As mentioned earlier, females do not begin to ovulate until they are in the presence of a novel male, so both the presence of scents from the mother and absence of novel males appear to limit reproduction by females. The only times when we observed two females pregnant in the same groups at the same time in wild cotton-top tamarins and common marmosets were after a novel male had joined the group.[39]

However, the same principles do not apply to young males. There is no reproductive suppression in males and adult males of two years of age acting as helpers have the same hormonal profile as fathers.[40] Puberty starts about twelve months of age and by twenty-four months sons have the same body weight and testicular size as fathers.[41] Furthermore, adult sons show erections and engage in sexual behavior as often as their fathers. However, adult sons more often engage in sexual activity with other members of the group, including brothers, sisters, and on occasion their own mothers.[42] This sexual activity of sons is not regulated by fathers and there is no aggression between father and son even in the minutes after the son has directed sexual behavior toward his mother.[43] Limited courtship and sexual behavior toward mothers by fully adult sons appears to be tolerated by both parents, and may be necessary for sons to learn how to interact appropriately with females in order to be prepared for their own future interaction with a mate.[44] Full copulations by sons with the mothers appear to be prevented by sons learning appropriate behavior over time and mothers physically rebuffing sons.[45]

Earlier, I mentioned the importance of grooming in pair bonding. We can also see the importance of grooming as a reward for infant care by helpers. In a field study of common marmosets, the breeding adults groomed subordinate helpers much more often than they were groomed by helpers.[46] In captive tamarins, we found that sons play a more important role in caregiving than daughters.[47] We also observed that pregnant mothers groomed their adult sons at a rate directly proportional to how much effort the sons had given with the previous infants. Sons who had done more infant care received grooming at higher rates. The opposite result was seen with fathers. They groomed most the sons who had contributed the least effort to previous infant care. We interpret these results in terms of the differential effects of helpers on each parent. The workload of mothers is reduced by having a single additional helper; thus, as long as the father is also present, it might make sense for her to invest in maintaining a cooperative, rewarding relationship with good caretakers who are already present.[48] However, the presence of multiple helpers affects fathers differently. In contrast to mothers, the workload of fathers is reduced further with each additional helper. Because the amount the father contributes to infant care can be continually offset, it may make sense for him to invest in cooperative relationships with as large a force of helpers as possible, including building good cooperative relationships with those sons who had not contributed as much to previous infant care.[49] Thus, mothers appear to be rewarding a good helper for past services and fathers appear to be recruiting poor helpers for future service.[50]

With daughters unable to ovulate and mothers deflecting copulation attempts by sons, the helpers in a group are prevented from reproducing. Positive rewards such as grooming and tolerance of nonconceptive sex in sons appear important in maintaining the services of helpers.[51] In other cooperatively breeding mammals (wolves, meerkats), parents often use aggression to coerce others into helping, but in marmosets and tamarins parents appear to reward helpers by increased tolerance and affiliation.[52]

HOW HELPERS BENEFIT AND FAMILY FEUDS

It is clear that parents benefit from the presence of helpers: Infant survival is high, fathers do not lose as much weight during infant care, and mothers have more energy to devote to nursing and gestation. But what are the benefits to helpers? As noted earlier, helpers that are full siblings of infants will gain as much reproductive success by helping siblings as they would by breeding on their own, but in many case in the wild, helpers are not full siblings. There are still other benefits that helpers might gain when they are not full siblings of the infants. First, in contrast to many other primate species, marmosets and tamarins need experience in caring for someone else's infants in order to become successful parents.[53] In some studies, the survival rate of infants born to parents with no prior infant care experience is zero! Young monkeys have to acquire infant care skills. Second, a male might use infant care as a courtship strategy.[54] If a female has a choice of mates, then selecting the one who demonstrates the greatest caretaking skills and interest in infants will help the female be more successful. Third, there may be no other option for breeding. In our field studies of cotton-top tamarins in Colombia and of common marmosets in Brazil, the number of groups remained stable over years suggesting that there is little suitable habitat for expansion. For a helper, the best route to reproduction may be staying home to inherit the parent's breeding area, or to keep close watch on neighboring groups for an opportunity to take over a breeding position.[55]

So far, I have painted a picture of family life in marmosets and tamarins as full of affiliation, positive social rewards, and a lack of aggression. But there is also a dark side to family life. In our captive tamarins, we occasionally observed tensions that predicted an outburst of aggression that required us to remove a group member. Tensions between mates were uncommon, with one male representing all of the cases where we had to separate reproductive adults from each other. The remaining cases of severe aggression were between brothers or between mothers and daughters.[56] The cases of mother-daughter aggression occurred only with daughters that began scent marking and showing sexual solicitation behavior, indicating that suppression of ovulation was not effective. The fights among brothers were typically instigated by older brothers, leading to expulsion of the younger brothers. These fights were possibly due to competition over carrying infants, but are curious in light of the fact that the same brothers who initiated aggression would several months earlier have been carrying their younger brothers and sharing food with them. Group size was also a factor in when aggression occurred, with captive groups at the upper limit of wild groups being the ones most likely to have serious aggression. In the wild, animals would be able to move away and avoid the severe aggression.

An extreme case of family violence occurred in a wild population of common marmosets. The reproductive female in two groups died, and over the course of the next months, the remaining groups became increasingly unstable with the daughters spending increasing time with some males from another group and the father and his sons spending time with the females of another group. Eventually four new groups were formed with the males and females of each of the original groups now in a separate group. Two daughters in each of the groups became pregnant shortly after the death of the mother and both daughters gave birth within two weeks of each other. Family life was anything but harmonious, with one sister attacking the other sister and eventually killing her nieces and nephews.[57] This continued for more than three successive pregnancies in each group with one sister killing the offspring of the other sister. Violence toward infants ceased only when two females could breed asynchronously, and the most parsimonious interpretation is that helpers are a scarce resource and multiple births are possible only when mothers can time-share helpers.[58]

HOW INFANTS BENEFIT

Are there any benefits to infants growing up in a cooperative care family? I have already noted that infant survival is greater. Multiple caregivers show a division of labor, taking turns in carrying infants, locating and attracting other group members to food, sharing food with infants, and providing vigilance against predators.[59] There is safety in numbers and with multiple caregivers sharing in all aspects of family life, infants will benefit.

However, there are more subtle benefits to multiple caregivers. Studies of rodents and of other primate species where mothers are the primary caregiver have found that the behavior of the mother has a profound effect on the behavior of the infant, and if the infant is a daughter on how the daughter will care for her own infants.[60] Two dimensions of maternal style have been identified in single-parent monkeys: (1) laissez-faire versus restricted mothers and (2) accepting versus rejecting mothers. Daughters tend to use with their own infants the style of infant response used by their own mothers. These maternal styles have consequences for infants. Infants of laissez-faire mothers are more confident and independent, but they are also more susceptible to predation since they take more risks.

Cooperative infant care raises the question of whether maternal style has any influence or whether there are family styles. We studied infants of three successive litters from ten tamarin families, five families that were well established and had many helpers and five families that were just starting families and typically had few helpers. There was great variability in how individual tamarins behaved toward infants, and family size and experience influenced the relative contribution of each family member. However, when we looked at caregiving from the perspective of the infant, we found to our surprise that each infant in each family received similar care, regardless of the number of helpers and experience of parents. Infants were carried as often, rejected as often, transferred as often, and received similar amounts of food transfers. There was no obvious "family style." Instead, it appeared that multiple caregivers served to buffer the variation of any one caregiver.[61] When we looked at infant behavior for markers of boldness or independence, there again were no effects of family size or experience. In fact, the variation in behavior between twins in the same litter was as great as variation between litters from different families. These findings suggest that by buffering the extremes of variation in infant care, behavioral development in tamarin infants is much less influenced by parental style and more influenced by intrinsic variation in temperament of each infant.

IMPLICATIONS FOR HUMAN PARENTING

There are several implications for human parenting that emerge from research on cooperatively breeding primates.

1. A strong relationship between mates is critical to establish trust between mother and father. This is important for mothers who need assurance that someone will help care for the infant, but may be even more important for fathers who can never be certain of their paternity.
2. Pair bonds are maintained through nonconceptive sex and physical contact. The role of positive physical interactions between mates is rarely emphasized. Such contact elicits release of hormones such as endogenous opioids and oxytocin that are involved in social reward.
3. Males can undergo physiological changes during the pregnancy of their mates that may make them more prepared to become involved in infant care.

The closer the interaction between parents during pregnancy, the greater the likelihood of a father being involved with infant care.

4. Parenting skills must be learned. If tamarins and marmosets need experience in caring for other infants in order to become successful parents, we should not assume that parenting is natural for humans. Before the modern era, virtually all children grew up in extended families where mothers and fathers could gain parenting skills. We need to create effective training programs for parents.

5. If mothers want fathers to be involved in infant care, they need to let go and allow fathers to be involved from the earliest stages. Men can learn quickly to avoid infant care if their offers of infant care are rejected.

6. If fathers receive physical rewards from their mates and are active participants in infant care, they are less likely to be distracted by other females.

7. Involving older siblings in infant care can decrease effort by both parents and develop the parenting skills of siblings.

8. Cooperative care benefits infants by buffering the variability in caretaking from a single individual. In the absence of extended families with multiple caregivers in modern society, high quality childcare outside of the home may provide an alternative means for cooperative childcare.

NOTES

1. Ziegler et al. 1987.
2. Tardif 1997:11–33.
3. Garber et al. 1984; Savage et al. 1996a; Savage et al. 1996b.
4. Snowdon 1996.
5. Sanchez et al. 1999; Achenbach and Snowdon 2002.
6. Savage et al. 1996b.
7. Elowson, Tannenbaum, and Snowdon 1991.
8. Roush and Snowdon 2001; Joyce and Snowdon 2007.
9. Hrdy 1999.
10. Carter, Getz, and Cohen-Parsons 1986.
11. Carter 1998.
12. Keverne, Martensz, and Tuite 1989; Uvnäs-Moberg 1998.
13. Widowski et al. 1992.
14. Savage, Ziegler, and Snowdon 1988.
15. Burley 1979.
16. Ziegler et al. 1993.

17. Washabaugh and Snowdon 1998.
18. Snowdon and Ziegler 2007.
19. Lazaro-Perea, Arruda, and Snowdon 2004.
20. Ziegler, Washabaugh, and Snowdon 2004.
21. Snowdon and Ziegler 2007.
22. Snowdon et al. 2010.
23. Evans 1983; Anzenberger 1985.
24. Ferris et al. 2001.
25. Ziegler et al. 2005.
26. Prudom et al. 2008.
27. Dixson and George 1982; da Silva Mota et al. 2006.
28. Ziegler, Wegner, and Snowdon 1996.
29. Ziegler et al. 2004.
30. Ziegler et al. 2006.
31. Ziegler, Washabaugh, and Snowdon 2004.
32. Almond, Ziegler, and Snowdon 2008.
33. Ziegler, Wegner, and Snowdon 1996.
34. Achenbach and Snowdon 1998.
35. Ziegler et al. 1987.
36. Savage et al. 1988.
37. Ibid.
38. Ziegler, Scheffler, and Snowdon 1995.
39. Savage et al. 1996a; Lazaro-Perea et al. 2000.
40. Ginther, Ziegler, and Snowdon 2001; Ginther et al. 2002.
41. Ginther et al. 2002.
42. Ginther, Ziegler, and Snowdon 2001; Ginther et al. 2002.
43. Anita J. Ginther and Charles T. Snowdon. In prep. "Nonconceptive sexual and post-sexual behavior of fathers and adult sons with females in breeding family groups of cotton-top tamarins."
44. Ginther 2008.
45. Anita J. Ginther and Charles T. Snowdon. In prep. "Nonconceptive sexual and post-sexual behavior of fathers and adult sons with females in breeding family groups of cotton-top tamarins."
46. Lazaro-Perea, Arruda, and Snowdon 2004.
47. Zahed, Kurian, and Snowdon 2010.
48. Ginther and Snowdon 2009.
49. Ibid.
50. Ibid.
51. Ginther 2008; Ginther and Snowdon 2009; Anita J. Ginther and Charles T. Snowdon. In prep. "Nonconceptive sexual and post-sexual behavior of fathers and adult sons with females in breeding family groups of cotton-top tamarins."

52. Ginther 2008; Ginther and Snowdon 2009.
53. Snowdon 1996.
54. Smuts and Gubernick 1992.
55. Snowdon 1996.
56. Snowdon and Pickhard 1999.
57. Lazaro-Perea et al. 2000.
58. Digby 1995.
59. Savage et al. 1996b.
60. Fairbanks 1996; Suomi 1987.
61. Washabaugh, Ziegler, and Snowdon 2002.

REFERENCES

Achenbach, Gretchen G. and Charles T. Snowdon. 1998. "Response to Sibling Birth in Juvenile Cotton-Top Tamarins (*Saguinus oedipus*)." *Behaviour* 135:845–862.

Achenbach, Gretchen G. and Charles T. Snowdon. 2002. "Costs of Caregiving: Weight Loss in Captive Adult Male Cotton-Top Tamarins (*Saguinus oedipus*) Following the Birth of Infants." *International Journal of Primatology* 23:179–189.

Almond, Rosamunde E. A., Toni E. Ziegler, and Charles T. Snowdon. 2008. "Changes in Prolactin and Glucocorticoid Levels in Cotton-Top Tamarin Fathers During Their Mate's Pregnancy: The Effect of Infants and Paternal Experience." *American Journal of Primatology* 70:560–565.

Anzenberger, Gustl. 1985. "How Stranger Encounters of Common Marmosets (*Callithrix jacchus jacchus*) Are Influenced by Family Members: The Quality of Behavior." *Folia Primatologica* 45:204–224.

Burley, Nancy. 1979. "The Evolution of Concealed Ovulation." *American Naturalist* 114:835–858.

Carter, C. Sue. 1998. "Neuroendocrine Perspectives on Social Attachment and Love." *Psychoneuroendocrinology* 23:779–818.

Carter, C. Sue, Lowell L. Getz, and Martha Cohen-Parsons. 1986. "Relationships Between Social Organization and Behavioral Endocrinology in a Monogamous Mammal." *Advances in the Study of Behavior* 16:109–145.

da Silva Mota, Maria Teresa, Celso Rodrigues Franci, and Maria Bernadete Cordeiro de Sousa. 2006. "Hormonal Changes Related to Paternal and Alloparental Care in Common Marmosets (*Callithrix jacchus*)." *Hormones and Behavior* 49:293–302.

Digby, Leslie. 1995. "Infant Care, Infanticide and Female Reproductive Strategies in Polygynous Groups of Common Marmosets (*Callithrix jacchus*)." *Behavioral Ecology and Sociobiology* 37:51–61.

Dixson, Alan F. and L. George. 1982. "Prolactin and Parental Behavior in a Male New World Primate." *Nature* 299:551–553.

Elowson, A. Margaret, Pamela L. Tannenbaum, and Charles T. Snowdon. 1991. "Food Associated Calls Correlate with Food Preferences in Cotton-Top Tamarins." *Animal Behaviour* 42:931–937.

Evans, Sian. 1983. "The Pair-Bond of the Common Marmoset, *Callithrix jacchus jacchus*: An Experimental Investigation." *Animal Behaviour* 31:651–658.

Fairbanks. Lynn A. 1996. "Individual Differences in Maternal Style: Causes and Consequences for Mothers and Offspring." In *Parental Care: Evolution, Mechanisms and Adaptive Significance*, ed. Jay S. Rosenblatt and Charles T. Snowdon, 579–611. San Diego: Academic.

Ferris, Craig F., Charles T. Snowdon, Jean A. King, Timothy Q. Duong, Toni E. Ziegler, Kamil Ugurbil, Reinhard Ludwig, Nancy J. Schultz-Darken, Zizi Wu, David P. Olson, John M Sullivan, Jr., Pamela L. Tannebaum, and J. Thomas Vaughn. 2001. "Functional Imaging of Brain Activity in Conscious Monkeys Responding to Sexually Arousing Cues." *NeuroReport* 12:2231–2236.

Garber, Paul A., Luis Moya, and Carlos Malaga. 1984. "A Preliminary Field Study of the Mustached Tamarin Monkey (*Saguinus mystax*) in Northeastern Peru: Questions Concerned with the Evolution of a Communal Breeding System." *Folia Primatologica* 42:17–32.

Ginther, Anita J. 2008. "Reproductive Biology and Social Strategies of Cooperatively Breeding Adult Male Cotton-Top Tamarins (*Saguinus oedipus oedipus*) in Two Life-History Phases: Fathers and Adult Sons." PhD thesis, University of Wisconsin-Madison.

Ginther, Anita J., Anne A. Carlson, Toni E. Ziegler, and Charles T. Snowdon. 2002. "Neonatal and Pubertal Development in Males of a Cooperatively Breeding Primate, the Cotton-Top Tamarin (*Saguinus oedipus oedipus*)." *Biology of Reproduction* 66:282–290.

Ginther, Anita J. and Charles T. Snowdon. 2009. "Expectant Parents Groom Adult Sons According to Previous Alloparenting in a Biparental Cooperatively Breeding Primate." *Animal Behaviour*, 78:287–297.

Ginther, Anita J., Toni E Ziegler, and Charles T. Snowdon. 2001. "Reproductive Biology of Captive Male Cotton-Top Tamarin Monkeys as a Function of Social Environment." *Animal Behaviour* 61:65–78.

Hrdy, Sarah Blaffer. 1999. *Mother Nature*. New York: Ballantine.

Joyce, Stella M. and Charles T. Snowdon. 2007. "Developmental Changes in Food Transfers in Cotton-Top Tamarins (*Saguinus oedipus*)." *American Journal of Primatology* 28:257–270.

Keverne, E. Barry, N. D. Martensz, and B. Tuite. 1989. "Beta-Endorphin Concentrations in Cerebrospinal Fluid of Monkeys as Influenced by Grooming Relationships." *Psychoneuroendocrinology* 14:155–161.

Lazaro-Perea, Cristina, M. Fatima Arruda, and Charles T. Snowdon. 2004. "Grooming as Reward? Social Functions of Grooming in Cooperatively Breeding Marmosets." *Animal Behaviour* 67:627–636.

Lazaro-Perea, Cristina, Carla S. S. Castro, Rebecca Harrison, Arrilton Araujo, M. Fatima Arruda, and Charles T Snowdon. 2000. "Behavioral and Demographic Changes Following the Loss of the Breeding Female in Cooperatively Breeding Marmosets." *Behavioral Ecology and Sociobiology* 48:137–146.

Prudom, Shelley L., Carrie A. Broz, Nancy J. Schultz-Darken, Craig T. Ferris, Charles T. Snowdon, and Craig F. Ferris. 2008. "Exposure to Infant Scent Lowers Serum Testosterone in Father Common Marmosets (*Callithrix jacchus*)." *Biology Letters* 4(6):603–605.

Roush, Rebecca S. and Charles T. Snowdon. 2001. "Food Transfers and the Development of Feeding Behavior and Food-Associated Vocalizations in Cotton-Top Tamarins." *Ethology* 107:415–429.

Sanchez, Susana, Fernando Peleaz, Carlos Gil-Burmann, and Wolfgang Kaumann. 1999. "Costs of Infant Carrying in the Cotton-Top Tamarin." *American Journal of Primatology* 48:99–111.

Savage, Anne, Humberto Giraldo, Luis Soto, and Charles T. Snowdon. 1996a. "Demography, Group Composition and Dispersal of Wild Cotton-Top Tamarin Groups." *American Journal of Primatology* 38:85–100.

Savage, Anne, Charles T. Snowdon, Humberto Giraldo, and Luis Soto. 1996b. "Parental Care Patterns and Vigilance in Wild Cotton-Top Tamarins (*Saguinus oedipus*)" In *Adaptive Radiations of Neotropical Primates*, ed. Marilyn Norconk, Alfred Rosenberger, and Paul A. Garber, 187–199. New York: Plenum.

Savage, Anne, Toni E. Ziegler, and Charles T. Snowdon. 1988. "Sociosexual Development, Pair Bond Formation and Mechanisms of Fertility Suppression in Female Cotton-Top Tamarins (*Saguinus oedipus oedipus*)." *American Journal of Primatology* 14:345–359.

Smuts, Barbara B. and David J. Gubernick. 1992. "Male-Infant Relationships in Nonhuman Primates: Paternal Investment or Mating Effort." In *Father-Child Relations: Cultural and Biosocial Contexts*, ed. Barry S. Hewlett, 1–30. Piscataway, NJ: Aldine.

Snowdon, Charles T. 1996. "Parental Care in Cooperatively Breeding Species." In *Parental Care: Evolution, Mechanisms and Adaptive Significance*, ed. Jay S. Rosenblatt and Charles T. Snowdon, 643–689. San Diego: Academic.

Snowdon, Charles T. and Jenifer J. Pickhard. 1999. "Family Feuds: Severe Aggression Among Cooperatively Breeding Cotton-Top Tamarins." *International Journal of Primatology* 20:651–663.

Snowdon, Charles T., Bridget A. Pieper, Katherine A. Cronin, Aimee V. Kurian, Carla Y. Boe, and Toni E. Ziegler. 2010. "Variation in Oxytocin Levels is Associated with Variation in Affiliative Behavior in Monogamous Pairbonded Tamarins." *Hormones and Behavior* 58:614–618.

Snowdon, Charles T. and Toni E. Ziegler. 2007. "Growing Up Cooperatively: Family Processes and Infant Care in Marmosets and Tamarins." *Journal of Developmental Processes* 2:40–66.

Suomi, Stephen J. 1987. "Genetic and Maternal Contributions to Individual Differences in Rhesus Monkey Biobehavioral Development." In *Perinatal Development: A Psychobiological Perspective*, ed. Norman A. Krasnegor, Elliott M. Blass, Myron A. Hofer, and William P. Smotherman, 397–419. Orlando: Academic.

Tardif, Suzette D. 1997. "The Bioenergetics of Parental Behavior and the Evolution of Alloparental Care in Marmosets and Tamarins" in *Cooperative Breeding in Mammals*, ed. Nancy G. Solomon and Jeffrey A. French, 11–33. New York: Cambridge University.

Uvnäs-Moberg, Kersten. 1998. "Oxytocin May Mediate the Benefits of Positive Social Interaction and Emotions." *Psychoneuroendocrinology* 23:819–835.

Washabaugh, Kate and Charles T. Snowdon. 1998. "Chemical Communication of Reproductive Status in Female Cotton-Top Tamarins (*Saguinus o. oedipus*)." *American Journal of Primatology* 45:337–349.

Washabaugh, Kate F., Toni E. Ziegler, and Charles T. Snowdon. 2002. "Variations in Care for Cotton-Top Tamarin (*Saguinus oedipus*) Infants as a Function of Parental Experience and Group Size." *Animal Behaviour* 63:1163–1174.

Widowski, Tina M., Teresa A. Porter, Toni E. Ziegler, and Charles T. Snowdon. 1992. "The Stimulatory Effect of Males on the Initiation, but Not the Maintenance, of Ovarian Cycling in Cotton-Top Tamarins (*Saguinus oedipus*)." *American Journal of Primatology* 26:97–108.

Zahed, Sofia R., Aimee V. Kurian, and C. T. Snowdon. 2010. "Social Dynamics and Individual Plasticity of Infant Care Behavior in Cooperatively Breeding Cotton-Top Tamarins." *American Journal of Primatology* 72:296–306.

Ziegler, Toni E., William E. Bridson, Charles T. Snowdon, and Svetlana Eman. 1987. "Urinary Gonadotropin and Estrogen Excretion During the Postpartum Estrous, Conception and Pregnancy in the Cotton-Top Tamarin (*Saguinus oedipus oedipus*)." *American Journal of Primatology* 12:127–140.

Ziegler, Toni E., Gisele Epple, Charles T. Snowdon, Teresa A. Porter, Ann Belcher, and Irmgard Kuederling. 1993. "Detection of the Chemical Signals of Ovulation in the Cotton-Top Tamarin, *Saguinus oedipus*." *Animal Behaviour* 45:313–322.

Ziegler, Toni E., Shelley L. Prudom, Nancy J. Schultz-Darken, Aimee V. Kurian, and Charles T. Snowdon. 2006. "Pregnancy Weight Gain: Marmoset and Tamarin Dads Show It Too." *Biology Letters* 2:181–183.

Ziegler, Toni E., Gunther Scheffler, and Charles T. Snowdon. 1995. "The Relationship of Cortisol Levels to Social Environment and Reproductive Functioning in Female Cotton-Top Tamarins, *Saguinus oedipus*." *Hormones and Behavior* 29:407–424.

Ziegler, Toni E., Nancy J. Schultz-Darken, Jillian J. Scott, Charles T. Snowdon, and Craig F. Ferris. 2005. "Neuroendocrine Response to Female Ovulatory Odors Depends Upon Social Condition in Male Common Marmosets, *Callithrix jacchus*." *Hormones and Behavior* 47:56–64.

Ziegler, Toni E., Kate F. Washabaugh, and Charles T. Snowdon. 2004. "Responsiveness of Expectant Male Cotton-Top Tamarins, *Saguinus oedipus*, to Mate's Pregnancy." *Hormones and Behavior* 45:84–92.

Ziegler, Toni E., Frederick H. Wegner, and Charles T. Snowdon. 1996. "A Hormonal Role for Male Parental Care in a New World Primate, the Cotton-Top Tamarin *(Saguinus oedipus)*." *Hormones and Behavior* 30:287–297.

3

HUMAN PARENTING FROM AN EVOLUTIONARY PERSPECTIVE

David F. Bjorklund and Ashley C. Jordan

CHILDREN ARE PROFOUNDLY INFLUENCED by their parents. In fact, parents and families have long been viewed "as the most significant influences on the developing child."[1] Children owe their very lives to their parents, and how and whether a child grows up will depend on the actions of his or her parents. Although parental effects extend to the genes that guide physical development, our primary focus here is on nongenetic, mainly postnatal, effects. We do not intend to imply that parents are the only significant factor in child development. Peers, for example, play a potent role in many aspects of a child's development, as does the greater culture in which children grow up.[2] Nonetheless, mothers and fathers, though not necessarily in equal degrees, significantly impact a child's development. Moreover, the patterns of childcare of modern men and women have deep evolutionary histories and share much in common with other mammals, making patterns of child-rearing only variations on a basic primate theme. Developing an appreciation of the evolutionary roots of parenting promises to provide insights into contemporary behavior.

We begin this chapter with a brief overview of some core concepts of evolutionary theory and a sketch of human evolution, particularly as it relates to childcare. We then present parental investment theory, a theory that explains male and female animals' decisions concerning the amount of nurturing, or investment, they provide to their offspring, with a special focus on humans.[3] We then examine the evolution of the human family, and conclude by looking at some of the factors that influence the care that mothers, fathers, and other people in a child's life provide.

EVOLUTIONARY THEORY AND *HOMO SAPIENS'* PLACE IN THE WORLD

EVOLUTION BY NATURAL SELECTION

Once considered taboo, evolutionary theory has gained the attention of social scientists trying to explain complex human behaviors. Although not without controversy, evolutionary psychology applies the basic principles of Darwin's theory of evolution by natural selection to human behavior.[4] The idea of evolution by natural selection rests on four basic premises. First, in any generation, more offspring are produced than will survive; second, there is naturally occurring variation in features or traits within members of a generation; third, these individual differences are heritable; and finally, individuals with collections of traits that fit well with the local environment are more apt to survive and have more offspring than individuals whose traits do not fit as well with the local environment.

Natural selection only works through variations that occur naturally within a population, and, even when there is strong selection pressure (i.e., intense competition associated with survival and reproduction), evolution is a slow process. The human mind/brain evolved over a period of hundreds of thousands of years, when ancestral hominids lived as hunter-gatherers and selection pressures were vastly different from what they are today. As a result, many adaptations that modern humans possess may not be as adaptive today as they would have been in ancient environments and may even be maladaptive. For example, humans' penchant for sweet and fatty foods was surely adaptive for our nomadic ancestors, who did not know where their next meal was coming from, but is associated with diabetes, obesity, and high blood pressure today for many people living in developed countries with easy access to grocery stores and fast food.

Central to modern evolutionary theory is the concept of *inclusive fitness*, which refers essentially to how many copies of one's genes persist into future generations.[5] This includes the offspring and grandoffspring one has, but also copies of one's genes that are possessed by siblings, nieces, and nephews, for example. Basically, individuals should have evolved psychological mechanisms that guide their behavior to enhance their inclusive fitness.

The modern definition of evolution relates to changes in gene frequency in populations over time. This, for some, implies a form of genetic determinism, which has been rightly rejected by modern behavioral and social scientists. In actuality, Darwin himself emphasized the importance of the fit between an individual and its environment, making evolutionary theory from its inception one that focused on organism-environment interactions, what contemporary scholars refer to as gene-environment interaction. (The concept of the gene was unknown to Darwin.) Recently, evolutionary theorists in both biology and psychology have stressed the role of development in evolution, with some emphasizing how modifications in experiences early in life, especially through maternal effects, can alter the course of development and possibly the course of evolution.[6] Such effects may be particularly important for a species such as *Homo sapiens*, whose extended period of immaturity and prolonged dependence makes them especially susceptible to variations in parenting behavior.

One misconception of evolutionary theory related to beliefs in genetic determinism is that if a behavior has evolved it is natural, and thus normal, or justifiable in some other way. The idea that something is "good" because it is natural is called *naturalistic fallacy*. The origins of a behavior, whether primarily biological or cultural, do not qualify the goodness or appropriateness of that behavior. Although stealing from a neighbor may have resulted in acquisition of valuable resources, and murdering one's rival may have produced substantial gains for our ancestors in some contexts, these and many other "natural" behaviors can be superseded by culture and humans' superior ability for social organization and cooperation. In this vein, differences in evolved biases that men and women may have toward children, parenting, and one another are not, in and of themselves, good or inevitable. Nonetheless, they are a part of our biological heritage, and an understanding of these biases will help us understand contemporary human behavior and possibly help ameliorate some "problem" behaviors in modern societies.

A BRIEF NATURAL HISTORY OF *HOMO SAPIENS*

The ancestral environment in which early humans evolved is often referred to as the *environment of evolutionary adaptedness*. Although it is impossible to pinpoint exactly what this environment was like and when it began, much information can be gained from fossil evidence. Humans last shared a common ancestor with modern chimpanzees (*Pan troglodytes*) and bonobos (*Pan paniscus*) approximately five to seven million years ago. Over this time, a number of hominid (or hominin) species lived in Africa, with modern humans (*Homo sapiens*) evolving from related species (e.g., *Homo ergaster*) and eventually migrating out of Africa and replacing all other members of the *Homo* genus (e.g., *Homo erectus*, *Homo neanderthalensis*).[7] Based on fossil evidence, the lifestyles of contemporary hunter-gatherers, and research on our primate cousins, paleoanthropologists have put together a sketch of how ancient humans may have lived. If modern chimpanzees and bonobos are any indication, humans have always been a social species. Our ancestors likely lived in groups of between thirty and sixty people, making a living as hunters, gatherers, and scavengers. There was likely substantial division of labor, with males involved in hunting and primitive warfare while females did most of the gathering and carried the bulk of the responsibility for childcare.

There are many special features about humans, but one of them is an extended juvenile period. Within mammals, the length of the juvenile period is associated with brain size, with animals having larger brains taking longer to attain sexual maturity.[8] Humans take longer to reach adulthood than any other mammal, and they also have the largest brain relative to body size.[9] Within primates, brain size and length of the juvenile period are also related to the size of the social group, and this relationship has caused some to speculate that it was the confluence of a big brain, an extended juvenile period, and living in socially complex groups that was the impetus for human intelligence.[10] An extended juvenile period is very costly. Parents must provide care and resources to their dependent offspring, possibly postponing having additional children, and there is the chance of dying before reproducing, the ultimate Darwinian dead end. Biologists assume that when aspects of an animal's life history, such as an extended juvenile period, have great costs, there must also be great benefits otherwise it would have been weeded out by natural selection. What might some of those benefits be? Some have argued that an extended juvenile period, in combination with a large brain and enhanced learning abilities afforded ancestral humans time to acquire technological skills needed for making and using tools, foraging, and hunting.[11] Others have emphasized that the most complicated tasks for most people are not technical but social, and that a prolonged period of immaturity was (and continues to be) necessary to learn about the complexities associated with group living.[12] This prolonged period of immaturity meant that mothers, the primary caretakers in (nearly) all mammals and in all human cultures, required help in rearing their offspring. Humans became what anthropologist Sara Hrdy calls cooperative breeders, with mothers receiving assistance from mainly female kin in rearing offspring.[13] However, the special needs of a slow-growing child also placed pressures on fathers to invest more in their children, or their children's mothers.[14] Thus, humans' long sojourn to adulthood not only contributed to our species' unique pattern of intellectual abilities, but also to the invention of the human family.[15]

THE ORIGIN OF HUMAN FAMILIES

The family is the social group that is principally responsible for the care and rearing of children. Although there are substantial cultural differences in how families are constituted (as reflected, for example, by monogamous or polygamous marriages), as a species, humans form *biparental* (both mother and father provide some support) and *extended families* (several genetically related adults typically help to tend the young).[16]

Families are not unique to humans, and scientists have looked at extant primates for the possible roots of the human family. Although of all the great apes, chimpanzees and bonobos most recently shared a common ancestor with humans, they are not likely the best models for the origins of human families. Both species display a promiscuous form of mating, leading to almost no paternity certainty, and as a result, like most mammals, males engage in no childcare. Evolutionary developmental psychologist David Geary and evolutionary anthropologist Mark Flinn proposed that goril-las might provide a better model for the family structure of our hominid ancestors.[17]

Gorilla social structures share many similarities with those of modern humans, most notably that gorillas often form long-term social relationships similar to those of adult human male-female partnerships. Gorillas are a polygamous species, with a single male having multiple mates. While pater-nity certainty is not as high for male gorillas as for humans, it does tend to be relatively higher than that of chimpanzees and bonobos. This is because gorilla harems generally consist of only one or two adult reproducing males, with the dominant male siring the majority of the offspring. Furthermore, their groups are generally isolated from other gorillas due to mountainous terrain and a lack of kin-based social networks.[18] As is expected when pater-nity certainty is high, male gorillas protect and play with their offspring, much as human fathers do (although they do not take midnight feedings as some human fathers do).

A major difference between gorillas and humans is that humans live in larger social groups with intricate social networks rooted in kin-based coalitions. Living in multi-male, multi-female communities creates com-plex social relationships and an increased risk of *cuckoldry* (the domestic father not being the genetic father). Geary and Flinn proposed that these differences caused humans' ancestors to diverge from the basic gorilla family model, resulting in the current human pattern, with females focusing more on parenting and males focusing more on mating (see discussion of parental investment theory that follows).[19]

According to Geary and Flinn, because females carry the burden of obligatory childcare, they evolved strategies to retain their mates so they could continue to reap the benefits of the resources males provide. Among these strategies are common mate-retention tactics—concealed ovulation, female aversion to casual sex, pair-bonding, and nonreproductive sexuality—that served to increase the affiliation between a man and woman, resulting in a family structure that includes some male parenting, similar to those seen in modern human societies.

Family structure is rare in nonhuman primates and the only identified cooperative breeders other than humans are tamarins and marmosets. Similar to humans, these primates work together to care for infants, thus increasing the chance of infant survival proportionately to the amount of care given and reducing the effect of individual differences in parenting style, since often times the entire family (generally between five to eight individuals) contributes to raising an infant. Studies of tamarins and marmosets have also found that they employ many of the aforementioned mate-retention tactics, suggesting that these human behaviors may have evolutionary ties to nonhuman primates as well.[20]

PARENTAL INVESTMENT THEORY

Debates about how much mothers and fathers should invest in childcare are not restricted to discussions among contemporary parents, but have been central to evolutionary theory. (Biologists use the term invest to reflect the amount of time and resources parents devote to their offspring. The term investment implies that we expect to get something back for our troubles. In evolutionary biology, that something is offspring who reach adulthood and reproduce themselves, passing some of the investor's genes to the next generation.) Although an offspring carries the genes of both its mother and father, suggesting that the payoff, and thus investment in, any offspring should be the same for the two sexes, that is not always the case. In most species, there is greater obligatory care of offspring for females than for males. For example, in mammals, conception and gestation occur within the female body, and she must invest the time associated with pregnancy as well as that required by postpartum suckling. Females in most mammalian species also engage in more childcare (e.g., carrying the infant, foraging for food for weanlings) than males. In contrast, at a bare minimum, males must only invest the time required for attracting a mate and the subsequent act of copulation. In fact, male parenting is observed in fewer than five percent of mammalian species.[21]

As a result of differences in obligatory investment in offspring, males and females developed different psychologies with respect to how much time and effort they devote to mating versus parenting. These differences are captured by biologist Robert Trivers' *parental investment theory*.[22] Males tend to focus more attention on mating, including efforts to compete for, attract, and retain potential mates, whereas females invest more time and attention in parenting than in mating. According to Trivers, the sex that invests more in parenting (usually females) becomes a limiting resource to the potential reproductive fitness of the lesser-investing sex (usually males).

Parental investment theory applies to all sexually reproducing animals, including humans. For example, while men have an almost unlimited supply of sperm and can reproduce from puberty almost until death, women have a limited number of ova and can only reproduce for a relatively short period of time beginning at puberty and extending no longer than through their forties, with fertility peaking in the mid-twenties.[23] Because the risk of pregnancy carries with it years of obligatory maternal investment for the offspring's survival, women are more generally selective in assenting to sex than are men.[24] In contrast, men need only invest the short time needed for copulation and are more inclined to compete, often vigorously, with one another for access to women. Although these statements may strike a sour chord with modern sensibilities, every female a male inseminates increases his potential inclusive fitness (the number of offspring he may have) and, at the same time, reduces the potential mates a female can have, at least while she is pregnant. From this perspective, males' fitness is best served by siring as many offspring as possible, rather than spending time and energy dedicated to investing in children. In contrast, females' reproductive success is better served by investing in offspring rather than investing in (multiple) mating efforts. This is at the extreme, of course, and the very nature of human development makes paternal investment, if not necessary, at least an asset. Men can increase their inclusive fitness by investing in their children, and most men do, providing, if not childcare, resources to their mates and their children.[25] However, in both traditional and contemporary cultures, and surely in our past, women provided the bulk of the childcare. Because human males can gain some benefit from investing in their children, even though it is not obligatory, conflict may arise between males and females as a result of clashing interests of the two sexes. "Females attempt to obtain more paternal investment than males prefer to give, whereas males attempt to reduce paternal investment and focus more resources on mating effort."[26]

We want to be clear that the mating and parenting decisions that men and women are purported to make are not necessarily conscious, but are based on implicit (that is, out of self-awareness) strategies that have evolved because, on average, they benefited the animals that possessed them. Humans, however, have consciousness, making them able to calculate the costs and benefits of any action and to override them if they see fit.

There are also apparent sex differences in the emotional patterns of men and women related to differences in parental investment. Although expressing all emotions other than anger stronger than men, women are better able to regulate emotions than men.[27] Women's superior ability to manage emotional expression may aid their relationships with men as well as with other women. Men have a physical advantage over women on average, and in the face of potentially hostile or aggressive men, women are able to rely on relationship-management skills that could potentially prove life saving; furthermore, better emotional regulation could help women with intrasexual (female-female) competition, which is characterized more by relational, or indirect, aggression (spreading malicious gossip, social exclusion, and reputation damage among other things) rather than direct, physical aggression as is typically seen in males.[28] These tactics serve as mate-retention devices, in that women are able to manage their relationships with mates, increasing the likelihood of continued investment in them and their offspring. Females are also better able to inhibit emotional expression than males, and this ability, in addition to helping them regulate social relations with men and other women, may serve to make them better mothers.[29] Caring for infants and young children often requires delaying one's own gratification and the inhibition of aggressive responses, areas in which a female advantage is consistently found.[30]

Sex differences related to parenting do not appear fully formed in adulthood but have developmental origins. Children tend to segregate themselves into same-sex groups from an early age, showing an increasing preference for children of their same sex in their school years, a trend that is found cross-culturally.[31] The types of play that boys and girls partake in are also very different. Boys frequently engage in rough-and-tumble play and competitive activities and frequently use a variety of aggressive strategies for gaining or maintaining leadership within their social group. Some have proposed that such play provides practice for fighting seen adolescence and adulthood and helps boys learn about maneuvering in the social hierarchy of other boys, with whom in traditional environments they would continue to interact with as adults.[32] Boys' fantasy play is also often focused on aggression, power, and dominance, and is frequently part of rough-and-tumble play.[33] Girls' play, in contrast, is less vigorous and more focused on social relationships. This is especially apparent in children's fantasy play, with common themes in girls' pretend play centering on topics such as playing house or school ("You be the baby and I'll be the mommy"). Such play is often focused on parenting.[34] This is related to girls' greater interest in infants, a pattern that has been found across cultures and for many primates.[35]

These different types of social behaviors reflect the different adaptive problems of each respective sex. This period of socializing helps children to learn valuable skills, specifically those associated with intrasexual competition that will gain importance in their lives especially as they reach adulthood.[36]

CARING FOR AND INVESTING IN CHILDREN

Although, as we noted, there are sex differences in how much mothers and fathers devote to childcare, there are also substantial individual differences in the investment men and women make in their children. Some of the investment decisions that mothers and fathers make have been honed by thousands, if not millions, of years of evolution. Some of the evolved biases people have toward investing in their children may actually be maladaptive in modern society, but, of course, they can be overridden by conscious decision-making. Nonetheless, contemporary men and women have essentially the same brains as their stone-age ancestors, and their decisions about parenting are affected, for the better or worse, by these evolved biases.

MATERNAL CARE

There is no other being as important to a mammal infant as its mother, and this includes humans. In traditional cultures, children without mothers usually die.[37] As we have seen, women are biased to care for and invest in their children; however, there is no maternal instinct of a kind that ensures a new mother will provide appropriate care for her infant. The work of the pioneering primatologist Harry Harlow with motherless mothers reflected this. When female monkeys who had been raised in social isolation for their first six months later became mothers themselves, they ignored, abused, and sometimes killed their helpless offspring.[38]

However, it is not only pathological mothers who invest less than is ideal (from the point of view of the infant) in their offspring. For the vast majority of our species' history, resources were scarce and survival uncertain. The chance of living to adulthood for our ancestors was about 50 percent. Given those odds, natural selection would favor women who could identify cues that signal the likelihood of a child reaching adulthood and then devoting the necessary care to those children, reducing care to riskier offspring. Such decisions may seem abhorrent to us, but given what we know about maternal behavior in other species and in traditional groups of humans, and the incidence in contemporary society of children being abused or neglected, we can be confident that such thinking surely characterized our foremothers. These are not necessarily conscious thoughts, but rather implicit, and perhaps automatic, cognitions that proved adaptive to our ancestors.[39]

Perhaps the most obvious cue to survivability mothers can use is a child's physical and mental health. Children with mental retardation or other congenital problems are two to ten times more likely to be abused sometime during childhood than nonafflicted children.[40] When these children are institutionalized, the amount of parental care often decreases sharply, with some parents rarely ever seeing their children again.[41] In most cases, differential care of unhealthy children is less severe and likely unconscious. For instance, in one study, mothers with low birth weight and sickly twins displayed more positive behaviors, such as looking at, talking to, playing with, kissing, holding, and soothing, toward the healthier of the two twins.[42]

Both a mother's and a child's age are also predictors of maternal neglect. Younger women have many childbearing years ahead of them and are less apt to devote considerable care to high-risk infants than older women, who have fewer opportunities to have more children.[43] Concerning children's age, because rates of infant mortality have traditionally been high, women should devote more care to older than younger children, particularly when resources are scarce and investment in a younger child can result in the deterioration and possibly death of an older child. Mother and child's ages are also predictors of the most extreme form of disinvestment, filicide, the killing of a child. Teenage mothers are more likely to kill their infants than older women, a pattern found in both developed and traditional societies.[44] And although fathers are overall more likely to kill a child than mothers, the exception is during infancy, especially the first month, when the culprit is most apt to be the mother.[45] Nearly all incidences of neonatalcide, the killing of a newborn, are performed by mothers. Although this is clearly criminal behavior in modern society, it is sanctioned, and sometimes expected, in many traditional societies when resources are scarce and the newborn or the more sickly twin will not likely survive or would take resources away from a mother's other children.[46] From an evolutionary perspective, this is not pathological behavior, but a life-or-death decision based on weighing a host of factors related to one's inclusive fitness.

Mothers are also sensitive to the amount of social support they can expect in helping rear their children. Recall that humans are cooperative breeders. Abuse, neglect, and even infanticide are more common when mothers have little prospect of social support, including support from the father.[47] Fortunately, modern society provides single mothers who lack extensive family support with assistance in rearing their children, but inadequate social support was surely a serious concern for our foremothers and remains a problem for many single mothers in the world today.

MATERNAL EFFECTS

Before we discuss factors that affect paternal investment, we would like to say a few things about the role of mothers in children's development. It goes without saying that mothers have a major influence on their children. Some of this influence can be attributed to prenatal effects. In mammals, where mothers provide nutrition to the fetus through the placenta, the effects on the fetus of malnutrition and teratogens, including alcohol, drugs, and infections, among many others, are well documented.[48] In humans, even the emotional state of a pregnant woman has been related to subsequent child development, with high levels of anxiety having a detrimental effect on offspring behavioral development, while moderate levels of stress have a somewhat positive effect on the child's later mental development.[49]

Mammal mothers also, of course, have substantial postnatal influence on their offspring. Freud famously blamed mothers for whatever ailed their adult children, but more recent research has examined specific aspects of emotional, social, and cognitive development, examining how individual differences in maternal behavior affects ontogeny. Although most contemporary studies talk of "parenting effects," the vast bulk of the observations are of mothers and their infants and children. Fathers are much more rarely studied.[50] Some of the topics in which maternal effects have been examined include intelligence as measured by IQ, stress reactivity, attachment, empathy, shared attention, referential communication, social learning, language, autobiographical memory, and theory of mind (understanding that people's behavior is motivated by what they know and what they want), among others.[51]

It is beyond the scope of this chapter to review the literature on postnatal maternal effects on children's development, but we will examine briefly two topics: attachment and stress reactivity. It has been well documented that individual differences in maternal behaviors are related to subsequent quality of attachment, which in turn is related to cognitive, social, and emotional functioning later in life.[52] For example, mothers of children described as securely attached are more sensitive and responsive to their infants' signals of physical, social, and emotional needs and enjoy close contact with them compared to mothers of infants with insecure attachment styles who are generally found to be less responsive to their infants.[53] In turn, securely attached infants display better psychological adjustment later in life. In fact, the research literature on the relation between quality of infant attachment and later development has been described as "dizzying"[54] and its effects are some of the most robust in developmental psychology, causing developmental psychologists Teresa McDevitt and Jeanne Ormond to describe secure attachment as a "multivitamin" that prevents problems and fosters healthy development.[55]

Early mothering may also play an important role in children's reactions to stress. The stress-related hormone cortisol has been linked to children who experience elevated levels of early life stressors. For example, children living in stultifying orphanages, foster care, or who experience other types of family trauma (e.g., living with a stepfather), have higher levels of cortisol and poorer health than children without such early stress experiences.[56] That these effects are mediated at least in part by mothers is illustrated by higher cortisol levels and more sick days for children who experienced stressors *prenatally* than for control children.[57]

That the effects of early maternal behavior can be long lasting is shown in research with rats. Mother rats display individual differences in the degree to which they engage in licking/grooming (LG) and arched-back nursing (ABN) of their pups. The offspring of mothers who engage in high levels of these behaviors display less fear of novelty and accompanying differences in hypothalamic-pituitary-adrenal (HPA) responses than the offspring of mothers who engage in lower levels.[58] Cross-fostering studies, in which pups born to mothers high in licking/grooming are raised by mothers low in licking/grooming and vice versa, make it clear that it is the mothers' behavior and not genetic disposition that is responsible for the differential response to stress in the offspring. Moreover, these maternal effects are passed on to subsequent generations, revealing an instance of nongenetic inheritance and a potential source of a behavioral mechanism for evolution.[59]

PATERNAL CARE

As already noted, where paternal investment is not obligatory, it rarely occurs. A notable exception is for those species where paternal investment is not required but can result in reproductive benefits for males. This is clearly the case for humans. For one thing, a willingness to invest in children may increase a male's mate value. In a survey on mate preferences conducted in thirty-seven cultures, it was found that the top three characteristics women sought were: love and commitment, dependability, and emotional stability.[60] There are good reasons that such preferences would have evolved in our female ancestors. The fact that love is lumped with commitment is quite telling of the way our wants and needs have evolved. Commitment implies fidelity; it implies a channeling of resources to one's partner and offspring; it implies support—emotional, physical, and economical. Considering the years of obligatory investment required by a woman if she were to become pregnant, it is reasonable that these mate preferences would develop. According to evolutionary psychologist, David Buss,[61] "Because sex is one of the most valuable reproductive resources women can offer, they have evolved psychological mechanisms that cause them to resist giving it away indiscriminately. Requiring love, sincerity, and kindness is a way of securing a commitment of resources commensurate with the value of the resource that women give to men."

By women requiring commitment and dependability in a mate, they solve a critical adaptive problem by ensuring that they and their offspring will continue receiving resources necessary for survival. That much of a man's investment in his children is actually for increased sexual access (mating effort) rather than for enhancing the lot of his children, is evidenced through numerous studies on paternal investment following divorce or separation. While divorce rarely weakens a mother's affection for her children, it does frequently result in a deterioration of the father-child relationship.[62] To further support the parenting-as-mating strategy of men, the quality of the spousal relationship affects fathers' more than mothers' investment in their children, meaning that "paternal parenting is more dependent on a supportive marital relationship than maternal parenting."[63] When men are in an unhappy marital relationship, they tend to withdraw from their children as well as their spouse. The withdrawal is sometimes physical, as in refraining from holding infants or playing with children, or sometimes emotional, such as abstaining from giving hugs, kisses, and outward expressions of emotion, or through some combination of both.

However, not all investment that human males make in their children is geared toward sexual access to their mothers. In humans, paternal investment is *facultatively* expressed, meaning that investment is not obligatory for offspring survival and, therefore, can vary according to ecological conditions.[64] Depending on the environment, a father's support can result in a better outcome for his children, and thus for his inclusive fitness. There are three main factors that have been identified to be associated with the facultative expression of paternal investment: offspring survival, mating opportunities, and paternity certainty.[65]

If the likelihood of offspring survival is greatly enhanced by paternal investment, natural selection will favor men who invest in their children. Conversely, if paternal investment does not at least moderately impact offspring survival, selection will favor males who abandon their offspring in search of additional mates.[66] If, however, the effects of paternal investment are moderate but not extreme, selection will tend to favor some form of mixed reproductive strategies incorporating some paternal investment as well as mating effort, as seen in table 3.1.

Sometimes social and ecological factors can reduce the number of possible mating opportunities for males. This was probably the case at least occasionally for our hunter-gatherer ancestors whose small groups could possibly be separated by vast geographical regions from other groups with potential mates. In these circumstances, selection would favor paternal investment if it would improve the chances of survival of offspring or if it did not inflict additional heavy costs.[67]

Paternal investment is also affected by paternity certainty. According to parental investment theory, the more certain a male is that an offspring is indeed his, the more likely he will be to provide support.[68] Maternal certainty has never been a problem for women, since humans have internal conception and gestation. Men, however, have recurrently faced the problem of paternity certainty over ancestral time, with the cuckoldry rate hovering around 10 percent.[69] This provides men with a moderate degree of certainty, enough to (usually) convince a man that caring for his wife's child is in his best interest, but not enough certainty to ignore hints that the child may not be his. Selection favors paternal investment if paternity certainty is high and the costs of investing are relatively low. If there are moderate costs to males, selection favors mixed reproductive strategies including seeking new mating opportunities and investing in offspring only to the extent that the costs to the male do not exceed the benefits to the offspring.[70]

TABLE 3.1 Factors associated with the evolution of paternal investment in species with internal fertilization

OFFSPRING SURVIVAL

1. If paternal investment is necessary for offspring survival, then it is obligatory; that is, selection will favor males who invest in offspring.

2. If paternal investment has little or no affect on offspring survival rate or quality, then selection will favor male abandonment, if additional mates can be found.

3. If paternal investment results in a relative but not an absolute improvement in offspring survival rate or quality, then selection will favor males who show a mixed reproductive strategy. Here, within-species variation is expected, with individual males varying their degree of emphasis on mating effort and parental effort, contingent on social (e.g., male status, availability of mates) and ecological (e.g., food availability, predator risks) conditions.

MATING OPPORTUNITY

1. If paternal investment is not obligatory and mates are available, then selection will favor the following:
   A. Male abandonment, if paternal investment has little affect on offspring survival rate and quality.
   B. A mixed male reproductive strategy, if paternal investment improves offspring survival rate and quality, that is, variation in degree of emphasis on mating effort and parental effort contingent on social and ecological conditions.

2. Social and ecological factors that reduce the mating opportunities of males, such as dispersed females or concealed (or synchronized) ovulation, will reduce the opportunity cost of paternal investment. Under these conditions, selection will favor paternal investment, if this investment improves offspring survival rate or quality, or does not otherwise induce heavy costs on the male.

PATERNITY CERTAINTY

1. If the certainty of paternity is low, then selection will favor male abandonment. Given that any level of parental investment is likely to be costly (e.g., in terms of reduced foraging time), indiscriminant paternal investment is not likely to evolve.

2. If the certainty of paternity is high, then selection will favor paternal investment, if
   A. Such investment improves offspring survival or quality, and
   B. The opportunity costs of investment (i.e., reduced mating opportunities) are lower than the benefits associated with investment.

3. If the certainty of paternity is high and the opportunity costs, in terms of lost mating opportunities, are high, then selection will favor males with a mixed reproductive strategy, that is, the facultative expression of paternal investment, contingent on social and ecological conditions.

Source: Adapted from Geary, D. C. 2000. "Evolution and Proximate Expression of Human Paternal Investment." *Psychological Bulletin* 126:55–77. Copyright 2000 by the American Psychological Association.

If, however, paternity certainty is low, selection almost certainly favors male abandonment, leaving men ample time to invest in mating strategies.[71]

In addition to the aforementioned factors affecting degree of paternal investment, social, cultural, and ecological conditions are also correlated with patterns of paternal investment. For example, in a study of Aka pygmy men (Aka pygmies are a modern hunter-gatherer group living in Africa), it was found that high-status men—those with large kin networks and high success rates hunting—hold their children less frequently than lower-status men.[72] The lack of physical care, however, is offset by the greater degree to which high-status men are able to provide food, especially those rich in fat and protein that are vital for nourishing offspring. Low-status men typically perform poorer in hunting due to a lack of kin network that would otherwise share in the hunting responsibilities. Although these low-status men provide less investment in terms of food items, they provide more direct investment—physically holding their children more than twice as often as higher-status men. These findings may be generalized to Western cultures, especially in the United States where such a high premium is placed on work ethic, and longer hours are typically put in at the office than in many cultures worldwide. While men who work long hours may provide less direct physical investment in their children, they may actually provide more indirect investment through monetary means. This indicates an inverse relationship between indirect and direct investment, such that as direct investment increases indirect investment decreases, and vice versa.[73]

Cultural factors also impact the proportion of paternal investment relative to mating effort. In cultures characterized by aloof husband-wife relationships, such as in polygamous societies, little direct male investment is typically afforded to offspring.[74] It is important to note, however, that cultures that embody these types of relationships are generally resource-rich. Because of this, it is unlikely that a lack of direct paternal investment will negatively affect offspring survival rates, in that mothers typically have enough resources to raise their offspring alone or with the help of co-wives.

In societies with socially imposed monogamy, as is the case in the majority of developed cultures, men are more likely to provide higher levels of paternal investment. This is also the case in unstable or harsh ecologies.[75] In harsh conditions, men are simply unable to secure enough resources to support multiple mates and many offspring; they are thus restricted to a monogamous lifestyle. Higher levels of paternal investment could also be due to the greater level of paternity certainty that monogamous relationships afford.

PATERNAL EFFECTS

The specific impact of fathers on child development has been less studied than that of mothers, in part because they spend considerably less time interacting with and caring for their children. On average, in all human cultures, fathers devote considerably less time to childcare than mothers, although some fathers in some developed countries spend as much, or even more, time with their children than do mothers.[76] However, while the model for a "good" father in these cultures includes increased childcare, many men have minimal or no contact with their children on a regular basis. For example, in the United States, the number of children born to single mothers, without the presence of a father in the household, has increased fourfold since 1960.[77]

In traditional societies, children without fathers have a higher mortality rate and achieve lower social status than children with fathers, although the impact of being fatherless is still substantially less than the impact of being motherless.[78] Nonetheless, individual differences in fathers' behavior have been shown to influence important aspects of child development. Geary and Flinn (2001) argue that paternal investment is correlated with later social competencies of children and that, due to the unique and unusual nature of paternal investment (occurring in fewer than 5 percent of mammalian species), the fact that humans display this behavior reflects male parenting as an "evolved reflection of social competition . . . [that] should be at least as strongly, perhaps more strongly, related to children's later social competitiveness than female parenting."[79] Furthermore, quality of paternal investment has been correlated with a delay in pubertal onset of pre-adolescent girls.[80] This lengthening of the juvenile period is associated with delayed onset of sexual activity, first childbirth, and higher educational attainment.[81] The flip side of this is that father absence accelerates pubertal attainment and sexual activity in girls.[82] One study reported that father absence was not only associated with earlier menarche, but also with greater interest in infants, suggesting that such girls are becoming prepared for early reproduction and parenting.[83]

Interestingly, the amount of parental investment mothers and fathers provide to their offspring may impact the longevity of males and females. Biologist John Allman compared the ratio of female-to-male survival as a function of the degree of paternal care that males in different primate species provide.[84] Several examples are shown in table 3.2. Higher numbers correspond to greater female longevity whereas lower numbers correspond to greater male longevity. On this scale, a ratio of 1.0 reflects a comparable survival rate

TABLE 3.2 Female and male survival rates as a function of degree of paternal care for selected primates

PRIMATE	SURVIVAL RATIO (FEMALE/MALE)	MALE CARE
Chimpanzee	1.42	Rare
Spider monkey	1.27	Rare
Orangutan	1.20	Rare
Gibbon	1.20	Pair living, but little direct role
Gorilla	1.13	Protects and plays with offspring
Human	1.07	Supports economically, some care
Goeldi's monkey	0.97	Both parents carry infant
Siamang	0.92	Carries infant in second year
Owl monkey	0.87	Carries infant from birth
Titi monkey	0.83	Carries infant from birth

Source: Adapted from Allman, J. M. 1999. *Evolving Brains*. New York: Scientific American Library.

for females and males. As can be seen, male survival rates increase relative to that of females as the amount of paternal care increases.

There are different speculations for why the discrepancy in survival rate as a degree of paternal care exists. Allman suggested that males who provide the bulk of the caregiving in their species may be naturally risk aversive.[85] This hypothesis extends beyond the aforementioned premise to include any sex that provides the majority of childcare for their species and suggests that they will take fewer risks since selection is likely to favor caregivers who are naturally avoidant of risks.[86] In contrast, species where males are not the primary caregivers tend to display riskier behavior, which is associated with increased mating opportunities and heightened social status.[87]

INVESTMENT BY GRANDPARENTS AND STEPPARENTS

Mothers and fathers are not the only people who invest in children. In fact, grandparents, especially maternal grandmothers, have likely played a critical role in childcare throughout human history. Most studies of contemporary people indicate that maternal grandmothers are perceived as emotionally closer and as providing more support, often in terms of gifts, than all other grandparents, with paternal grandfathers being the least supportive.[88] As you may have discerned, genetic certainty is assured for maternal mothers (they know their daughters are theirs and that their daughter is the genetic mother of their grandchild), whereas paternal grandfathers have the least genetic certainty.

Consistent with these findings, the presence of a maternal grandmother has been associated with increased chances of child survival, based both on historical records (e.g., 150 years of German birth/death records), and from contemporary cultures.[89] For example, in rural Ethiopia, help provided by maternal grandmothers was associated with lower child mortality.[90] Other research has shown that the presence of a mother's mother was associated with higher fertility and survival rates for Canadian and Finish farm families.[91]

Childcare is also often provided by people not genetically related to children, particularly stepparents. Stepfamilies were likely a recurrent feature of our evolutionary heritage. Mothers sometimes died in childbirth and fathers died in battle or on hunts, leaving their spouses and children with a single parent.[92] Stepparents are also a fact of modern life.

Why should stepparents invest at all? Unlike fathers and grandparents, they share no genes with their stepchildren. For stepfathers, at least, investment in stepchildren has been viewed as actually being investment in mating: Men provide care for their stepchildren to gain sexual access to their mothers.[93]

Stepparents do invest in their stepchildren, but usually less than genetic parents do. In studies across a wide range of cultures, stepparents have been found to spend less money on education and food, and to spend less time interacting with their stepchildren than their biological children.[94] Stepparents also report finding it difficult to form emotional bonds with their stepchildren. For example, in one study, only 53 percent of stepfathers and 25 percent of stepmothers claimed to have any "parental feelings" whatsoever for their stepchildren.[95] And perhaps most telling of all, the single best predictor of child abuse is the presence of a stepparent in the home.[96] Similar patterns are found for filicide.[97] In fact, the risk of even unintentional deaths, such as drowning, is greater in stepfamilies than in intact or single-parent families.[98]

Most stepparents do not abuse or kill their stepchildren, of course, and perhaps we should be emphasizing the fact that only humans regularly adopt and care for nongenetically related children. Adoption in other animals, such as monkeys, is rare, and usually done by a mother whose infant has just died, the result of a particular hormonal state focused on the wrong target (an unrelated infant rather than her own).[99] Humans are more magnanimous, and many stepparents love their stepchildren and provide them with substantial resources. Nonetheless, stepparental investment is less than that of genetic parents, and, as predicted by parental investment theory, stepparents are more apt to disinvest in their step-offspring in certain ecological situations.

SOME CONCLUDING REMARKS

Humans are mammals, and like all mammals, infants are highly dependent on their mothers for survival. However, aspects of human natural and life history made it impossible for mothers to rear children alone, and *Homo sapiens* thus evolved to be cooperative breeders, with mothers receiving help rearing their children from mainly female kin and their mates. Although the ancient environments in which human families and patterns of child-rearing evolved are long gone, modern men and women are born with essentially the same brains and some of the same biases that influenced the mating and parenting decisions of our ancestors, and these are often reinforced over the course of childhood.

Although the survival and success of their children is in the best interest of both mothers and fathers, men and women's self-interests are not identical, and they evolved to be sensitive to different cues when making mating and parenting decisions. This often produces conflict between men and women, but also often results in cooperation and a supportive environment in which children can develop.

Mothers and fathers are not interchangeable. Millions of years of natural selection have shaped male and female psychologies to be somewhat different. However, humans also evolved a large brain and intellectual abilities that permit them to rise above the inherited biases that direct the behavior of other animals and influenced the actions of their ancestors. Patterns of parenting evolved because they were associated with success for our ancestors. In many respects, the evolved biases of modern men and women continue to enhance the survival and success of their children, although cultural changes, also enabled by humans' evolved intelligence, have and will continue to shape these biases. An understanding of the biological

underpinnings of human parenting can help promote social policies to foster the development of children in diverse and evolutionarily-novel environments, which are far different from anything our ancestors experienced.

NOTES

1. Bjorklund and Pellegrini 2002a:3–30.
2. Harris 1995:458–489; Bronfenbrenner and Morris 2006:793–828.
3. Trivers 1972:136–179.
4. Darwin 1859; Buller 2005.
5. Hamilton 1964:1–52.
6. Meany 2001:1161–1192; Bjorklund and Pellegrini 2002b; West-Eberhardt 2003; Bjorklund 2006:213–242; Bjorklund, Ellis, and Rosenberg 2007; Ploeger, Vand der Maas, and Raijmakers 2008:41–48.
7. Tattersall 1988; Olson 2002; Springer and Andrews 2005.
8. Bonner 1988; Kaplan and Gangestad 2005:68–95.
9. Jerrison 1973; Jerrison 2002:251–288.
10. Dunbar 1995:388–389; Joffee 1997:593–605; Bjorklund and Bering 2003: 133–151; Bjorklund, Cormier, and Rosenberg 2005.
11. Kaplan and Gangestad 2005:68–95
12. Bjorklund, Cormier, and Rosenberg 2005.
13. Hrdy 2007:39–68.
14. Whiting and Whiting 1975; Eibl-Eibesfeldt 1989; Clutton-Brock 1991.
15. Bjorklund and Yunger 2002:63–66.
16. Emlen 1995:8092–8099.
17. Geary and Flinn 2001:5–61.
18. Robbins 1999:1013–1020; Geary and Flinn 2001:5–61; Bradley, et al. 2005: 9418–9423.
19. Geary and Flinn 2001:5–61.
20. Clutton-Brock 1991; Snowdon and Ziegler 2007:40–66; Snowdon 2011.
21. Clutton-Brock 1991.
22. Trivers 1972:136–179.
23. Campbell and Ellis 2005:419–442.
24. Oliver and Hyde 1993:29–51.
25. Geary 2007.
26. Geary 2000:55.
27. Geary 1998.
28. Ibid.
29. Bjorklund and Kipp 1996:163–88; Bjorklund and Kipp 2002:27–53.
30. Slaby and Parke 1971:40–47; Bjorklund and Kipp 1996; Kochanska, Murry, Jacques, Koenig, and Vandegeest 1996:490–507.
31. Maccoby and Jacklin 1987:239–287.

32. Pellegrini and Smith 1998:577–98; Pellegrini (in press).

33. Pellegrini and Bjorklund 2004:23–43; Pellegrini (in press).

34. Geary 1998.

35. Maestripieri and Pelka 2002:327–344; Maestripieri and Roney 2006:120–137.

36. Geary 1998; Bjorklund and Pellegrini 2002b.

37. Geary 1998.

38. Harlow, Harlow, and Dodsworth 1966:58–66.

39. Bugental and Beaulieu 2003:329–361.

40. Daly and Wilson 1981:405–416.

41. Daly and Wilson 1988.

42. Mann 1992:367–390.

43. Beaulieu and Bugental 2008:249–255; Lee and George 1999:755–80.

44. Bugos and McCarthy 1984:503–520; Daly and Wilson 1988; Overpeck et al. 1998:1211–1216.

45. Overpeck et al. 1998:1211–1216; Harris et al. 2007.

46. Schiefenhövel 1988.

47. Daly and Wilson 1988.

48. Fifer 2005.

49. Ellis, Jackson, and Boyce 2006.

50. Parke 2002:27–73.

51. Bjorklund, Causey, and Periss 2009; Bjorklund, Grotuss, and Csinady 2009.

52. Belsky 1999:141–161; Thompson 2006:24–98; Belsky 2007:454–468.

53. Ainsworth, Blehar, Waters, and Wall 1978; Thompson 2006:24–98.

54. Thompson 2006:24–98.

55. McDevitt and Ormrod 2004.

56. Gunner et al. 2001:611–628; Flinn and England 2003:107–147; Dozier et al. 2006:189–197; Flinn 2006:138–174.

57. Flinn 2006:138–174.

58. Caldji et al. 1998:5335–5340; Francis et al. 1999:1155–1158; Champagne and Curley 2008.

59. Meany 2001:1161–1192; Bjorklund and Rosenberg 2005:45–75; Champagne and Curley 2008.

60. Buss 1994.

61. Ibid.

62. Geary 2000:55.

63. Parke 1995:27–63.

64. Clutton-Brock 1991.

65. Geary 2000:55.

66. Trivers 1972:136–179; Geary 2005:483–505.

67. Trivers 1972:136–179; Clutton-Brock 1991; Geary 2005:483–505

68. Trivers 1972:136–179.

69. Trivers 1972:136–179; Geary 2005:483–505.

70. Geary 2000:55.
77. Trivers 1972:136–179; Geary 2005:483–505.
72. Hewlett 1988:263–276.
73. Geary 1998.
74. Ibid.
75. Ibid.
76. Whiting and Whiting 1975; Eibl-Eibesfeldt 1989; Parke 2002:27–73.
77. Cabera et al. 2000:127–136.
78. Geary 1998.
79. Geary and Flinn 2001:5–61.
80. Ellis et al. 1999:387–401.
81. Ellis 2004:920–958; Belsky 2007:454–468; Del Guidice 2009.
82. Wierson, Long, and Forehand 1993:913–924; Ellis et al. 2003:376–390.
83. Maestripieri et al. 2004:560–566.
84. Allman 1999.
85. Ibid.
86. Campbell 1999:203–252.
87. Daly and Wilson 1988.
88. Oliver and Hyde 1993:29–36; Michalski and Shackelford 2004:293–305; Euler and Michalski 2007:230–255; Pashos and McBurney 2008:311–330.
89. Beise and Voland 2002:469–498.
90. Gibson and Mace 2005:469–482.
91. Lahdenpera et al. 2004.
92. Buss 1994.
93. Anderson, Kaplan, and Lancaster 1999a:405–431; Rowher, Herron, and Daly 1999:367–390.
94. Flinn 1988:335–369; Anderson, Kaplan, and Lancaster 1999a:405–431; Anderson, Kaplan and Lancaster; Anderson et al. 1999b:433–451; Marlowe 1999:391–404; Rowher, Herron, and Daly 1999:367–390; Case, Lin, and McLanahan 2000:781–804.
95. Duberman 1975.
96. Daly and Wilson 1988; Daly and Wilson 1996:77–81.
97. Bugos and McCarthy 1984:503–520; Daly and Wilson 1988; Overpeck et al. 1998:1211–1216; Harris et al. 2007.
98. Tooley et al. 2006:224–230.
99. Maestripieri 2001:93–120.

REFERENCES

Ainsworth, M. S., M. C. Blehar, E. Waters, and S. Wall. 1978. *Patterns of Attachment: A Psychological Study of the Strange Situation*. Hillsdale, NJ: Lawrence Erlbaum.

Allman, J. M. 1999. *Evolving Brains*. New York: Scientific American.

Anderson, K. G., H. Kaplan, D. Lam, and J. Lancaster. 1999b. "Paternal Care by Genetic Fathers and Stepfathers II: Reports by Xhosa High School Students." *Evolution and Human Behavior* 20:433–451.

Anderson, K. G., H. Kaplan, and J. Lancaster. 1999a. "Paternal Care by Genetic Fathers and Stepfathers I: Reports from Albuquerque Men." *Evolution and Human Behavior* 20:405–431.

Beaulieu, D. A. and D. Bugental. 2008. "Contingent Parental Investment: An Evolutionary Framework for Understanding Early Interaction Between Mothers and Children." *Evolution and Human Behavior* 29:249–255.

Beise, J. and E. Voland. 2002. "A Multilevel Even History Analysis of the Effects of Grandmothers on Child Mortality in a Historical German Population (Krummhorn, Ostfriesland, 1720–1987)." *Demographic Research* 7:469–498.

Belsky, J. 1999. "Modern Evolutionary Theory and Patterns of Attachment." In *Theory, Research, and Clinical Applications*, ed. J. Cassidy and P. R. Shaver, 141–161. New York: Guilford.

Belsky, J. 2007. "Experience in Childhood and the Development of Reproductive Strategies." *Evolutionary Psychology* 39:454–468.

Bjorklund, D. F. 2006. "Mother Knows Best: Epigenetic Inheritance, Maternal Effects, and the Evolution of Human Intelligence." *Developmental Review* 26: 213–242.

Bjorklund, D. F. and J. M. Bering. 2003. "Big Brains, Slow Development, and Social Complexity: The Developmental and Evolutionary Origins of Social Cognition." In *The Social Brain: Evolutionary Aspects of Development and Pathology*, ed. M. Brüne, H. Ribbert, and W. Schiefenhövel, 133–151. New York: John Wiley.

Bjorklund, D. F., K. Causey, and V. Periss. 2009. "The Evolution of Human Social-Cognitive Development." In *Mind the Gap: Tracing the Origins of Human Universals*, ed. P. Kappeler and J. Silk. 351–372. Berlin: Springer Verlag.

Bjorklund, D. F., C. A. Cormier, and J. S. Rosenberg. 2005. "The Evolution of Theory of Mind: Big Brains, Social Complexity, and Inhibition." In *Young Children's Cognitive Development: Interrelationships Among Executive Functioning, Working Memory, Verbal Ability, and Theory of Mind*, ed. W. Schneider, R. Schumann-Hengsteler, and B. Sodian. 147–174. Mahwah, NJ: Lawrence Erlbaum.

Bjorklund, D. F., B. J. Ellis, and J. S. Rosenberg. 2007. "Evolved Probabilistic Cognitive Mechanisms." In *Advances in Child Development and Behavior*, vol. 35, ed. R. V. Kail. 1–39. New York: Academic.

Bjorklund, D. F., J. Grotuss, and A. Csinady. 2009. "Maternal Effects, Social Cognitive Development, and the Evolution of Human Intelligence." In *Maternal Effects in Mammals*, ed. D. Maestripieri and J. Mateo. 292–321. Chicago: Chicago University.

Bjorklund, D. F. and K. Kipp. 1996. "Parental Investment Theory and Gender Differences in the Evolution of Inhibition Mechanisms." *Psychological Bulletin* 120:163–188.

Bjorklund, D. F. and K. Kipp. 2002. "Social Cognition, Inhibition, and Theory of Mind: The Evolution of Human Intelligence." In *The Evolution of Intelligence*, ed. R. J. Sternberg and J. C. Kaufman, 27–53. Mahwah, NJ: Lawrence Erlbaum.

Bjorklund, D. F. and A. D. Pellegrini. 2002a. "The Evolution of Parenting and Evolutionary Approaches to Childrearing." In *Handbook of Parenting: The Biology of Parenting*, vol. 1, 2nd ed., ed. M. Bornstein, 3–30. Mahwah, NJ: Lawrence Erlbaum.

Bjorklund, D. F. and A. D. Pellegrini. 2002b. *The Origins of Human Nature: Evolutionary Developmental Psychology*. Washington, DC: American Psychological Association.

Bjorklund, D. F. and J. S. Rosenberg. 2005. "The Role of Developmental Plasticity in the Evolution of Human Cognition." In *Origins of the Social Mind: Evolutionary Psychology and Child Development*, ed. B. Ellis and D. F. Bjorklund, 45–75. New York: Guilford.

Bjorklund, D. F. and J. L. Yunger. 2002. "Evolutionary Developmental Psychology: A Useful Framework for Evaluation the Evolution of Parenting." *Parenting: Science and Practice* 1:63–66.

Bonner, K. M. 1988. *The Evolution of Complexity by Means of Natural Selection*. Princeton, NJ: Princeton University.

Bradley, B. J., M. M. Robbins, E. A. Williamson, H. D. Steklis, N. G. Steklis, N. Eckhardt, C. Boesch, and L. Vigilant. 2005. "Mountain Gorilla Tug-of-War: Silverbacks Have Limited Control Over Reproduction in Multimale Groups." *Proceedings of the National Academy of Sciences* 102:9418–9423.

Bronfenbrenner, U. and P. A. Morris. 2006. "The Bioecological Model of Human Development." In *Handbook of Child Psychology*, 6th ed., ed. W. Damon and R. M. Lerner, in *Theoretical Models of Human Development*, vol. 1, ed. R. M. Lerner, 793–828. New York: John Wiley.

Bugental, D. B. and D. A. Beaulieu, 2003. "A Bio-Social-Cognitive Approach to Understanding and Promoting the Outcomes of Children with Medical and Physical Disorders." In *Advances in Child Development and Behavior*, vol. 31, ed. R. V. Kail, 329–361. New York: Elsevier.

Bugos, P. E. and L. M. McCarthy. 1984. "Avoreo Infanticide: A Case Study." In *Infanticide: Comparative and Evolutionary Perspectives*, ed. G. Hausfater and S. B. Hrdy, 503–520. New York: Aldine de Gruyter.

Buller, D. J. 2005. *Adapting Minds: Evolutionary Psychology and the Persistent Quest for Human Nature*. Boston: MIT.

Buss, D. M. 1994. *The Evolution of Desire: Strategies of Human Mating*. New York: Perseus.

Cabera, N. J., C. S. Tamis-LeMonda, R. H. Bradley, S. Hofferth, and M. E. Lamb. 2000. "Fatherhood in the Twenty-First Century." *Child Development* 71:127–136.

Caldji, C., B. Tannenbaum, S. Sharma, D. Francis, P. M. Plotsky, and M. J. Meany. 1998. "Maternal Care During Infancy Regulates the Development of Neural Systems Mediating the Expression of Fearfulness in the Rat." *Proceedings of the National Academy of Science USA* 95:5335–5340.

Campbell, A. 1999. "Staying Alive: Evolution, Culture, and Women's Intrasexual Aggression." *Behavioral and Brain Sciences* 22:203–252.

Campbell, L. and B. J. Ellis. 2005. "Commitment, Love, and Mate Retention." In *The Handbook of Evolutionary Psychology*, ed. D. M. Buss, 419–442. Hoboken, New Jersey: John Wiley.

Case, A., I. F. Lin, and S. McLanahan. 2000. "How Hungry is the Selfish Gene?" *Economic Journal* 110:781–804.

Champagne, F. A. and J. P. Curley. 2008. "The Trans-Generational Influence of Maternal Care on Offspring Gene Expression and Behavior in Rodents." In *Maternal Effects in Mammals*, ed. D. Maestripieri and J. Mateo. Chicago: Chicago University.

Clutton-Brock, T. H. 1991. *The Evolution of Parental Care*. Princeton, NJ: Princeton University.

Daly, M. and M. Wilson. 1981. "Abuse and Neglect of Children in Evolutionary Perspective." In *Natural Selection and Social Behavior*, ed. R. D. Alexander and D. W. Tinkle, 405–416. New York: Chiron.

Daly, M. and M. Wilson. 1988. *Homicide*. Hawthorne, NY: Aldine.

Daly, M. and M. Wilson. 1996. "Violence Against Stepchildren." *Current Directions in Psychological Science* 5:77–81.

Darwin, C. 1959. *On the Origin of Species by Means of Natural Selection, or the Preservation of Favoured Races in the Struggle for Life*. New York: W. W. Norton.

Del Giudice, M. 2009. "Sex, Attachment, and the Development of Reproductive Strategies." *Behavioral and Brain Sciences* 32:1–21.

Dozier, M., E. Peloso, M. K. Gordon, M. Manni, M. R. Gunnar, K. C. Stovall-McClough, and S. Levine. 2006. "Foster Children's Diurnal Production of Cortisol: An Exploratory Study." *Child Maltreatment* 11:189–197.

Duberman, L. 1975. *The Reconstituted Family: A Study of Remarried Couples and Their Children*. Chicago: Nelson-Hall.

Dunbar, R. I. M. 1995 "Neocortical Size and Language." *Journal of Human Evolution* 32:388–389

Eibl-Eibesfeldt, I. 1989. *Human Ethology*. New York: Aldine de Gruyter.

Ellis, B. J. 2004. "Timing of Pubertal Maturation in Girls: An Integrated Life History Approach." *Psychological Bulletin* 130:920–958.

Ellis, B. J., J. E. Bates, K. A. Dodge, D. M. Fergusson, L. J. Horwood, G. S. Pettit, and L. Woodward. 2003. "Does Father Absence Place Daughters at Special Risk for Early Sexual Activity and Teenage Pregnancy?" *Child Development* 74:801–821.

Ellis, B. J., S. McFadyen-Ketchum, K. A. Dodge, G. S. Pettit, and J. E. Bates. 1999. "Quality of Early Family Relationships and Individual Differences in the Timing of Pubertal Maturation in Girls: A Longitudinal Test of an Evolutionary Model." *Journal of Personality and Social Psychology* 77:387–401.

Emlen, S. T. 1995. "An Evolutionary Theory of the Family." *Proceedings of the National Academy of Sciences* 92:8092–8099.

Euler, H. A. and R. L. Michalski. 2007. "Grandparental and Extended Kin Relationships." In *Family Relationships: An Evolutionary Perspective*, ed. C. Solomon and T. K. Shackelford, 230–255. New York: Oxford University.

Fifer, W. P. 2005. "Normal and Abnormal Prenatal Development." In *The Cambridge Encyclopedia of Child Development*, ed. B. Hopkins. Cambridge, UK: Cambridge University.

Flinn, M. V. 1988. "Step- and Genetic Parent/Offspring Relationships in a Caribbean Village." *Ethology & Sociobiology* 9:335–369.

Flinn, M. V. 2006. "Evolution and Ontogeny of Stress Response to Social Challenges in the Human Mind." *Developmental Review* 26:138–174.

Flinn, M. V. and B. G. England. 2003. "Childhood Stress: Endocrine and Immune Responses to Psychosocial Events." In *Social and Cultural Lives of Immune Systems*, ed. J. M. Wilce, 107–147. London: Routledge.

Francis, D. D., J. Diorio, D. Liu, and M. J. Meany. 1999. "Nongenomic Transmission across Generations in Maternal Behavior and Stress Response in the Rat," *Science* 286:1155–1158.

Geary, D. C. 1998. *Male,Female: The Evolution of Human Sex Differences*. Washington, DC: American Psychological Association.

Geary, D. C. 2000. "Evolution and the Proximate Expression of Human Paternal Investment." *Psychological Bulletin* 126:55–77.

Geary, D. C. 2005. "Evolution of Paternal Investment." In *The Handbook of Evolutionary Psychology*, ed. D. M. Buss, 483–505. Hoboken, NJ: John Wiley.

Geary, D. C. 2007. "Evolution of Fatherhood." In *Family Relationships: Evolutionary Perspectives*, ed. C. Solomon and T. K. Shackelford. New York: Oxford University.

Geary, D. C. and M. Flinn. 2001. "Evolution of Human Parental Behavior and the Human Family." *Parenting: Science and Practice* 1:5–61.

Gibson, M. A. and R. Mace. 2005. "Helpful Grandmothers in Rural Ethiopia: A Study of the Effect of Kin on Child Survival and Growth." *Evolution and Human Behavior* 26:469–482.

Gunner, M. R., S. J. Morison, K. Chisholm, and M. Schuder. 2001. "Salivary Cortisol Levels in Children Adopted from Romanian Orphanages." *Development and Psychopathology* 13:611–628.

Hamilton, W. D. 1964. "The Genetical Theory of Social Behavior." *Journal of Theoretical Biology* 7:1–52.

Harlow, H. F., M. K. Harlow, and R. O. Dodsworth. 1966. "Maternal Behavior of Rhesus Monkeys Deprived of Mothering and Peer Associations in Infancy." *Proceedings of the American Philosophical Society* 110:58–66.

Harris, G. T., N. Z. Hilton, M. E. Rice, and A. W. Eke. 2007. "Children Killed by Genetic Parents Versus Stepparents." *Evolution and Human Behavior* 28:85–95.

Harris, J. R. 1995. "Where is the Child's Environment?" *Psychological Review* 102:458–489.

Hewlett, B. S. 1988. "Sexual Selection and Paternal Investment among Aka Pygmies." In *Human Reproductive Behavior: A Darwinian Perspective*, ed. L. Betzig, M. Borgerhoff-Mulder, and P. Turke, 263–276. Cambridge, UK: Cambridge University.

Hrdy, S. B. 2007. "Evolutionary Context of Human Development: The Cooperative Breeding Model." In *Family Relationships: An Evolutionary Perspective*, ed. C. Salmon and T. Shackelford, 39–68. New York: Oxford University.

Jerrison, H. J. 1973. *Evolution of the Brain and Intelligence.* New York: Academic.

Jerrison, H. J. 2002. "On Theory in Comparative Psychology." in *The Evolution of Intelligence*, ed. R. J. Sternberg and J. C. Kaufman, 251–288. Mahwah, NJ: Lawrence Erlbaum.

Joffee, T. H. 1997. "Social Pressures Have Selected for an Extended Juvenile Period in Primates." *Journal of Human Evolution* 32:593–605.

Kaplan, H. S. and S. W. Gangestad. 2005. "Life History Theory and Evolutionary Psychology." In *The Handbook of Evolutionary Psychology*, ed. D. M. Buss, 68–95. Hoboken, NJ: John Wiley.

Kochanska, G., K. Murry, T. Y. Jacques, L. A. Koenig, and K. A. Vandegeest. 1996. "Inhibitory Control in Young Children and its Role in Emerging Internalization." *Child Development* 67:490–507.

Lahdenpera, M., V. Lummaa, S. Helle, M. Tremblay, and A. F. Russell. 2004. "Fitness Benefits of Prolonged Post-Reproductive Lifespan in Women." *Nature* 428:178–181.

Lee, B. J. and R. M. George. 1999 "Poverty, Early Childbearing and Child Maltreatment: A Multinomial Analysis." *Children & Youth Services Review* 21:755–780.

Maccoby, E. E. and C. N. Jacklin, "Gender Segregation in Childhood." In *Advances in Child Development and Behavior*, ed. H. Reese, 239–287. San Diego, CA: Academic.

Maestripieri, D. 2001. "Is There Mother-Infant Bonding in Primates?" *Developmental Review* 21:93–120.

Maestripieri, D. and S. Pelka. 2002. "Sex Differences in Interest in Infants Across the Lifespan: A Biological Adaptation for Parenting." *Human Nature* 13:327–344.

Maestripieri, D. and J. R. Roney. 2006. "Evolutionary Developmental Psychology: Contributions from Comparative Research with Nonhuman Primates." *Developmental Review* 26:120–137.

Maestripieri, D., J. R. Roney, N. DeBias, K. M. Durante, and G. M. Spaepen. 2004. "Father Absence, Menarche and Interest in Infants Among Adolescent Girls." *Developmental Science* 7:560–566.

Mann, J. 1992. "Nurture or Negligence: Maternal Psychology and Behavioral Preference Among Preterm Twins." In *The Adapted Mind: Evolutionary Psychology and the Generation of Culture*, ed. J. Barkow, L. Cosmides, and J. Tooby, 367–390. New York: Oxford University.

Marlowe, F. 1999. "Showoffs or Providers? The Parenting Effort of Hazda Men." *Evolution and Human Behavior* 20:391–404.

McDevitt, T. M. and J. E. Ormrod. 2004. *Child Development: Educating and Working with Children and Adolescents*, 2nd ed. Upper Saddle River, NJ: Pearson.

Meany, M. J. 2001. "Maternal Care, Gene Expression, and the Transmission of Individual Differences in Stress Reactivity Across Generations." *Annual Review of Neuroscience* 24: 1161–1192.

Michalski, R. L. and T. S. Shackelford. 2004. "Grandparental Investment as a Function of Relational Uncertainty and Emotional Closeness with Parents." *Human Nature* 16:293–305.

Oliver, M. B. and J. S. Hyde. 1993. "Gender Differences in Sexuality: A Meta-Analysis." *Psychological Bulletin* 114:29–51.

Olson, S. 2002. *Mapping Human History: Genes, Race, and Our Common Origins*. Boston: Houghton Mifflin.

Overpeck, M. D., R. A. Brenner, A. C. Trumble, L. B. Trifiletti, and H. W. Berendes. 1998. "Risk Factors for Infant Homicide in the United States." *New England Journal of Medicine* 339:1211–1216.

Parke, R. D. 1995. "Fathers and Families." In *Handbook of Parenting: Status and Social Conditions of Parenting*, vol. 3, ed. M. H. Bornstein, 27–63. Hillsdale, NJ: Lawrence Erlbaum.

Parke, R. D. 2002. "Fathers and Families." In *Handbook of Parenting: Being and Becoming a Parent*, vol. 3, 2nd ed., ed. M. H. Bornstein, 27–73. Mahwah, NJ: Lawrence Erlbaum.

Pashos, A. and D. H. McBurney. 2008. "Kin Relationships and the Caregiving Biases of Grandparents, Aunts, and Uncles." *Human Nature* 19:311–330.

Pellegrini, A. D., in press. "Play." In *Oxford Handbook of Developmental Psychology*, ed. P. Zelazo. New York: Oxford University.

Pellegrini, A. D. and D. F. Bjorklund. 2004. "The Ontogeny and Phylogeny of Children's Object and Fantasy Play." *Human Nature* 15:23–43.

Pellegrini, A. D. and P. K. Smith. 1998. "Physical Activity Play: The Nature and Function of Neglected Aspect of Play." *Child Development* 69:577–98.

Ploeger, A., H. L. J. Vand der Maas, and M. E. J. Raijmakers. 2008. "Is Evolutionary Psychology a Metatheory for Psychology? A Discussion of Four Major Issues in Psychology from an Evolutionary Developmental Perspective." *Psychological Inquiry* 19:41–48.

Quinlan, R. J. 2003. "Father Absence, Parental Care, and Female Reproductive Development." *Evolution and Human Behavior* 24:376–390.

Robbins, M. M. 1999. "Male Mating Patterns in Wild Multimale Mountain Gorilla Groups." *Animal Behavior* 57:1013–1020.

Rowher, S., J. C. Herron, and M. L. Daly. 1999. "Stepparental Behavior as Mating Effort." *Evolution and Human Behavior* 20:367–390.

Schiefenhövel, W. 1988. "Geburtsverhalten und reproduktiver Strategien der Eipo. Ergebnisse humanethologischer und ethnomedizinischer Untersuchungen im zentralen Bergland von Irian Jaya (West-Neuguinea), Indonesien." [Fertility behavior and reproductive strategies of the Eipo: Human-ethnomedical studies and results in the central highlands of Irian Jaya (West New Guinea]. *Mensch, Kultur und Umwelt im zentralen Bergland von Westneuguinea [People, Culture, and Environment in the Highlands of Western New Guinea]* 16. Berlin: Reimer.

Slaby, R. G. and R. D. Parke 1971. "Effect on Resistance to Deviation of Observing a Model's Affective Reaction to Response Consequences." *Developmental Psychology* 5:40–47.

Snowdon, C. T. and T. E. Ziegler. 2007. "Growing Up Cooperatively: Family Processes and Infant Care in Marmosets and Tamarins." *Journal of Developmental Processes* 2:40–66.

Springer, C. and P. Andrews. 2005. *The Complete World of Human Evolution.* New York: Thames & Hudson.

Tattersall, I. 1988. *Becoming Human: Evolution and Human Intelligence.* San Diego: Harcourt Brace.

Thompson, R. A. 2009. "The Development of the Person: Social Understanding, Relationships, Conscience, Self." In *Handbook of Child Psychology,* 6th ed., ed. W. Damon and R. M. Lerner, in *Social, Emotional, and Personality Development,* vol. 3, ed. N. Eisenberg, 24–98. New York: John Wiley.

Tooley, G. A., M. Karakis, M. Stokes, and J. Ozanne-Smith. 2006. "Generalizing the Cinderella Effect to Unintentional Childhood Fatalities." *Evolution and Human Behavior* 27:224–230.

Trivers, Robert. 1972. "Parental Investment and Sexual Selection." In *Sexual Selection and the Descent of Man: 1871–1971,* ed. B. Campbell, 136–179. Chicago: Aldine.

West-Eberhardt, M. J. 2003. *Developmental Plasticity and Evolution.* NY: Oxford University.

Whiting, J. W. and B. B. Whiting. 1975. *Children of Six Cultures: A Psycho-Cultural Analysis.* Cambridge, MA: Harvard University Press.

Wierson, M., P. Long, and R. Forehand. 1993. "Toward a New Understanding of Early Menarche: The Role of Environmental Stress in Pubertal Timing." *Adolescence* 28:913–924.

4

PARENTING × GENDER × CULTURE × TIME

Marc H. Bornstein

GENETICS AND ANATOMY PLAY undeniable and consequential parts in defining the self and our roles in life, but being a "girl" or a "boy" has implications that carry considerably beyond the biological. Most of what we believe and how we behave are gendered. Apart from biological influences, socialization pressures, and cultural variation, children universally and normatively develop a reasonably clear sense of self as female or male and master all of the roles generally associated with their assigned gender.[1] Some illustrations bring this point home. Children's self-perceptions of their strengths in domains such as physical appearance, academics, and athletics contribute to their global sense of self-worth, and all vary with gender (Harter 2006), and children are motivated to build on their ideas about gender and to develop gendered standards for their own behavior. Children commonly rely on their ideas about gender to appraise and explicate behavior. When told about a girl or boy who spilled some milk, children evaluate the behavior of boys more negatively than girls, which is interpreted in terms of gender stereotypes (Heyman 2001; Giles and Heyman 2004). The influence of gender roles is played out in educational attainment and employment choices. Children around the world typically follow academic courses as well as future occupations that are taken to be "traditional" or important or relevant for their gender.

(A LITTLE) BIOLOGY

When the human organism first starts out as a zygote, the whole difference between female and male consists of the fact that one has two X chromosomes and the other one X and one Y. Natural selection shapes the morphology of an organism, which in turn inclines behavioral and psychological tendencies (Kenrick and Luce 2000). Females and males are biologically prepared to experience their environments differently, and their experiences mold gender-appropriate behaviors. However, biology is neither a necessary nor a sufficient cause of gender. Biological factors are not deterministic because even features of self with a strong genetic, anatomical, or hormonal influence may be modifiable. Gender results from genetically, anatomically, or hormonally influenced predispositions, but its ultimate expression is shaped by experience with the social environment (Wallen 1996). Biology and experience coproduce gender.

EXPERIENCE

Parents constitute initial influences on the development of their children's gender. Parents have a strong tendency to treat children differently by gender. Classic "Baby X" studies (where the gender of the infant is not known to study participants) in the United States have shown that parents (and other adults) conceive of and behave toward infants differently depending on whether they think they are interacting with a girl or a boy (Seavey, Katz, and Zalk 1975; Sidorowicz and Lunney 1980). Boys are described as "big" and "strong" and are bounced and handled more physically than girls who are described as "pretty" and "sweet" and are handled more gently. Even before birth, after finding out their child's gender via ultrasound, parents describe girls as "finer" and "quieter" than boys who are described as "more coordinated" than girls (Sweeney and Bradbard 1989). It is important to note that such experiential influences do not imply free will and easy malleability because social forces may be significant and robust in themselves (Best 2010).

This brief chapter focuses on the roles of parenting and culture in children's gender development. After an overview of prominent psychological mechanisms of socialization (parenting), the chapter focuses on variation by gender of parent and gender of child (parenting × gender). The chapter then introduces culture to parenting and gender (parenting × gender × culture). Finally, developmental and historical time are discussed as moderating factors in the parenting by gender by culture formulation (parenting × gender × culture × time). Several excellent and extended historical, theoretical, and empirical reviews of gender development are available (see, e.g., Russell and Saebel 1997; Leaper 2002; Ruble, Martin, and Berenbaum 2006; Best 2010).

PARENTING

Parents influence children (Collins et al. 2002; Maccoby 2002; Vandell 2002; Bornstein 2006), including their gender development, and differences between girls and boys are often attributed to differences in parental socialization. Overall, however, differences in how parents treat girls and boys vary due to which parent is doing the socializing, which child is being socialized, the ways socialization is measured, and so forth. Parenting exerts its active and direct effects through cognitions and practices; other effects may be indirect, such as peer and neighborhood choice. As it is not feasible to review the entire literature, this chapter confines itself to central points and select illustrations.

MECHANISMS OF PARENTING GENDER

How does parenting contribute to children's gender development? How do we conceptualize the direct and interactive effects of various influences? Which features from the environment are noticed and incorporated into gender development, and by what processes? Scholars have identified a surprisingly small number of likely mechanisms.

SOCIALIZATION

A direct avenue of influence is posited to flow through parents' differential treatment of daughters and sons. Differential treatment may take various forms. One type of differential treatment is through parenting cognitions, for instance, the various expectations that parents have for their children. As an illustration, parents may convey gender-related expectations about science and math. Parents tend to expect boys to do better than girls in science and math (Eccles et al. 2000; Tenenbaum and Leaper 2003), despite a lack of actual gender difference in performance (Tenenbaum and Leaper 2003; Hyde et al. 2008). Parents hold different beliefs about (their) girls and boys in a wide array of domains. Mothers of eleven-month-olds underestimate girls' motor skills and overestimate boys' motor skills even when objective tests show no gender differences in children's motor performance (Mondschein, Adolph, and Tamis-LeMonda 2000). These messages are apt to influence children's own self-concept and motivation.

A second type of differential treatment occurs through parenting practices—direct interactions with the child. Examples (instruction or guided participation) include a mother teaching a daughter how to nurse a baby or a father teaching a son how to build a model. Parents on outings to museums focus on explanations of scientific content with their boys more than with their girls and so may foster boys' greater interest in and knowledge about science (Crowley at al. 2001). Many family studies indicate that parents treat females and males differently and encourage girls and boys to accept distinctive and often "traditional" gender roles. Lytton and Romney (1991) examined 158 North American studies of parental socialization in diverse domains and found that the only significant effect obtained was for the encouragement of gender-typed behaviors in children. Parenting practices themselves are of different kinds; some are active, some are passive.

MODELING

Parents also offer children different role models. To the extent that mothers, fathers, or other caregivers are important and powerful figures in children's lives, often to be emulated or feared, they shape children's impressions of what it means to be a woman or a man simply by acting like a woman or a man (Bussey and Bandura 1999). As an illustration, mothers' tendency to be more talkative with daughters than sons may contribute to gender-differentiated language learning and development in girls and boys (Leaper, Anderson, and Sanders 1998). Mothers and fathers have traditionally differed in multiple roles and status.

SCAFFOLDING

Vygotsky (1978) emphasized the crucial importance of interaction with others in child development. He contended that the more advanced or expert partner (the caregiver) influences the behavior of the less advanced or expert partner (the child) through their social interaction. Wood, Bruner, and Ross (1976) identified the informal teaching roles adults adopt in interactions with children under the rubric of "scaffolds." As carpenters would in constructing a building, caregivers sometimes use temporary aids to support and guide a child's development. Scaffolding strategies vary in their effectiveness depending on the nature and age of the child and the actual activity, and caregivers can be expected to vary too in the scaffolds they favor. Mothers and fathers tend to scaffold children's learning differently (Power 1985; Tenenbaum and Leaper 1998), and they encourage girls' and boys' participation in different learning activities and assigned household chores in anticipation of later gender role differences in adulthood (see Goodnow 1988; Leaper 2000).

REINFORCEMENT

Mischel's (1970) social learning perspective on the development of gender pointed to parents' and others' direct reinforcement of children's conformity to expected or desired gender norms, as when adults compliment a girl when she nurses a doll and a boy when he builds a model airplane. Children's execution of different behaviors often depends on rewards or injunctions associated with their outcomes. As an illustration, gender-differentiated patterns of parent-child interaction in the domain of emotions may contribute to girls learning to express their emotions versus boys learning to mute them (Eisenberg, Cumberland, and Spinrad 1998). Through such experiences, children develop expectancies and beliefs about themselves that link to gender-related behaviors that, in turn, encourage and regulate their expressed gender roles.

OPPORTUNITY STRUCTURES

Another important way that parents treat daughters and sons differently is through the types of opportunities they provide or promote (Lytton and Romney 1991; Bussey and Bandura 1999). Access to certain settings gives children chances to develop certain conceptions of themselves and to engage in particular activities as well as to receive encouragement for repeating those activities (Lott and Maluso 1993). As an illustration, feminine-stereotyped toys tend to induce caregiving behaviors (e.g., nursing a doll), whereas masculine-stereotyped toys generate instrumental behaviors (e.g., building a model). Furthermore, stereotyped girls' toys (e.g., dolls) provide girls with practice learning rules, imitating behaviors, and using adults as sources of help, whereas stereotyped boys' toys (e.g., models) refine visual/spatial skills, problem-solving, independent learning, self-confidence, and creativity (Martin and Dinella 2002). Parents further influence gender development in their children by tending to place girls and boys in gender-distinctive contexts (e.g., rooms with certain furnishings; Pomerleau et al. 1990). Gender-typed environments also guide children's gender development. To the extent that gender-differentiated situations become customary in their lives, all features of children's gender-related knowledge, expectations, abilities, and activities are likely to be biased. These kinds of control of children's opportunity structures mean that parents do not need to differentially socialize, model, scaffold, or reinforce gendered beliefs or behaviors in their children because opportunity structures per se may elicit or ordain desired gendered beliefs or behaviors.

Socialization practices are subtle, complex, and context-dependent, but parents follow many customs in differentially socializing daughters and sons. Every culture is characterized (and distinguished from others) by thoroughgoing, deep-seated, and consistent themes that inculcate what one needs to know to think and behave as an appropriately functioning member of the culture. One major domain of this thematicity (the repetition of the same cultural idea across mechanisms and in a variety of contexts) is gender. Thus, parents' cognitions and practices communicate about gender in many convergent ways. Parents socialize, model, scaffold, and reinforce their children's gendered beliefs and behaviors, as they also organize and align their children's activities and environments within and outside the family. An illustration of how all these forces join was provided by Fredricks and Eccles (2002), who reported that parents who hold stronger stereotypes regarding the general differential capabilities of girls and boys in English, math, and sports had specialized expectations regarding their own children's abilities in these areas, which in turn related to their children's self-perceptions of competence and performance, even when actual ability levels were controlled. These relations were mediated, in part, by parents' tendencies to provide different experiences for daughters and sons.

TRANSACTION

Parents' cognitions and practices as well as those of peers, teachers, and other socialization agents promote gender-appropriate beliefs and behaviors that come to define "girlhood" and "boyhood." However, in the socializer-child transactions through time, children also contribute to their own development. In this regard, the influence of gender constancy is exemplary. Kohlberg (1966) proposed that children's developing sense of the permanence of categorical gender ("I am a girl and will always be a girl") critically organizes and motivates their learning gender beliefs and behaviors. Indeed, children appear to transit a series of cognitive stages in regard to understanding the nature of gender (Slaby and Frey 1975): first identifying their own and others' gender (basic gender identity or labeling), next accepting that gender remains stable through time (gender stability), and finally understanding that gender is an immutable characteristic that is not altered by superficial transformations in appearance or activities (gender consistency). Furthermore, the putative universality of these stages has been established in cross-cultural research (De Lisi and Gallagher 1991). Gender development, therefore, importantly entails active construction of the meaning of gender categories that is internal to the child. In this respect, research confirms associations between levels of gender constancy and gender development in terms of selective attention to same-gender models, same-gender imitation (activity, clothing, and peer preferences), gender-stereotype knowledge, and heightened responsiveness to gender cues. As an illustration, children's own developing cognitive structures influence their gender-role orientation and growth.

Although parents do the socializing, modeling, scaffolding, and reinforcing, children do the learning, and gender-typing and stereotypes pass from parent to child, and from one child to another, only when children attend to, accept, and adopt them (Hoyenga and Hoyenga 1993). Children may engage in more same- than other-gender beliefs and behaviors because they are differentially exposed to same-gender models (Crouter, Manke, and McHale 1995). Children's tendency to segregate themselves by gender reinforces the influence of same-gender peers vis-à-vis other-gender peers (Maccoby 1998; Martin and Fabes 2001), and children may not learn from one same-gender model but from many same-gender models engaged in the same activity. That is, modeling and observational learning are not necessarily confined to a single model or a specific belief or behavior; instead, children may learn abstract rules and styles. Indeed, by attending to models of both genders, children construct ideas of what is gender appropriate to themselves across a range of domains. Thus, a boy may develop the notion of gender-acceptable games based on observations of multiple boys engaging in different games and girls not participating in those games but in other games. Even if these learning processes are initially externally moderated, they eventually become internalized as children approve or sanction themselves in relation to personal standards of gender conduct (Bussey and Bandura 1999).

In summary, parents provide their children with many types of socialization experiences vis-à-vis gender, including models of gender roles and differential treatment of daughters and sons. We tend to assume that parents and other adult caregivers are responsible for gender-differentiated conduct with children, but it is also the case that daughters elicit more feminine stereotypes (nurturance) and sons more masculine ones (instrumentality). Child effects on parents are in play and are not mutually exclusive with parent effects on children. Moreover, child characteristics and parent influences interact to consolidate gender differences in children. In the end, effects in the socialization of child gender run in both directions—parent-to-child and child-to-parent. This consistency is mutually reinforcing to child gender development.

PARENTING × GENDER

Gender shapes parent–child relationships in multiple ways. Starrels (1994:160) asserted that "parenting is undoubtedly a gendered activity" because both parent and child gender are of essence. Beliefs, behaviors, and structures are all organized by gender. Parent and child gender alike moderate influences.

MOTHERS VS. FATHERS

Mothers and fathers have different relationships with their children (Barnard and Solchany 2002; Parke 2002) and socialize girls and boys differently (Siegal 1987; Lytton and Romney 1991). Collins and Russell (1991), Parke (2002), and Pleck (2012) have all identified mother–father contrasts. Social and scientific concerns begin at the level of initial childcare. In nearly 100 percent of mammalian species, females take responsibility for early childcare, whereas males provide little direct investment in offspring (Clutton-Brock 1989, 1991). For two species most closely related to humans—chimpanzees (*Pan troglodytes*) and bonobos (*Pan paniscus*)—males are not typically invested in care and only rarely even affiliate with juveniles (Goodall 1986; Whitten 1987; de Waal and Lanting 1997). By many accounts, several cross-cultural in nature, human mothers provide more direct care to their children than fathers do (Whiting and Edwards 1988). Indeed, analyzing data from 186 societies worldwide, Weisner and Gallimore (1977) found that in the vast majority mothers (and female adult relatives and female children) served as the primary caregivers of infants. These observations cannot be attributed to a general inability of men to care for young children. When fathers interact with infants and children, for example, they show many of the same characteristics as mothers (e.g., they switch to child-directed speech), and fathers can provide competent routine care (Belsky et al. 1989; Eibl-Eibesfeldt 1989; Parke 2002; Pleck 2012). These gender differences also cannot be attributed to paternal absence because fathers tend to be away hunting or working outside of the home. When both parents are present, for example, U.S. mothers spontaneously engage their infants 1.5 to 2 times more frequently and provide routine care 3 to 4 times more frequently than do their husbands (Belsky, Gilstrap, and Rovine 1984). (These differences may have narrowed somewhat in recent years at least for some men; see following and Pleck 2012.)

Nontraditional families are those in which fathers take leave from work to care for children and express a desire to be the primary caregiver. On a self-report measure, nontraditional fathers rated parenthood more highly than did nontraditional mothers; the opposite pattern was found for traditional families. Despite differences in expressed attitudes toward childcare, however, mothers constitute children's primary caregivers in traditional and nontraditional families alike. In fact, traditional and nontraditional fathers differ little in the ways in which they actually interact with their children; the primary distinction being that traditional fathers more likely play more often with their children than do nontraditional fathers.

Notably, observations of parental care in preindustrial traditional societies, such as the !Kung San (Botswana), reveal the same pattern found in modern and Western nations (West and Konner 1976; Flinn 1992; Griffin and Griffin 1992;). Studies of the !Kung San are particularly telling because their social customs center on equality among group members and because they have sometimes been described as enjoying the type of social structure representative of the one in which human beings evolved (Eibl-Eibesfeldt 1989). Observations of caregiving activities—for children younger than two years of age—indicate !Kung San fathers provide less than 7 percent of care, with the majority of the remaining care provided by mothers (West and Konner 1976; Katz and Konner 1981). In another hunter–gatherer society— the Aka pygmies (Central African Republic)—fathers provide more direct care to their infants and children than do fathers in any other society that has been studied (Hewlett 1988, 1992). One reported observation indicated that Aka fathers held their one- to four-month-old infants 22 percent of the time, on average, in which the fathers were in camp. Nevertheless, during the course of the day, "the father would on average hold his infant for a total of 57 minutes while the mother would hold the infant 490 minutes" (Hewlett 1988:268).

Evolutionary psychology attributes such stark and consistent mother-father differences in child tending principally to maternal internal gestation and obligatory postpartum suckling (Clutton-Brock 1989). Gender differences in the relative costs and benefits of producing offspring are argued to play a key part in understanding the evolution of gender differences in reproductive strategies and in parental investment (Williams 1966; Trivers 1972).

In a nutshell, the gender with the higher potential rate of reproduction typically invests more in "mating effort" than in "parenting effort," whereas the gender with the lower potential rate of reproduction invests more in parenting than in mating (Trivers 1972; Clutton-Brock and Vincent 1991).

In overview, in almost all species and all regions of the world, across a wide diversity of subsistence activities and social ideologies, observational studies indicate more maternal than paternal investment in parenting. The common mammalian pattern is for the reproductive strategy of females to focus on parenting efforts and the reproductive strategy of males to focus on mating efforts.

DAUGHTERS VS. SONS

Daughters and sons are traditionally reared differently. Many studies suggest that parents treat females and males in singular ways and encourage them to accept unique and conventional gender roles. Lytton and Romney (1991) examined the differential socialization of girls and boys; they focused on parental treatment of children; and they considered especially the interaction between parent gender and child gender by investigating whether mothers and fathers distinguish between daughters and sons. The clearest effect they found was parents' disparate encouragement of gender-typed activities (versus areas such as personality traits). Parental behaviors appear fairly consistently to be gender-related. Parents have been reported to purchase gender-stereotyped toys for their children within a few months of the child's birth—prior to when children could express gender-typed toy preferences themselves (Pomerleau et al. 1990). As an illustration, tend not only to give their children gender-typed toys but also to encourage gender-typed play (Rheingold and Cook 1975; Eisenberg et al. 1985; Robinson and Morris 1986; Pomerleau et al. 1990; Fisher-Thompson 1993). Parents tend to discuss more emotional experiences and use more frequent and varied emotional words and references with their daughters than with their sons (Dunn, Bretherton, and Munn 1987; Adams et al. 1995; Fivush 1998; Flanagan and Perese 1998; Eisenberg 1999). Fathers reward daughters for displays of sadness and fear, whereas they discourage sons from expressing the same emotions. As children grow, parents also assign household chores along gender stereotyped lines that may (as we have seen) have implications beyond children's locally learning particular skills (Antill et al. 1996).

The dynamics of mother-father daughter-son socialization practices are intricate and complex. They are not fully understood either. On the one hand, parents may feel a greater affinity, commonality, and responsibility for same-gender children, and thereby exert closer control over them. On the other hand, differential treatment may occur through reciprocal role enactment processes in which fathers encourage femininity in daughters and mothers encourage masculinity in sons. On the third hand, children of both genders spend more time in the formative years of their lives with female than male caregivers, and such circumstances may represent a significant type of differential treatment.

MOTHERS VS. FATHERS AND DAUGHTERS VS. SONS

If gender has a powerful and pervasive influence on relationships within the family, then it follows that individual parent–child dyad combinations might betray distinct features of its dynamics. Indeed, considering gender alone, one would then posit four separate parent–child dyad types. In this vein, Steinberg (1987:194) asked "if the 'adolescent–parent relationship' might not be more accurately characterized as four very different relationships;" Collins and Russell (1991:128) concluded that understanding mother–child and father–child relationships in middle childhood and adolescence might "require distinctions according to gender of offspring, as well as gender of parents;" and Cowan, Cowan, and Kerig (1993) posited the presence of the four dyad types in their study of family formation. In short, relationships in the four dyads of mother–son, mother–daughter, father–son, and father–daughter could be distinct. Notably, among all the studies and all the analyses contained in the literature up until 1997, Russell and Saebel (1997) could find only one that clearly showed the four dyads to differ significantly from each other. In the study in question, Noller and Callan (1990) investigated the effects of gender of adolescent and gender of parent (as well as age) on adolescents' perceptions of communication with their parents. Six dimensions of parent–adolescent communication (e.g., frequency of communication, self-disclosure, and so forth) were examined in relation to fourteen content areas (e.g., adolescents' interests, politics, and so forth), with separate analyses conducted on each dimension, and then on each content area. For the dimensions of frequency of communication, self-disclosure, domination, and satisfaction, interactions of parent gender and child gender emerged. For example, an interaction between parent gender and child gender was obtained for the measure of frequency of interaction between adolescent and parent. Follow-up tests on the content areas dealing with frequency of interaction yielded different patterns of gender differences from one analysis to another. From the analyses of the data for the frequency of adolescents discussing their interests with their parents, it was possible to conclude that the four dyads were distinct. Reported rates of talking with parents about interests were highest in mother–daughter dyads, followed in turn by mother–son dyads, father–son dyads, and father–daughter dyads.

In summary, parenting and childhood are both gendered, and both parent gender and child gender have consequences for children's gender development. Parents differ in their parent investment strategies by their own gender, and they parent their children differently relative to their child's gender. The result is a fourfold taxonomy of distinctive intrafamilial relationships of mother-daughter, mother-son, father-daughter, and father-son pairs.

PARENTING × GENDER × CULTURE

Many factors influence child development, parenting, and parent–child relationships (Belsky 1984; Bornstein 2002, 2006; Bronfenbrenner and Morris 2006). These factors can be grouped into three broad categories: (a) individual child characteristics, such as gender, age, temperament, and social competence; (b) individual parent characteristics, such as gender, personality, social competence, beliefs, and values; and (c) social-contextual factors, such as the marital relationship, sources of stress, social networks, and social class as well as culture. In the prevailing ecological model of human development (Bronfenbrenner and Morris 2006), these spheres of influence range from the distal macrosystem to the proximal microsystem. Microsystems refer to particular physical and social circumstances that operate on the child individual at close range. The parent-child relationship typifies the microsystem. The macrosystem refers to remote but still influential circumstances that are thought to shape individual development through microsystems. Cultural factors that define a society, such as its form of economy, political structure, traditions, and laws, constitute the macrosystem of individual development.

Culture has profound effects on gender-related beliefs and behaviors, prescribing how children are socialized and by whom, how they are dressed, what behavior is considered adaptive and what maladaptive, which tasks children are taught, and what roles as adult women and men they will adopt. Thus, culture can be expected to mold parents' cognitions about child gender and shape their child-rearing practices vis-à-vis child gender (Whiting and Edwards 1988; Best and Williams 1997). Parents are principal agents for transmitting culture. With respect to gender, cultural forces pressure conformity to gender roles and influence how people think about themselves in terms of gender, their perceptions of femininity and masculinity generally—in themselves as well as in other people—and not insignificantly their child gender-related socialization. The cultural forces that engender gender contrasts in a society take many guises and include the relative statuses of women and men, the social division of labor, involvement in caregiving, economic opportunities, and religious values.

Child-rearing strategies reflect adaptations by parents (and other caregivers) meant most to help prepare children for success in their specific culture. The types of socialization practices directed toward girls and boys in large measure reflect the existing opportunity structures for women and men in a particular community at a particular time in history. As an illustration, if women in the society are expected to assume primary responsibility for rearing children, childcare practices in the society would incline to emphasize the practice of nurturant behaviors in girls more than in boys. If men are expected to take primary responsibility for providing economic subsistence outside of the home, childcare practices would tend to emphasize independent and constructive behaviors in boys more than in girls. Thus, roughly speaking, division of labor according to gender tends to correlate with child-rearing emphases in the society (Weisner 1979; Whiting 1986; Hewlett 1991; Best and Williams 1997). The meaning of gender is communicated through the cultural flavoring and accents of the macrosystem (e.g., power and economic differentials between women and men) that in turn influence the microsystems a child directly experiences at home, in the school, and around the neighborhood (Low 1989).

It follows, then, that stories of culture and gender are largely (although not wholly) ones of cultural stereotypes of gender transmitted by parents. Mothers throughout the world show a much greater availability to and engagement with their children than fathers do. Observations of families in Liberia, Kenya, India, Guatemala, and Peru reveal that fathers rarely (if ever) engage in the care of children younger than one year of age (Whiting and Edwards 1988). In the United States, (especially contemporary) fathers may provide more care to their infants than fathers in these other settings, although U. S. fathers still do considerably less baby tending than infants' mothers (Belsky et al. 1989; Harkness and Super 1992). Draper and Harpending (1988) characterized human cultures as inclined to be father absent or father present, reflecting differences in the relative emphasis of men on mating and parenting, respectively. As indicated earlier, the biology of mammalian reproduction appears to condition higher levels of maternal than paternal investment especially in early childcare (Clutton-Brock and Vincent 1991; Andersson 1994).

Parents typically adopt dominant and prevailing cultural prescriptions for their girls and boys. In many cultures, more positive evaluations apply to men and "masculine" activities than to women and "feminine" activities (Berscheid 1993). "Strong," "aggressive," "cruel," "coarse," and "adventurous" are consistently associated with men by people of all age groups; "weak," "appreciative," "softhearted," "gentle," and "meek" are consistently associated with women. Traditionally, fathers are seen as more powerful and separated from the family, whereas mothers are cast as caregivers and home managers embedded in the family (Goldman and Goldman 1983; Weisner, Garnier, and Loucky 1994).

Household chores and access to diverse opportunities constitute common activities and situations around the world that further reinforce culturally meaningful practices and circumstances for children. Studies of children's household work indicate patterns that are pertinent to considerations of gender socialization. First, mothers and fathers typically model a traditional gender-stereotyped division of labor in their own household work (Hilton and Haldeman 1991). Second, parents tend to allocate gender-typed chores to children. They typically assign childcare and cleaning to daughters and allot maintenance work to sons (Burns and Homel 1989; Antill et al. 1996). As an illustration, in rural agrarian societies, older daughters are typically charged with childcare and older sons with helping outside of the home (Whiting 1986). Moreover, third, children tend to prefer being delegated with gender-stereotyped chores (Etauh and Liss 1992). In Chile, for example, prevalent cultural standards of women as caregivers and men as providers operate early in the primary socialization contexts of families and schools (Martinez, Cumsille, and Thibaut 2008). Traditional cultural gender stereotypes for children transcend the confines of the family as well. Thus, sisters have less educational opportunity, especially in poorer settings, than their brothers. Many more boys attend school in the Peruvian highlands, for example, because girls are often in charge of house chores and younger siblings (Pinzas 2008).

Nonetheless, several important factors moderate cultural influences on parenting by gender. One is intercultural variability. Parental attitudes and activities toward daughters and sons are far from absolutely uniform, but vary across cultures (Hobbs and Wimbish 1977), and there is considerable variability in men's focus on mating versus parenting (L. C. Miller and

Fishkin 1997; Parke and Buriel 1998). In sedentary, high-food-accumulating societies, for example, female-male socialization tends to differ greatly with females being trained to be nurturant and compliant. In low-food-accumulating societies, by contrast, the division of labor by gender tends to be less rigid, and both males and females contribute to subsistence so socialization is similar for females and males (Van Leeuwen 1978). One dimension on which cultures are thought to differ is collectivism-individualism. Children's peer experiences vary across cultures in part because of different expectations regarding individual independence versus social interdependence. In so-called collectivist or sociocentric societies, tensions in the pursuits of independence versus personal identity, and the commitment to group undertakings, may be less evident than in so-called individualist or idiocentric societies. In collectivist cultures, children are expected and encouraged to identify with the group (Sharabany 2006). It is likely that collectivist cultural values facilitate and reinforce the regulatory effect of the peer group on children's behavior and development (Chen et al. 2003, 2006). Stereotyped knowledge, rigidity/flexibility, and inferences of many kinds about gender also vary across cultures. Even countries that share a European background differ with respect to degree of their stereotyping. As an illustration, Italian children are more likely to gender stereotype toys and activities than Dutch children (Zammuner 1987).

Child factors constitute a second important constellation of variables that moderate cultural influences on parenting by gender. The two genders differ in their susceptibility to cultural socialization re gender, for example. Perhaps because of the higher status generally afforded men in different cultures, boys are more resistant to nontraditional gender attitudes than are girls (Bussey and Bandura 1999; Leaper 2000). Child age also moderates culture effects. An examination of gender stereotypes of five-, eight-, and eleven year olds in twenty-five countries revealed a general developmental pattern of stereotype acquisition beginning prior to age five, accelerating during the early school years, and becoming complete during adolescence (Williams and Best 1982, 1990).

Third, is intracultural variability. Cultures are not monolithic entities. Within a given culture, there may be social-structural variations in gender relationships depending on people's education, social class, ethnic and religious tradition as well as other characteristics particular to specific communities. In the United States, as an illustration, gender emphases appear to vary depending on socioeconomic factors such as income, education, and ethnicity (Reid and Comas-Diaz 1990; Chow, Wilkinson, and Baca Zinn 1996; Leaper and Valin 1996) as well as structural factors such as marital status or maternal employment (Stevenson and Black 1988; Etaugh 1993; Leaper et al. 1995; Risman 2001). Each of these factors influences the relative amounts of power, status, and resources that women and men enjoy in a society (Kimmel 2000). Distinctive gender differences in beliefs and behaviors appear to be less prominent among African American children (Kane 2000) than among European American (Bardwell, Cochran, and Walker 1986; Albert and Porter 1988) or Latin American (Bailey and Nihlen 1990; Raffaelli and Ontai 2004) or Asian American children (Lobel et al. 2001).

Finally, all of these factors may interact in different combinations to affect the influence of culture in gender development. European American children's knowledge of adult-defined gender stereotypes (e.g., women are "emotional" and "gentle" and men are "strong" and "dominant") increases from kindergarten through high school with the most dramatic gains during the elementary school years; whereas African American children's knowledge of the same stereotypic traits also increases with age, but at a slower rate, suggesting that different ethnic or national groups within one country vary in their stereotype knowledge according to their developmental status (Williams and Best 1982, 1990).

In summary, culture shapes gendered parenting and gender development in children pervasively and in both subtle and manifest ways. However, effects of culture are moderated by various factors, including intercultural variability, child individual differences, and intracultural variability.

PARENTING × GENDER × CULTURE × TIME

We live in the moment, but a principal (and often neglected) component of the bioecological model of human development is time (Bronfenbrenner and Morris 2006). Two main temporal issues arise in considering the intersection of parenting, gender, and culture. One is developmental time. As an illustration, adolescence is often viewed as a period of gender intensification (Hill and Lynch 1983; Crouter, Manke, and McHale 1995; Steinberg and Silk 2002). A second is historical time. As an illustration, although gender continues to be portrayed in stereotypic ways, some diachronic changes appear to be underway (Huston and Wright 1998). I explore each of these construals of time briefly in connection with parenting, gender, and culture.

DEVELOPMENTAL TIME

Influences on gender development subtly and not so subtly modulate from parents to peers and school as children grow. In early childhood, parents (mostly) are children's primary caregivers and special influences on their development. When children are young and still at home, parents socialize, model, scaffold, and reinforce gendered beliefs or behaviors in their children as well as construct most of their children's formative experiences. As children develop, however, influences beyond the family begin to rival parents for sway over children's development. Parents do not relinquish their responsibilities or authority entirely, and good parent-child relationships maintain parent input life-long. However, children's friends and the establishments with which they now associate come to hold waxing authority. These two forces, one interpersonal (peers) and one institutional (school), play increasingly central roles in children's gender development.

Once they enter the world of peers, children in many cultures are encouraged to learn independence and self-direction while establishing and maintaining positive relationships with others; eventually, they are expected to acquire a sense of gender identity within peer contexts (Mead 1934). Children learn some standards for gender-appropriate behavior through observation, as we have learned, and like parents peers socialize gender development by serving as role models. Young children spend significant amounts of time with other children of their own gender; in this way they selectively learn more about the behaviors and interaction styles associated with their own gender and less about other-gender interactions and styles (Thorne 1986; Leaper 1994; Maccoby 1998). Gender segregation appears to be universal and is typical of the young in many higher species of nonhuman primates (Wallen 1996) as well as children in Western and non-Western societies. The extent of peer influences appears to depend on a number of factors, including the number of children available, their ages, and the setting—highest when children have more playmate choices and in less structured situations (Whiting and Edwards 1988; Maccoby 1998). Gender segregation of play groups leads to different activities and opportunity structures that in turn may lead to differences in intellectual and emotional development (Block 1983). Examination of peer interactions of two- to ten year olds from the Six Culture Study and from additional cultural samples shows that a robust and cross-culturally universal preference for affiliating with children of the same gender emerges as early as age two (Edwards 1992; Edwards and Whiting 1993). By middle childhood, gender segregation is pervasive (Edwards 1992).

Agemates who resemble the child in abilities and activity preferences also provide opportunities for competition and conflict. This circumstance is referred to as the "separate cultures" perspective. Indeed, gender-segregated interactions can move girls and boys in gender-typed directions with relatively limited exposure. A social dosage effect is common too in children's socialization by peers. Children with high levels of same-gender play early in the school year increase in gender-typed behaviors later in the school year, with effects beyond those that initially drew children into gender-segregated groups. Boys increase in rough-and-tumble play, aggression, and playing away from teachers, and girls decrease activity and aggression and increase affiliative play and play near to adults. Peers further serve as gender enforcers or "gender police" (Martin and Fabes 2001). It is the rare child who crosses the gender line in some way in front of her or his peers.

Adolescence in particular marks a crossroads that is associated with gender intensification and increases in gender traditionalism (Hill and Lynch 1983). Adolescence is a period of increasing pressures to conform to gender (as well as other) stereotypes in preparation for future independent roles and adult status (Eccles 1987; Katz and Ksansnak 1994). Just a few domains of gender development that are transformed in adolescence include gender schemas, body image, athletic participation, school achievement, and emotional autonomy and closeness.

Children's school attendance institutionalizes and consolidates some of these peer influences and adds others of its own. In many contemporary societies, schools provide children with a primary context for social interaction because they congregate large numbers of nonkin, same-age children and thereby breed gender-segregated peer groups. Classrooms provide children with additional opportunities to learn about gender behavior through observing and associating with peers. Insofar as teachers hold differential expectations of girls' and boys' abilities and treat them differently, they too channel schools' influences on gender development. Finally, gender-biased themes, descriptions, images, and characters commonly populate school textbooks.

In brief overview, peers have a major role in gender development because of the opportunities they provide to learn interactional styles and because children's increasing time with same-gender peers exposes them more to same-gender than other-gender behaviors and interaction styles, narrowing their behavioral repertoire. With same-gender peers, children practice gender-typed play, learn behavioral patterns that facilitate interaction with their own gender, and limit interaction with the other gender. Schools reinforce gender segregation and further gender differentiation in myriad ways.

HISTORICAL TIME

"Traditional" gender-role prescriptions characterize women as interpersonally sensitive and men as independent problem solvers; women as soft and nurturant, men as hard and demanding; gatherers versus hunters; homemakers as opposed to breadwinners; and so forth. Many places around the world still cling to these traditional gender and role views; in other places, for a variety of reasons, more egalitarian gender and role beliefs are emergent or prevail. Even if the world as a whole is in the midst of diachronic change, there are still many places where traditional gender roles reign and continue to permeate conceptions of female and male, similarities and differences between the genders, and expectations for girls and boys. Cross-national surveys indicate that traditional attitudes tend to correlate with women's degree of dependence on men in the society (Baxter and Kane 1995).

Elsewhere, the way of the world is moving toward more egalitarian social and economic relationships between the genders. Maternal employment, which is on the rise worldwide, is associated with less stereotyped beliefs and behaviors (Ruble et al. 2006). As an illustration, the socioeconomic situation of middle-class and working-class Peruvians has forced men and women to change their views about gender roles (Pinzas 2008). Andean and migrant families are mostly patriarchal. In the coastal urban areas, this "macho" family culture is still present, even among educated Peruvians. The father is the main authority in the house and the last word in decision-making. He chooses rewards and punishments, and his wife will be his advisor. However, the behavior of families and adolescents has been radically changing. Many female adolescents, young adults, and mothers today work outside the house or at home. Egalitarian attitudes are more likely in countries where wives and husbands share relatively equal economic power. Furthermore, globalization of the mass media has led to the rapid transmission of information and values in general and for youth in particular. (In some societies, however, the diachronic change is not from traditionalism to egalitarianism, but to stagnation in traditionalism or even toward greater cultural and religious conservatism.)

Many factors appear to be driving these changing conditions. In a given culture, low-socioeconomic status or more religious respondents tend to endorse more traditional gender-restrictive views of family roles. As an illustration, in Chile, 53 percent of men with elementary education or less believe women are mainly responsible for household chores, compared to only 10 percent of college educated men (Martinez, Cumsille, and Thibaut 2008).

A countrywide study of 13,200 girls in the age range seven to eighteen years and their mothers drawn from fourteen states of India revealed a complex web of familial and cultural factors that determine the course of a girl's life (Anandalakshmy 1994). Social class, level of economic development of her village/district, parental education levels, her birth order, number and gender of siblings, and family's caste all influenced girls' status within the family and in the community.

With the spread of Western styles of schooling, gender differences in overall peer interactions are diminishing. However, Western values are not always adopted completely in their original forms, but instead tend to integrate with cultural traditions of the society. In Argentina, a macho attitude has steadily decreased, and the gap between the genders in work, education, and political activity has been narrowing (Facio and Resett 2008). Although women are highly regarded for their maternal role, Argentine young people of both genders consider "being capable of caring for children" as important for defining an adult man as it is for defining an adult woman.

In summary, two temporal factors moderate the intersection of parent, gender, and culture. As children develop, initially friends and later school supplement, if not spell, parents as significant influences on children's gender development. Overall and around the globe as well, historical forces are at work that are moving some cultures in a modernizing egalitarian direction with respect to gender and freezing others in more traditional gender role differences.

CONCLUSIONS

This chapter overviews thinking and evidence regarding the impact on gender development of socialization processes in the family and culture (separate from peers, school, and other factors, like media, which all contribute to gender differentiation). Parenting is gendered and a gendered activity. It appears that parents must overcome barriers to rear children in a gender-neutral manner, and even similar parenting behaviors may affect daughters and sons differently due to gender-related differences in children's dispositions or their prior socialization. Childhood gender differences pave the way for later adult gender differences in roles and status.

Cultural influences on children's gender are dynamic and reflected at three levels: the changing cultural context, the developing child, and the mediating role of social interaction between children and parents as well as peers and others. Peer influence increases as children grow, helping to structure the transition between childhood and adulthood, and peers may play as important a role as parents, if not more so, in the eventual socialization of gender. Nonetheless, parents set children down initial pathways of their gender development. In spite of the fact that females and males are biologically and psychologically more similar than different (Hyde 2005), children growing up in traditional or modern societies alike can continue to expect to live qualitatively different lives based on their gender.

ACKNOWLEDGMENTS

This chapter summarizes selected aspects of my research, and portions of the text have appeared in previous scientific publications cited in the references. This research was supported by the Intramural Research Program of the NIH, NICHD.

NOTES

1. Sex is often used for biological differences and gender for learned behaviors between females and males. Using separate terms for sex and gender sets up an arbitrary, unnecessary dichotomy between biological and experiential influences (Fausto-Sterling 2000; Best 2010). In this chapter, therefore, I adopt "gender" passim. This chapter is also concerned exclusively with what is conventionally accepted as normal and heterosexual gender differentiation and development, and not with issues of gender identity duality, ambiguity, or homosexuality.

REFERENCES

Adams, S., J. Kuebli, P. A. Boyle, and R. Fivush. 1995. "Gender Differences in Parent–Child Conversations About Past Emotions: A Longitudinal Investigation." *Sex Roles* 33:309–323.

Albert, A. A. and J. R. Porter. 1988. "Children's Gender-Role Stereotypes: A Sociological Investigation of Psychological Models." *Sociological Forum* 3(2):184–210.

Anandalakshmy, S., ed. 1994. *The Girl Child and the Family: An Action Research Study*. New Delhi: Department of Women and Child Development, Ministry of Human Resource Development, Govt. of India.

Andersson, M. 1994. *Sexual Selection*. Princeton, NJ: Princeton University Press.

Antill, J. K., J. J. Goodnow, G. Russell, and S. Cotton. 1996. "The Influence of Parents and Family Context on Children's Involvement in Household Tasks." *Sex Roles* 34:215–236.

Bailey, B. A. and A. S. Nihlen. 1990. "Effect of Experience with Nontraditional Workers on Psychological and Social Dimensions of Occupational Sex-Role Stereotyping by Elementary School Children." *Psychological Reports* 66:1273–1282.

Bardwell, J. R., S. W. Cochran, and S. Walker. 1986. "Relationship of Parental Education, Race, and Gender to Sex Role Stereotyping in Five-Year-Old Kindergartners." *Sex Roles* 15:275–281.

Barnard, K. E. and J. E. Solchany. 2002. "Mothering." In *Handbook of Parenting: Becoming a Parent*, ed. M. H. Bornstein, 3:3–26. Mahwah, NJ: Erlbaum.

Baxter, J. and E. W. Kane. 1995. "Dependence and Independence: A Cross-National Analysis of Gender Inequality and Gender Attitudes." *Gender & Society* 9:193–215.

Belsky, J. 1984. "The Determinants of Parenting: A Process Model." *Child Development* 55:83–96.

Belsky, J., B. Gilstrap, and M. Rovine. 1984. "The Pennsylvania Infant and Family Development Project: I. Stability and Change in Mother–Infant and Father–Infant Interaction in a Family Setting at One, Three, and Nine Months." *Child Development* 55:692–705.

Belsky, J., M. Rovine, and M. Fish. 1989. "The Developing Family System." In *Systems and Development: The Minnesota Symposia on Child Psychology*, ed. M. R. Gunnar and E. Thelen, 22:119–166. Hillsdale, NJ: Erlbaum.

Berscheid, E. 1993. "Forward." In *The Psychology of Gender*, ed. A. E. Beall and R. J. Sternberg, 1–17. New York: Guilford.

Best, D. L. 2010. "Gender." In *The Handbook of Cultural Developmental Science. Part 1. Domains of Development Across Cultures*, ed. M. H. Bornstein, 209–237. New York: Taylor & Francis.

Best, D. L. and J. E. Williams. 1997. "Sex, Gender, and Culture." In *Handbook of Cross-Cultural Psychology: Vol. 3. Social Behavior and Application*, ed. J. W. Berry, M. H. Segall, and C. Kagitcibasi, 163–212. Boston: Allyn and Bacon.

Block, J. H. 1983. "Differential Premises Arising from Differential Socialization of the Sexes: Some Conjectures." *Child Development* 54:1335–1354.

Bornstein, M. H., ed. 2002. *Handbook of Parenting*, 2nd ed., vols. 1–5. Mahwah, NJ: Lawrence Erlbaum.

Bornstein, M. H. 2006. "Parenting Science and Practice." In *Handbook of Child Psychology*, vol. 4, 6th ed., ed. K. A. Renninger, I. E. Sigel, W. Damon, and R. M. Lerner, 893–949. Hoboken, NJ: John Wiley.

Bronfenbrenner, U. and P. A. Morris. 2006. "The Bioecological Model of Human Development." In *Theoretical Models of Human Development. Handbook of Child Psychology*, vol. 1, 6th ed., ed. R. M. Lerner, 793–828. Hoboken, NJ: John Wiley.

Burns, A. and R. Homel. 1989. "Gender Division of Tasks by Parents and Their Children." *Psychology of Women Quarterly* 13:113–125.

Bussey, K. and A. Bandura. 1999. "Social Cognitive Theory of Gender Development and Differentiation." *Psychological Review* 106:676–713.

Chen, X., L. Chang, and Y. He. 2003. "The Peer Group as a Context: Mediating and Moderating Effects on the Relations Between Academic Achievement and Social Functioning in Chinese Children." *Child Development* 74:710–727.

Chen, X, D. French, and B. Schneider. 2006. *Peer Relationships in Cultural Context.* New York: Cambridge University.

Chow, E., D. Y. Wilkinson, and Baca Zinn, M., ed. 1996. *Race, Class, and Gender: Common Bonds, Different Voices.* Thousand Oaks, CA: Sage.

Clutton-Brock, T. H. 1989. "Mammalian Mating Systems." *Proceedings of the Royal Society of London B,* 236:339–372.

Clutton-Brock, T. H. 1991. *The Evolution of Parental Care.* Princeton, NJ: Princeton University.

Clutton-Brock, T. H. and A. C. J. Vincent. 1991. "Sexual Selection and the Potential Reproductive Rates of Males and Females." *Science* 351:58–60.

Collins, W. A., S. D. Madsen, and A. Susman-Stillman. 2002. "Parenting During Middle Childhood." In *Handbook of Parenting: Children and Parenting,* vol. 1, 2nd ed., ed. M. H. Bornstein, 73–101. Mahwah, NJ: Lawrence Erlbaum.

Collins, W. A. and G. Russell. 1991. "Mother–Child and Father–Child Relationships in Middle Childhood and Adolescence: A Developmental Analysis." *Developmental Review* 11:99– 136.

Cowan, P. A., C. P. Cowan, and P. K. Kerig. 1993. "Mothers, Fathers, Sons, and Daughters: Gender Differences in Family Formation and Parenting Style." In *Family, Self, and Society: Toward a New Agenda for Family Research,* ed. P. A. Cowan, D. Field, D. A. Hansen, A. Skolnick, and G. E. Swanson, 165–195. Hillsdale, NJ: Erlbaum.

Crouter, A. C., B. A. Manke and S. M. McHale. 1995. "The Family Context of Gender Intensification in Early Adolescence." *Child Development* 66:317–329.

Crowley, K., M. A. Callanan, H. R. Tenenbaum, and E. Allen. 2001. "Parents Explain More Often to Boys Than to Girls During Shared Scientific Thinking." *Psychological Science* 12:258–261.

De Lisi, R. and A. M. Gallagher. 1991. "Understanding of Gender Stability and Constancy in Argentinean Children." *Merrill Palmer Quarterly* 37:483–502.

de Waal, F. and F. Lanting. 1997. *Bonobo: The Forgotten Ape.* Berkeley, CA: University of California.

Draper, P. and H. Harpending. 1988. "A Sociobiological Perspective on the Development of Human Reproductive Strategies." In *Sociobiological Perspectives on Human Development,* ed. K. B. MacDonald, 340–372. New York: Springer-Verlag.

Dunn, J., I. Bretherton, and P. Munn. 1987. "Conversations About Feeling States Between Mothers and Their Young Children." *Developmental Psychology* 23: 132–139.

Eccles, J. S. 1987. "Adolescence: Gateway to Gender-Role Transcendence." In *Current Conceptions of Sex Roles and Sex Typing: Theory and Research,* ed. D. B. Carter, 225–241. New York: Praeger.

Eccles, J. S., C. Freedman-Doan, P. Frome, J. Jacobs, and K. S. Yoon. 2000. "Gender-Role Socialization in the Family: A Longitudinal Approach." In *The Developmental Social Psychology of Gender*, ed. T. Eckes and H. M. Trautner, 333–360. Mahwah, NJ: Lawrence Erlbaum.

Edwards, C. P. 1992. "Cross-Cultural Perspectives on Family-Peer Relations." In *Family-Peer Relationships: Modes of Linkages*, ed. R. D. Parke and G. W. Ladd, 285–315. Mahwah, NJ: Lawrence Erlbaum.

Edwards, C. P. and B. B. Whiting. 1993. "Mother, Older Sibling, and Me: The Overlapping Roles of Caretakers and Companions in the Social World of 2–3 Year Olds in Ngeca, Kenya." In *Parent-Child: Descriptions and Implications*, ed. K. MacDonald, 305–329. Albany: State University of New York.

Eibl-Eibesfeldt, I. 1989. *Human Ethology*. New York: Aldine de Gruyter.

Eisenberg, A. R. 1999. "Emotion Talk Among Mexican American and Anglo American Mothers and Children from Two Social Classes." *Merrill–Palmer Quarterly* 45:267–284.

Eisenberg, N., A. Cumberland, and T. L. Spinrad. 1998. "Parental Socialization of Emotion." *Psychology Inquiry* 9:241–273.

Eisenberg, N., S. A. Wolchik, R. Hernandez, and J. Pasternak. 1985. "Parental Socialization of Young Children's Play: A Short-Term Longitudinal Study." *Child Development* 56:1506–1513.

Etaugh, C. 1993. "Maternal Employment: Effects on Children." In *The Employed Mother and the Family Context*, ed. J. Frankel, 68–88. New York: Springer.

Etauh, C. and M. B. Liss. 1992. "Home, School, and Playroom: Training Grounds for Adult Gender Roles." *Sex Roles*, 26:129–147.

Facio, A. and S. Resett. 2008. "Argentina." In *International Encyclopedia of Adolescence*, ed. J. J. Arnett, 1–15. New York: Routledge.

Fausto-Sterling, A. 2000. *Sexing the Body: Gender Politics and the Construction of Sexuality*. New York: Basic.

Fisher-Thompson, D. 1993. "Adult Toy Purchase for Children: Factors Affecting Sex-Typed Toy Selection." *Journal of Applied Developmental Psychology* 14:385–406.

Fivush, R. 1998. "Gendered Narratives: Elaboration, Structure, and Emotion in Parent-Child Reminiscing Across the Preschool Years." In *Autobiographical Memory: Theoretical and Applied Perspectives*, ed. C. P. Thompson and D. J. Hermann, 79–103. Mahwah, NJ: Lawrence Erlbaum.

Flanagan, D. and S. Perese. 1998. "Emotional References in Mother-Daughter and Mother-Son Dyads' Conversations About School." *Sex Roles* 39:353–367.

Flinn, M. V. 1992. "Paternal Care in a Caribbean Village." In *Father–Child Relations: Cultural and Biosocial Contexts*, ed. B. S. Hewlett, 57–84. New York: Aldine de Gruyter.

Fredricks, J. A. and J. S. Eccles. 2002. "Children's Competence and Value Beliefs from Childhood Through Adolescence: Growth Trajectories in Two Male-Sex-Typed Domains." *Developmental Psychology* 38:519–533.

Giles, J. W. and G. D. Heyman. 2004. "When to Cry Over Spilled Milk: Young Children's Use of Category Information to Guide Inferences About Ambiguous Behavior." *Journal of Cognition and Development* 5:359–386.

Goldman, J. D. and R. J. Goldman. 1983. "Children's Perceptions of Parents and Their Roles: A Cross-National Study in Australia, England, North America, and Sweden." *Sex Roles* 9:791–812.

Goodall, J. 1986. *The Chimpanzees of Gombe: Patterns of Behavior.* Cambridge, MA: Belknap.

Goodnow, J. J. 1988. "Children's Household Work: Its Nature and Functions." *Psychological Bulletin* 103:5–26.

Griffin, P. B. and M. B. Griffin. 1992. "Fathers and Childcare Among the Cagayan Agta." In *Father–Child Relations: Cultural and Biosocial Contexts*, ed. B. S. Hewlett, 297–320. New York: Aldine de Gruyter.

Harkness, S. and C. M. Super. 1992. "The Cultural Foundations of Fathers' Roles: Evidence from Kenya and the United States." In *Father–Child Relations: Cultural and Biosocial Contexts*, ed. B. S. Hewlett, 191–211. New York: Aldine de Gruyter.

Harter, S. 2006. "The Self." In *Handbook of Child Psychology*, vol. 3, ed. W. Damon, R. M. Lerner, and N. Eisenberg, 505–570. New York: John Wiley.

Hewlett, B. S. 1988. "Sexual Selection and Paternal Investment Among Aka Pygmies." In *Human Reproductive Behaviour: A Darwinian Perspective*, ed. L. Betzig, M. Borgerhoff Mulder, and P. Turke, 263–276. Cambridge, England: Cambridge University.

Hewlett, B. S. 1991. *Intimate Fathers: The Nature and Context of Aka Pygmy Paternal Infant Care.* Ann Arbor: University of Michigan.

Hewlett, B. S. 1992. "Husband–Wife Reciprocity and the Father–Infant Relationship Among Aka Pygmies." In *Father–Child Relations: Cultural and Biosocial Contexts*, ed. B. S. Hewlett, 153–176. New York: Aldine de Gruyter.

Heyman, G. D. 2001. "Children's Interpretation of Ambiguous Behavior: Evidence for a 'Boys Are Bad' Bias." *Social Development* 10:230–247.

Hill, J. P. and M. E. Lynch. 1983. "The Intensification of Gender-Related Role Expectations During Early Adolescence." In *Girls at Puberty: Biological and Psychosocial Perspectives*, ed. J. Brooks-Gunn and A. C. Petersen, 201–228. New York: Plenum.

Hilton, J. M. and V. A. Haldeman. 1991. "Gender Differences in the Performance of Household Tasks by Adults and Children in Single-Parent and Two-Parent, Two-Earner Families." *Journal of Family Issues* 12:114–130.

Hobbs, D. F. and J. M. Wimbish. 1977. "Transition to Parenthood by Black Couples." *Journal of Marriage and Family* 39(4):677–689.

Hoyenga, K. B. and K. T. Hoyenga. 1993. *Gender-Related Differences: Origins and Outcomes.* Boston: Allyn & Bacon.

Huston, A. C. and J. C. Wright. 1998. "Mass Media and Children's Development." In *Handbook of Child Psychology: Child Psychology in Practice*, vol. 4, 5th ed., ed. I. E. Sigel and K. A. Renninger. 999–1058. New York: John Wiley.

Hyde, J. S. 2005. "The Gender Similarities Hypothesis." *American Psychologist* 60:581–592.

Hyde, J. S., S. M. Lindberg, M. C. Linn, A. B. Ellis, and C. C. Williams. 2008. "Diversity: Gender Similarities Characterize Math Performance." *Science* 321: 494–495.

Kane, E. W. 2000. "Racial and Ethnic Variations in Gender-Related Attitudes." *Annual Review of Sociology* 26:419–439.

Katz, M. M. and M. J. Konner. 1981. "The Role of the Father: An Anthropological Perspective." In *The Role of the Father in Child Development*, 2nd ed., ed. M. E. Lamb, 155–186. New York: John Wiley.

Katz, P. A. and K. R. Ksansnak. 1994. "Developmental Aspects of Gender Role Flexibility and Traditionality in Middle Childhood and Adolescence." *Developmental Psychology* 30(2):272–282.

Kenrick, D. T. and C. L. Luce. 2000. "An Evolutionary Life-History Model of Gender Differences and Similarities." In *The Developmental Social Psychology of Gender*, ed. T. Eckes and H. M. Trautner, 35–63. Mahwah, NJ: Lawrence Erlbaum.

Kimmel, M. S. 2000. *The Gendered Society*. New York: Oxford University.

Kohlberg, L. A. 1966. "A Cognitive-Developmental Analysis of Children's Sex Role Concepts and Attitudes." In *The Development of Sex Differences*, ed. E. E. Maccoby, 82–173. Stanford, CA: Stanford University.

Leaper, C. 1994. "Exploring the Consequences of Gender Segregation on Social Relationships." In *Childhood Gender Segregation: Causes and Consequences*, ed. C. Leaper, 67–86. San Francisco: Jossey-Bass.

Leaper, C. 2000. "Gender, Affiliation, Assertion, and the Interactive Context of Parent-Child Play." *Development Psychology* 36(3):381–393.

Leaper, C. 2002. "Parenting Girls and Boys." In *Handbook of Parenting: Children and Parenting*, ed. M. H. Bornstein, 189–225. Mahwah, NJ: Lawrence Erlbaum.

Leaper, C., K. J. Anderson, and P. Sanders. 1998. "Moderators of Gender Effects on Parents' Talk to Their Children: A Meta-Analysis." *Developmental Psychology* 34(1):3–27.

Leaper, C., L. Leve, T. Strasser, and R. Schwartz. 1995. "Mother-Child Communication Sequences: Play Activity, Child Gender, and Marital Status Effects." *Merrill-Palmer Quarterly* 41:307–327.

Leaper, C. and D. Valin. 1996. "Predictors of Mexican-American Mothers' and Fathers' Attitudes Toward Gender Equality." *Hispanic Journal of Behavioral Sciences* 18:343–355.

Lobel, T. E., R. Gruber, N. Govrin, and S. Mashraki-Pedhatzur. 2001. "Children's Gender-Related Inferences and Judgments: A Cross-Cultural Study." *Developmental Psychology* 37:839–846.

Lott, B. and D. Maluso. 1993. "The Social Learning of Gender." In *The Psychology of Gender*, ed. A. E. Beall and R. J. Sternberg, 99–123. New York: Guilford.

Low, B. S. 1989. "Cross-Cultural Patterns in the Training of Children: An Evolutionary Perspective." *Journal of Comparative Psychology* 103(4):311–319.

Lytton, H. and D. M. Romney. 1991. "Parents' Differential Socialization of Boys and Girls: A Meta-Analysis." *Psychological Bulletin* 109:267–296.

Maccoby, E. E. 1998. *The Two Sexes: Growing Apart and Coming Together*. Cambridge, MA: Harvard University.

Maccoby, E. E. 2002. "Gender and Group Process: A Developmental Perspective." *Current Directions* 11:54–58.

Martin, C. L. and L. M. Dinella. 2002. "Children's Gender Cognitions, the Social Environment, and Sex Differences in Cognitive Domains." In *Biology, Society, and Behavior: The Development of Sex Differences in Cognition*, ed. A. McGillicuddy-De Lisi and R. De Lisi, 207–239. Westport, CT: Ablex.

Martin, C. L. and R. A. Fabes. 2001. "The Stability and Consequences of Young Children's Same-Sex Peer Interactions." *Developmental Psychology* 37:431–446.

Martinez, M. L., P. Cumsille, and C. Thibaut. 2008. "Chile." In *International Encyclopedia of Adolescence*, ed. J. J. Arnett, 167–178. New York: Routledge.

Miller, L. C. and S. A. Fishkin. 1997. "On the Dynamics of Human Bonding and Reproductive Success: Seeking Windows on the Adapted-for-Human-Environmental Interface." In *Evolutionary Social Psychology*, ed. J. A. Simpson and D. T. Kenrick, 197–235. Mahwah, NJ: Lawrence Erlbaum.

Mischel, W. 1970. "Sex-Typing and Socialization." In *Carmichael's Manual of Child Psychology*, vol. 2, ed. P. H. Mussen, 3–72. New York: John Wiley.

Mondschein, E. R., K. E. Adolph, and C. S. Tamis-LeMonda. 2000. "Gender Bias in Mothers' Expectations About Infant Crawling." *Journal of Experimental Child Psychology* 77(4):304–316.

Noller, P. and V. J. Callan. 1990. "Adolescents' Perceptions of the Nature of Their Communication with Parents." *Journal of Youth and Adolescence* 19:349–362.

Parke, R. D. 2002. "Fathers and Families." In *Handbook of Parenting: Being and Becoming a Parent*, vol. 3, 2nd ed., ed. M. Bornstein, 27–73. Hillsdale, NJ: Lawrence Erlbaum.

Parke, R. D. and R. Buriel. 1998. "Socialization in the Family: Ethnic and Ecological Perspectives." In *Handbook of Child Psychology*, vol. 3, 5th ed., ed. W. Damon and E. Eisenberg, 463–552. New York: John Wiley.

Pinzas, J. 2008. "Peru." In *International Encyclopedia of Adolescence*, ed. J. J. Arnett, 764–773. New York: Routledge.

Pleck, J. 2012. "Integrating Father Involvement in Parenting Research." *Parenting; Science and Practice* 12: 243–253.

Pomerleau, A., D. Bolduc, G. Malcuit, and L. Cossette. 1990. "Pink or Blue: Environmental Gender Stereotypes in the First Two Years of Life." *Sex Roles* 22:359–367.

Power, T. G. 1985. "Mother- and Father-Infant Play: A Developmental Analysis." *Child Development* 56:1514–1524.

Raffaelli, M. and L. L. Ontai. 2004. "Gender Socialization in Latino/a Families: Results from Two Retrospective Studies." *Sex Roles* 50:287–299.

Reid, P. T. and L. Comas-Diaz. 1990. "Gender and Ethnicity: Perspectives on Dual Status." *Sex Roles* 22:397–408.

Rheingold, H. L. and K. V. Cook. 1975. "The Contents of Boys' and Girls' Rooms as an Index of Parents' Behavior." *Child Development* 46:445–463.

Risman, B. J. 2001. "Necessity and the Invention of Mothering." In *Gender and Social Life*, ed. R. Satow, 26–31. Boston: Allyn and Bacon.

Robinson, C. C. and J. T. Morris. 1986. "The Gender-Stereotyped Nature of Christmas Toys Received by 36-, 48-, and 60-Month-Old Children: A Comparison Between Nonrequested vs. Requested Toys." *Sex Roles* 15:21–32.

Ruble, D. N. and C. Martin. 1998. "Gender Development." In *Handbook of Child Psychology: Personality and Social Development*, vol. 3, 5th ed., ed. N. Eisenberg, 933–1016. New York: John Wiley.

Ruble, D. N., C. L. Martin, and S. A. Berenbaum. 2006. "Gender Development." In *Handbook of Child Psychology: Social, Emotional, and Personality Development*, vol. 3, 6th ed., ed. W. Damon, R. M. Lerner, and N. Eisenberg, 858–931. New York: John Wiley.

Russell, A. and J. Saebel. 1997. "Mother–Son, Mother–Daughter, Father–Son, and Father-Daughter: Are They Distinct Relationships?" *Developmental Review* 17:111–147.

Seavey, C. A., P. A. Katz, and S. R. Zalk. 1975. "Baby X: The Effect of Gender Labels on Adult Responses to Infants." *Sex Roles* 1:103–110.

Sharabany, R. 2006. "The Cultural Context of Children and Adolescents: Peer Relationships and Intimate Friendships Among Arab and Jewish Children in Israel." In *Peer Relationships in Cultural Context*, ed. X. Chen, D. C. French, and B. H. Schneider, 452–478. New York: Cambridge University.

Sidorowicz, L. S. and G. S. Lunney. 1980. "Baby X Revisited." *Sex Roles* 6:67–73.

Siegal, M. 1987. "Are Sons and Daughters Treated More Differently by Fathers Than by Mothers?" *Developmental Review* 7:183–209.

Slaby, R. G. and K. S. Frey. 1975. "Development of Gender Constancy and Selective Attention to Same-Sex Models." *Child Development* 52:849–856.

Starrels, M. E. 1994. "Gender Differences in Parent–Child Relations." *Journal of Family Issues* 15:148–165.

Steinberg, L. 1987. "Recent Research on the Family at Adolescence: The Extent and Nature of Sex Differences." *Journal of Youth and Adolescence* 16:191–197.

Steinberg, L. and J. S. Silk. 2002. "Parenting Adolescents." In *Handbook of Parenting: Children and Parenting*, vol. 1, 2nd ed., ed. M. H. Bornstein, 103–133. Mahwah, NJ: Lawrence Erlbaum.

Stevenson, M. R. and K. N. Black. 1988. "Paternal Absence and Sex-Role Development: A Meta-Analysis." *Child Development* 59:793–814.

Sweeney, J. and M. R. Bradbard. 1989. "Mothers' and Fathers' Changing Perceptions of Their Male and Female Infants Over the Course of Pregnancy." *Journal of Genetic Psychology* 149:393–404.

Tenenbaum, H. R. and C. Leaper. 1998. "Gender Effects on Mexican-Descent Parents' Questions and Scaffolding During Play: A Sequential Analysis." *First Language* 18:129–147.

Tenenbaum, H. R. and C. Leaper. 2003. "Parent-Child Conversations About Science: Socialization of Gender Inequities." *Developmental Psychology* 39:34–47.

Thorne, B. 1986. "Girls and Boys Together, but Mostly Apart." In *Relationship and Development*, ed. W. W. Hartup and Z. Rubin, 167–184. Hillsdale, NJ: Lawrence Erlbaum.

Trivers, R. L. 1972. "Parental Investment and Sexual Selection." In *Sexual Selection and the Descent of Man 1871–1971*, ed. B. Campbell, 136–179. Chicago: Aldine.

Van Leeuwen, M. S. 1978. "A Cross-Cultural Examination of Psychological Differentiation in Males and Females." *International Journal of Psychology* 13:87–122.

Vandell, D. 2002. "Early Childcare and Children's Development Prior to School Entry: Results from a NICHD Study of Early Childcare." *American Educational Research Journal* 39:133–164.

Vygotsky, L. S. 1978. *Mind in Society: The Development of Higher Mental Processes*. Cambridge, MA: Harvard University.

Wallen, K. 1996. "Nature Needs Nurture: The Interaction of Hormonal and Social Influences on the Development of Behavioral Sex Differences in Rhesus Monkeys." *Hormones and Behavior* 30:364–378.

Weisner, T. S. 1979. "Some Cross-Cultural Perspectives on Becoming Female." In *Becoming Female: Perspectives on Development*, ed. C. B. Kopp, 313–332. New York: Plenum.

Weisner, T. S. and R. Gallimore. 1977. "My Brother's Keeper: Child and Sibling Caretaking." *Current Anthropology* 18:169–190.

Weisner, T. S., H. Garnier, and J. Loucky. 1994. "Domestic Tasks, Gender Egalitarian Values and Children's Gender Typing in Current and Nonconventional Families." *Sex Roles* 30(1/2): 23–54.

West, M. M. and M. J. Konner. 1976. "The Role of Father: An Anthropological Perspective." In *The Role of the Father in Child Development*, ed. M. E. Lamb, 185–217. New York: John Wiley.

Whiting, B. B. 1986. "The Effect of Experience on Peer Relationships." In *Process and Outcome in Peer Relationships*, ed. E. C. Mueller and C. R. Cooper, 79–99. Orlando, FL: Academic.

Whiting, B. B. and C. P. Edwards. 1988. *Children of Different Worlds: The Formation of Social Behavior*. Cambridge, MA: Harvard University.

Whitten, P. L. 1987. "Infants and Adult Males." In *Primate Societies*, ed. B. B. Smuts, D. L. Cheney, R. M. Seyfarth, R. W. Wrangham, and T. T. Struhsaker, 343–357. Chicago: University of Chicago.

Williams, G. C. 1966. *Adaptation and Natural Selection: A Critique of Some Current Evolutionary Thought*. Princeton, NJ: Princeton University.

Williams, J. E. and D. L. Best. 1990. *Measuring Sex Stereotypes: A Multination Study*. Newbury Park, CA: Sage.

Wood, D. J., J. S. Bruner, and G. Ross. 1976. "The Role of Tutoring in Problem Solving. *Journal of Child Psychology and Psychiatry* 17:89–100.

5

GENDER DIFFERENCES AND SIMILARITIES IN PARENTAL BEHAVIOR

Ross D. Parke

PARENTING IS A GENDERED ACTIVITY, and a variety of differences in the parenting behavior of mothers and fathers have been documented for both humans and animals. The overarching aim of this chapter is to provide an overview of both similarities and differences in parenting behavior of mothers and fathers. The first aim of this chapter is to explore these differences. Since any discussion needs to recognize patterns of similarity as well as differences between parents of different genders, the second aim is highlight the ways in which there is overlap between mothers and fathers in caregiving competence, and in style and levels of involvement. It is assumed that patterns of differences and similarities are not fixed but undergo modification as a function of a variety of biological, social, cultural, and historical factors. Therefore, a third aim is to explore the factors that may help explain the variability among fathers and mothers in the extent to which they adhere to stereotypic patterns of interactive style and to culturally expected patterns of involvement. The fourth aim is to examine the implications of stylistic differences between mothers and fathers for children's development. Finally, we ask whether we need to recognize that style of interaction typically covaries with gender of parent in our culture but that no single gender "owns" a particular style of parenting. Work on reversed role families and same-gender parent families will be examined to begin to address this issue.

Our review includes a wide range of studies that uses a variety of sampling strategies and data collection approaches. To the extent possible, we base our conclusions on random nationally representative samples in which participants are surveyed and self-report on their parenting; this approach is characteristic of studies concerning levels of involvement of mothers and fathers in their children's lives. However, these studies often rely on single reporters for both parenting measures and child outcomes and are limited in their capacity to examine issues of parental interactive processes. Therefore, to address issues pertaining to qualitative differences between mothers and fathers in their interactive styles, we rely on nonrepresentative smaller sample studies that employ mixed methods including observational assessments, interviews, and /or questionnaires. In many cases, reports of parenting and measures of dependent outcomes such as child adjustment are based on independent sources. Although the samples are often nonrepresentative, conclusions are drawn only when there have been replications of the pertinent findings across independent samples both within laboratories and across laboratories at different national and international sites. This reliance on replicability across time and location increases our confidence in the patterns of findings that are highlighted in this review. Moreover, both nationally representative as well as small sample studies include both cross-sectional and longitudinal designs. The reliance on findings from longitudinal studies in combination with experimental intervention studies in our review provides a reasonable basis for inferring direction of causality between parenting and child outcomes.

SIMILARITIES BETWEEN MOTHERS AND FATHERS IN PARENTING

Both parents are capable of providing the basic caregiving that infants and children need for survival such as nurturance/affection, feeding, and stimulation that are necessary to ensure appropriate development and the teaching/guidance needed for infants and children to become competent participants in their cultural milieu. These basic similarities are evolutionarily adaptive and ensure that infants and children will flourish if one parent of either gender is unable to provide adequate caregiving support. As an example, let us consider the overlap in maternal and paternal styles of interaction with infants. In a set of studies in which we observed fathers and mothers interacting with their newborns, we found that mothers and fathers showed patterns of striking similarity: they touched, looked, vocalized, rocked, and kissed their newborns equally (Parke and O'Leary 1976). If this cluster of behaviors can be termed nurturant, it is clear that mothers and fathers are capable of and clearly do provide similar levels of this critical parental input. Only in smiling did the mother surpass the father—an often observed gender difference in which females routinely are higher than males across a variety of settings and social partners. Similarly, in observations of thirty-month-old children at home, Clarke-Stewart (1980) found that fathers and mothers were similar in their stimulation, affection, and teaching. However, successful/competent parenting involves more than providing nurturance and stimulation. Decades of research have shown that the delivery of this stimulation in a manner that is contingent, sensitive, and responsive to the infant's signals and behaviors is critical (Tamis-LeMonda, Bornstein, and Baumwell 2001). Competent parenting is dependent on the parent's ability to correctly read or interpret the infant's behavior so that they can regulate their own behavior in order to achieve some interactional goal such as feeding. To illustrate, the aim of the parent in the feeding context is to facilitate the food intake of their infant. The infant, in turn, by a variety of behaviors such as sucking, drooling, spitting, coughing, or moving provides the parent with feedback concerning the effectiveness and/or ineffectiveness of the caregiver's efforts to maintain the smooth flow of the food intake process. In this context, parental competence can be assessed by examining how well the parent tracks and appropriately responds to infant cues in this feeding situation; and fathers were as competent as mothers in their ability to sensitively respond to changes in the newborn infant's behavior (Parke and Sawin 1979, 1980). In response to an auditory distress cue—sneeze, spit up, cough—fathers like mothers adjusted their behavior by momentarily ceasing their feeding activity, looking more closely to check on the infant, and vocalizing to the infant. Moreover, there are other similarities as well. Fathers were just as responsive as mothers to other infant cues such as vocalizations and mouth movements. Parents of either gender increased their rate of vocalizations following an infant vocal sound and touched and looked more closely in response to an infant vocalization. In short, both mothers and fathers reacted to newborn infant cues in a contingent and functional manner. Even more important from an evolutionary perspective was the fact that the amount of milk consumed by the infant when either the father or the mother was the bottle feeding agent was comparable (Parke and O'Leary 1976). Fathers and mothers are not only similar in their parental sensitivity but are equally competent in feeding the infant based on the amount of milk consumed by the infant. More recent evidence tells a similar story: Mothers and fathers showed similar levels of sensitivity to their twenty-four- and thirty-month-old children's behavior during a play interaction (Tamis-LeMonda, Shannon, Cabrera, and Lamb 2004), responded to the smiles and cries of their toddlers (Berman 1987), and were responsive to their twelve month olds when engaged in a task (Notaro and Volling 1999).

When parents talk to their infants, they adjust their speech patterns in well-documented ways; in contrast to adult-directed speech, when talking to infants, parents talk slower, use more repetitions, use shorter phrases, and a higher pitch. Although it has been common to label this pattern of infant-directed speech as "motherese," fathers as well as mothers show similar characteristic adjustments in their speech patterns when talking to newborns or their three-month-olds (Parke 1981). Others report similar patterns of mother and father child directed speech (Golinkoff and Ames 1979; Dalton–Hummel 1982). In view of the similarities across mothers and fathers, perhaps "parentese" would be a more accurate descriptor for this pattern. Clearly maternal and paternal caregiving are similar in a variety of ways which, in turn, provide a safety net for the child in case either parent is incapacitated or unavailable.

Nor is it simply similarities in parenting. There is ample evidence that infants develop similar critical social relationships with both mothers and fathers. For example, infants form attachments not only to their mothers but to their fathers too. Many decades ago, Schaffer and Emerson (1964) showed that infants formed emotional attachments to fathers as well as mothers (see Lamb and Lewis 2004 for a review). However, as Lamb (1976) showed, the mothers were preferred as a source of comfort in times of stress while fathers were sought out as a source of stimulation and play. Similarly, studies of social referencing indicate that fathers as well as mothers are used as objects of emotional reassurance in ambiguous situations such as an approaching unfamiliar figure (Dickstein and Parke 1988).

In spite of this overlap, there are clear gender differences in both the levels of involvement of mothers and fathers in the parenting of children, in the parenting tasks for which parents of each gender are typically responsible, the style of interaction that parents adopt as they carry out their parenting responsibilities, and the degree to which maternal and paternal parenting is culturally scripted.

QUANTITATIVE ASSESSMENTS OF MOTHER AND FATHER INVOLVEMENT IN INTACT FAMILIES

In this section, we consider descriptive studies of differences in both the quantity of mother versus father involvement with their children as well as qualitative differences in styles of interaction.

Not all forms of parental involvement are conceptually equivalent. Lamb, Pleck, and Levine (1985) have distinguished various types of parental involvement: interaction, availability, and responsibility (see Lamb 2004). Interaction refers to the parent's direct contact with their child through caregiving and shared activities. Availability is a related concept concerning the parents' potential availability for interaction, by virtue of being present or accessible to the child whether or not direct interaction is occurring. Responsibility refers to the role that the parent takes in ascertaining that the child is taken care of and arranging for resources to be available for the child. It is important to distinguish among domains of involvement, since fathers and mothers vary in their distribution of time across different child and household activities. Several further distinctions have been offered, including involvement in childcare activities and involvement in play, leisure, or affiliative activities with the child. The need for this distinction flows from the fact that there are different determinants of these two types of parental involvement (Beitel and Parke 1998; Palkovitz 2002; Pleck and Masciadrelli 2004). Absolute and relative involvement need to be distinguished because prior work suggests that these indices are independent and may affect both children's and adults' views of role distributions in different ways (Pleck and Masciadrelli 2004). Others have expanded the domain list to include not just personal care and play but achievement-related activities, (i.e. homework, reading) household activities (i.e., housework, shopping), social activities (conversation, social events), and other activities, and have found that the determinants of involvement in these domains vary across parents (Yeung et al. 2001). Finally, estimates of parental involvement have usefully distinguished between weekdays and weekends since both the types of activities and levels of parental involvement vary as a function of the time period being assessed (Yeung et al. 2001).

In spite of current shifts in cultural attitudes concerning the appropriateness and desirability of shared roles and equal levels of participation in routine caregiving and interaction of mothers and fathers, the shifts toward parity are small. Fathers spend less time with their infants and children than mothers not only in the United States (Pleck and Masciadrelli 2004), but in other countries such as Great Britain, Australia, France, Belgium, and Japan as well (Zuzanek 2000). Mothers and fathers differ in the amount of time that they spend in actual interaction with their children. However, Pleck and Masciadrelli (2004) document that fathers' involvement in the United States has increased, albeit slowly but is nonetheless real in the majority of intact families. This pattern of change even if modest underscores the plasticity and modifiability of maternal and paternal roles. Compared to the 1970s, proportional engagement (relative to mothers) was about 33 percent while accessibility/availability was approximately 50 percent. In contrast, estimates for the 1990s suggest that proportional engagement had increased to approximately 70 percent, while availability was more than 70 percent. Mothers continue to assume more managerial responsibility than fathers such as arranging social contacts, organizing schedules, taking the child for medical checkups, and monitoring homework and school-related tasks. However, these patterns change as a function of the time of the week and the age of the child. For example, fathers are more involved in household activities (shopping) and social activities on weekends than weekdays and play as the focus of fathering decreases as the child develops (Yueng et al. 2001).

Studies of African-American and Hispanic-American families confirm the pattern found for Euro-Americans. Middle-class as well as lower-class African-American and Latino fathers were less involved in caregiving their infants than mothers (Roopnarine 2004). Comparisons across ethnic groups (African, Hispanic, and Euro-American) revealed few differences in level of father involvement (Yeung et al. 2001). These findings are important in light of past negative characterizations of low income African-American and Hispanic-American fathers as uninvolved. Clearly the stereotype surrounding fathers of different ethnic backgrounds is inaccurate and outdated and needs to be revised in light of recent evidence (Roopnarine 2004). Much of the earlier work concerning fathering among ethnic minority fathers was based on single-parent families and/or on young unwed fathers and failed to recognize differences within cultural or racial groups.

The differences in patterns of contact time between mothers and fathers with their children in infancy continue into middle childhood and adolescence (Collins and Russell 1991). In middle childhood (six- to seven year olds), Russell and Russell (1987) found that Australian mothers were available to children 54.7 hours/week compared to 34.6 hours/week for fathers. Mothers also spent more time alone with children (22.6 hours/week) than did fathers (2.4 hours/week). However, when both parents and child were together, mothers and fathers initiated interactions with children with equal frequency and children's initiations toward each parent were similar. Adolescents spend less time with their parents than younger children and less time alone with their fathers than their mothers (Larson and Richards 1994).

From infancy through adolescence, mothers and fathers clearly differ in their degree of involvement with their children.

Part of the explanation for the greater involvement of mothers versus fathers is due to the fact that the maternal parenting role is more mandatory and more clearly scripted by our culture, while paternal parenting is still more discretionary and less clearly scripted and proscribed by the culture. A further illustration of the culturally mandated nature of motherhood is in the nature of custody arrangements following divorce. Although historically fathers were unequivocally favored in custody decisions, for nearly a century courts have viewed mothers as the "natural" parent in part due to the assumption of biological predisposition and in part due to the tender years doctrine, which held that infants and young children should be raised by their mothers (Clarke-Stewart and Brentano 2006). Since the 1980s, there has been a shift away from the presumption that mothers are automatically the best parent and an increase in the proportion of children in joint custody arrangements in recognition of the fact that children need a continuing relationship with both their mothers and fathers. However, the vast majority of custodial parents are mothers and more mothers than fathers have physical custody in joint custody arrangements. In a study with a national probability sample of 13,017 individuals age nineteen and over, representing 9,643 U.S. families and households, Kelly, Redenbach, and Rinaman (2005) found that in 80 percent of the cases, the mother received sole physical custody of the minor child or children. The remaining 20 percent of the cases were evenly divided between the father having sole physical custody and joint custody. Of those cases designated as joint custody cases, about half of the cases involved situations where the children were spending approximately 50 percent of the time with each parent and the remaining were sharing physical custody but to a lesser degree (e.g., school year with the mother and summer with the father). However, the number of fathers with sole custody has increased over the last several decades as a result of the growing national fatherhood movement, the growing recognition of fathers as significant parental figures, and perhaps father-friendlier courts (Clarke-Stewart and Brentano 2006). These general demographic trends in custody are evident not only in the United States but internationally as well. Nonetheless, mothers continue to have more opportunities for involvement in their children's lives after divorce than do fathers. This is further evidence of the cultural assumption, albeit a questionable one, that mothers are a more central socialization agent for children than fathers.

QUALITATIVE EFFECTS: STYLISTIC DIFFERENCES
IN MOTHER AND FATHER INTERACTION

Fathers participate less than mothers in caregiving such as feeding and diapering in infancy and in providing meals, school lunches, and clothing as the child develops. Instead, they spend a greater percentage of the time available for interaction with their children in play activities than mothers do. In North American families, fathers regardless of ethnicity (Euro-American, African-American, and Hispanic-American) spent a greater percentage of their time with their infants in play than mothers; although, in absolute terms, mothers spent more time than fathers in play with their children (Yeung et al. 2001). The quality of play across mothers and fathers differs too. In infants and toddlers, fathers' hallmark style of interaction is physical play that is characterized by arousal, excitement, and unpredictability in terms of the pace of the interaction. In contrast, mothers' playful interactive style is characterized by a more modulated and less arousing tempo. Moreover, mothers play more conventional motor games or toy-mediated activities, and are more verbal and didactic (Clarke-Stewart 1980; Hossain and Roopnarine 1994; Parke 1996, 2002a). In a study of eight-month-olds (Power and Parke 1982), for example, fathers engaged in more lifting and tossing play bouts even when toys were available. In fact, when playing with toys, fathers tended to use them in unconventional ways—to physically stimulate their infants. Others report higher rates of teasing during physical play with young children as well (Labrell 1996). Mothers, in contrast, present a toy and make it salient for the baby by moving and shaking it, but do not use it to poke or physically stimulate the infant (Power and Parke 1982). And they engage in more pretend play and role play (Crawley and Sherrod 1984) as well as more teaching activities than fathers by labeling colors and shapes as they engage their infant in play (Power and Parke 1982). Fathers engage in more physical play with sons than daughters (Power and Parke 1982; Jacklin, DiPietro, and Maccoby 1984) while mothers facilitate pretend play of their daughters more than of their sons (Tamis-LeMonda and Bornstein 1991).

Nor are these effects evident only in infancy. MacDonald and Parke (1984) found that fathers engaged in more physical play with their three- and four-year-old children than mothers, while mothers engaged in more object-mediated play than fathers. According to a survey (MacDonald and Parke 1986), fathers' distinctive role as a physical play partner changes with age. Physical play was highest between fathers and two year olds, and between two and ten years of age father-child physical play decreases. In spite of the decline in physical play across age, fathers remain more physical in their play than mothers. In an Australian study of parents and their six- to seven-year-old children (Russell and Russell 1987), fathers were more involved in physical/outdoor play interactions and fixing things around the house and garden than mothers. In contrast, mothers were more actively involved in caregiving and household tasks, in school work, reading, playing with toys, and helping with arts and crafts.

In adolescence, the quality of maternal and paternal involvement continues to differ. Just as in earlier developmental periods, mothers and fathers may complement each other and provide models that reflect the tasks of adolescence—connectedness and separateness. Across development, the focus on physical play on the part of fathers declines and is replaced in adolescence by verbal playfulness in the form of sarcasm, humor, and word play even though this often increases emotional distance but perhaps encourages independence as well. Evidence suggests that fathers may help adolescents develop their own sense of identity and autonomy by being more "peer-like" and more playful (joking and teasing), which is likely to promote more equal and egalitarian exchanges (Shulman and Klein 1993). "Fathers, more than mothers conveyed the feeling that they can rely on their adolescents, thus fathers might provide a 'facilitating environment' for adolescent attainment of differentiation from the family and consolidation of independence" (Shulman and Klein 1993:53). Mothers, on the other hand, are more emotionally available to their adolescents and mother adolescent dyads spend more time together than father adolescent dyads (Larson and Richards 1994; Larson and Sheeber 2007). Mothers continue to be more involved in arts, crafts, and reading, and maintain more open communication and emotional closeness with their offspring during adolescence. Although the style of fathers' involvement as a play or recreational partner appears to have reasonable continuity from infancy through adolescence, the meaning and function of this interaction style shifts across development. The positive affect associated with fathers' play in infancy is not as evident in adolescence, although other goals of this age period such as autonomy development may be facilitated by this more playful egalitarian style.

Why do mothers and fathers play differently? Both biology and environment are probably contributing factors. Experience with infants, the amount of time spent with infants, and the usual kinds of responsibilities that a parent assumes are all factors that influence parents' style of play. For example, as a result of spending less time with infants and children than mothers, fathers may use their distinctive arousing style as a way to increase their salience to compensate for their more limited interaction time. Biological factors cannot be ignored in light of the fact that male monkeys show the same rough-and-tumble physical style of play as American human fathers and infant male monkeys tend to respond more positively to bids for rough-and-tumble play than females (Parke and Suomi 1981). "Perhaps [both monkey and human] males may be more susceptible to being aroused into states of positive excitement and unpredictability than females" (Maccoby 1988:761)—speculation that is consistent with gender differences in risk-taking and sensation-seeking. In addition, human males, whether boys or men, tend to behave more boisterously and show more positive emotional expression and reactions than females (Maccoby 1998). Together these threads of the puzzle suggest that predisposing biological differences between males and females may play a role in the play patterns of mothers and fathers. At the same time, the cross-cultural data underscore the ways in which cultural and environmental contexts shape play patterns of parents and remind us of the high degree of plasticity of human social behaviors.

IMPLICATIONS OF MATERNAL VERSUS PATERNAL QUALITY OF INVOLVEMENT FOR CHILDREN'S DEVELOPMENT

In this section, we briefly review the argument that mothers' and fathers' distinctive interactive styles make unique contributions to children's development and examine whether a combination of clearly gender-based styles has any developmental advantages for children. Once this has been established we address factors that either reduce or sharpen mother/father differences in the quantity or quality of parental involvement in children's lives.

IMPACT OF NORMAL VARIATIONS IN INTACT FAMILIES ON CHILDREN'S DEVELOPMENT

A voluminous literature has emerged that clearly demonstrates relations between quality of and to a lesser degree the quantity of parental involvement and children's social, emotional, and cognitive development (Parke and Buriel 2006). At the same time, considerable evidence shows a good deal of redundancy between fathers' and mothers' impact on children. There is less evidence that fathers make a unique contribution to children's development.

In a review of the effects of fathers on children, Marsiglio, Amato, Day, and Lamb (2000) examined seventy-two studies published in the 1990s with the majority involving young children or adolescents and the remaining concerning young adults. Their review revealed moderate negative associations between authoritative fathering and internalizing and externalizing problems. The relations held for children and adolescents regardless of age. Moreover, Amato and Rivera (1999) found that positive influence on children's behavior was similar for European-American, African-American, and Latino fathers. Marsiglio et al. (2000:1183) offer three important caveats to their conclusion that "positive father involvement is generally beneficial to children." First, most studies rely on a single data source, which raises the problem of shared method variance. Second, many researchers do not control for the quality of the mother-child relationship when examining father effects. Since the behavior and attitudes of parents are often highly related, this step is critical. Only eight of the seventy-two studies reviewed by Marsiglio et al. (2000) did, in fact, control for the quality of the mother-child relationship; five of the eight studies continued to show a father effect after taking into account mother-child effects. For example, Isley, O'Neil, and Parke (1996) found that fathers' level of affect and control predicted children's social adaptation with peers both concurrently and one year later after controlling for maternal effects (see also Mosley and Thomson, 1995; Hart, Nelson, Robinson, Olsen, and McNeilly-Choque 1998).

Pleck and Masciadrelli (2004) cited several other studies that controlled for maternal involvement and avoided the same reporter problem. For example, Aldous and Mulligan (2002) using a national data set found that positive paternal engagement is linked to lower frequency of later behavior problems for boys and for "difficult to rear" children. Similarly, in a large sample of British teenagers, positive paternal engagement predicted positive school attitudes (Flouri, Buchanan, and Bream 2002). Pleck and Masciadrelli (2004) concluded that in more than 70 percent of the studies that were methodologically sound (controlled for maternal effects and used independent data sources), there was evidence of a positive correlation between positive child outcomes and paternal involvement. Although there is overlap between the effects of mothers and fathers on their children's academic, emotional, and social development, evidence is emerging that fathers and mothers make unique contributions to their children's development (Rohner 1998; Parke 2002b).

A third caveat concerns problems of inferring direction of causality because studies are correlational and involve concurrent rather than longitudinal assessments (Marsiglio et al. 2000). However, two strands of evidence suggest that the direction of effects can plausibly flow from parental behavior to child outcomes. First, longitudinal studies support the view that fathers and mothers influence their children (see Amato and Rivera 1999; Pleck and Masciadrelli 2004; Parke and Buriel 2006 for reviews). For example, Gottman, Katz, and Hooven (1997) found that fathers' acceptance of and assistance with their children's emotions (sadness, anger) at five years of age were related to higher levels of social acceptance with peers at age eight. Positive father engagement in tenth grade was related to fewer behavior problems one year later (Zimmerman, Salem, and Notaro 2000). Nor are the effects of fathering on developmental outcomes restricted to childhood. In a follow up of the classic child-rearing study of Sears, Maccoby, and Levin (1957), Koestner, Franz, and Weinberger (1990) reassessed a sample of the original children when they were thirty-one years old. The most powerful predictor of empathy in adulthood for both men and women was paternal child-rearing involvement at age five. In a further follow up at age forty-one, men and women with better social relationships (marriage quality, extra-familial ties) in mid-life had experienced more paternal warmth as children (Franz, McClelland, and Weinberger 1991). Although these studies support a parent effects perspective, it is likely that reciprocal relationships are operative, in which children and parents mutually influence each other across the life course (Parke 2002b). Second, experimental intervention studies (Cowan and Cowan 1992, 2002) in which parenting skills are taught show that changes in both maternal and paternal parenting behavior are related to enhanced social and cognitive development in children in comparison to children in a control group whose parents did not receive the intervention.

BEYOND DESCRIPTION: PROCESSES THAT LINK FATHERING, MOTHERING, AND CHILD OUTCOMES

FATHERING, EMOTIONAL PROCESSES, AND CHILD OUTCOMES

Recent work that has focused on fathers' special style of interaction, namely play, has begun to reveal the processes through which fathers influence children's development (Parke 1996; see Paquette 2004; Parke et al. 2004 for reviews). Parke and his colleagues, for example, examined the relation between father-toddler physical play and children's adaptation to peers. In one study (MacDonald and Parke 1984), fathers and their three- and four-year-old girls and boys were observed in twenty minutes of structured play in their homes. Teachers ranked these sample children in terms of their popularity among their preschool classmates. For both girls and boys, fathers who were rated as exhibiting high levels of physical play with their children, and elicited high levels of positive affect in their children during the play sessions, had children who received the highest peer popularity ratings. For boys, however, this pattern was qualified by the father's level of directiveness. Boys whose fathers were both highly physical and low in directiveness received the highest popularity ratings, and the boys whose fathers were highly directive received lower popularity scores. Possibly, children who interact with a physically playful father and at the same time have an opportunity to regulate the pace and tempo of the interaction, a characteristic of low-directive fathers, learn how to recognize and send emotional signals during social interactions. Later studies confirmed these findings and showed a link between children's emotional encoding and decoding abilities that are presumably acquired, in part, in these playful interchanges and children's social adaptation to peers (Parke et al. 1994). In addition, fathers' affect displays, especially father anger, seem to be a potent correlate of children's social acceptance. In studies in both the laboratory (Carson and Parke 1996) and the home (Boyum and Parke 1995), fathers' negative affect is inversely related to preschool and kindergarten children's sociometric status. Mize and Pettit (1997) found that preschool children whose play with fathers is characterized by mutuality or balance in making play suggestions and following partners' suggestions were less aggressive, more competent, and better liked by peers. Similarly, Hart and his colleagues (1998, 2000) found that greater playfulness, patience, and understanding with children, especially on the part of the father, were associated with less aggressive behavior with peers. Later work has isolated other emotional processes such as emotional regulation (McDowell, Kim, O'Neil, and Parke 2002; Parke, McDowell, Kim, and Leidy 2006) and knowledge and use of display rules (McDowell and Parke 2000) that are influenced by paternal interaction patterns and are predictive of children's social acceptance. Other aspects of children's development that may be influenced by fathers arousing and unpredictable play style include risk-taking (Kromelow, Harding, and Touris 1990; Le Camus 1995), the capacity to manage unfamiliar situations (Grossmann et al. 2002), and the skill to manage competition (Bourçois 1997); however, these topics have received less attention than social competence with peers. Although father involvement in infancy and childhood is quantitatively less than mother involvement, the data suggest that both mothers as well as fathers nevertheless do have an important impact on their offspring's socio-emotional development.

MOTHERING, VERBAL AND LANGUAGE PROCESSES, AND CHILD OUTCOMES

At the same time, there is a long history of documentation that maternal involvement is related to child outcomes independently of paternal effects (Bornstein 2002; Parke and Buriel 2006). More interesting is evidence suggesting that mothers' verbal style of interaction may enhance children's intellectual development including memory, problem-solving, and language advancement (Bornstein 2002; Cabrera, Shannon, West, and Brooks-Gunn 2006) and perhaps children's knowledge of internal emotional states—a consequence of maternal labeling of emotions and feeling states during social and caregiving interactions (Denham 1998).

DIFFERENTIATION VERSUS SIMILARITY BETWEEN PARENTS

It is important to look beyond the independent effects of mothers and fathers on children's outcomes and examine the relative merits of family arrangements in which there is either little differentiation between the styles of parents of different genders or marked differences in parental style. Several French investigators have addressed this issue. Bourçois (1997) compared the social adjustment of children from two-parent families in which mothers and fathers had either differentiated roles with mother as caregiver and father as playmate or in which parental roles were less clearly differentiated. Children from the differentiated families were more interactive, more involved, and more open with their peers than children from the less differentiated families. In another study, Ricaud (1998) showed that it is parental differentiation in combination with involvement that is important for children's social adaptation. In a comparison among highly differentiated parents but less involved fathers, highly involved but undifferentiated parents, and highly involved and highly differentiated parents, children in the last family configuration in which parental roles were clearly demarcated in a context of high involvement had the most successful relationships with peers. These children had more friendly exchanges, fewer conflicts, better conflict resolution skills, and fewer aggressive interactions.

More attention to the ways in which stylistic differences in interaction between mothers and fathers map onto unique and specific developmental outcomes for children and/or the extent to which there is overlap in developmental outcomes emanating from maternal and paternal style is needed. Perhaps both mothers and fathers influence a wide range of children's developmental domains including motoric, cognitive, linguistic, and social-emotional but do so through different process-based pathways that are linked with their distinctive styles of interaction. Moreover as others (Paquette 2004; Parke and Buriel 2006) have argued, we need more work that involves a family systems approach if we are to understand not simply the individual contributions of mothers and fathers but the effects of complementarity of maternal and paternal styles on children as well.

DETERMINANTS OF VARIABILITY IN MATERNAL AND PATERNAL BEHAVIOR: FROM CATEGORICAL ANALYSES TO INDIVIDUAL AND SITUATIONAL INFLUENCES

The patterns of similarities and differences between mothers and fathers as classes of actors that we have summarized so far address only one aspect of the issue; the other issue that needs to be addressed is the variability within groups of mothers and fathers that either increases or decreases the size of the differences and the degrees of similarity between opposite gender parents. To explore this second aspect of the issue, we briefly outline a multilevel framework that recognizes that a variety of factors operate in concert to determine how mothering and fathering roles are enacted and, in turn, alter the degree to which individual mothers and fathers vary in terms of their similarities and differences. These factors include individual (biological predispositions, gender of child, socialization history, family of origin, parental age), familial (maternal/paternal attitudes concerning spousal involvement, marital relationships), extra familial influences (availability of social support, extended family ties), work (hours of employment, job-related characteristics and stress), and culture (norms, attitudes, and beliefs about appropriate roles and responsibilities for mothers and fathers). Only by recognizing the complex interplay among these determinants will we begin to understand the striking degree of variability in the patterns of similarities and differences across the parenting of sets of mothers and fathers.

BIOLOGICAL DETERMINANTS OF PARENTING

Parenting behavior is clearly influenced by a set of evolutionary and biological processes. Evolutionary theorists argue that women's greater investment in caregiving activities is due in part to the fact that relative to men their reproductive cycle is shorter and they therefore can have fewer children. In turn, women are more likely to ensure the survival of their offspring by a high expenditure of caregiving effort (Bjorklund and Pelligrini 2000). Second, women invest nine months carrying their fetus, an investment that is enormous in comparison to men's burden. Moreover, women undergo a variety of biological changes in hormonal patterns during pregnancy, childbirth, and subsequent nursing experiences that "prime" maternal behavior. For example, estradiol and progesterone increase throughout pregnancy and drop at birth, oxytocin and prolactin levels rise around the birth of the baby, while cortisol levels increase throughout pregnancy. Considerable evidence suggests that these changing hormonal patterns are related to maternal responsiveness to their infants (Corter and Fleming 2002). To illustrate this hormonal effect, nursing mothers showed an increase in oxytocin in response to infant crying and displayed more positive behavior toward their infant than bottle-feeding mothers (Carter and Altemus 1997). Similarly mothers with higher cortisol levels displayed more affectionate and stimulating behavior toward their infants, were superior at recognizing the odor signature of their infants, and responded more sympathetically to infant cries than mothers with lower cortisol levels (Fleming et al. 1997; Stallings et al. 2001).Clearly mothers are biologically as well as culturally prepared for parenthood and this biological priming may be one reason for higher levels of maternal involvement with infants and children (see Corter and Fleming 2002 for a review).

Although much attention has been devoted to the role of biologically-related changes in women that prepares them for parenting activities (Fleming and Li 2002; Rosenblatt 2002), until recently the recognition of biological factors in shaping fathering behavior has been neglected. In part, this was due to the assumption that the lack of biological preparedness accounted for fathers' lack of involvement in caregiving of children. In fact, early evidence (Lamb 1975) suggested that the tyranny of hormones as a constraint on father involvement was not well founded and that hormones did not play a necessary role in paternal behavior in either rats or humans. Instead, social factors such as exposure to young offspring increased paternal activity without any changes in hormonal levels in either rats or humans (Fleming and Li 2002). For example, studies of father-infant relationships in the cases of adoption clearly suggest that hormonal shifts are unnecessary for the development of positive father-infant relationships (Brodzinsky and Pinderhughs 2002).

More recent evidence has challenged the assumption that hormonal levels are unimportant determinants of paternal behavior by examining this issue in species other than rats, which is not a natural paternal species. In naturally paternal species such as canid species, which constitute less than 10 percent of mammalian species (Storey, Walsh, Quinton, and Wynne-Edwards 2000), researchers have found that males experience hormonal changes, including increases in prolactin and decreases in testosterone, prior to the onset of parental behavior and during infant contact (Fleming and Li 2002; Rosenblatt 2002). Human fathers, too, undergo hormonal changes during pregnancy and childbirth. Storey et al. (2000) found that men experienced significant pre-, peri-, and postnatal changes in each of three hormones—prolactin, cortisol, and testosterone—a pattern of results that was similar to the women in their study. Specifically, prolactin levels were higher for both men and women in the late prenatal period than in the early postnatal period, and cortisol levels increased just before and decreased in the postnatal period, which corresponds to the first opportunity for interaction with their infants. Hormonal levels and changes were linked with a variety of social stimuli as well. Men with lower testosterone held test baby dolls longer and were more responsive to infant cues (crying) than were men with higher testosterone. Men who reported a greater drop in testosterone also reported more pregnancy or couvade symptoms. Together these findings suggest that lower testosterone in the postnatal period may increase paternal responsiveness to infant cries and in men reporting more couvade symptoms during pregnancy. Finally, Storey et al. (2000:91) argue that the "cortisol increases in late pregnancy and during labor may help new fathers focus on and become attached to their newborns." Men's changes in hormonal levels are linked not only with baby cries and the time in pregnancy cycle but also to the hormonal levels of their partners. Women's hormonal levels were closely linked with the time remaining before delivery, but men's levels were linked with their partner's hormone levels, not with time to birth. This demonstrates that contact with the pregnant partner may play a role in paternal responsiveness, just as the quality of the marital relationship is linked with paternal involvement in later infancy. This suggests that social variables need to be considered in understanding the operation of biological effects. Perhaps intimate ties between partners during pregnancy stimulate hormonal changes, which, in turn, are associated with more nurturance toward babies.

Other evidence is consistent with a psychobiological view of paternal behavior. Fleming, Corter, Stallings, and Steiner (2002) found that fathers with lower baseline levels of testosterone are more sympathetic and show a greater need to respond when hearing infant cries than men with higher baseline testosterone levels. Moreover, fathers with higher baseline prolactin levels are more positive and alert in response to infant cries. However, experience also plays a role. At two days after the birth of a baby, fathers show lower levels of testosterone than nonfathers. Moreover, fathers who have more experience with babies have lower testosterone and higher prolactin levels than first-time fathers (Corter and Fleming 2002), even after controlling for paternal age. This perspective recognizes the dynamic or transactional nature of the links between hormones and behavior in which behavior changes can lead to hormonal shifts and vice versa. In contrast to the myth of the biologically unfit father, this work suggests that men may be more prepared—even biologically—for parenting than previously thought. More work is needed to explore the implications of these hormonal changes for the long-term relationship between fathers and their offspring. For example, are the ties between children and fathers who do not experience hormone-related changes at birth weaker, or can experience compensate for this lack of hormonal shift? However, for our purposes, namely the determinants of gender differences in parenting, it is clear that hormonal, in combination with social, factors are an important class of factors to recognize since the shifts in paternal hormones may decrease differences in maternal versus paternal parenting behavior. Next we turn to a discussion of the social determinants of parental involvement.

SOCIAL DETERMINANTS OF PARENTING BEHAVIOR

There are a host of individual, family background, and marital relationship factors that influence the degree of similarity or difference between maternal and paternal involvement. These determinants have been extensively reviewed elsewhere (see Pleck and Masciadrelli 2004; Parke and Buriel 2006) and will be only briefly examined here.

INDIVIDUAL LEVEL DETERMINANTS OF PARENTAL INVOLVEMENT

Age of Parent   Several studies show that timing of entry into parenthood is a determinant of both maternal and paternal roles. First, patterns of parental responsibilities for mothers and fathers are more egalitarian in late-timed parents than on-time parents (Daniels and Weingarten 1982). Second, style of interaction varies by parental age. Specifically, even after controlling for the age of the child as they age, fathers and mothers engage in less robust physical play and fathers become more maternal in their style (cognitively stimulating activities such as reading) (Cooney et al. 1993; Neville and Parke 1997).

Maternal and Paternal Attitudes   At the individual level, attitudes toward the parental role, role identity, and perceived competence on the part of mothers and fathers predict levels of quality and quantity of parental involvement (Beitel and Parke 1998; Rane and McBride 2000). For example, men with more liberal gender ideology (Bonney, Kelley, and Levant 1999), those who value the fathering role (Beitel and Parke 1998), and those who regard the nurturing role as central to their self-identity (Rane and McBride 2000) were more involved in parenting. Similarly women who value the maternal role and view it as an important part of their self concept are more involved mothers (Barnard and Solchany 2002). Individual differences in perceived caregiving competence are related to parental involvement as well; changes in perceived competence as a result of parenting skills interventions are linked with increases in paternal and maternal involvement (Fagan and Hawkins 2000).These factors alter the magnitude of the differences between mothers' and fathers' involvement in parenting.

FAMILY LEVEL DETERMINANTS OF PARENTAL INVOLVEMENT   Individual factors are not the only determinants of maternal or paternal involvement. Family-level variables, including maternal attitudes concerning father involvement and the marital relationship, are both factors that require examination.

Maternal Attitudes as a Determinant of Father Involvement   Consistent with a family systems view, maternal attitudes need to be considered as a determinant of paternal participation in childcare. In spite of advances in women's participation in the workplace, many women still feel ambivalent about father involvement in domestic issues (Coltrane 1996). As Allen and Hawkins (1999:202) suggest, their ambivalence "may be because increased paternal involvement intrudes on a previously held monopoly over the attentive and intuitive responsibilities of family work, which if altered may compromise female power and privilege in the home." Work on maternal gatekeeping suggests that maternal attitudes toward father involvement can suppress levels of father involvement (Beitel and Parke 1998; Allen and

Hawkins 1999). These maternal attitudes may lead to behavior which, in turn, limit father involvement and constitute a form of gatekeeping (Beitel and Parke 1998; Bonney et al. 1999). However, two qualifications to our discussion of gatekeeping are needed. First, the term is gender-neutral and fathers as well as mothers engage in gatekeeping activities in other domains of family life (Allen and Hawkins 1999). Second, gates can open as well as close and the term needs to be broadened to recognize that parents — mothers and fathers — can facilitate as well as inhibit the type and level of domestic involvement of each other. Work on "parental gatekeeping" needs to include gate opening as well as gate closing in order to underscore the dual nature of the inhibitory and faciliatory processes that are in part of the co-parenting enterprise (Parke 2002b).

Marital Relationships and Parental Involvement   Models that limit examination of the effects of interaction patterns to only the father-child and mother-child dyads and the direct effects of one individual on another are inadequate for understanding the impact of social interaction patterns in families (Belsky 1984; Parke 1996; Parke and Buriel 2006). From a family systems viewpoint, the marital relationship needs to be considered as well. Several studies in both the United States (Pedersen 1975; Dickie and Matheson 1984) and other cultures (e.g., Japan; Durrett, Otaki, and Richards 1984) support the conclusion that the degree of emotional/social support that fathers provide mothers is related to both indices of maternal caregiving competence as well as measures of the quality of infant-parent attachment. Other evidence suggests that the quality of the marital relationship is related to father-child involvement (Booth and Amato 1994; Coley and Chase-Lansdale 1999; Cummings et al. 2004) Fathers in high satisfaction marriages are more involved than those in unhappy marital relationships (Cummings et al. 2004). Moreover, the evidence suggests that the father-child relationship is altered more than the mother-child relationship by the quality of the marriage (Belsky et al. 1984). A number of factors may aid in explaining this relation. First, there is prior evidence that the father's level of participation is, in part, determined by the extent to which the mother permits participation (Beitel and Parke 1998; Allen and Hawkins 1999). Second, because the paternal role is less well articulated and defined than the maternal role, spousal support may serve to help crystallize the boundaries of appropriate role behavior. Third, men have fewer opportunities to acquire and practice skills that are central to caregiving activities during childhood socialization and therefore may benefit more than mothers from informational (e.g., cognitive) support (Parke and Brott 1999).

ECOLOGICAL DETERMINANTS OF PARENTAL INVOLVEMENT

Our search for patterns of gender of parent similarities and differences needs to be viewed as embedded in a set of contexts including work and culture. In this section, as illustrative examples of ecological determinants, we consider shifts in work patterns of mothers and fathers as well as cultural background as factors that organize both the amount and type of parental behavior. A variety of other factors influence parental involvement and style including legal, medical, educational, and government policies as well as media portrayals of mothers and fathers, but these will not be reviewed in this chapter (see Parke and Brott 1999; Parke 2002; Pleck and Masciadrelli 2004 for reviews).

PARENTAL WORK AS A DETERMINANT OF PARENTAL INVOLVEMENT

In terms of work, two issues are relevant. First, does father involvement shift with increases in maternal employment? Second, how does the quality of work alter maternal and paternal parenting behavior? Maternal employment is a robust predictor of paternal involvement (Pleck and Masciadrelli 2004). For example, Bailey (1992) and Bonney, Kelley, and Levant (1999) found that among European Americans, father participation in childcare was higher when mothers were employed outside the home. Similar findings are evident for African-American and Mexican-American fathers as well. Fagan (1998) found that as the number of hours that wives work increased, the amount of time African-American fathers spend playing, reading, and directly interacting with their preschoolers increased. Other evidence (NICHD Early Child Care Research Network 2000) suggests that the relation between maternal employment and father involvement is, in part, dependent on fathers' childbearing beliefs. When mothers do not work or work only part-time, fathers were more likely to participate in caregiving if they held nontraditional views of parenting; when mothers were employed full-time, father participation in caregiving is higher regardless of fathers' beliefs. However, there are exceptions to this overall pattern. Yeung et al. (2001), in their national sample, found no evidence of an increase in fathers' childcare responsibilities on weekdays as a function of the number of hours of maternal employment. In sum, maternal employment is a possible factor that may diminish to some degree the differences between mothers and fathers in terms of their involvement with their children.

Although there has been an increase in the number of parents who are employed in recent years, many workers experienced increases in work hours, a decrease in job stability, a rise in temporary jobs, and especially among low wage workers, a decrease in income (Mishel, Bernstein, and Schmitt 1999). As a result of these changes, the theoretical questions have shifted. More recently, instead of examining whether or not one or both parents are employed, researchers have begun to address the issue of the impact of the quality and nature of work on the parenting of both mothers and fathers (Perry-Jenkins, Repetti, and Crouter 2000). Both how much and when parents work, matter for children. Not only are heavy parental work schedules associated with negative outcomes for children (Parcel and Menaghan 1994) but nonoverlapping work hours for husbands and wives has negative effects on marital relationships (Perry-Jenkins, Repetti, and Crouter 2000). Job loss and underemployment has serious effects on family life, including marital relationships, parent-child relationships, and child adjustment (White and Rogers 2000; Conger et al. 2002; Parke et al. 2004).

In terms of the impact of work on families, Crouter (1994) suggests two types of linkage. One type of research focuses on work as an "emotional climate" that in turn, may have carryover effects to the enactment of roles in home settings. The focus is generally on short-term or transitory effects. A second type of linkage focuses on the types of attitudes and values that adults acquire in the workplace and on how these variations in job experience alter their behavior in family contexts. In contrast to the short-term perspective of the spillover of emotional climate research, this second type examines more enduring and long-lasting effects of work on family life.

Work in the first tradition has been conducted by Repetti (1994), who studied the impact of working in a high stress job (air traffic controller) on subsequent family interaction patterns. She found that the male air traffic controllers were more withdrawn in marital interactions after high-stress shifts and tended to be behaviorally and emotionally withdrawn during interactions with their children as well. Although high workload is associated with withdrawal, negative social experiences in the workplace have a different effect. In addition, distressing social experiences at work were associated with higher expressions of anger and greater use of discipline during interaction with the child later in the day. Repetti and Wood (1997) found similar effects for mothers who withdrew from their preschoolers on days when the mothers experienced greater workloads or interpersonal stress on the job. Repetti views this as a "spillover effect" in which there is transfer of negative feeling across settings. Similarly, Crouter, Bumpus, Maguire, and

McHale (1999) found that parents who reported high work pressure and role overload had more conflicts with their adolescents.

Research in the second tradition of family-work linkages, namely the effects of the nature of men's occupational roles on their parenting behavior, dates back to the classic work of Kohn (1997). Men who experience a high degree of occupational autonomy value independence in their children, consider children's intentions when considering discipline, and use reasoning and withdrawal of rewards instead of physical punishment. In contrast, men who are in highly supervised jobs with little autonomy value conformity and obedience, focus on consequences rather than intentions, and use more physical forms of discipline. In short, they repeat their job-based experiences in their parenting roles. Several researchers extended this work by focusing on the outcomes of job characteristics for children's development. Cooksey, Menaghan, and Jokielek (1997) found that children had fewer behavior problems when their mothers' work involved more autonomy, working with people, and more problem-solving opportunities. Similarly, others found that fathers with greater job complexity and autonomy were less authoritarian (Grimm-Thomas and Perry-Jenkins 1994), responded with greater warmth to their children, and provided more verbal explanations (Greenberger and O'Neil 1990).

Together these studies underscore the importance of quantity, schedule, and quality of work as a further set of situational factors that may alter the profile of similarities and differences between maternal and paternal parenting.

THE CULTURAL EMBEDDEDNESS OF PARENTING

Cultural factors also play an important role in determining both the quantity and quality of parental involvement. In spite of this recognition, a universalist assumption underlies much of the theorizing in the social sciences. This assumes that the processes noted in studies of Western parents—or more narrowly, Euro-American and middle-class parents—will be generalizable both to other cultures and to non-Euro-American groups in the United States. In the last several decades, this assumption has been challenged on several fronts. Theoretically, there has been a revival of interest in cross-cultural and intracultural variations, in large part due to the rediscovery of Vygotskian theory with the strong focus on the cultural embeddedness of families (Rogoff 2003). This is reflected in renewed interest in cross-cultural variations in parenting (Bornstein 1991; Parke and Buriel 2006).

To illustrate how cross-cultural work can inform our discussion of mother–father stylistic differences in interactions with their offspring, we consider work on the universality of paternal physical play. A cross-cultural perspective on fathers has not only forced us to confront the variability in fathering behaviors but also challenged some of our assumptions about central features of the father role. For example, the well-established finding that physical play is the hallmark of fathers' interactive style has been questioned (Parke 2002a). While in some cultures that are similar to U.S. culture, such as Great Britain and Australia, where there are similar parental sex or parent differences in play, findings from several other cultures do not find that physical play is a central feature of the father-infant relationship (Roopnarine 2004). Neither in Sweden nor among Israeli kibbutz families were fathers more likely to play with their children or to engage in different types of physical play (Hwang 1987). Similarly, Chinese Malaysian, Indian, and Aka pygmy (Central Africa) mothers and fathers rarely engaged in physical play with their children (Hewlett 1991; Roopnarine 2004). Instead, both display affection and engage in plenty of close physical contact. Perhaps societies who value sharing and cooperation will be less likely to encourage a physical playful interactive style, whereas industrialized societies that are characterized by a high degree of competition and value independence and assertiveness would commonly support this interactive style (Paquette 2004). In fact, Western technologically advanced and highly individually-oriented societies are likely to have the highest levels of competition in their children's play (Hughes 1999). However, there is less competitive play among North American children raised in cooperation-oriented communes (Plattner and Minturn 1975) and perhaps less prevalence of physical play between fathers and children, although this has not been established.

In other cultures, such as in Italy, neither mothers nor fathers but other women in the extended family or within the community are more likely to play physically with infants (New and Benigni 1987), while in Mexico this physical play role often falls to siblings (Zukow-Goldring 2002). These findings suggest that the physical play role of the father is not universal and that the play role may be assumed by other social agents in some cultures. Moreover, these cross-cultural differences suggest that cultural context is one of the factors that may reduce the differences—in this case, in terms of play style—between mother and father interaction patterns. These cross-cultural observations may lead to a reevaluation of the pathways through which fathers influence their children and may force us to rethink the father's physical play role as a major contributor to children's emotional regulation—at least in non-Western cultures. Nor are the cultural differences restricted to style of interaction; instead cultural factors influence levels or quantity of involvement between mothers and fathers as well. Although it is assumed that differences in level of involvement of mothers and fathers in caregiving, for example, are universally found, the Aka data suggest otherwise (Hewlett 1991). Among the Aka, mothers and fathers share much of the caregiving responsibilities, which suggests that even this assumed universal mother/father difference may be dependent on the cultural context.

Demographic shifts in North America have fueled interest in intracultural variation in mother and father parenting roles. In 2003, 31 percent of the population belonged to a racial minority group. Currently, 13 percent of the U.S. population are Hispanic (37 million), 12.7 percent are African-American (36.7 million), 1 percent are Asian-American, Indian, or Alaska Natives (2.7 million), and another 4.1 percent are of two or more races (4.1 million) (U.S. Census Bureau 2003). In view of these demographic shifts, there is an opportunity to evaluate the generalizability of our assumptions about similarities and differences in parenting of mothers and fathers. A detailed review of these variations is beyond the scope of this chapter but a few examples will suffice to underscore that ethnicity is an important factor to consider in trying to understand similarities and differences across parents of opposite genders (see Parke et al. 2005; Parke and Buriel 2006 for reviews).

Studies of African-American and Hispanic-American families, for example, suggest that the size of differences in maternal and paternal involvement varies in subtle ways from white households. For example, Hofferth (2003) using a nationally representative sample of African-American and white fathers found that in comparison to white fathers, African-American fathers, spend less time with their children on a regular basis, although the differences are relatively modest (12.76 hours per week versus 15.35 hours per week for African-American and white fathers respectively). In turn, this suggests a larger difference in maternal versus paternal involvement in African-American households. In spite of these differences in level of involvement, African-American fathers assumed greater responsibility for routine care of their children than white fathers. This level of responsibility is consistent with the less traditional attitudes of black fathers toward caregiving roles than white fathers. Similarly, African-American fathers were higher in monitoring their children than white fathers. As others (Dodge, McLoyd, and Landsford 2005) have argued, neighborhood characteristics may account for these patterns. African-American fathers control and monitor their children more because their neighborhoods are more dangerous. Family size may explain this difference as well since African-Americans have larger families than white families and larger families require more parental control.

Empirical research on Hispanic-Americans has found that these fathers are more likely to be engaged in caregiving, and household and personal care than European Americans (Toth and Xu 1999; Yeung et al. 2001), which suggests a reduction in the differences between mother-father involvement among Latino parents. However, Latino fathers spend more time in play with their children relative to mothers (Toth and Xu 1999; Yeung et al. 2001) just as we noted earlier for Euro-American families.

Asian- and Asian-American fathers, in comparison with mothers, have typically been viewed as aloof and uninvolved with their children. Again, this stereotype has some historical basis, but the portrait of the modern Asian father is changing due to both patterns of immigration and acculturation as well as shifting economic conditions in some Asian countries (for detailed discussions see Ishii-Kuntz 2000; Chao and Tseng 2002). In both Asian American and Asian families, there are two general findings that characterize maternal and paternal roles in the family. First, the strong commitment to the breadwinner role among Asian fathers has resulted in men's limited involvement with the care of their children (Ishii-Kuntz 2000) compared to mothers, as well as to men in other cultures. For example, Japanese fathers are less involved with their children compared to mothers and less than fathers in other countries (Ishii-Kuntz 2000). While Japanese fathers, according to a 1994 survey, spend 3.8 hours per day with their young children (three years or younger), fathers in other cultures were higher (United States, 5.35 hours; Korea, 4.12 hours; Thailand, 7.17 hours; United Kingdom, 6.45 hours). As in many countries, Japanese fathers engaged in play more than routine physical care (Ishii-Kuntz 2000). Similar levels of father involvement have been reported for Chinese families (Jankowiak 1992) as well as Taiwanese families (Sun and Roopnarine 1996). Taiwanese fathers were less involved in childcare with their infants; in China, fathers were not viewed as sufficiently competent or trustworthy to care for infants. Instead, in Chinese families, a father's role was focused on children's education when children entered middle school.

However, as Ishii-Kuntz (2000) notes, the centrality of the men's bread-winning role among Japanese fathers is changing. In one study, 81 percent of Japanese fathers ranked the paternal role as first or second in importance among five paternal roles—evidence that the importance of the worker role is lessening (Shwalb, Kawai, Shoji, and Tsunetsugu 1997). Second, the economic recession, in combination with an increase in the labor force participation of women, has contributed to this decline as well. While not universal, there are trends among some segments of Japanese society for men to become more involved in fathering (Ishii-Kuntz 2000). Similarly, in the United States as Asian families become more acculturated, there is a trend toward greater equality in the division of household labor including more sharing of childcare responsibilities (Ishii-Kuntz 2000). However, the patterns are not uniform across Asian subgroups that vary in terms of immigration patterns and levels of economic participation.

Stylistic differences as well as level of involvement need to be considered. As Chao and Tseng (2002:73) observed, "Parenting differences purported between Asian fathers and mothers have been based on the traditional adage 'strict father, kind mother'—wherein fathers exert high degrees of authoritarian control and mothers manifest high degrees of warmth." Consistent with this view, in a study of Chinese adolescents' perceptions, maternal parenting was viewed as being more positive than paternal parenting (Shek 2000). Adolescents stated that fathers showed less concern, less responsiveness, and higher levels of harshness than mothers. Also, father-adolescent communication was perceived less positively and as occurring less frequently than mother-adolescent communication (Shek 2000). In contrast to the general picture that emerges for East Asian families, studies of Asian immigrant families in the United States have found few differences between mothers and fathers in levels of authoritarian parenting control and warmth (Chao and Kim 2000). Again, acculturation clearly plays a role in helping to understand differences and similarities in mother-father child-rearing styles. These patterns present a clear challenge to our stereotype of the maternal and paternal child-rearing styles among Asian-American families.

The role of Native American parents has been largely neglected in research. While one cannot generalize across all Native Americans since there are 280 tribal groups and 161 different linguistic groups (Staples 1988), Mirandé's 1991 discussion of the Navajo experience is illustrative. Traditionally, Navajo women exercised the role that was equal to, if not greater than, the role of men. Women were responsible for the care and maintenance of children. Many teaching and disciplinary functions were carried out by the mother's brothers, not the father. As the society came in contact more with Euro-American culture, the father became increasingly important within the family and the mother lost much of her influence (Mirandé 1991). Native American families rely heavily on the community as a whole. Children are protected, loved, and nurtured not only by parents, but also by siblings, aunts, uncles, grandparents, cousins, and other extended family

(Mirandé 1991). Parenting in the traditional Native-American community must also be examined in the context of the extended family (Burgess 1980). Among the Hopi, the family is considered to be the whole clan. The sisters of the child's mother are also called mothers. The brothers of the child's father are called fathers. The child knows which is his/her real mother and father, but is surrounded by many relatives who are very close to him/her. The siblings of the child's grandparents are called grandparents. All members consider themselves to be related to one another and have obligations to each other. This glimpse at Native American families challenges our reliance on discrete and bounded categories of parents as mothers and fathers. In cultures where there is a network of "parental" figures, the utility of these labels of mother and father are brought into question. Just as Kessen (1979) argued that the child is a "cultural invention," it will be well to remember that the concepts of parent, father, mother, and family are cultural inventions as well.

It is clear from these brief examples that cultural factors will either enhance or diminish differences between mothers and fathers and underscores the plasticity of parental roles.

RECENT CHALLENGES TO FATHERS AND/OR MOTHERS AS ESSENTIAL SOCIALIZATION AGENTS

Although it is common to assume that fathers and mothers are essential to the successful socialization of children, evidence concerning the impact of gay and lesbian parents on children's development challenges this basic assumption. Work by Golombok, Patterson, and their colleagues suggests that the development of children raised by lesbian parents is well within normal limits (Golombok 2000, 2006; Patterson 2000, 2006). Although the amount of research on the effects of being reared by two male parents is even more limited than the work on two female parents, the limited available data suggest that the gender identities of children of gay fathers are similar to those of children of heterosexual fathers (Bailey and Zucker 1995; Patterson 2006). Moreover, the relationships that children develop with their gay fathers are positive (Patterson 2006). If children reared in homes with two parents of the same gender are developing well, it raises the question about the necessity of fathers and/or mothers in the socialization mix. As Silverstein and Auerbach (1999) and Golombok (2000) suggest, our focus on the gender of the parent may be too narrow a conceptualization of the issue. Instead, it may be helpful to recast the issue to ask whether exposure to male and female parents is the key, or whether it is exposure to the interactive style typically associated with either mothers or fathers that matters. An experimental study by Ross and Taylor (1989) is relevant. They found that boys prefer the paternal play style, whether it is mothers or fathers who engage in the physical and active stimulation. Their work suggests that boys may not necessarily prefer their fathers but rather their physical style of play.

In another body of work relevant to this issue, fathers and mothers reversed their customary roles (Radin 1994). In this case, the primary care-giving functions typically fulfilled by women were undertaken by men. Evidence from both the United States (Field 1978) and Australia (Russell 1999) suggests that the style of interaction of primary caregiving fathers is more like that of primary care-giving mothers. For example, Russell found that role-sharing fathers engaged in a less stereotypically masculine style of parenting and instead exhibited a more maternal interactive style (e.g., more indoor recreational activities and less exclusive focus on roughhousing and outdoor games). Finally, Israeli primary care-giving fathers were more nurturant as reported by both themselves and their children relative to traditional fathers (Sagi 1982). Together, this evidence indicates that the style of parenting and the gender of the parent who delivers or enacts this style can be viewed as at least partially independent. These types of data will help us eventually address the uniqueness of fathers' and mothers' roles in the family and in their children's development. Moreover, they will help provide needed clarity on the important issue of how essential fathers (Silverstein and Auerbach 1999) or mothers (Parke 2002b) are for children's development.

At the same time, it seems premature to conclude that fathers or mothers are replaceable based on this evidence. Two key issues need to be addressed. More needs to be understood about the extent to which role division in lesbian or gay families approximates role division in heterosexual families, and more needs to be understood about the degree to which same-gender couples expose their children to opposite-sex role models. In the first case, evidence suggests that lesbian couples share household tasks and decision-making responsibilities more equally than do heterosexual couples (Patterson 2000). Similarly, gay parental couples are more likely to share child-rearing duties evenly (McPherson 1993). At the same time, however, lesbian biological mothers viewed their parental role as more salient than either nonbiological lesbian mothers or heterosexual mothers (Hand 1991). Moreover, despite the more egalitarian divisions of household labor in lesbian households, there also exists some traditionality in roles. Biological lesbian mothers are more involved in childcare than are their partners; these nonbiological lesbian mothers spent more time working outside the family (Patterson 2000, 2006). This raises the possibility that even in same-gender families, the usual role division concerning childcare, which characterizes heterosexual partnerships, may be evident. Whether the nonbiological mothers enact other aspects of more traditional male roles, such as a physical play style, remains to be established. Moreover, we know little about the ways in which gay men enact their family roles and whether one partner is likely to enact a more traditional maternal role. In short, children may be afforded opportunities to experience both maternal and paternal interactive styles in same-gender households, but more work is needed to evaluate this possibility. Moreover the critical issue is whether differentiation of roles between co-parents in same-gender parent families is associated with the apparent advantages that this bestows in heterosexual families (Ricaud 1998). Again this allows us to address the issue raised earlier, namely the relative importance of parental style versus gender of parent who is the delivery agent of this style.

There are other strategies for providing a child with exposure to a range of stylistic experiences not only in same-gender parent households but in otherwise undifferentiated traditional opposite-gendered parent households as well. Parents have increasingly been recognized as managers of their children's social environments (Furstenberg, Cook, Eccles, Elder, and Sameroff 1999; Parke et al. 2003). In this role, lesbian parents can choose to deliberately expand their children's range of experiences with male or, in the case of gay parents, female figures. Or nonplay-oriented fathers in heterosexual households such as older fathers can elect to expose their child to either more playful males or to vigorous play activities such as wrestling or karate classes. At this point, we simply do not have extensive data on how much exposure children raised by lesbian or gay couples have to males or females outside the family, or whether lesbian mothers intentionally provide this exposure as a means of compensating for the absence of a male figure in the household (Parke 2002b). Moreover, nothing is known about the duration and frequency necessary to confer any potential developmental advantage if such exposure were found to be beneficial. Perhaps most fundamentally, we lack data on the kind of relationship needed if exposure is to prove beneficial for the child's development. And of course, the larger question is whether this exposure, after controlling for parent effects, makes a difference in child outcomes. Work on adult mentors confirms conventional wisdom and past research on nonparental adult influence: The positive effect of nonfamilial mentors on adolescents' social behavior is independent of the effect of parent-child relationships (Greenberger, Chen, and Beam 1998).

CONCLUDING THOUGHTS AND FUTURE QUESTIONS

Our aim in this chapter has been to provide an overview of the similarities and differences across opposite gender caregivers in their parental styles of interaction with their children. However, in recognition of the complexity of this issue, this chapter has been less an attempt to provide a definitive answer to the question of whether there are differences in parenting between mothers and fathers and more of an effort to reframe the question to be "What factors contribute to differences and similarities between mothers and fathers and what are the implications for children of exposure to these patterns of similarities and differences?" It is clear that the many similarities between parents are evolutionarily sensible and provide a practical, protective benefit for the child in case of the loss of one parent. At the same time, there are differences in parental interactive style between mothers and fathers at least in North American and similar Western cultures. Evidence suggests that these differing styles of maternal and paternal interaction may provide unique opportunities to learn different kinds of cognitive-linguistic and/or emotional regulatory skills that are important for children's intellectual and social competence. Whether this style of interaction needs to be delivered by a caregiver of a particular gender, however, is an issue that merits further empirical examination since it raises important policy as well as scientific issues about our definitions of family and parenthood.

REFERENCES

Aldous, J. and G. M. Mulligan. 2002. "Fathers' Child Care and Children's Behavior Problems." *Journal of Family Issues* 54:699–707.

Allen, J. and A. Hawkins. 1999. "Maternal Gatekeeping: Mothers' Beliefs and Behaviors That Inhibit Greater Father Involvement in Family Work." *Journal of Marriage and Family* 61:199–212.

Amato, P. A. and J. G. Gilbreth. 1999. "Nonresident Fathers and Children's Well-Being: Media Analysis." *Journal of Marriage and Family* 61:557–573.

Amato, R. R. and F. Rivera. 1999. "Paternal Involvement and Children's Behavior." *Journal of Marriage and Family* 61:375–384.

Bailey, J. M. and K. J. Zucker. 1995. "Childhood Sex-Typed Behavior and Sexual Orientation: A Conceptual Analysis and Quantitative Review." *Developmental Psychology* 31:43–55.

Bailey, W. T. 1992. "Psychological Development in Men: Generativity and Involvement with Preschool Young Children." *Psychological Reports* 71:929–930.

Barnard, K. and J. E. Solchany. 2002. "Mothering." In *Handbook of Parenting*, vol. 2, 2nd ed., ed. M. Bornstein, 3–26. Mahwah, NJ: Lawrence Erlbaum.

Beitel, A. and R. D. Parke. 1998. "Paternal Involvement in Infancy: The Role of Maternal and Paternal Attitudes." *Journal of Family Psychology* 12:268–288.

Belsky, J. 1984. "The Determinants of Parenting: A Process Model." *Child Development* 55:83–96.

Belsky, J., M. Rovine, and M. Fish. 1989. "The Developing Family System." In *Systems and Development, Minnesota Symposia on Child Psychology*, vol. 22, ed. M. Gunnar and E. Thelen, 119–166. Hillsdale NJ: Lawrence Erlbaum.

Belsky, J., H. J. Ward, and M. Levine. 1986. "Perspectives on the Family." In *Prenatal Expectations, Postnatal Experiences and the Transition to Parenthood*, ed. R. Ashmore and D. Brodinsky, 111–146. Hillsdale, NJ: Lawrence Erlbaum.

Berman, P. W. 1987. "Young Children's Response to Babies: Do They Foreshadow Differences Between Maternal and Paternal Styles?" In *Origins of Nurturance*, ed. A. Fogel and G. Melson, 25–26. Hillsdale, NJ: Lawrence Erlbaum.

Bjorklund, D. F. and A. D. Pellegrini. 2000. "Child Development and Evolutionary Psychology." *Child Development* 71:1687–1708.

Bonney, J. F., M. L. Kelley, and R. F. Levant. 1999. "A Model of Fathers' Involvement in Child Care in Dual-Earner Families." *Journal of Family Psychology* 13:401–415.

Booth, A. and P. Amato. 1994. "Parental Marital Quality, Divorce and Relations with Offspring in Young Adulthood." *Journal of Marriage and Family* 56:21–34.

Bornstein, M. H., ed. 1991. *Cultural Approaches to Parenting*. Hillsdale, NJ: Lawrence Erlbaum.

Bornstein, M. H. and C. S. Tamis-LeMonda. 1989. "Maternal Responsiveness and Cognitive Development in Children." In *Maternal Responsiveness: Characteristics and Consequences. New Directions for Child Development*, no. 43, ed. M. H. Bornstein, 49–61. San Francisco: Jossey-Bass.

Bourçois, V. 1997. "Modalités de présence du père et développement social de l'enfant d'âge préscolaire." ["Forms of Father Involvement and Social Development in Preschoolers."] *Enfance* 3:389–399.

Boyum, L. and R. D. Parke. 1995. "The Role of Family Emotional Expressiveness in the Development of Children's Social Competence." *Journal of Marriage and Family* 57:593–608.

Brodzinsky, D. M. and E. Pinderhughes. 2002. "Parenting and Child Development in Adoptive Families." In *Handbook of Parenting*, vol. 1, 2nd ed., ed. M. Bornstein, 279–312. Mahwah, NJ: Lawrence Erlbaum.

Burgess, B. J. 1980. "Parenting in the Native-American Community." In *Parenting in a Multicultural Society*, ed. M. R. Fantini and R. Cárdenas, 63–73. New York: Longman.

Cabrera N., J. Shannon, and C. Tamis-LaMonda. 2007. "Fathers' Influence on Their Children's Cognitive and Emotional Development: From Toddlers to Pre-K." *Applied Developmental Science* 11:208–213.

Carson, J. and R. D. Parke. 1996. "Reciprocal Negative Affect in Parent-Child Interactions and Children's Peer Competency." *Child Development* 67:2217–2226.

Carter, C. S. and M. Altemus. 1997. "Integrative Functions of Lactational Hormones in Social Behavior and Stress Management." *Annals of the New York Academy of Sciences, Integrative Neurobiology of Affiliation* 807:164–174.

Chao, R. K. and K. Kim. 2000. "Parenting Differences Among Immigrant Chinese Fathers and Mothers in the United States." *Journal of Psychology in Chinese Societies* 1:71–91.

Chao, R. and V. Tseng. 2002. "Parenting of Asians." In *Handbook of Parenting*, vol. 4, 2nd ed., ed. M. Bornstein, 59–94. Mahwah, NJ: Lawrence Erlbaum.

Clarke-Stewart, K. A. 1980. "The Father's Contribution to Children's Cognitive and Social Development in Early Childhood." In *The Father-Infant Relationship*, ed. F. Pedersen, 111–146. New York: Praeger.

Clarke-Stewart, K. A. and C. Brentano. 2006. *Divorce: Causes and Consequences*. New Haven, CT: Yale University.

Coley, R. L. and P. L. Chase-Lansdale. 1999. "Stability and Change in Paternal Involvement Among Urban African-American Fathers." *Journal of Family Psychology* 13:416–435.

Collins, W. A. and A. Russell, A. 1991. "Mother-Child and Father-Child Relationships in Middle Childhood and Adolescence." *Developmental Review* 11:99–136.

Coltrane, S. 1996. *Family Man*. New York: Oxford.

Coltrane, S., R. D. Parke, and M. Adams. 2004. "Complexity of Father Involvement in Low-Income Mexican American Families." *Family Relations* 53:179–189.

Conger, R. and G. Elder. 1994. *Families in Troubled Times*. New York: Aldine de Gruyter.

Conger, R. D., L. E. Wallace, Y. Sun, R. L. Simons, V. C. McLoyd, and G. H. Brody. 2002. "Economic Pressure in African-American Families: A Replication and Extension of the Family Stress Model." *Developmental Psychology* 38:179–193.

Cooksey, E. C., E. G. Menaghan, and S. M. Jokielek. 1997. "Life Course Effects of Work and Family Circumstances on Children." *Social Forces* 76:637–667.

Cooney, T. M., F. A. Pedersen, S. Indelicato, and R. Palkovitz. 1993. "Timing of Fatherhood: Is 'On Time' Optimal?" *Journal of Marriage and Family* 55:205–215.

Corter, C. and A. S. Fleming. 2002. "Psychobiology of Maternal Behavior in Human Beings." In *Handbook of Parenting*, vol. 2, 2nd ed., ed. M. Bornstein, 141–182. Mahwah, NJ: Lawrence Erlbaum.

Cowan, P. A. and C. P. Cowan. 1992. *When Partners Become Parents*. New York: Basic.

Cowan, P. A. and C. P. Cowan. 2002. "Interventions as Tests of Family Systems Theories: Marital Family Relationships in Children's Development and Psychopathology." *Development and Psychopathology* 14:731–759.

Crawley, S. B. and K. B. Sherrod. 1984. "Parent-Infant Play During the First Year of Life." *Infant Behavior and Development* 7:65–75.

Crouter, A. C. 1994. "Processes Linking Families and Work: Implications for Behavior and Development in Both Settings." In *Exploring Family Relationships with Other Contexts*, ed. R. D. Parke and S. Kellam, 9–28. Hillsdale, NJ: Lawrence Erlbaum.

Crouter, A. C., M. F. Bumpus, M. C. Maguire, and S. M. McHale. 1999. "Linking Parents' Work Pressure and Adolescents' Well Being: Insights Into Dynamics in Dual-Earner Families." *Developmental Psychology* 35:1453–1461.

Cummings, E. M., M. C. Goeke-Morey, and J. Raymond. 2004. "Fathers in Family Context: Effects of Marital Quality on Child Adjustment." In *The Role of the Father in Child Development*, 4th ed., ed. M. E. Lamb. New York: John Wiley.

Daly, K. 1997. "Reshaping Fatherhood: Finding the Models." In *Fatherhood Contemporary Theory, Research and Social Policy*, ed. W. Marsiglio, 21–40. Thousand Oaks, CA: Sage.

Dalton-Hummel, D. 1982. "Syntactic and Conversational Characteristics of Fathers' Speech." *Journal of Psycholinguistic Research* 11:465–483.

Dancy, B. and P. Handal. 1984. "Perceived Family Climate, Psychological Adjustment, and Peer Relationship of Black Adolescents: A Function of Parental Marital Status or Perceived Family Conflict." *Journal of Community Psychology* 12:222–229.

Deater-Deckard, K. and K. Dodge. 1997. "Externalizing Behavior Problem and Discipline Revisited: Nonlinear Effect and Variation by Culture, Context and Gender." *Psychological Inquiry* 8:161–175.

Denham, S. 1998. *Emotional Development in Young Children*. New York: Guilford.

Dickie, J. R. and P. Matheson. 1984. "Mother-Father-Infant: Who Needs Support?" Paper presented at the meeting of the American Psychological Association, August 1984, Toronto, Ontario.

Dickstein, S. and R. D. Parke. 1988. "Social Referencing: A Glance at Fathers and Marriage." *Child Development* 59:506–511.

Dienhart, A. and K. Daly. 1997. "Men and Women Co-Creating Father Involvement in a Nongenerative Culture." In *Generative Fathering*, ed. A. J. Hawkins and D. C. Dollahite, 147–164. Thousand Oaks, CA: Sage.

Dodge, K. A., V. C. McLoyd, and J. E. Lansford. 2005. "The Cultural Context of Physically Disciplining Children." In *African-American Family Life*, ed. V. C. McLoyd, N. E. Hill and K. A. Dodge, 245–263. New York: Guilford.

Doherty, W. E. J., E. F. Kouneski, and M. Erikson. 1998. "Responsible Fathering: An Overview and Conceptual Framework." *Journal of Marriage and Family* 60:277–292.

Durrett, M. E., M. Otaki, and P. Richards. 1984. "Attachment and the Mother's Perception of Support from the Father." *International Journal of Behavioral Development* 7:167–176.

Fagan, J. 1998. "Correlates of Low-Income African American and Puerto Rican Fathers' Involvement with Their Children." *Journal of Black Psychology* 24:351–367.

Fagan, J. and A. J. Hawkins, ed. 2000. *Clinical and Educational Interventions with Fathers*. New York: Hawkins.

Field, T. M. 1978. "Interaction Behaviors of Primary and Secondary Caretaker Fathers." *Developmental Psychology* 14:183–185.

Fleming, A. S., C. Corter, J. Stallings, and M. Steiner. 2002. "Testosterone and Prolactin are Associated with Emotional Responses to Infant Cues in New Fathers." *Hormones and Behavior* 42:399–413.

Fleming, A. S. and M. Li. 2002. "Psychobiology of Maternal Behavior and Its Early Determinants in Nonhuman Mammals." In *Handbook of Parenting*, vol. 2, 2nd ed., ed. M. Bornstein, 61–98. Mahwah, NJ: Lawrence Erlbaum.

Fleming, A. S., D. Ruble, H. Krieger, and P. Y. Wong. 1997. "Hormonal and Experimental Correlates of Maternal Responsiveness During Pregnancy and the Puerperium in Human Mothers." *Hormones and Behavior* 31:145–158.

Flouri, E., A. Buchanan, and V. Bream. 2002. "Adolescents' Perceptions of Their Fathers' Involvement: Significance to School Attitudes." *Psychology in the Schools* 39:575–582.

Franz, C. E., D. McClelland, and J. Weinberger. 1991. "Childhood Antecedents of Conventional Social Accomplishment in Midlife Adults: A 26-Year Prospective Study." *Journal of Personality and Social Psychology* 58:709–717.

Frone, M. R., J. K. Yardley, and K. S. Markel. 1997. "Developing and Testing an Integrative Model of the Work-Family Interface." *Journal of Vocational Behavior* 50:145–167.

Furstenberg, F. F., T. D. Cook, J. Eccles, G. Elder, and A. J. Sameroff. 1999. *Managing to Make It*. Chicago: University of Chicago.

Furstenberg, F. F. and K. M. Harris. 1993. "When and Why Fathers Matter: Impacts of Father Involvement on Children of Adolescent Mothers." In *Young Unwed Fathers*, ed. R. I. Lerman and T. J. Ooms, 117–138. Philadelphia: Temple University.

Gadsen, V. 1999. "Black Families in Intergenerational and Cultural Perspective." In *Parenting and Child Development in "Nontraditional" Families*, ed. M. E. Lamb, 221–246. Mahwah, NJ: Lawrence Erlbaum.

Golinkoff, R. M. and G. Ames. 1979. "A Comparison of Fathers' and Mothers' Speech to Their Young Children." *Child Development* 50:28–32.

Golombok, S. 2000. *Parenting: What Really Counts*. London: Routledge.

Golombok, S. 2006. "New Family Forms." In *Families Count: Effects on Child and Adolescent Development*, ed. K. A. Clarke -Stewart and J. Dunn, 273–298. Cambridge, UK: Cambridge University.

Gottman, J. M. 1994. *Why Marriages Succeed or Fail.* New York: Simon and Schuster.

Gottman, J. M., L. Katz, and C. Hooven. 1997. *Meta-Emotion.* NJ: Lawrence Erlbaum.

Greenberger, E., C. Chen, and M. K. Beam. 1998. "The Role of 'Very Important' Nonparental Adults in Adolescent Development." *Journal of Youth and Adolescence* 27:321–343.

Greenberger, E. and R. O'Neil. 1990. "Parents' Concerns About Their Child's Development: Implications for Fathers' and Mothers' Well-Being and Attitudes Toward Work." *Journal of Marriage and Family* 52:621–635.

Greenberger, E., R. O'Neil, and S. K. Nagel. 1994. "Linking Workplace and Home Place: Relations Between the Nature of Adults' Work and Their Parenting Behaviors." *Developmental Psychology* 30:990–1002.

Grimm-Thomas, K. and M. Perry-Jenkins. 1994. "All in a Day's Work: Job Experiences, Self-Esteem and Fathering in Working-Class Families." *Family Relations* 43:174–181.

Grossman, F. K. 1987. "Separate and Together: Men's Autonomy and Affiliation in the Transition to Parenthood." In *Men's Transition to Parenthood,* ed. P. W. Berman and F. A. Pedersen, 89–114. Hillsdale, NJ: Lawrence Erlbaum.

Grossmann, K., K. E. Grossmann, E. Fremmer-Bombik, H. Kindler, H. Scheuerer-Englisch, and P. Zimmerman. 2002. "The Uniqueness of the Child-Father Attachment Relationship: Fathers' Sensitive and Challenging Play as a Pivotal Variable in a 16-Year Longitudinal Study." *Social Development* 11:307–331.

Hand, S. 1991. *The Lesbian Parenting Couple.* Unpublished dissertation. California Professional School of Psychology, San Francisco, CA.

Hart, C. H., D. A. Nelson, C. C. Robinson, S. F. Olsen, and M. K. McNeilly-Choque. 1998. "Overt and Relational Aggression in Russian Nursery-School-Age Children: Parenting Style and Marital Linkages." *Developmental Psychology* 34:687–697.

Hart, C. H., D. A. Nelson, C. C. Robinson, S. F. Olsen, M. K. McNeilly-Choque, C. L. Porter, and T. R. McKee. 2000. "Russian Parenting Styles and Family Processes: Linkages with Subtypes of Victimization and Aggression." In *Family and Peers: Linking Two Social Worlds,* ed. K. A. Kerns, J. M. Contreras, and A. M. Neal-Barnett. Westport, CT: Praeger.

Heiss, J. 1996. "Effects of African American Family Structure on School Attitudes and Performance." *Social Problems* 43:246–265.

Hewlett, B. S. 1991. *Intimate Fathers.* Ann Arbor: University of Michigan.

Hochschild, A. and A. Machung. 1989. *The Second Shift: Working Parents and the Revolution at Home.* New York: Viking.

Hofferth, S. L. 2003. "Race/Ethnic Difference in Father Involvement in Two-Parent Families: Culture, Context, or Economy?" *Journal of Family Issues* 24:185–216.

Hossain, T., I. Field, J. E. Malphurs, C. Valle, and J. Pickens. 1997. "Father Caregiving in Low Income African-American and Hispanic American Families." Unpublished manuscript. University of Miami Medical School, Miami, Florida.

Hossain, Z. and J. L. Roopnarine. 1994. "African-American Fathers' Involvement with Infants: Relationship to Their Functional Style, Support, Education, and Income." *Infant Behavior and Development* 17:175–184.

Hwang, P. 1987. "The Changing Role of Swedish Fathers." In *The Father's Role: Cross-Cultural Perspectives*, ed. M. E. Lamb, 115–138. Hillsdale, NJ: Lawrence Erlbaum.

Hyde, B. L. and M. S. Texidor. 1988. "A Description of the Fathering Experience Among Black Fathers." *Journal of Black Nurses Association* 2:67–78.

Ishii-Kuntz, M. 1993. "Japanese Fathers: Work Demands and Family Roles." In *Men, Work and Family*, ed. J. C. Hood, 45–67. Newbury Park, CA: Sage.

Ishii-Kuntz, M. 1997. "Paternal Involvement and Perception Toward Fathers' Roles: A Comparison Between Japan and the United States." In *Fatherhood: Contemporary Theory, Research, and Social Policy*, ed. W. Marsiglio, 102–118. Newbury Park, CA: Sage.

Ishii-Kuntz, M. 2000. "Diversity Within Asian American Families." *Handbook of Family Diversity*, 274–292. New York: Oxford University.

Isley, S., R. O'Neil, and R. D. Parke. 1996. "The Relation of Parental Effect and Control Behavior to Children's Classroom Acceptance: A Concurrent and Predictive Analysis." *Early Education and Development* 7:7–23.

Jacklin, C. N., J. A. DiPietro, and E. E. Maccoby. 1984. "Sex-Typing Behavior and Sex-Typing Pressure in Child/Parent Interaction." *Archives of Sexual Behavior* 13:413–425.

Jain, A., J. Belsky, and K. Crnic. 1991. "Beyond Fathering Behavior: Types of Dads." *Journal of Family Psychology* 10:431–442.

Jankowiak, W. 1992. "Father-Child Relations in Urban China." In *Father-Child Relations: Cultural and Biosocial Contexts*, ed. B. S. Hewlett, 345–363. New York: Aldine De Gruyter.

Katz, L. F. and J. M. Gottman. 1993. "Patterns of Marital Conflict Predict Children's Internalizing and Externalizing Behaviors." *Developmental Psychology* 29:940–950.

Kelly, R., L. Redenbach, and W. Rinaman. 2005. "Determinants of Custody Arrangements in a National Sample." *American Journal of Family Law* 19:25–43.

Kessen, W. 1979. "The American Child and Other Cultural Inventions." *American Psychologist* 34:815–820.

Knight, G., J. Tein, J. H. Prost, and N. A. Gonzales. 2002. "Measurement Equivalence and Research on Latino Children and Families: The Importance of Culturally Informed Theory." In *Latino Children and Families in the United States*, ed. J. M. Contreras, K. K. Kerns, and A. M. Neal-Barnett, 181–202. Westport, CT: Praeger.

Koestner, R., C. Franz, and J. Weinberger. 1990. "The Family Origins of Empathic Concern: A 26-Year Longitudinal Study." *Journal of Personality and Social Psychology* 58:709–717.

Kohn, M. 1997. "Social Structure and Personality Through Time and Space." In *Examining Lives in Context: Perspectives on the Ecology of Human Development*, ed. P. Moen, G. H. Elder, and K. Luscher, 141–168. Washington, DC: American Psychological Association.

Kromelow, S., C. Harding, and M. Touris. 1990. "The Role of the Father in the Development of Stranger Sociability During the Second Year." *American Journal of Orthopsychiatry* 60:521–530.

Labrell, F. 1996. "Paternal Play with Toddlers: Recreation and Creation." *European Journal of Psychology of Education* 11:43–54.

Lamb, M. E. 1975. "Fathers: Forgotten Contributors to Child Development." *Human Development* 18:245–266.

Lamb, M. E. 1976. "Effects of Stress and Cohort on Mother and Father-Infant Interaction." *Developmental Psychology* 12:435–443.

Lamb, M. E. 1977. "Father-Infant and Mother-Infant Interaction in the First Year of Life." *Child Development* 48:167–181.

Lamb, M. E., ed. 1987. *The Father's Role: Cross-Cultural Perspectives*. Hillsdale, NJ: Lawrence Erlbaum.

Lamb, M. E., ed. 2004. *The Role of the Father in Child Development*, 4th ed. New York: John Wiley.

Lamb, M. E., A. M. Frodi, C. P. Hwang, M. Frodi, and J. Steinberg. 1982. "Effects of Gender and Caretaking Role on Parent-Infant Interaction." In *Attachment and Affiliative Systems*, ed. R. M. Emde and R. J. Harmon. New York: Plenum.

Lamb, M. E. and C. Lewis. 2004. "The Development and Significance of Father-Child Relationships in Two-Parent Families." In *The Role of the Father in Child Development*, 4th ed., ed. M. E. Lamb. New York: John Wiley.

Lamb, M. E., J. Pleck, E. L. Charnov, and J. A. Levine. 1987. "A Biosocial Perspective on Paternal Behavior and Involvement." In *Parenting Across the Life Span: Biosocial Perspectives*, ed. J. B. Lancaster, J. Altmann, A. Rossi, and L. R. Sherrod. Chicago: Aldine.

Lamb, M. E., J. H. Pleck, and J. A. Levine. 1985. "The Role of the Father in Child Development: The Effects of Increased Paternal Involvement." In *Advances in Clinical Child Psychology*, vol. 8, ed. B. Lahey and E. E. Kazdin. New York: Plenum.

Lamborn, S. D., S. M. Dornbusch, and L. Steinberg. 1996. "Ethnicity and Community Context as Moderators of the Relations Between Family Decision Making and Adolescent Adjustment." *Child Development* 67:283–301.

Larson R. and M. Richards. 1994. *Divergent Realities*. New York: Basic.

Larson, R. W., S. Wilson, and A. Rickman. 2007. "Globalization, Societal Change, and Adolescence Across the World." In *Handbook of Adolescent Psychology*, ed. R. M. Lerner and L. Steinberg. New York: John Wiley.

Le Camus, J. 1995. "Le dialogue phasique: Nouvelles perspectives dans l'étude des interactions pèrebébé." [Phasic Dialogue: New Perspectives in the Study of Father-Infant Interactions.] *Neuropsychiatrie de l'Enfance* 43:53–65.

Lerman, R. and T. Ooms, ed. 1993. *Young Unwed Fathers*. Philadelphia: Temple University.

Maccoby, E. E. 1988. "Gender as a Social Category." *Developmental Psychology* 24:755–765.

Maccoby, E. E. 1998. *The Two Sexes: Growing Up Apart Coming Together*. Cambridge, MA: Harvard University.

Maccoby, E. E. and J. A. Martin. 1983. "Socialization in the Context of the Family: Parent-Child Interaction." In *Handbook of Child Psychology*, vol. 4, 4th ed., ed. E. M. Hetherington, 1–101. New York: John Wiley.

MacDonald, K. and R. D. Parke. 1984. "Bridging the Gap: Parent-Child Interaction and Peer Interactive Competence." *Child Development* 55:1265–1277.

MacDonald, K. and R. D. Parke. 1986. "Parent-Child Physical Play: The Effects of Sex and Age of Children and Parents." *Sex Roles* 78:367–379.

Marsiglio, W., P. Amato, R. D. Day, and M. E. Lamb. 2000. "Scholarship on Fatherhood in the 1990s and Beyond." *Journal of Marriage and Family* 62:1173–1191.

McAdoo, J. L. 1981. "Black Father and Child Interaction." In *Black Men*, ed. L. E. Gary, 115–130. Beverly Hills, CA: Sage.

McAdoo, J. L. 1988. "The Roles of Black Fathers in the Socialization of Black Children." In *Black Families*, ed. H. P. McAdoo, 257–269. Newbury Park, CA: Sage.

McBride, B. A. 1989. "Stress and Fathers' Parental Competence: Implications for Family Life and Parent Educators." *Family Relations* 38:385–389.

McDermid, S. M., T. Huston, and S. McHale. 1990. "Changes in Marriage Associated with the Transition to Parenthood: Individual Differences as a Function of Sex-Role Attitudes and Changes in the Division of Household Labor." *Journal of Marriage and Family* 52:475–486.

McDowell, D. J., M. Kim, R. O'Neil, and R. D. Parke. 2002. "Children's Emotional Regulation and Social Competence in Middle Childhood: The Role of Maternal and Paternal Interactive Style." *Marriage and Family Review* 34:345–364.

McDowell, D. J. and R. D. Parke. 2000. "Differential Knowledge of Display Rules for Positive and Negative Emotion: Influence from Parents, Influences on Peers." *Social Development* 9:415–432.

McLanahan, S. S. and G. Sandefur. 1994. *Growing Up with a Single Parent: What Helps, What Hurts*. Cambridge, MA: Harvard University.

McPherson, D. 1993. *Gay Parenting Couples: Parenting Arrangements, Arrangement Satisfaction and Relationship Satisfaction*. Unpublished doctoral dissertation. Professional School of Psychology, San Francisco.

Meany, M. J., J. Stewart, and W. W. Beatty. 1985. "Sex Differences in Social Play: The Socialization of Sex Roles." In *Advances in the Study of Behavior*, vol. 15, ed. J. S. Rosenblatt, C. Bear, C. W. Bushnell, and P. Slater, 1–58. New York: Academic.

Mirandé, A. 1991. "Ethnicity and Fatherhood." In *Fatherhood and Families in Cultural Context*, ed. F. W. Bozett and S. M. H. Hanson, 53–82. New York: Springer.

Mirandé, A. 1997. *Hombres y Machos: Masculinity and Latino Culture*. Boulder, CO: Westview.

Mishel, L., J. Bernstein, and J. Schmitt. 1999. *The State of Working America*. Ithaca, NY: Cornell University.

Mize, J. and G. S. Pettit. 1997. "Mothers' Social Coaching, Mother-Child Relationship Style and Children's Peer Competence: Is the Medium the Message?" *Child Development* 68:312–332.

Montemayor, R. 1982. "The Relationship Between Parent-Adolescent Conflict and the Amount of Time Adolescents Spend Alone with Parents and Peers." *Child Development* 68:312–332.

Montemayor, R. and J. Brownlee. 1987. "Fathers, Mothers, and Adolescents: Gender Based Differences in Parental Roles During Adolescence." *Journal of Youth and Adolescence* 16:281–291.

Mosley, J. and E. Thomson. 1995. "Fathering Behavior and Child Outcomes: The Role of Race and Poverty." In *Fatherhood: Contemporary Theory, Research and Social Policy*, ed. W. Marsigllo, 158–165. Thousand Oaks, CA: Sage.

Neville, B. and R. D. Parke. 1997. "Waiting for Paternity: Interpersonal and Contextual Implications of the Timing of Fatherhood." *Sex Roles* 37:45–59.

New, R. and L. Benigni. 1987. "Italian Fathers and Infants: Cultural Constraints on Paternal Behavior." In *The Father Role: Cross-Cultural Perspectives*, ed. M. E. Lamb. New York: John Wiley.

NICHD Early Child Care Research Network. 2000. "Factors Associated with Fathers' Caregiving Activities and Sensitivities with Young Children." *Journal of Family Psychology* 14:200–219.

Notaro, B. and B. Volling. 1999. "Parental Responsiveness and Infant-Parent Attachment: A Replication Study with Fathers and Mothers." *Infant Behavior and Development* 22:345–352.

Palkovitz, R. 2002. *Involved Fathering and Men's Adult Development*. Mahwah, NJ: Lawrence Erlbaum.

Paquette, D. 2004. "Theorizing the Father-Child Relationship: Mechanisms and Developmental Outcomes." *Human Development* 47:193–219.

Parcel, J. L. and E. G. Menaghan. 1994. *Parents' Jobs and Children's Lives*. New York: Aldine de Gruyter.

Parke, R. D. 1981. *Fathers*. Cambridge, MA: Harvard University.

Parke, R. D. 1988. "Families in Life-Span Perspective: A Multi-Level Developmental Approach." In *Child Development in Life Span Perspective*, ed. E. M. Hetherington, R. M. Lerner, and M. Perlmutter, 159–190. Hillsdale, NJ: Lawrence Erlbaum.

Parke, R. D. 1996. *Fatherhood*. Cambridge, MA: Harvard University.

Parke, R. D. 2000. "Father Involvement: A Developmental Psychological Perspective." *Marriage and Family Review* 29:43–58.

Parke, R. D. 2002a. "Fathers and Families." In *Handbook of Parenting*, vol. 3, 2nd ed., ed. M. Bornstein, 27–73. Mahwah, NJ: Lawrence Erlbaum.

Parke, R. D. 2002b. "Parenting in the New Millennium: Prospects, Promises and Pitfalls." In *Retrospect and Prospect in the Psychological Study of Families*, ed. J. P. McHale and W. S. Grolnick, 65–94. Mahwah NJ: Lawrence Erlbaum.

Parke, R. D. and A. Brott. 1999. *Throwaway Dads*. Boston: Houghton-Mifflin.

Parke, R. D. and R. Buriel. 2006. "Socialization in the Family: Ecological and Ethnic Perspectives." In *Handbook of Child Psychology*, vol. 3, 6th ed., ed. W. Damon and R. Lerner, 429–504. New York: John Wiley.

Parke, R. D., S. Coltrane, S. Borthwick-Duffy, J. Powers, M. Adams, W. Fabricius, S. Braver, and D. Saenz. 2004. "Assessing Father Involvement in Mexican-American Families." In *Conceptualizing and Measuring Father Involvement*, ed. R. Day and M.E. Lamb, 1–14. Mahway, NJ: Lawrence Erlbaum.

Parke, R. D., C. Killian, J. Dennis, M. Flyr, D. J. McDowell, S. Simpkins, M. Kim, and M. Wild. 2003. "Managing the External Environment: The Parent and Child as Active Agents in the System." In *Handbook of Dynamics in Parent-Child Relations*, ed. L. Kuczyaski. Thousand Oaks, CA: Sage.

Parke, R. D., D. J. McDowell, M. Kim, C. Killian, J. Dennis, M. L. Flyer, and M. N. Wild. 2002. "Fathers' Contribution to Children's Peer Relationships." In *Handbook of Father Involvement*, ed. C. S. Tamis-LeMonda and N. Cabrera, 141–168. Mahwah, NJ: Lawrence Erlbaum.

Parke, R. D. and S. O'Leary. 1976. "Family Interaction in the Newborn Period: Some Findings, Some Observations, and Some Unresolved Issues." In *The Developing Individual in a Changing World: Social and Environmental Issues*, vol. 2, ed. K. Riegel and J. Meacham, 653–663. The Hague: Mouton.

Parke, R. D. and R. O'Neil. 2000. "The Influence of Significant Others on Learning About Relationships: From Family to Friends." In *The Developmental Psychology of Personal Relationships*, ed. R. Mills and S. Duck, 15–47. London: John Wiley.

Parke, R. D., T. G. Power, and J. M. Gottman. 1979. "Conceptualization and Quantifying Influence Patterns in the Family Triad." In *Social Interaction Analysis: Methodological Issues*, ed. M. E. Lamb, S. J. Suomi, and G. R. Stephenson. Madison: University of Wisconsin.

Parke, R. D. and D. B. Sawin. 1980. "The Family in Early Infancy: Social, Interactional, and Attitudinal Analyses." In *The Father-Infant Relationship: Observational Studies in a Family Context*, ed. F. Pedersen, 44–70. New York: Praeger.

Parke, R. D. and S. J. Suomi. 1981. "Adult Male-Infant Relationships: Human and Non Human Primate Evidence." In *Behavioral Development: The Bielefeld Interdisciplinary Project*, ed K. Immelmann, G. Barlow, M. Main, and L. Petrinovich, 700–725. New York: Cambridge University.

Patterson, C. J. 2000. "Sexual Orientation and Family Life: A Decade Review." *Journal of Marriage and Family* 62:1052–1069.

Patterson, C. J. 2006. "Children of Lesbian and Gay Parents." *Current Directions in Psychological Science* 15:241–244.

Perry-Jenkins, M., R. L. Repetti, and A. C. Crouter. 2000. "Work and Family in the 1990s." *Journal of Marriage and Family* 62:981–989.

Plattner, S. and L. Minturn. 1975. "A Comparative and Longitudinal Study of the Behavior of Communally-Raised Children." *Ethos* 3:469–480.

Pleck, J. H. and B. P. Masciadrelli. 2004. "Paternal Involvement: Levels, Sources and Consequences." In *The Role of the Father in Child Development*, 4th ed., ed. M. E. Lamb, 222–271. New York: John Wiley.

Power, T. G. and R. D. Parke. 1982. "Play as a Context for Early Learning: Lab and Home Analyses." In *The Family as a Learning Environment*, ed. L. M. Laosa. and I. E. Sigel, 147–178. New York: Plenum.

Radin, N. 1994. "Primary Caregiving Fathers in Intact Families." In *Redefining Families*, ed. A. Gottfried and A. Gottfried, 11–54. New York: Plenum.

Rane, T. R. and B. A. McBride. 2000. "Identity Theory as a Guide to Understanding Fathers' Involvement with Their Children." *Journal of Family Issues* 21:347–366.

Repetti, R. and J. Wood. 1997. "Effects of Daily Stress at Work on Mothers' Interactions with Preschoolers." *Journal of Family Psychology* 11:90–108.

Repetti, R. L. 1994. "Short-Term and Long-Term Processes Linking Perceived Job Stressors to Father-Child Interactions." *Social Development* 3:1–15.

Ricaud, H. 1998. "Influence de l'implication diférenciée du couple parental sur les modalités de resolution des conflits interpersonnels des enfants de 3 à 5 ans en milieu scolaire." ["Influence of the Differential Involvement of the Parental Couple on the Terms of Resolution on Interpersonal Conflict in Infants from 3 to 5 Years Old in Schools."] Ph.D. thesis. University of Toulouse, France.

Rogoff, B. 2003. *The Cultural Nature of Human Development*. New York: Oxford University.

Rohner, R. P. 1998. "Father Love and Child Development: History and Current Evidence." *Current Directions in Psychological Science* 7:157–161.

Roopnarine, J. 2004. "African American and African Caribbean Fathers: Level, Quality, and Meaning Involvement." In *The Role of the Father in Child Development* 4th ed., ed. M. E. Lamb, 58–97. Hoboken, NJ: John Wiley.

Roopnarine, J. C., F. H. Hooper, M. Ahmdezzaman, and B. Pollack. 1993. "Gentle Play Partners: Mother-Child, Father-Child Play in New Delhi, India." In *Parent-Child Play*, ed. K. MacDonald, 287–304. Albany: State University of New York.

Rosenblatt, J. 2002. "Hormonal Basis of Parenting in Mammals." In *Handbook of Parenting*, vol. 2, ed. M. Bornstein, 3–25. Mahwah, NJ: Lawrence Erlbaum.

Ross, H. and H. Taylor. 1989. "Do Boys Prefer Daddy or His Physical Style of Play?" *Sex Roles* 20:23–33.

Russell, G. 1999. "Primary Caregiving Fathers." In *Parenting and Child Development in "Nontraditional" Families*, ed. M. E. Lamb, 57–82. Mahwah, NJ: Lawrence Erlbaum.

Russell, G. and A. Russell. 1987. "Mother-Child and Father-Child Relationships in Middle Childhood." *Child Development* 58:1573–1585.

Sagi, A. 1982. "Antecedents and Consequences of Various Degrees of Paternal Involvement in Child Rearing: The Israeli Project." In *Nontraditional Families: Parenting and Child Development*, ed. M. E. Lamb, 205–232, Hillsdale, NJ: Lawrence Erlbaum.

Sagi, A., M. E. Lamb, R. Shoham, R. Dvir, and K. S. Lewkowicz. 1985. "Parent-Infant Interaction in Families on Israeli Kibbutzim." *International Journal of Behavioral Development* 8:273–284.

Sandberg, J. F. and S. L. Hofferth. 2001. "Changes in Children's Time with Parents: United States, 1981–1997." *Demography* 38:423–436.

Schaffer, H. R. and P. E. Emerson. 1964. "The Development of Social Attachment in Infancy." *Monographs of the Society for Research in Child Development* 29.

Sears, R. R., E. E. Maccoby, and H. Levin. 1957. *Patterns of Childrearing*. Evanston, IL: Row Peterson.

Shek, D. L. T. 2000. "Differences Between Fathers and Mothers in the Treatment of, and Relationship with, Their Teenage Children: Perceptions of Chinese Adolescents." *Adolescence* 35:135–146.

Shelton, B. A. 1992. *Women, Men and Time: Gender Differences in Paid Work, Housework and Leisure*. New York: Greenwood.

Shulman, S. and M. M. Klein. 1993. "Distinctive Role of the Father in Adolescent Separation-Individuation." In *Father-Adolescent Relationships: New Directions for Child Development*, ed. S. Shulman and A. W. Collins, 41–57. San Francisco: Jossey-Bass.

Shwalb, D. W., H. Kawai, J. Shoji, and K. Tsunetsugu. 1997. "The Middle Class Japanese Father: A Survey of Parents of Preschoolers." *Journal of Applied Developmental Psychology* 18:497–511.

Silverstein. L. B. and C. F. Auerbach. 1999. "Deconstructing the Essential Father." *American Psychologist* 54:397–407.

Smith, P. K. and L. Daglish. 1977. "Sex Differences in Parent and Infant Behavior in the Home." *Child Development* 48:1250–1254.

Stallings, J., A. S. Fleming, C. Corter, C. Worthman, and M. Steiner. 2001. "The Effects of Infant Cries and Odors on Sympathy, Cortisol, and Autonomic Responses in New Mothers and Nonpostpartum Women." *Parenting: Science and Practice* 1:71–100.

Staples, R. 1988. "The Black American Family." In *Ethnic Families in America: Patterns and Variations*, ed. C. H. Mindel, R. W. Habenstein, and R. W. Wright, Jr., 173–195. New York: Elsevier.

Storey, A. E., C. J. Walsh, R. L. Quinton, and K. E. Wynne-Edwards. 2000. "Hormonal Correlates of Paternal Responsiveness in New and Expectant Fathers." *Evolution and Human Behavior* 21:79–95.

Sun, L. C. and J. L. Roopnarine. 1996. "Mother-Infant, Father-Infant Interaction and Involvement in Child Care and Household Labor Among Taiwanese Families." *Infant Behavior and Development* 19:121–129.

Tamis-LeMonda, C. S., M. H. Bornstein, and L. Baumwell. 2001. "Maternal Responsiveness and Children's Achievement of Language Milestones." *Child Development* 72:748–767.

Tamis-LeMonda, C. S. and N. Cabrera. ed., 2002. *Handbook of Father Involvement*. Mahwah, NJ: Lawrence Erlbaum.

Tamis-LeMonda, C. S., J. D. Shannon, N. Cabrera, and M. Lamb. 2004. "Fathers and Mothers at Play with Their 2- and 3-Year-Olds: Contributions to Language and Cognitive Development." *Child Development* 75:1806–1820.

Toth, J. F. and X. Xu. 1999. "Ethnic and Cultural Diversity in Fathers' Involvement: A Racial/Ethnic Comparison of African American, Hispanic, and White Fathers." *Youth and Society* 31: 76–99.

U.S. Census Bureau 2003. *Population Reports*. Washington, DC: Government Printing Office.

White, L. and B. Keith. 1990. "The Effect of Shift Work on the Quality and Stability of Marital Relations." *Journal of Marriage and Family* 52:453–462.

White, L. and S. L. Rogers. 2000. "Economic Circumstances and Family Outcomes: A Review of the 1990s." *Journal of Marriage and Family* 62:1035–1051.

Williams, E., N. Radin, and K. Coggins. 1996. "Paternal Involvement in Childrearing and the School Performance of Ojibwa Children: An Exploratory Study." *Merrill-Palmer Quarterly* 42:578–595.

Yang, J. 1999. "An Exploratory Study of Korean Fathering of Adolescent Children." *Journal of Genetic Psychology* 160:55–68.

Yeung, W. J., J. F. Sandberg, P. E. Davis-Kean, and S. L. Hofferth. 2001. "Children's Time with Fathers in Intact Families." *Journal of Marriage and Family* 63:136–154.

Zimmerman, M. A., D. A. Salem, and P. C. Notaro. 2000. "Make Room for Daddy II: The Positive Effects of Fathers' Role in Adolescent Development." In *Resilience Across Contexts: Family, Work, Culture, and Community*, ed. R. D. Taylor and M. C. Wang, 233–258. Mahwah, NJ: Lawrence Erlbaum.

Zukow–Golding, P. 2002. "Sibling Caregiving." In *Handbook of Parenting*, 2nd ed., ed. M. Bornstein, 253–286. Mahwah, NJ: Lawrence Erlbaum.

Zuzanek, J. 2000. *The Effects of Time Use and Time Pressure on Child Parent Relationships*. Waterloo, Ontario, Canada: Otium.

6

GENDER AND PARENTING ACROSS THE FAMILY LIFE CYCLE

Ayelet Talmi

ACROSS DIFFERENT LIFE STAGES, families experience dynamic relational and organizational shifts driven by children's developmental needs, demographic forces, historical trends, and economic circumstances. Parenting at each stage involves balancing the internal nurturing needs of the family and its members against external factors including resource attainment, education and employment demands, and the sociopolitical context. Here, the underlying assumption is made that both familial and contextual factors interact to impact child outcomes (Bronfenbrenner 1979). With respect to gender differences and similarities across the family life course, questions emerge regarding negotiating division of labor (domestic and paid), child-rearing responsibilities, and the suitability of partners in providing certain types of care and resources at different points in development of the child and family. The family serves as "an organization and a setting for facilitating growth and development of its members" (Hill 1986:20) across different life stages, thereby necessitating exploration of structural and relational components that drive family development.

Families continually reorganize to meet individual member's needs within the context of available resources and environment factors. Both internal (e.g., the age of children, the addition of a family member) and external factors (e.g., employment, historical events) drive renegotiation of roles and responsibilities and alter expectations regarding partner contributions. The current chapter examines the manner in which gender differences in parenting manifest across the life course. These gender differences interact with developmental and sociocultural factors to impact roles, responsibilities, allocation of resources, and child outcomes. The development of families in modern, industrialized societies will be explored using economic (Hill 1986), demographic (Glick 1989), and stage perspectives (Duvall and Hill 1948; McGoldrick and Carter 2003).

ECONOMIC PERSPECTIVE ON FAMILIES

The economic conceptualization of family life course development posits that the periods prior to having children and after children have left home are times of "net accumulation" (Hill 1986). During these periods, males and females gather assets and have greater ability to save assets because their resource needs are fewer. In contrast, the period of child-rearing (parenting) and the period after retirement are conceptualized as times of "deficit financing" (Hill 1986). During child-rearing, accumulation of resources is accompanied by higher resource needs and greater depletion of resources that are allocated to the care of offspring. While parents continue to gather assets to support their offspring, they are simultaneously less able to store assets for future use. In retirement, while child-rearing is typically completed and resources are no longer being allocated to offspring, asset accrual also slows or stops and adults deplete saved assets to meet their resource needs.

An economic analysis of the family life course provides a mechanism for examining asset contributions and resource needs during distinct periods of family development. From this perspective, the cost of parenting includes not only material support of offspring, unpaid domestic labor, and childcare but also confers risks including decreased earnings, decreased retirement income, and decreased access to health and social resources as time for workforce participation becomes restricted. Because of competing demands between domestic and employment roles and responsibilities, parenting may ultimately lessen the societal contribution of adults to the extent contributions are measured through workforce enterprise. For professionals, the timing of parenthood often coincides with generative and productive phases of employment thereby necessitating decisions about whether to delay having children in order to focus on careers. Moreover, having children significantly increases the domestic burden in households (McDonald 2006) with additional members creating more chores and siphoning time and resources that otherwise could be invested in accomplishing tasks. These domestic burdens have traditionally fallen to women and have become increasingly more difficult to negotiate as more women move into the workforce (Craig and Mullan 2010).

The economic perspective is based on the assumption that families can accrue assets at various points in the life course. For the more than forty million Americans living in chronic poverty, asset accrual is not possible. In 2008, 8,147,000 families (10.3 percent) and 13,507,000 children (18.5 percent) were living in poverty (U.S. Bureau of the Census 2011). Families in poverty struggle to afford basic needs such as food and shelter

(Wood, Valdez, Hayashi, and Shen 1990) and substantial evidence documents adverse effects of poverty on child outcomes including achievement (Duncan and Brooks-Gunn 2000). Additionally, poverty compounds the costs of parenting by impacting parental well-being (Elder, Eccles, Ardelt, and Lord 1995) and decreasing parental involvement in children's lives (Waanders, Mendez, and Downer 2007). As a result, families in poverty find themselves in positions of instability and need that may ultimately alter the life course trajectories of both the adult and child members of the family.

Finally, family structure significantly impacts the economic well-being of children and their parents. Numerous studies document economic risks associated with single-parent households and in particular, for those headed by females (Wong, Garfinkel, and McLanahan 1992; Hilton, Desrocher, and Devall 2001; Biblarz and Stacey 2010). In one study, children in households with cohabiting adults had lower rates of poverty, food insecurity, and housing insecurity than their counterparts living in single-parent households (Manning and Brown 2003). In comparison to single-parent households headed by males (13.8 percent), significantly more female-headed (28.7 percent) single-parent households where no spouse is present reported living in poverty in 2008 (U.S. Bureau of the Census 2011).

DEMOGRAPHIC PERSPECTIVE ON FAMILIES

Demographic studies of family life course use national (e.g., U.S. Census Bureau) and international data sources to determine the frequency, timing, and duration of family characteristics and predict changes based on population trends and historical factors (Glick 1989). This research endeavors to detail how families have changed over time and in response to sociocultural and political events, illuminating similarities and differences in family characteristics including age at marriage, age at birth of first child, family size, and duration of widowhood by sociodemographic factors like race, ethnicity, nationality, and age.

Recent sociodemographic trends confirm increases in childlessness, delayed fertility, delayed marriage, smaller families, and increased divorce (Schnittker 2007). Current divorce rates, estimated at 3.6 divorces per 1,000 marriages (U.S. Census Bureau 2005), combined with the fact that women are less likely to remarry post-divorce, have contributed to a significant increase in the number of single-parent families. Beyond examining broad population trends, family demographers conduct in-depth analyses that illuminate shifts in family life course and necessitate redefining characterizations of family life. Bumpass and Raley (1995) distinguished between single parent families and single-parent households on the basis of data suggesting that single parents may reside in households with other family members (e.g., grandparents) or cohabitating partners. According to this line of research, single parent status cannot be determined solely on the basis of marital status but rather must be established by examining parent relationship status (i.e., does the parent have a partner who co-parents) and household composition.

Population shifts including delayed onset of marriage and increased life expectancies have dramatically altered the family life course. More than a century ago, at least one parent was likely to die before their last child was married, while in 1940 couples had a 50 percent chance of spending an average of eleven years in an "empty nest" (Glick 1989). Other demographic trends demonstrate generational effects, such as the growth in the number of married couples without children at home, which resulted from baby boomers launching their children to independence (Day 1996). The demographic perspective identifies periods during the life cycle where gender differences in parenting differentially impact child and adult development, and during which additional social supports are necessary to promote optimal family outcomes.

STAGES OF FAMILY LIFE COURSE DEVELOPMENT

Finally, studies from social and biological sciences have extensively documented the stages of family development and posited models of family life course for varying species. Duvall and Hill (1948) described the formation, expansion, contraction, and eventual dissolution of families. Stage changes are precipitated by changes in the roles, responsibilities, and positions of family members that occur when other family members are added (e.g., birth) or lost (e.g., leaving home, death). Shifts between family life course stages also coincide with significant role alterations for members based on age or developmental level. For example, when children start school caregiving demands decrease, often driving reorganization of family structure and of the roles and responsibilities of specific family members (e.g., a parent who was a primary caregiver of a young child may return to the workforce when that child enters school). The literature applies the following criteria in determining specific family life course stages: change in family size (e.g., birth of a child), developmental age of oldest child (e.g., beginning to attend school), and work status of primary earners (e.g., retirement).

In light of the dynamic nature of families and the myriad factors impacting family life course development, life cycle norms can be utilized to characterize family patterns across cultures, classes, sociocultural circumstances, and global realities. McGoldrick and Carter (2003) identified life cycle changes denoted by fundamental reorganization of the family system. Their model of family life course stages does not inherently link stages to specific ages, nor does it assume traditional family structures (e.g., married, heterosexual couples). Instead, McGoldrick and Carter posit that a uniform, sequential path across the family life course stages does not adequately characterize the significant variability in family life course development.

The process by which families transition between stages requires consideration. According to Rapoport (1963), stressors and precipitating events lead to stage disruptions and changes in roles and responsibilities for family members. Events such as the youngest child leaving home to attend college or live on his/her own may trigger a reorganization of the family, require changes in roles and responsibilities of the remaining family members, and ultimately lead to a stage transition. Similarly, family systems theorists have documented that points of transition across the family life course are often the most stressful and can lead to manifestation of psychopathology (Carter and McGoldrick 1988). Therefore, as families move from one stage to another, both the transition itself and navigating the challenges of the next stage require significant adjustment. To remain stable and organized within a given stage, family members must achieve consensus about numerous issues including division of labor, allocation of resources, ability of members to perform required tasks, and the urgent needs of members (Hill 1986).

The remainder of this chapter describes family life course stages, highlighting gender differences in parenting when relevant. Within each stage, particular attention is paid to interactions among the specific needs of children, parents, and the family unit in shaping the division of labor, negotiation of roles and responsibilities, and parenting practices. An extensive literature documents that effective parenting practices include providing high levels of support and monitoring and using less harsh discipline techniques across diverse sociodemographic contexts and family structures (Amato and Fowler 2002; Browne et al. 2010; Randolph and Radey 2011).

The chapter considers similarities and differences in gendered parenting behaviors across the life span and within varying family constellations.

THE YOUNG COUPLE

From a historical and evolutionary perspective, parenting behaviors are sex-dimorphic and, as such, gender differences in parenting are to be expected. Evolutionary biology studies find that selectivity in choosing a mate is adaptive for females, while males are at an advantage if they seek as many mates as possible, unless their paternal contribution significantly enhances the survival of their offspring (Lancaster 1976; Rossi 1984; Bjorklund and King, chapter 3, this volume). Beyond gendered biological imperatives in coupling, historical factors over the last fifty years have dramatically altered coupling, marriage, and parenthood. First, advances in medicine have led to increased human longevity, enabling women and men to delay parenting and still have ample time to raise children into adulthood (Rossi 1984; Glick 1989). Medical advances have also improved contraceptive options at a time when sexual relations outside of marriage and use of contraception are accepted social norms in broad segments of the population. Second, since World War II, American women have been prominent in the workforce. Notably, it is easier for women to obtain higher levels of education and establish themselves more securely in the workforce when they do not have children (Schnittker 2007). In certain sociodemographic subgroups, greater educational attainment actually contributes to the decisions of single mothers to remain unmarried or unpartnered as their criteria for suitable partners increase (Holland 2009). The confluence of increased longevity, availability of contraception, a tolerant sociocultural context, and an open labor market has enabled women to delay child-rearing, focus on educational attainment, postpone marriage and childbearing, and participate in the workforce.

The family life course itself has been truncated by longer life expectancy and a compressed period of childbearing and child-rearing. Historically, when adult life spans were considerably shorter, parenting consumed a much greater proportion of the life span. Census projections suggest that the number of never-married adults in the Unites States is growing and will continue to do so, with the proportion of single younger adults increasing steadily (Day 1996). Forces including modern gender ideologies, increased presence of women in the workforce, greater educational attainment for women, improved contraception, and a longer latency to parenthood, have reconfigured the desired or ideal contemporary family life cycle in Western cultures.

TRANSITION TO PARENTHOOD

The transition to parenthood results in significant biological, physical, psychological, and emotional changes for males and females (Cowan and Cowan 2000; Gottman and Gottman 2007; McHale 2007; Pruett and Kline Pruett 2009). This transition is associated with decreased marital satisfaction, assumption of more traditional gender roles and responsibilities (even in egalitarian, dual-earner partnerships), and increased risk for perinatal mood disorders for mothers and depression for both partners (Cox, Paley, Payne, and Burchinal 1999; Cowan and Cowan 2003). Although the biological connection between mother and infant is stronger in the newborn period than the bond between father and newborn (e.g., Swain et al. 2008; Doucet 2009a) fathers are essential caregivers during pregnancy and infancy (Yogman, Kindlon, and Earls 1995), providing support to mothers and caring for newborns and young infants.

Newborn behaviors and needs elicit parenting behaviors and function to keep intimate caregivers close. From feeding every few hours, to holding, cleaning, soothing, regulating, and maintaining physiologic (e.g., temperature) and motoric stability (e.g., staying in a tucked, comfortable position), adults must remain in close proximity to their newborn. In a study of mothers' and fathers' attachment status during pregnancy in relation to co-parenting after a baby's birth, Talbot, Baker, and McHale (2009) found that parenting dyads where both partners reported secure attachment patterns in pregnancy exhibited the highest levels of co-parenting cohesion and that prenatal marital quality also predicted co-parenting cohesion. Such findings demonstrate powerful intergenerational transmission of parenting behaviors that actively contribute to the interpersonal experience of newborns and young children in the context of their families.

Social and cultural expectations significantly impact how males and females parent (McMahon 1995; Ruddick 1995; Fox and Worts 1999). While gender socialization produces automatic response patterns and habits (Doucet 2009b) resulting from repeated enactment across the life cycle, gender differences in caregiving of newborns and infants are also influenced by proximity to and experience with newborns and infants. Increased certainty of paternity, shared parental resource attainment, and partnership with a female that encourages involvement with offspring all function to promote paternal involvement with offspring (Rossi 1984; Bjorklund and Jordan, chapter 3, this volume).

In early caregiving of human infants, patterns of initial maternal regulation followed by more egalitarian and communal caregiving emerge.

In general, co-parenting in two-parent families tends to occur after eighteen months of age and follows a period of female primary caregiving. While fathers are as capable of being highly involved and sensitively attuned to their young infants (Parke and Tinsley 1984), mothers more frequently responded to, stimulated, expressed positive affection toward, and took basic care of their infants while fathers engaged in other activities over the course of the first nine months of life (Belsky, Gilstrap, and Rovine 1984). When subsequent children were born to these families, mothers were less involved with their second children but still took primary responsibility for the infants while fathers were taking care of the older children.

Findings from numerous studies of parenting behaviors suggest that mothers are the gatekeepers and primary caregivers of newborns and young infants, regulating the amount of caregiving provided by others, including fathers, until they deem it appropriate for others to participate in care or until they require assistance. Bell and colleagues (2007) found that families transitioned from undifferentiated units (e.g., mothers and fathers providing care) early in the newborn period to having highly differentiated gender stereotypical roles and responsibilities at six weeks of life and ultimately, shifted back to a more integrated and balanced family unit by sixteen weeks. Not surprisingly, integration and balance coincided with the end of parental leave periods, a time when the primary caregiver may be returning to work and caregiving responsibilities must be redistributed.

The conditions under which mothers turn over the care of infants to fathers and other intimate caregivers vary considerably depending on factors including child, maternal, and paternal characteristics, the environment in which the family lives, and resource availability (e.g., suitable caregivers). For example, a first-time mother in a stable, committed relationship with a supportive partner who is egalitarian, interested in caring for the baby, and available, may relinquish nighttime feedings of a newborn to her partner very early in the baby's life. Another mother, whose family depends on her income to survive and is forced to return to work shortly after delivering her baby, may also relinquish nighttime feedings to her partner, but for different reasons than those of the first mother. In contrast, mothers of babies with special health care needs may take longer to share caregiving responsibilities due to concerns that others will not be able to adequately meet their babies' complex needs.

Negotiating the return to work after having a baby requires reconciling ideological principles, expectations, and needs for employment and income. These work-family strategies (Singley and Hynes 2005) are impacted by local, state, and national policies that may inadvertently reinforce traditional division of labor. Families must weigh the benefit of being the full-time primary caregivers of their young children with the costs of income loss, job loss, and financial strain. For many families, returning to work is not optional; it is a financial necessity. Cultural expectations about the definitions of motherhood, fatherhood, and role expectations also shape decision making around workforce re-entry. Because of gender inequities in the labor market, with women earning less and having fewer job opportunities than men, the cost of women staying at home to raise children is less than the cost of men doing so. Women may also be more likely to stay at home after giving birth because their jobs may not offer the flexibility that allows them to meet familial obligations while continuing to participate in the workforce (e.g., breastfeeding-friendly work environments).

Other gender differences in workforce participation emerge during the transition to parenthood. During early parenthood, mothers tend to take leave or reduce their workload and, on average, are slower than fathers to return to work during their child's infancy even when they have a history of previous employment. In contrast, a father's work involvement stays the same or increases during the transition to parenthood (Kaufman and Uhlenberg 2000). Some dual-earner families balance their work-family responsibilities through shift work and turn-taking. In these families, parents take turns being at work and being available for childcare. Negotiating schedules that allow for alternating work and parenting responsibilities between partners enables mothers and fathers to maintain their caregiving primacy and reduces the financial burden of paying for childcare. However, in such cases, a significant toll is exacted on the couple's relationship and on the children's experience of family because less time is available for joint family activities.

In interviews with couples about their employment decisions after the birth of their first child, Singley and Hynes (2005) found that during the period immediately following birth, the majority of women took six to eight weeks of leave using a combination of vacation time, sick leave, and disability. Fathers took one to two weeks off from work using vacation time and sick leave. After the initial transition, mothers made greater changes to their work schedules, moving to part-time schedules, transitioning out of the labor force, or making multiple arrangements. Additionally, couples reorganized their work lives to incorporate new family obligations through changing jobs, refusing extra work or travel, changing work schedules, or decreasing the total number of hours worked. Overall, work-family strategies were shaped by either strong parenting role ideologies or by practical and financial considerations. Singley and Hynes concluded that "couples' use of policies appeared to flow from interactional processes that defined women's jobs and careers as more flexible and their role in family life as more primary" (2005:390).

FAMILIES WITH YOUNG AND SCHOOL AGE CHILDREN

As families transition from infancy and early childhood, their world expands considerably. The expansion is driven, in part, by the presence of a young child who is striving for autonomy and independence while at the same time attempting to acquire the skills necessary for self-care and relationship formation and maintenance. Having established strong relationships with intimate caregivers, preschoolers are ready to make efforts at connecting to a wider range of relationship partners including peers and other adults (Mueller and Cohen 1986). While mothers continue to play a key role in the lives of preschoolers, serving as coordinators, mediators, and navigators of the broader social circles in which preschoolers find themselves, these expanding circles provide opportunities for other caregivers and relationship partners to take on a more prominent role.

Research suggests that fathers of young children feel more able to freely display physical affection (e.g., kisses, hugs, cuddling) than fathers of older children (Doucet 2009a). During early childhood, both mothers and fathers have been found to frequently engage in a variety of parenting behaviors, including educational guidance, physical caretaking, emotional support, discipline-administrative, active-recreational (Kellerman and Katz 1978), and personal interaction (Moon and Hoffman 2008). However, mothers typically engage in physical care and emotional support more frequently than fathers, with fathers also reporting lower levels of personal interaction with their children (Moon and Hoffman 2008).

In a study of paternal engagement in early childhood, Cowdery and Knudson-Martin (2005) found that it was not fathers' inability or lack of knowledge that prevented them from actively caring for their young children, but rather paternal beliefs that mothers were better able to do the job. The more fathers left caregiving tasks to mothers, the less aware they were of what needed to be done and how to engage with their children. Consequently, fathers who were more distally involved had children who were less responsive to them.

Families in this stage continue to strive for balance between family life and the demands of work. Working parents of young children reported feeling rushed, pressed for time, and more strained than parents who do not work (Craig and Mullan 2009). Given the traditional role of fathers as breadwinners, it is not surprising that men spend more time engaged in activities with children on weekends than they do on weekdays (Yeung, Sandberg, David-Kean, and Hofferth 2001). Schnittker (2007) reported that for women, working was associated with better overall health across the life span, although having a child under age six decreased the health benefits of being employed due to the stress of managing multiple demands. The negative impact of combining work and family diminished for mothers when their children were old enough to attend school. In contrast, fathers with young children reported better health outcomes when working full-time as compared to part-time. Fathers who work full-time are likely to have higher paying jobs with better benefits than those who are only able to secure part-time employment, suggesting that socioeconomic differences may also underlie these health outcomes.

In an ethnographic study of Canadian fathers identified as primary caregivers of their young children (e.g., single fathers, stay-at-home fathers, parental leave, or shared caregiving) Doucet (2009a) reported gender differences in paternal manifestation of parental responsibilities. Fathers in this study displayed emotional responsibility through daily interactions with children (e.g., activities, involvement in sports) and by actively promoting independence through expectations of self-sufficiency and teaching life skills. According to Lamb (2000), fathers' nurturance traditionally manifests in play as a way of connecting to children. Research also suggests that in some nontraditional families where fathers are the primary caregivers of young children, both parents reported not fulfilling role expectations for which they were socialized (Radin 1982). In this study, mothers reported not spending enough time taking care of their children and fathers reported not meeting societal expectations of professional achievement and earning. According to Doucet (2009b;113–114), "There is a strong sense that women feel guilty about leaving their child to go back to work and men feel guilty about leaving their work to care for their child. Put differently, mothers feel pulled toward care and connection while fathers feel pulled toward paid work and autonomy."

In childhood, parenting behaviors of mothers and fathers may differentially impact child behaviors and outcomes. Illustrating this, Puustinen and colleagues (2008) found that paternal emotional warmth impeded problem solving for boys, while for girls it was associated with improved problem solving strategies and greater self-confidence.

It is also important to note the bidirectional influence of children and parents on each other. Not only do parent practices affect child outcomes, but child characteristics (e.g., temperament, behavior) affect parent outcomes (e.g., self-efficacy, mood). Coleman and Karraker (2000) reported that mothers who perceived their school-age children as less emotional and more sociable and who had experience with children other than their own endorsed greater parenting self-efficacy than their counterparts who perceived their children as having more difficult temperaments and less sociable and with less experience caring for other children. In this study, higher maternal parenting self-efficacy was also associated with having an older child, higher maternal education, and greater family income. Taken together, these findings highlight the importance of examining the transactional nature of parent-child relationships when considering the impact of parenting across the family life course.

FAMILIES WITH ADOLESCENTS

Adolescence is a time of upheaval and renegotiation of family structure for children and their parents. As young people mature, grow, and develop, their cognitive capacities expand tremendously enabling them to tackle more complex challenges and problems, engage in more sophisticated discourse, and entertain more nuanced perspectives on various social issues. Adolescents become increasingly autonomous, separating from parents and families to spend more time in other social realms including school, extracurricular activities, and peer relationships. These other environments and social realms can exert a powerful influence on an adolescent's opinions, decision making, and behavior.

With the onset of adolescence, family boundaries become more permeable as adolescents bring new friends, activities, and ideas into the family and exert more control over their schedules and relationships. Even with greater permeability in family boundaries, parents remain gatekeepers, helping guide and shape the choices adolescents make about their peers, activities, and driving outcomes including educational attainment (Kan and Tsai 2004). Although teenagers are increasingly independent in their choices and behaviors, their parents maintain a supervisory role, ensuring that adolescents abide by both family and societal rules. An extensive literature documents the relationship between parenting styles and adolescent outcomes. Gordon Simons and Conger (2007) found that having at least one authoritative parent significantly reduced delinquency and depression and increased the likelihood of greater commitment to school, while having two authoritative parents resulted in the best adolescent outcomes. Similarly, adolescents reported higher rates of delinquency and drug use when their parents engaged in less monitoring and supervision, they lived in homes with more conflict, reported less attachment to their parents, and their parents had more lax attitudes about offending (Fagan, Van Horn, Antaramian, and Hawkins 2011). Adolescence is a time when family rituals might change, with adolescents preferring to spend time with friends on weekends rather than spending time with their families. Adolescents are also increasingly capable of and interested in defining their relationships with family and nonfamily members and exert greater influence on what these relationships look like.

With respect to gender differences in parenting, research has shown that fathers may have more challenges relating to and remaining close with their daughters during adolescence as puberty and sexuality become more salient (McGoldrick and Carter 2003; McKinney and Renk 2008). On the whole, adolescents report decreased parental monitoring as they get older, with females reporting greater monitoring and closer attachment to their mothers and males reporting less family conflict and closer relationships with their fathers (Fagan, Van Horn, Antaramian, and Hawkins 2011). However, even in late adolescence, females and males report that their well-being is related to both mother's and father's parenting and expectations, the family environment in which they live, and conflict with both parents (McKinney and Renk 2008). With these and other changes in the parent-child relationship during adolescence, there is an increased capacity for distancing and disconnection. However, it is important to note that on the whole, both male and female adolescents remain close to their parents and do not experience the severe conflict and rebellion described in developmental theories of adolescents (Tavris 1992).

In African-American families, the presence of mothers and fathers has been shown to differentially impact male and female adolescents. When both mothers and fathers are present in the home, adolescents of both sexes displayed similar psychological outcomes, whereas in father-absent homes, boys are at greater risk than girls for mental health and behavioral problems (Mandara and Murray 2000, 2006; Mandara, Murray, and Joyner 2005). Mandara, Varner, and Richman (2010) predicted that differential socialization patterns would emerge for unmarried African-American mothers, who traditionally give girls responsibilities and have higher educational expectations of them than they do of boys—"raise" their daughters and "love" their sons. Their results confirmed this hypothesis, showing that girls reported the highest levels of household responsibilities, expectations, and rules and also the highest achievement. Firstborn boys reported similar socialization to the firstborn girls, with slightly fewer rules about their whereabouts. However, later-born boys reported greater conflict with their mothers, fewer responsibilities, more freedom, less ability to make decisions for themselves, less cognitive stimulation (e.g., going to a museum, playing an instrument), and lower achievement as compared to girls. Taken together, these results suggest that for African-American adolescents, gender and birth order contribute to socialization experiences when they are being raised by their mothers. In African-American communities where, on average, females outperform males in achievement and education, differential parental investment in children may maximize the success of girls, for whom mothers have higher expectations.

FAMILIES AT MIDLIFE

The pattern of active, daily parenting characteristic of infancy, early childhood, and adolescence typically changes during the midlife stage for adults. As life expectancies have increased, parents find themselves preparing and launching their young adult children twenty years before they are eligible for or interested in retirement, making this stage the longest in the family life course. In families where divorce, remarriage, and the birth of additional children occurs, parents may find themselves launching different sets of children at different times. Regardless of the timing, when children leave home, family roles and responsibilities are reconstituted.

The daily burdens and domestic demands in the family of origin decrease as young adults establish their own households. However, young adults may still be financially dependent on their parents and continue to require financial and emotional resources even if they do not live in the same household. Additionally, many families make significant contributions to the educational expenses of young adults. In times of economic stress and uncertainty, many families find themselves unable to launch young adults, as finding employment that affords economic self-sufficiency is difficult and setting up a separate household can be prohibitively expensive. For some families, it may be beneficial to have young adults remain in the household and contribute some of their earnings to keep families financially solvent. Even in cases where young adults leave home, changes in their own family life course (e.g., a divorce or break-up) may result in returning to live with their parents. Finally, as young adults leave their families of origin and renegotiate relationships with their parents, opportunities emerge for the introduction of new members into the family system—the partners and, eventually, spouses of young adults.

Mothers, who have functioned as primary caregivers for many years, may look forward to cultivating other interests, focusing on work, and developing relationships with time afforded to them by decreased caregiving demands (DeVries, Kerrick, and Oetinger 2007). In contrast, fathers may find themselves yearning for closeness with children who are no longer within arm's reach (McGoldrick and Carter 2003). Whereas mothers tend to remain closer with their children (especially their daughters) than fathers (Rossi and Rossi 1990), fathers in this stage of the family life cycle tend to invest more time in their work. Both husbands and wives hold the belief that women should maintain family relationships with children who no longer live at home.

THE FAMILY IN LATER LIFE

In the last stage of the family life course, the nest is empty, parents are aging, and retirement may be on the horizon. Parents may find themselves with fewer formal societal obligations and roles to fulfill. As the family decreases in size, parents may relocate the family home (Bures 2009), downsizing to a space that better fits their needs or relocating to be closer to their children and extended families. This stage has become increasingly important because with longer life expectancies, families are in a period of contraction for many more years than in the past. Today, empty-nest baby boomers are a rapidly growing demographic, representing more than seven million households (Day 1996). As these baby boomers continue to age, there will be a corresponding growth of people in this stage of the family life course.

More than 80 percent of adults over age sixty-five live within an hour of at least one of their children (Walsh 1999). Ongoing connection to children is facilitated through proximity, health and social needs, and with the arrival of grandchildren. Many grandparents continue to provide considerable assistance to their children by helping to care for the grandchildren. Contrary to the idea that family relationships become less frequent and intense during this phase in the family life course, relationships may become more intense and require more frequent contact depending on parental and familial needs. During this stage, roles may be reversed, with children taking care of the long-term health needs of their aging parents and becoming more central to their parents' support systems. Intergenerational caregiving patterns emerge, which improve well-being and buffer depressive symptoms in elders (Whitbeck, Hoyt, and Tyler 2001). For instance, aging fathers who have a caring relationship with an adult child report fewer depressive symptoms.

Gender differences exist in the amount of time spent by adults caring for their parents. Women spend more hours providing care to parents and in-laws than do men, and aging mothers are more likely to be receiving help from their children than are fathers (Hammer and Neal 2008). Research on gender differences has shown that men are more likely to help their parents with instrumental activities of daily living (IADLs) such as grocery shopping, writing checks, and mowing lawns, than activities of daily living (ADLs) such as bathing, dressing, and feeding, which are usually done by females. Thus, while both males and females engage in elder care, females are more likely to engage in tasks that are physically draining and that interrupt their daily activities and routines when compared with males whose assistance and involvement is more periodic, circumscribed, and can be done more flexibly. Unlike child-rearing, wherein the child's physical and emotional dependency gradually diminishes as their competence and skill increases, parent-caring involves the caregiver meeting the sustained or increasing physical and emotional needs of the older person who is in decline (Singleton 2000).

A recent national telephone screening survey revealed that between 9 and 13 percent of American households with adults over age thirty had dual-earner couples who were caretaking for both children and their parents (Neal and Hammer 2007). Especially for women sandwiched between their familial roles and responsibilities and the obligations of caretaking for their elderly parents, this increased pressure to provide for the needs of multiple generations of family members can cause increased role strain and stress, depleting them of the requisite energy to properly meet the needs of all those for whom they are responsible. Studies have shown that employed caregivers of elderly parents report more absenteeism, more distractions at work, more physical and mental health problems, and loss of career advancements. In one study, 22 percent of men and 35.6 percent of women reported depression scores above the clinical cutoff (Hammer and Neal 2008). Women in this study reported higher levels of work-family conflict than men while simultaneously reporting higher levels of positive spillover from family to work. They also reported more absenteeism due to child or parent care responsibilities than did their husbands.

In general, women in this stage of life are more likely to be cared for by their children, which may increase the likelihood that these grandmothers will play an important caregiving role in the lives of their grandchildren. Aging fathers may have fewer opportunities to contribute to their children's families, particularly if they do not have a spouse to mediate the relationship. Nonetheless, even at this last phase of the family life course, contraction of the family back to the original couple does not preclude connection and involvement with the growing and evolving families created by their children.

SINGLE-PARENT FAMILIES, DIVORCE, AND REMARRIAGE

In 2010, more than twelve million American households were headed by single mothers and more than three million by single fathers (U.S. Bureau of the Census 2010). Thirty-one percent of all families can be classified as single-parent, with 85 percent of these households being headed by mothers (Cunningham and Knoester 2007), a trend that likely reflects the tendency for women to bear the brunt of child-rearing responsibilities post-divorce. What these data do not adequately represent is the diversity in types of single-parent households. Some single-parent households result from divorces or dissolutions of partnerships. In these cases, children may be raised in two separate single-parent households, one headed by their mother and the other headed by their father. Other single-parent households are headed by women or men who have children without being in a committed relationship. Widowers comprise another group of single-parent households. Households headed by single grandparents raising their grandchildren represent yet another demographic.

In single-parent households, parents are limited in their ability to divide roles and responsibilities. The burden of parenting typically falls to one person who is responsible for the emotional, instrumental, and financial support of children. This reduction in available members to assume roles places additional burdens on the remaining family members, including children being raised in these households. Children in single-parent families may be expected to take on some of the domestic work (e.g., chores, caring for younger children) to decrease the burden on the only adult in the family.

While single mothers and fathers have to be "all-in-one" parents, some gender differences emerge when considering quality of life. For example, poverty rates are higher in families headed by single mothers than those headed by single fathers due to higher male earning capacity (Biblarz and Stacey 2010; Hilton, Desrocher, and Devall 2001). In times of national economic strain, the impact on single-parent households may be even more profound because only one adult is providing the sole financial support for the family.

Cunningham and Knoester (2007) found that single parents reported more symptoms of depression and alcohol abuse than married parents. Mothers in this study reported more traditional depressive symptoms while fathers were more likely to abuse alcohol. Depressive symptoms for parents were associated with experiencing economic strain and with the amount of time spent doing domestic work. More importantly, spending time with children was negatively associated with depression symptoms, suggesting that parents who spent more time with their children were less depressed. Contrasting single and married parenthood, the authors concluded that marriage confers a benefit of greater well-being and provides parents with a sense of meaning and purpose in their lives. Consistent with these findings, women reported greater life satisfaction around having children when they were in relationships (Kohler, Behrman, and Skytthe 2005). Indeed, the benefits of two-parent households appear to extend beyond support, division of labor, and ability to rely on a partner for assistance, reaching into the realm of adult psychological and emotional well-being.

While single fathers and mothers experience social isolation, decreased standard of living, and restricted workforce options because of child-rearing responsibilities, some gender differences emerge (Rossi 1984; Biblarz and Stacey 2010). Rossi (1984) found that fathers received more help from the community and relatives than mothers but were less likely to ask for help if they were not receiving sufficient support. Single fathers made fewer social contacts than single mothers given that male social contacts are made primarily through work and their greater domestic burden limited the time available for socialization with colleagues. Single fathers also reported more worries about meeting the emotional needs of their children, especially daughters. In contrast, single mothers reported greater anxiety around maintaining standards of living and were more concerned about discipline and structure than were fathers.

The literature suggests that additional gender differences between single mothers and fathers exist. In one study, single mothers spent more time with their children, exhibited more skilled parenting, and displayed more affection and warmth than single fathers (Biblarz and Stacey 2010). Single mothers were more actively engaged in their child's life, knowing the names of friends, participating in school-related activities, and attending to homework and academic responsibilities than were single fathers. Single mothers also had higher levels of parental control than single fathers, which might help explain increased levels of conflict with their children. In other research, maternal partnership transitions in the first five years of a child's life have been associated with decreases in children's verbal abilities and increased behavioral problems, especially for boys (Cooper et al. 2011).

In families where single parents remarry, they may find themselves simultaneously working on their marital and parenting relationships. Childbearing may also accompany remarriage, thereby putting the family back to an earlier stage and expanding the time from having children to launching them. In some cases, families may end up launching two sets of children with several years separating the launchings. Without remarriage, the cycle for a single woman more closely parallels the trajectory of intact families, but is more difficult due to financial and domestic burdens and social isolation (Hill 1986).

Taken together, the literature on single parenting suggests that single-parent households face numerous challenges, not the least of which is the increased responsibility of caring for children alone and the greater likelihood that female-headed households will experience greater financial and economic strain. Undoubtedly, single parents experience more parenting stress than do couples. Research on child outcomes in single-parent families presents mixed results. Some studies demonstrate the negative effects of a father's absence, others report worse outcomes for boys and girls in single-parent families, and yet others find no differences in child outcomes when comparing children being raised by single-parent versus coupled parents.

NONTRADITIONAL FAMILY CONSTELLATIONS

Today, many children are being raised by same-sex couples and by single females and males who choose to parent without being in partnered relationships. Lesbian and gay couples account for 1 percent of families (O'Connell and Lofquist 2009), though these figures likely underestimate the number of households with same-sex parents who are raising children. Some have arrived at parenthood through adoption, some through assistive reproductive technology (e.g., donor insemination), and some as stepparents. However, the vast majority of the literature on gender differences in parenting has been based on studies of married, heterosexual couples and studies of single parents. These studies confound family structure (e.g., married/ unmarried, two-parent household/single-parent household) with gender. A smaller literature exists with data on same-sex and different-sex parenting and on single-mother versus single-father families.

The literature on same-sex parenting reveals higher levels of co-parenting satisfaction for lesbian couples and more positive parenting practices including greater parental awareness and concern, better parent/child interaction, more time spent in play and shared interests, and greater warmth, affection, and attachment than for heterosexual couples (Biblarz and Stacey 2010). In both same-sex and heterosexual relationships, mothers engaged in more caregiving than their partners and spent more time caregiving than in paid work. The transition to parenthood exacted a similar toll on heterosexual and lesbian couples, with increased stress and decreased relationship satisfaction reported in both groups. Gay male parents exhibit parenting that is more similar to mothers than fathers in part because when gay men parent, they are actively choosing to be the primary caregivers. In fact, more gay fathers are stay-at-home dads than gay mothers. In considering child outcomes, the majority of studies find similarities in well-being of children raised by heterosexual or lesbian parents (Crowl, Ahn, and Baker 2008; Tasker 2010). Some benefits conferred to children being raised by lesbian parents included greater attachment security, fewer behavioral problems, greater perceptions that parents are available and dependable, and increased capacity for discussing emotional issues.

PARENTING AND WORK

Extensive research demonstrates a greater domestic and psychological burden associated with parenting (Bird 1997). While on the whole, women engage in more domestic duties than men, the largest gender gap is evidenced in married couples (South and Spitze 1994). In fact, being married creates an additional seven hours of work each week for women (Panel Study of Income Dynamics April 2008). When caring for children is added, the gender gap widens further. Research comparing household time spent in paid work, domestic work, and childcare for males and females with and without children in the United States, Australia, Italy, France, and Denmark, found that in all five countries, total time demands were higher for households with children than those without (Craig and Mullan 2010). In households with children, men did more paid work and women did more domestic work and childcare than in households without children. Even when mothers worked outside the home, they spent significantly more time in childcare activities than fathers in all of the countries studied. On weekdays, mothers in the United States spent an average of 3.6 hours caring for children in contrast to fathers' 1.3 hours. On weekends, mothers spent 4.2 hours each day caring for children while fathers spent 3.2 hours each day. This study clearly demonstrates that in industrialized societies around the world, parents spend more time doing paid and domestic work than nonparents. Moreover, the time demands are more pronounced for women than for men and as such, women's daily lives are more significantly impacted when they have children than are the daily lives of men.

Achieving the elusive work-family balance may be less relevant for families in financial distress. Families that depend on two incomes or that rely exclusively on the income of a single parent have fewer degrees of freedom with respect to parenting responsibilities. In dual-earner families, both mothers and fathers reported less parenting distress with more egalitarian division of labor (Deater-Deckard and Scarr 1996). In a period of high unemployment and underemployment, caregiving responsibilities may default to the parent who is not currently in the labor force or who is working less. More and more fathers are finding themselves in positions of head of domestic household due to unemployment. As domestic heads of household, fathers assume the roles and responsibilities related to scheduling, child-rearing, and maintaining a household while their partners are out in the workforce earning income that is used to support the family. In times of severe financial stress, the drive to ensure family survival by providing food, shelter, and clothing supersedes other important parental activities such as playing, encouraging achievement, supporting emotional needs, spending time together. Parents under such duress become preoccupied with worries, stress, and needing to work, and may be unavailable at a time when their children might require additional support and reassurance. At the very least, they have less emotional energy and less time available to foster healthy relationships with their children.

CONCLUSION: SUPPORTING PARENTING AND FAMILY SHIFTS ACROSS THE LIFE COURSE

Families are constantly evolving, dynamic systems. Economic, demographic, and stage models of family life course have been used to capture how families change over time. This chapter explored gender differences and partner contributions in parenting across the family life course. Life stage theories are instructive in characterizing the stages through which families move as they form, expand, stabilize, and contract. Using these stages of family development also helps illuminate the periods during which gender differences in parenting are more or less salient and influential with respect to child and family outcomes. Importantly, even within a particular life course stage, families continually reorganize and renegotiate roles, responsibilities, and expectations to meet the needs of different members. These within stage fluctuations are driven by internal factors and external factors.

The magnitude and influence of gender differences in parenting on child and family outcomes depends, in part, on the stage of the family life course. Throughout child-rearing, mothers assume greater responsibility for scheduling, child-rearing, and domestic work while fathers engage in more paid work. However, the literature as a whole suggests that both mothers and fathers assume critical parenting responsibilities throughout a child's life and over the course of the family life cycle. Both fathers and mothers can and do assume similar parenting roles and responsibilities. When two parents are available, roles and responsibilities may be divided and be complementary. When one parent is available, he or she may provide what a child needs to grow and thrive, utilizing more androgynous parenting practices.

It is of the utmost importance that strategies and policies that promote optimal parenting across the family life course be implemented and sustained for both mothers and fathers. Fostering parenting confidence and competence through repeated experiences with children across the family life course is critical to both mothers' and fathers' skills and to developing positive and enduring relationships with their children. Repeated, daily interactions — micro-interactions — that occur routinely across different stages of a child and family's development are woven into the fabric that becomes the family's relationships. Focusing on these relationships promotes enhanced fathering, mothering, and collaborative parenting. Developing and implementing family-friendly parental leave and workforce policies that take into account the unique circumstances and family constellations in today's world are necessary to maintain family economic stability and nurture the development of healthy, strong relationships throughout the family life cycle.

REFERENCES

Amato, P. and F. Fowler. 2002. "Parenting Practices, Child Adjustment, and Family Diversity." *Journal of Marriage and Family* 64(3):703–716.

Belsky J., B. Gilstrap, and M. Rovine. 1984. "The Pennsylvania Infant and Family Development Project, I: Stability and Change in Mother-Infant and Father-Infant Interaction in a Family Setting at One, Three, and Nine months." *Child Development* 55:692–705.

Biblarz, T. J. and J. Stacey. 2010. "How Does Gender of Parents Matter?" *Journal of Marriage and Family* 72:3–22.

Bird, C. E. 1997. "Gender Differences in the Social and Economic Burdens of Parenting and Psychological Distress." *Journal of Marriage and Family* 59(4):809–823.

Bronfenbrenner, U. 1979. *The Ecology of Human Development.* Cambridge: Harvard University.

Browne, D. T., A. Odueyungbo, L. Thabane, C. Byrne, and L. A. Smart. 2010. "Parenting-by-Gender Interactions in Child Psychopathology: Attempting to Address Inconsistencies with a Canadian National Database." *Child and Adolescent Psychiatry and Mental Health* 4(5):1–13.

Bumpass, L. L. and R. K. Raley. 1995. "Redefining Single-Parent Families: Cohabitation and Changing Family Reality." *Demography* 32(1):97–109.

Bures, R. M. 2009. "Moving the Nest: The Impact of Coresidential Children on Mobility in Later Midlife." *Journal of Family Issues* 30:837–851.

Carter, B. and M. McGoldrick. 1988. "Overview the Changing Family Life Cycle: A Framework for Family Therapy." In *Family Life Cycle: A Framework for Family Therapy*, 2nd ed., ed. B. Carter and M. McGoldrick, 3–28. New York: Gardner.

Coleman, P. K., and K. H. Karraker. 2000. "Parenting Self-Efficacy Among Mothers of School-Age Children: Conceptualization, Measurement, and Correlates." *Family Relations* 49(1):13–24.

Cooper, C. E., C. A. Osborne, A. N. Beck, and S. S. McLanahan. 2011. "Partnership Instability, School Readiness, and Gender Disparities." *Sociology of Education* 84(3):246–259.

Cowan, C. P. and P. A. Cowan. 2000. *When Partners Become Parents.* New York: Lawrence Erlbaum.

Cowan, P. A. and C. P. Cowan. 2003. "Normative Family Transitions, Normal Family Processes, and Healthy Child Development." In *Normal Family Processes: Growing Diversity and Complexity*, 3rd ed., ed. F. Walsh, 424–459. New York: Guilford.

Cox, M. J., B. Paley, C. C. Payne, and M. Burchinal. 1999. "The Transition to Parenthood: Marital Conflict and Withdrawal and Parent-Infant Interactions." In *Conflict and Cohesion in Families: Causes and Consequences*, ed. M. J. Cox and J. Brooks-Gunn, 87–104. Mahwah, NJ: Lawrence Erlbaum.

Craig, L. and K. Mullan. 2009. "The Policeman and the Part-Time Sales Assistant: Household Labour Supply, Family Time and Subjective Time Pressure in Australia 1997–2006." *Journal of Comparative Family Studies* 40:545–560.

Craig, L. and K. Mullan. 2010. "Parenthood, Gender and Work-Family Time in the United States, Australia, Italy, France, and Denmark." *Journal of Marriage and Family* 72:1344–1361.

Crowl, A. L., S. Ahn, and J. Baker. 2008. "A Meta-Analysis of Developmental Outcomes for Children of Same-Sex and Heterosexual Parents." *Journal of GLBT Family Studies* 4:385–407.

Cunningham, A. and C. Knoester. 2007. "Marital Status, Gender, and Parents' Psychological Well-Being." *Sociological Inquiry* 77:264–287.

Day, J. C. 1996. *Projections of the Number of Households and Families in the United States: 1995 to 2010.* U.S. Bureau of the Census, Current Population Reports, 25–1129. Washington, DC: U.S. Government Printing Office.

Deater-Deckard, K. and S. Scarr. 1996. "Parenting Stress Among Dual-Earner Mothers and Fathers." *Journal of Family Psychology* 10(1):45–59.

Doucet, A. 2009a. "Dad and Baby in the First Year: Gendered Responsibilities and Embodiment." *The ANNALS of the American Academy of Political and Social Science* 624:78–98.

Doucet, A. 2009b. "Gender Equality and Gender Differences: Parenting, Habitus, and Embodiment." The 2008 Porter Lecture. *CRS/RCD* 46(2):103–121.

Duncan, G. J. and J. Brooks-Gunn. 2000. "Family Poverty, Welfare Reform, and Child Development." *Child Development* 71(1):188–196.

Fagan, A. A., M. L. Van Horn, S. Antaramian, and J. D. Hawkins. 2011. "How Do Families Matter? Age and Gender Differences in Family Influences on Delinquency and Drug Use." *Youth Violence and Juvenile Justice* 9(2):150–170.

Glick, P. C. 1989. "The Family Life Cycle and Social Change." *Family Relations* 38:123–129.

Gordon Simons, L. and R. D. Conger. 2007. "Linking Mother-Father Differences in Parenting to a Typology of Family Parenting Styles and Adolescent Outcomes." *Journal of Family Issues* 28(2):212–241.

Gottman, J. and J. Gottman. 2007. *And Baby Makes Three.* New York: Crown.

Hammer, L.B. and M. B. Neal. 2008. Working Sandwiched-Generation Caregivers: Prevalence, Characteristics, and Outcomes. *The Psychologist-Manager Journal* 11:93–112.

Hill, R. 1986. "Life Cycle Stages for Types of Single Parent Families: Of Family Development Theory." *Family Relations* 35:19–29.

Hilton, J. M., S. Desrocher, and E. Devall. 2001. "Comparison of Role Demands. Relationships and Child-Functioning in Single-Mother, Single-Father, and Intact Families." *Journal of Divorce and Remarriage* 35:29–57.

Holland, R. 2009. "Perceptions of Mate Selection for Marriage Among African American, College-Educated, Single Mothers." *Journal of Counseling & Development* 87:170–178.

Kan, K. and W. Tsai. 2004. "Parenting Practices and Children's Education Outcomes." *Economics of Education Review* 24(1):29–43.

Kaufman, G. and P. Uhlenberg. 2000. "The Influence of Parenthood on the Work Effort of Married Men and Women." *Social Forces* 78:931–947.

Kellerman, J. and E. R. Katz. 1978. "Attitudes Toward the Division of Child-Rearing Responsibility." *Sex Roles* 4:505–512.

Kohler, H., J. R. Behrman, and A. Skytthe. 2005. "Partner + Children = Happiness? The Effect of Fertility and Partnerships on Well-Being." *Population and Development Review* 31:407–445.

Lamb, M. E. 2000. "The History of Research on Father Involvement: An Overview." *Marriage and Family Review* 29:23–42.

Lancaster, J. B. 1976. "Sex Roles in Primate Societies." In *Sex Differences: Social and Biological Perspectives*, ed. M. S. Teitlebaum, 22–62. Garden City, NY: Doubleday-Anchor.

Mandara, J. and C. B. Murray. 2000. "The Effects of Parental Marital Status, Family Income, and Family Functioning on African American Adolescent Self-Esteem." *Journal of Family Psychology* 14:475–490.

Mandara, J. and C. B. Murray. 2006. "Father's Absence and African American Adolescent Drug Use." *Journal of Divorce and Remarriage* 46:1–12.

Mandara, J., C. B. Murray, and T. Joyner. 2005. "The Impact of Fathers' Absence on African American Adolescents' Gender Role Development." *Sex Roles* 53:207–220.

Mandara, J., F. Varner, and S. Richman. 2010. "Do African American Mothers Really 'Love' Their Sons and 'Raise' Their Daughters?" *Journal of Family Psychology* 24:41–50.

Manning, W. D. and S. L. Brown. 2003. "Children's Economic Well-Being in Cohabiting Parent Families: An Update and Extension." Paper presented at the annual meeting of the Population Association of America, Minneapolis, Minnesota.

McDonald, P. 2006. "Low Fertility and the State: The Efficacy of Policy." *Population and Development Review* 32:485–510.

McGoldrick, M. and B. Carter. 2003. "The Family Life Cycle." In *Normal Family Processes: Growing Diversity and Complexity*, 3rd ed., ed. F. Walsh, 375–398. New York: Guilford.

McHale, J. P. 2007. *Charting the Bumpy Road of Coparenthood: Understanding the Challenges of Family Life*. Washington, DC: Zero to Three.

McKinney, C. and K. Renk. 2008. "Multivariate Models of Parent-Late Adolescent Gender Dyads: The Importance of Parenting Processes in Predicting Adjustment." *Child Psychiatry and Human Development* 39(2):147–170.

Mendoza, S. P. and W. A. Mason. 1986. "Parental Division of Labour and Differentiation of Attachments in a Monogamous Primate (*Callicebus moloch*)." *Animal Behavior* 34:1336–1347.

Moon, M. and C. D. Hoffman. 2008. "Mothers and Fathers' Differential Expectancies and Behaviors: Parent x Child Gender Effects." *The Journal of Genetic Psychology* 164:261–279.

Neal, M. B. and L. B. Hammer. 2007. *Working Couples Caring for Children and Aging Parents: Effects on Work and Well-Being*. Mahwah, NJ: Lawrence Erlbaum.

O'Connell, M. and D. Lofquist. 2009. "Counting Same-Sex Couples: Official Estimates and Unofficial Guesses." Paper presented at the Annual Meeting of the Population Association of America, Detroit, Michigan.

Parke, R. D. and B. J. Tinsley. 1984. "Fatherhood: Historical and Contemporary Perspectives." In *Life-Span Developmental Psychology: Historical and Generational Effects*, ed. K. McCluskey and H. W. Reese. New York: Academic Press.

Pruett, K. and M. Kline Pruett. 2009. *Partnership Parenting*. Cambridge, MA: Da Capo.

Puustinen, M., A. L. Lyyra, R. L. Metsäpelto, and L. Pulkkinen. 2008. "Children's Help Seeking: The Role of Parenting." *Learning and Instruction* 18(2):160–171.

Radin, N. 1982. "Primary Caregiving and Role-Sharing Fathers." In *Non-Traditional Families: Parenting and Child Development*, ed. M. E. Lamb, 173–204. Hillsdale, NJ: Lawrence Erlbaum.

Randolph, K. A. and M. Radey. 2011. "Measuring Parenting Practices Among Parents of Elementary School-Aged Youth." *Research on Social Work Practice* 21:88–97.

Rapoport, R. 1963. "Normal Crises, Family Structure and Mental Health." *Family Process* 2:68:80.

Rossi, A. S. 1984. "Gender and Parenthood." *American Sociological Review* 49:1–19.

Rossi, A. S. and P. H. Rossi. 1990. *Of Human Bonding: Parent-Child Relations Across the Life Course*. New York: Aldine de Gruyter.

Schnittker, J. 2007. "Working More and Feeling Better: Women's Health, Employment, and Family Life, 1974–2004." *American Sociological Review* 72:221–238.

Singleton, J. 2000. "Women Caring for Elderly Family Members: Shaping Non-Traditional Work and Family Initiatives." *Journal of Comparative Family Studies* 31:367–375.

Singley, S. G. and K. Hines. 2005. "Transitions to Parenthood: Work-Family Policies, Gender, and the Couple Context." *Gender and Society* 19:376–397.

South, S. J. and G. Spitze. 1994. "Housework in Marital and Non-Marital Households." *American Sociological Review* 59:327–347.

Swain, J., E. Taskgin, L. Mayes, R. Feldman, R. Constable, and J. Leckman. 2008. "Maternal Brain Response to Own Baby Cry." *Journal of Child Psychology and Psychiatry* 49:1042–1052.

Tasker, F. 2010. "Same-Sex Parenting and Child Development: Reviewing the Contribution of Parental Gender." *Journal of Marriage and Family* 72(1):35–40.

Tavris, C. 1992. *The Mismeasure of Women*. New York: Simon & Schuster.

U.S. Bureau of the Census. 2005. "Marital History for People 15 Years and Older, by Age and Sex: 2004—All Races [Data File]." United States Census Bureau, Housing and Household Economic Statistics Division, Fertility & Family Statistics Branch.

U.S. Bureau of the Census. 2010. "America's Families and Living Arrangements: 2010." www.census.gov/population/www/socdemo/hh-fam/cps2010.html. Accessed January 4, 2010.

U.S. Bureau of the Census. 2011. "Income, Poverty, and Health Insurance Coverage in the United States: 2008." In *Current Population Reports, P60-236*, ed. Carmen DeNavas-Walt, Bernadette D. Proctor, and Jessica C. Smith. Washington, DC: U.S. Government Printing Office.

Waanders, C., J. L. Mendez, and J. Downer. 2007. "Parent Characteristics, Economic Stress, and Neighborhood Context as Predictors of Parent Involvement in Preschool Children's Education." *Journal of School Psychology* 45:619–636.

Walsh, F. 1999. "Families in Later Life: Opportunities and Challenges." In *The Expanded Family Life Cycle*, ed. B. Carter and M. McGoldrick. Boston: Allyn & Bacon.

Whitbeck, L.B., D. R. Hoyt, and K. A. Tyler. 2001. "Family Relationship Histories, Intergenerational Relationship Quality, and Depressed Affect Among Rural Elderly People." *The Journal of Applied Gerontology* 20:214–229.

Wong, Y. L., I. Garfinkel, I., and S. McLanahan. 1992. "Single-Mothers in Eight Countries: Economic Status and Social Policy." *Luxembourg Income Studies Working Papers*, Working Paper No. 76.

Wood, D., R. B. Valdez, T. Hayashi, and A. Shen. 1990. "Homeless and Housed Families in Los Angeles: A Study Comparing Demographic, Economic, and Family Function Characteristics." *American Journal of Public Health* 80:1049–1052.

Yeung, J., J. F. Sandberg, P. David-Kean, and S. Hofferth. 2001. "Children's Time with Fathers in Intact Families." *Journal of Marriage and Family* 63:136–154.

Yogman, M. W., D. Kindlon, and F. Earls. 1995. "Father Involvement and Cognitive/Behavioral Outcomes of Preterm Infants." *Journal of the American Academy of Child and Adolescent Psychiatry* 34:58–66.

PART TWO

IMPLICATIONS FOR CHILDREN, COUPLES, AND FAMILIES

7

ESSENTIAL ELEMENTS OF THE CARETAKING CRUCIBLE

Kathleen Kovner Kline and Brian Stafford

THIS CHAPTER WILL EXAMINE the essential elements of the "caretaking crucible," that is, the developmental context that appears to support optimal early child development. We will attempt to provide a dynamic portrait in which the neurophysiological trajectory of child development that begins at conception is shaped by the physical, social, emotional, and cultural contexts in which the young person progresses. Development will be viewed as a multi-layered feedback system, in which a child's genetic and biological possibilities are shaped by concentric layers of proximal and distant environments, which in turn shape the next stage of genetic and biological possibility.

We will begin our discussion with a review of current models of child development. Next, we examine the neuroanatomical development of the child's brain, elucidating the basic pattern of early neural brain growth from fetal life into the preschool years. We will then examine the ways in which early brain growth—and overall health—can be affected by the child's earliest environment, the womb, noting the ways in which the maternal fetal environment is affected by familial, social, and cultural influences. Moving on from the womb, we will look closely at the child's early attachment system, the first extrauterine system of caregiving experienced. Next, we will take on a more elaborate discussion of the ways in which one's original genetic nature is shaped by the experience of one's environmental nurture to produce behaviors that can be adaptive or appear pathological in our current technological and information oriented culture.

Finally, we will consider evidence from pathological and suboptimal child-rearing environments. By examining these deficient contexts, together with results from interventions to remediate their deleterious outcomes, we come closer to identifying some of the critical ingredients for optimal child development.

This chapter will touch upon issues of gender in parenting and caretaking only obliquely, and somewhat asymmetrically, as mothers have a biologically more intimate relationship with their offspring and our research models have focused much more intensively on the socioemotional aspects of mothering more than fathering. However, the overarching principle of multilayered systems of care sheds light on the potential impact of fathers, from their genetic contribution, to their direct physical and emotional support of children and their mothers, to their role in engaging and sustaining extended familial, social, institutional, and cultural systems that promote optimal child development.

DEVELOPMENTAL THEORIES AND MODELS

For many decades, untested theories of development guided our understanding of early childhood. These theories have been revised, disposed of, or replaced by scientific evidence from cognitive psychology, behavioral genetics, neuro-imaging, neurobiology, and ethology, among many other disciplines. This research into early childhood development and the study of its contexts in the past forty years has afforded greater understanding of development and allowed for greater insight into cultural and clinical issues, including optimal, suboptimal, and pathologic contexts. Formerly unapproachable constructs have been elucidated by collaboration among researchers, clinicians, and theoreticians and inform current clinical insights.

In this section, we present a brief overview of some models of infant development. Three overarching points are emphasized throughout. First, infants are not passive recipients in the developmental crucible; in fact, they are active participants in their development, and individual differences in their characteristics and capacities have important implications for how infants are experienced by their caregivers. Second, the caregiving environment is the crucible within which individual differences in development in the first three years of life are shaped, preparing infants for transition to the broader influences of the preschool years and beyond. Finally, development occurs within the enabling or limiting multiple dynamic contexts of biology, relationships, culture, and technology.

Whereas theories of development describe the evolution of particular developmental lines such as cognition, language, and moral development, models of development are more concerned with the process by which development proceeds. How do individuals change or remain the same over time? What drives both continuities and discontinuities in development? And how do the biological and environmental influences interplay with development? Although extremist positions in the debate about nature and nurture are much more rare, the debate about the role of environmental and genetic influences continues to this day. We highlight several useful models, including behavioral genetics, sensitive period, experience expectant, transactional, risk factor, and developmental programming.

Behavioral genetics attempts to describe the respective contributions of genes and environment to a specific behavior. Studies of identical, fraternal, and adopted siblings are able to determine some measure of variance in the outcomes explained by genes, the shared environment, and the nonshared environment. The current evidence suggests that for the broad areas of intellectual capacities, personality traits, and many types of psychopathology, nonshared environmental contributors are more important than previously recognized. Some studies suggest that what appear to matter most for a particular infant's development are not the general characteristics of family size, income, or warmth, but instead the very particular ways in which the family relates to that child in the relationship domain.

The sensitive period and experience expectant models derive primarily from animal studies but also from observations of human sensory and perceptual functioning. These models propose that there is a developmental window in the organism's life during which critical environmental input is needed for normal development to proceed. Birds and rodents appear to have well-defined sensitive periods for learning critical sounds and smells essential for communication and survival, while nonhuman primates and humans may have broad windows and broad interspecies' differences in the lengths of sensitive periods, and the critical environmental input needed to initiate a new capacity.

Risk factors analysis has been another avenue for predicting developmental outcomes and dissecting their causes. Longitudinal studies of development suggest that environmental factors are often more predictive of outcomes than biological risks.[1] The current risk factor model indicates that it is not necessarily a specific risk that is detrimental to outcome, but rather it is the crucial accumulation of risk factors in many developmental domains that most powerfully affects outcome, since early biological or environmental adversity alone is not necessarily associated with the poorest outcomes.[2]

For example, Sameroff and colleagues studied the following risks in a set of infants and then tested whether poor preschool cognitive function and social–emotional resilience, defined as competence, was related to the risk factors associated with low socioeconomic circumstances. The ten environmental risk variables were: (1) a history of maternal mental illness, (2) high maternal anxiety, (3) parental perspectives that reflected rigidity in the attitudes, beliefs, and values that mothers had in regard to their child's development, (4) few positive maternal interactions with the child observed during infancy, (5) head of household in unskilled occupations, (6) minimal maternal education, (7) disadvantaged minority status, (8) single parenthood, (9) stressful life events, and (10) large family size. Each of these risk factors has a large literature documenting their potential for deleterious developmental effects, but there are many others not included in the list. Each of the ten variables turned out to be a risk factor for poor preschool competence. On the intelligence test, children with no environmental risks scored more than thirty points higher than children with eight or nine risk factors. No preschoolers in the zero-risk group had intelligence quotients (IQ) below 85, while 26 percent of those in the high-risk group did. On average, each risk factor reduced the child's IQ score by four points. Four year olds in the high-risk group (five or more risk factors) were 12.3 times as likely to be rated as having clinical mental health symptoms. They have continued these studies to age twenty and have found that risk factors continue to be relatively unchanged in these families. In addition, for those children who demonstrated early competence, remaining in a difficult environment led to poor outcomes at later assessment compared to those children who exhibited lesser early competence, but faced fewer risks and challenges.

It now appears that gene-environment interactions are incredibly complex, with genes switching on and off at various points in development, often in response to various environmental perturbations.[3] In 1975, Arnold Sameroff and Michael Chandler,[4] psychologists at the University of Rochester, proposed the transactional model of development in which genetic and environmental regulators of an individual's behavior transact continually over time, mutually influencing one another. In fact, Sameroff[5] has posited that much as the genotype acts as the biological regulator of infants' behavior, the environtype acts as the social regulator of infants' behavior. For infants, the environtype comprises the parental, familial, and cultural characteristics that regulate infants' experiences and opportunities. This model describes individuals transacting continually with genotypic and environtypic regulators over time. Behavior at any point in time is a result of the dynamic interplay of genotype, environtype, and individual. This model appears to account reasonably well for most developmental outcomes that have been studied except for those that follow the extremes of biological insults, such as certain chromosomal disorders or extreme environmental adversities, such as intense deprivation. Still, the transactional model does not give predictive weight to any particular set of risk or protective factors, and the search for more precise predictive models continues.

The developmental programming model posits that the biology of the fetus and child adapts to the early environment. These adaptations are referred to as programming because they set the biological system (which is not interminably mutable) so that the effects persist into adulthood. Importantly, these adaptations to environmental input occur during a particular period in development. The hypothesis is that variation in early environmental exposure determines an individual's "set point." This model is often used in examinations of the influence of early stress. The concept of adaptation or preparedness implies a focus on the behavioral fit between the organism and its current or later environment rather than normal versus deviant behavior.

Now we will move from conceptual models of developmental processes to tour the construction of the developmental hardware, the brain.

BRAIN STRUCTURAL AND FUNCTIONAL DEVELOPMENT

In general, neural development proceeds from neurogenesis (nerve birth) to migration (the nerve cell moves to where it needs to be), to differentiation (becoming the kind of nerve cell it is supposed to be), to synaptogenesis (where it makes connections with other nerve cells), to pruning (when excess cells are eliminated), and myelination (when the cells are insulated to improve efficiency). The brain develops from that single fertilized cell into a complex network of billions of interconnected cells. The cells for brain development begin neurogenesis at around week seven of gestation and continue through week twenty. All of the eighty billion neurons that form the mature cortex are present by four and a half months' gestation. This means that on some days, 250,000 neurons are created. Cell migration from lower layers of the brain to the upper layers continues until seven months' gestation. The gross anatomy of the brain looks human by week fourteen, but continues to develop its characteristic convolutions from months seven to nine of the mother's pregnancy. Hence, structural brain anomalies occur in utero and may impact future functioning. Genetic abnormalities or mutations can lead to suboptimal development in the case of genetic syndromes leading to mental retardation from too few neurons, and migrational deficits may result in gross pathological anomalies leading to lissencephaly (too smooth a brain, without the usual curves and folds), schizencephaly (too many clefts in the brain), and more subtle disorders such as tic disorders and possibly schizophrenia.

Cell differentiation follows and, over the course of development, cells develop axons and dendrites, make an overabundance of synapses, and prune some synapses and myelinate others. Overall, the structural development of the brain is completed largely before birth. However, the functional development of the brain is made possible by the selective strengthening and pruning of synapses and circuits through experience with the environment.[6] "Neurons that wire together, fire together." Structure, function, and behavior go hand in hand.

Structurally, in the first three years of a child's life, brain growth continues at a rapid pace. In the first six months, synaptic growth is primarily responsible. Head circumference and brain growth occur rapidly after the biobehavioral shift that occurs between seven and nine months of age, and coincides with the expansion of dendritic fields, increased frontal lobe capillary density, and selective myelination in the limbic (emotional) system and structures associated with language.

Synaptogenesis, the creating of connections between neurons, creates potentiality for the human infant and is thought to be both genetically programmed as well as experience dependent.[7] Studies placing cortical neurons in a tissue culture dish result in reproduced cortical anatomy and random synapses where dendrites and axons come into contact. Most synaptogenesis occurs postnatally through random and nonrandom events. The number of actual connections in the brain approaches an order of 10^{14} from 10^{11} neurons.

The next two steps, myelinization and synaptic pruning, are necessary for specialization and efficiency of the brain. Synapses persist if they receive environmental input from sensory organs; this leads to the formation of neural circuits that use some of the randomly formed synapses. After one year of age, synaptic pruning occurs and deletes incorrect or unnecessary synapses. In some cases up to 100,000 synapses are lost per second, but this is still a fraction of the final total of 10^{14} synapses.

The concept of neural plasticity incorporates the process by which experience is incorporated into the structure of the brain. Plasticity can either be adaptive or maladaptive depending on the experience and the brain's response to the experience. This can also occur at multiple levels, including physiologic, anatomic, metabolic, and possibly genetic. Sensitive periods are ones when experience critically matters because of the timing of pruning, or the energy required to overcome missing the sensitive period. Myelination occurs for those persistent circuits and leads to improved speed of impulse. Environmental variables such as poor nutrition can lead to poor myelination and other insults, such as premature birth, can damage the myelin in vulnerable areas of the brain, leading to cerebral palsy, cognitive difficulties, and visual disturbances.

PET scan glucose metabolism studies inform our knowledge of the brain's early functional development.[8] As with structural development, functional development also appears to occur in a hierarchical manner with a relatively early and high level of metabolism in the evolutionarily older parts of the brain such as the cingulate gyrus, amygdala, hippocampus, and basal ganglia, and a relative paucity of activity over the cerebral cortex. These findings are consistent with the relatively limited behavioral repertoire of the newborn infant's brain stem reflex and limited visual-motor integration. After the two- to three-month developmental transition, maturation of patterns of glucose metabolism are apparent for the first time in large parietal, occipital, and temporal areas of the brain and correlate with the infant's improved visual-motor and visual-spatial integration and the disappearance and reorganization of brain stem reflexes. After the baby's developmental transition between seven to nine months of age, a new rise in glucose metabolism in the frontal lobes occurs and resembles rates of adult patterns by one year of age, though typical adult levels are reached in the second year of life.

Although much remains to be learned about specific dimensions of brain development, evidence suggests that there are important associations between changes in structure and function and changes in the spurt in capacities in other important domains such as language, socioemotional, and cognitive development.[9]

Brain development, however, does not occur in a vacuum; it occurs in the nested contexts of proximal dyadic and family interactions, and distal cultural and historical contexts. The role of the caregiving environment during these times is to facilitate the appropriate developmental task occurring in the biological and other developmental realms.

In the first several months, the caregiving environment facilitates physiologic regularity, particularly in the realm of sleep, feeding, alertness, and other biologic rhythms. Dyadic interaction, or reciprocal behavior between an infant and a caregiver—once considered superfluous during this period of development—is probably of significant importance in regulating development of neural mechanisms that modulate and control brain arousal and regulate the newborn's behavioral, neurochemical, autonomic, and hormonal functions. This regulation occurs through different aspects of the relationship, such as the provision of nutrition, warmth, sensory stimulation, and rhythmical responsiveness.

MATERNAL-FETAL ENVIRONMENT

The human embryo does not begin its life alone. From the moment of conception, the embryo begins life as part of a dyad, a dynamic living system in which it is in constant reciprocal interaction with the neurobiochemical entity that is the mother. Conception begins a cascade of changes affecting multiple maternal systems, including her hormones; fluid balance; immune, gastrointestinal, and cardiac functions; appetites; moods; and interests. All of these changes can occur without the mother's conscious knowledge that she is pregnant.

From the other end of the dyad, many aspects of the mother's health and behavior have impact on the developing embryo. While optimal health and well-being in the mother generally promote optimal prenatal development, poor maternal nutritional status, as well as exposures to medications, alcohol, nicotine, drugs of abuse, infections, or excessive stress,[10] can all have detrimental effects on the embryo and developing fetus. There are certain times in development when the fetus or embryo seems to be particularly vulnerable to toxic maternal exposures or deficits in maternal nutrients.[11] For example, lack of folic acid in the maternal environment in the first trimester has been linked to infant neural tube deficits. Fortunately, in many countries, folic acid supplementation in the mothers' diets through the first and second trimester has clearly reduced the incidence of spinal birth defects such as spina bifida, and appears to have reduced other threats to maternal and neonatal health such as preeclampsia.[12] However, not everything that is good for mother is good for baby. As was tragically discovered in the 1960s, thalidomide used to successfully treat pregnant women's nausea resulted in devastating limb abnormalities in their children. While we think of the first trimester as a particularly vulnerable time, maternal herpes infections causes the greatest risk to infants when occurring late in the third trimester.

Most people can easily understand how maternal nutrition, infections, and drug exposures might affect fetal health. However, fewer appreciate the role of maternal stress on fetal development. A number of studies correlate severe acute stress experienced by pregnant women, such as death of a loved one, war, trauma, or famine, with increased risk that some of the children born to those women will develop schizophrenia in adolescence or adulthood. In one study, the authors pinpoint the increased risk of schizophrenia to those who were embryos in the second month of pregnancy, and note an increased risk for other psychiatric impairments for individuals whose mothers were in the third month of pregnancy when the brief, but traumatic conflict occurred.[13]

There is increasing knowledge from experimental biology that profound prenatal stress affects the development of neural systems in the offspring's brain, affecting animal models of behaviors that appear to be relevant to human depression, anxiety, aggression, and cognition.[14] In addition, there is concern that prenatal stress in humans can contribute to attention deficits, autism, and learning disorders.[15] Severe stress also appears to affect an offspring's' metabolic and cardiovascular systems. By influencing the hypothalamic-pituitary axis (HPA) and other systems, stress alters the endocrine system, increasing proclivity toward type 2 diabetes, hypertension, and metabolic syndrome, which in turn can affect life span.[16] There is even some evidence, following the September 11th terrorist attacks, that suggests that severe maternal stress can increase the risk of spontaneous pregnancy loss (miscarriage), especially for male fetuses.[17]

Certainly not all stresses in life are bad, or cause prenatal injury. In fact, in adults, a certain amount of "good stress" is associated with increased alertness, learning, and performance. The point here is to understand that, in the prenatal period, the developing human is particularly vulnerable to the psychophysiological state of the mother, and she in turn, is powerfully affected by her environment. The impact of the pregnant mother's experience on her child may not be appreciated until several decades later, when that embryo has become an adult.[18]

While assaults to prenatal health can cause impairments in a child's neurocognitive and physical development, these impairments further challenge the postnatal environment, increasing the likelihood of injury, abuse, or neglect. For example, children with neurocognitive and physical impairments can be difficult to care for. They are more likely to be irritable and difficult to console, and have difficulty achieving regular feeding and sleeping routines. Their care can be especially frustrating, and their special needs sometimes invoke considerable hostility in their tired and taxed parents. Some of the most common characteristics of the abused child include prematurity, low birth weight,[19] difficult temperament, behavior disorders,[20] and mental retardation.[21] Improving prenatal health therefore improves the likelihood that children will be more easily cared for, and that parents will find caregiving more rewarding.

THE ATTACHMENT SYSTEM

At birth, the locus of infant life support is transferred from the immediacy of the womb to the responsibility of the caregivers, principally the mother, who through the course of pregnancy has been physically and emotionally primed to assume the role. The attachment system is a biologically rooted motivational system in human infants and their caregivers, thought to have evolved to ensure proximity between a caregiver and its dependent/defenseless offspring, thereby increasing the likelihood of the offspring's and, therefore, the species' survival. The attachment system motivates young children to seek comfort, support, nurturance, and protection from particular attachment figures. Infants become attached to caregivers with whom they have had significant social interaction.

Young children develop a preference for a caregiver through multiple interactions and protest when separation is threatened. The caregiver also serves as a secure base from which to explore the environment and a safe haven to return to when distressed. Although the evolutionary behavioral goal of this motivational system is proximity-seeking, other functions of this system include physiological and behavioral regulation, and the creation of a template of an inner working model of relationships.

Attachment develops in stages that correlate with specific behaviors, and as of yet, undetermined neurological correlates. The first stage occurs during the first two months of life, and is described as "undiscriminating responsiveness." It is followed by the stages of "differential responsiveness" between the infant's months two to six, "proximity maintenance" during months seven through twenty-four, and the "goal corrected partnership" from two years of age through five. In addition, from twelve to fourteen months, the infant begins to show developing attachments to figures other than the primary caregiver, usually the father or another caregiver, and may develop a hierarchy of attachment figures.

Caregiving is more than food and shelter, and more than attention, nurturance, structure, and stimulation. The quality of caregiving appears to correlate with optimal, or what is known as "secure" attachment. Subsequent research continues to refine caregiving associations with infant behavior, highlighting sensitive caregiving,[22] and the caregiver's capacity to recognize the infant's signals, accurately interpret the signals, and to appropriately and promptly respond to them.[23] It appears as if the cognitive and emotional ability to see the child as a unique individual and the ability to appropriately respond leads to the optimal secure attachment.

NATURE AND NURTURE

Animal studies have provided the first elegant models of the powerful inter-action of environmental modulation of genetic strengths and vulnerabili-ties. For example, Stephen Soumi, of the National Institute of Child Health and Human Development, has identified a subgroup of rhesus monkeys that carry a genetic variation that appears to frequently correlate with a behavioral profile resembling human anxiety and depression. Under nor-mal circumstances, these young monkeys are much more timid in their interactions with others, behaviorally inhibited in new situations, and more prone to decompensate in the face of normal developmental stressors, such as separation from the mother. In addition, they exhibit certain physiological markers associated with anxiety and depression, such as higher levels of the stress hormone, cortisol, and less appropriate responsivity in heart rate, other cardiovascular measures, and immune function. However, Soumi found that if these at risk rhesus infants were cross-fostered at birth (meaning given to the care of rhesus mothers who were identified as particularly nurturing, responsive, and attentive to their infants) these genetically vulnerable rhesus youngsters would grow up to be indistinguishable from their average peers, and express none of the behavioral or physiological markers of anxiety and depression that were seen in those at genetic risk, but who were raised with-out an enriched nurturing environment. In this model, there was even some suggestion that intensive maternal nurturing of these vulnerable offspring can turn a potential liability into a strength, allowing these individuals to rise to the top of the social hierarchy.[24]

Animal and human data appear remarkably congruent in findings that sensitive and responsive caregiving—likely affecting changes in the hypo-thalamic-pituitary axis—has positive effects on memory, cognition, stress tolerance, emotional and behavioral regulation, and cardiovascular, meta-bolic, and immune function.[25]

Genetic and environmental risk factors have complex interactions. For example, alcohol and nicotine exposure in utero is well known to affect preterm delivery, low birth weight, and a host of subtle and more serious neurocognitive impairments leading to emotional, behavioral, and learning disorders in childhood. Some genes appear to increase the risk for these difficulties. For example, maternal alcohol use is more likely to cause ADHD in the child who carries the dopamine transporter (DAT) gene.[26] Maternal smoking is more likely to increase impulsive and oppositional behavior in the child with the same genetic variation.[27] In the presence of a variant of the GSTTI gene,[28] maternal smoking increases the risk of low birth weight infants, and low birth weight children, in turn, carry a higher risk of a number of chronic psychiatric difficulties[29] and physical health problems including hypertension, type 2 diabetes, and other metabolic disorders.[30]

Researchers who examined males with a particular variant, or polymorphism, of the monoamineoxidase gene, identified another very powerful illustration of gene and environment interactions. This genetic variant had been associated with increased risk of maladaptive aggressive behavior. Avshalom Caspi, currently professor of psychology and neuroscience at Duke University, identified a group of males in New Zealand who carried this genetic risk, and whose histories had been followed from age three into adulthood. In addition, Caspi and colleagues examined data concerning the environment in which these children were raised, particularly regarding levels of maltreatment.[31] In these individuals, the extent of childhood maltreatment directly correlated with the chance of these boys demonstrating disorders of conduct in adolescence, showing a propensity for violence, being convicted for violent offenses, and exhibiting symptoms of antisocial personality disorder in adulthood. A recent study demonstrated that women who carry this same gene, and have experienced the environmental stressor of childhood sexual abuse, are at higher risk for alcoholism and antisocial personality disorder as adults.[32]

LESSONS FROM PATHOLOGICAL AND SUBOPTIMAL ENVIRONMENTS

Now that we have reviewed some of the basic principles behind healthy child development, including the physiology of brain growth, the influence of the prenatal environment, the importance of healthy attachment to caregivers, and an exploration of the interactions between genes and environment, our task is to learn about some of the ingredients for optimal child development, by examining children who are born into pathological and suboptimal environments, that is, environments that have many of the risks associated with poor outcomes.

THE ROMANIAN ORPHANAGES

Children raised in institutions are known to be at dramatically increased risk for a variety of social, emotional, and behavioral problems including disturbance in attachment and relatedness, externalizing behaviors, impulsivity and hyperactivity, and a "quasi-autistic" syndrome.[33] These problems are believed to result from the deprivation in care. Although there is a wide variability among and within institutions, the common features of these environments include (1) regimented daily schedule, (2) high child/caregiver ratio, (3) lack of individualized care, (4) lack of psychological investment by caretakers, and (5) rotating shifts.[34] These features make it nearly impossible for a caretaker to provide sensitive care to an infant or toddler. To study the effects of this, Charles Zeanah, professor of psychiatry and pediatrics at Tulane University, and his colleagues first compared signs of disturbed social relatedness (attachment disorder behavior) in young children on a standard unit, in the community, and on a novel orphanage unit where the caregiving ratios and continuity were increased. They found a continuum of results with an increase in attachment disorder behavior, aggression, stereotypical behaviors, and language delay when moving from a never institutionalized group to the enriched pilot unit to the typical orphanage unit.

In a major study that documented baseline data on all children entering the orphanages, and randomized institutional children to a new, enhanced foster care system created by the research team, they found a number of important results.[35] Children reared in institutions showed greatly diminished intellectual performance (borderline mental retardation) relative to children reared in their families of origin. Second, as a group, children randomly assigned to foster care experienced significant gains in cognitive function. Third, the younger a child is when placed in foster care, the better the outcome. Indeed, there was a continuing cost to children who remained in the institution over the course of the study, and those that were placed after two years of age had little cognitive recovery. These results are compatible with the notion of a sensitive period for early cognitive and socioemotional development of the brain.

The researchers also found these institutionalized infants had poorer physical growth and marked deficits in competence.[36] In the realm of attachment, they found that these infants and toddlers had very abnormal attachments with only three percent having classic attachment patterns and the remainder either having anomalies or suffering from significant lack of preference.[37] Ten percent of the sample had no preference or attachment at all.

The researchers also assessed the individual caretaking environment using standardized measures for each child and found that the individual caregiving environment was also associated with cognitive development, competence, and negative behavior among these young children being reared in institutions. From these groundbreaking studies, we see the "continuum of caretaking casualty," in which the lack of available caregiving relationships leads to catastrophic outcomes in the attachment system, delays in the cognitive growth, and abnormal brain development.[38] It also demonstrates that in spite of such deprivation, early interventions enabling these children to consistently receive more sensitive and responsive care in the first two years of life improves their intellectual and social functioning.

THE NURSE-FAMILY PARTNERSHIP

Next, we will examine an intervention for children who are born into what risk factor analysis would deem as suboptimal environments. The Nurse-Family Partnership (NFP) program[39] has three decades of research that demonstrates the sequela of growing up in particular high risk homes in the United States, as well as the measurable gains made when the family environment is enriched and supported in particular ways. This program is especially significant to our task of identifying the basic requirements for optimal child development because it focuses its entire intervention on young families from pregnancy through the first two years of life. It takes an ecological approach, simultaneously addressing biological, familial, and social systems that affect the life course trajectory of the child and the family.[40]

Because it addresses family life beginning in the prenatal period, it is able to intervene in those very biological aspects of the maternal fetal dyad that have such important implications for long-term child and maternal health. Early intervention in maternal behavior to promote fetal health does not only decrease the chance of a child having psychiatric, learning, and physical impairments that directly lead to poor outcomes. Reducing the risk of these disabilities has multiple secondary environmental effects, including decreasing the risk of maltreatment, decreasing the risk of divorce, and increasing the likelihood that the child will receive the benefits of growing up in a two-parent family.[41]

Increasing prenatal health is one way in which the NFP first focuses on improving neurodevelopmental, cognitive, and behavioral function in children. It next focuses on the emotional and behavioral interactions between mother and child, and when present, father, that promote healthy attachment, optimal cognitive stimulation, and a safe environment. These interventions include such practical guidance as how to "baby-safe" a home to decrease accidents and injuries, and how to provide developmentally appropriate toys. They also entail more interactional interventions, such as teaching parents to provide verbal stimulation to their babies by talking to them, increasing parental emotional sensitivity and responsiveness to a baby's moods and needs, and helping baby and parent to delight in each other's presence, setting in process a healthy attachment system that will continue to reward and motivate parents to be attentive and responsible in the care of their children.

The nurses attempt to enhance the family system by improving relations between family members, particularly the father and other relatives, and by linking the family with other health and human services. By promoting healthy family systems, the program has decreased the incidence of abuse and neglect that leads to further negative outcomes. Finally the program helps the young family itself, and particularly the mother, to become more confident in her ability to make decisions and take actions that are associated with a positive life trajectory for herself and her child, by enhancing economic self-sufficiency, planning future pregnancies, finishing education, and finding work.

The Nurse-Family Partnership has achieved remarkable outcomes in three similarly young, but ethnically dissimilar communities. Each setting recruited pregnant women who were having their first births, and included large numbers of single and teenage mothers. The Elmira, New York, group was primarily white and semirural from a variety of socioeconomic backgrounds; the Memphis, Tennessee, group was primarily black, urban, and low-income; and the Denver, Colorado, group recruited similarly low-income mothers, the majority of whom were Hispanic. The duration of the intervention is less than three years with each mother-child dyad, but families are followed through adolescence. A number of common outcomes are seen in all three locations, including improved prenatal health, a reduction in children's injuries, greater intervals between subsequent births, increases in fathers' involvement with their children, increases in maternal employment, reduction in mothers' use of welfare and food stamps, improvement in school readiness, and reduction in substance use initiation and related problems. Overall this intervention appears to have provided the greatest benefit to those families with the lowest psychological resources.

Some of the most striking benefits to children in some groups have included decreased frequency and severity of prenatal complications, decreased child mortality, decreased maltreatment, improved IQ scores and academic performance in reading and mathematics, greater emotional and behavioral regulation, and—as the children have reached adolescence—less delinquency, fewer arrests, and less high-risk sexual behavior. Benefits to families have included longer relationships with partners and more father involvement, less dependency on welfare and food stamps, and less domestic violence.[42]

CONCLUSION

The psychological literature has assumed that early experiences have greater and perhaps different effects on later behavior than do experiences in adolescence or adulthood. Neuroscience confirms that the potential for brain growth and behavioral development is broad in infancy. Experience, however, can either modify the brain by altering existing circuits or by creating novel circuits. Some circuits will never develop fully if they do not receive requisite experiences within the appropriate time frame. Some of these circuits will persist if relevant for the subsequent environment, and unfortunately, some will persist even if they are no longer relevant or adaptive. Experience, therefore, alters synaptic organization of the brain, and this organization is associated with changes in capacity and behavior. Once organized, these circuits serve as the templates for the expression of cognition, emotion, and behavior, and alter future perception and interpretation of experience beyond the caregiver infant dyad.

So what do these developmental models and intervention programs teach us about the ingredients that promote optimal childhood outcomes? First, they underline the fact that the foundations of childhood emotional and behavioral health are laid during pregnancy. The maternal-fetal dyad is a remarkable, but vulnerable system. The maternal lifeline to the fetus requires fundamental physical and emotional nourishment, as well as protection from environmental toxins. The social and cultural support and guidance provided to mothers has significant influence on child outcomes.[43] Secondarily, the family crucible into which the child is born continues to support or retard growth depending not only on its material resources, but also on its emotional and educational climate. While later childhood appears to benefit from authoritative styles of parenting including parental demands, structure, and expectations in addition to emotional support and responsiveness,[44] safe, supportive, responsive, appropriately stimulating, and low-conflict environments encourage early childhood development. Mothers, fathers, and committed others who support the caregiving system provide the essential elements of the caregiving crucible.

NOTES

1. Broman, Nichols, and Kennedy 1975. Broman reports results from a study in which the importance of 169 biomedical and behavioral variables assessed in infancy was examined in relation to cognitive outcome of over 25,000 children four years later and found that, although only 11 of the 169 variables involved family factors, parental social class, and mother's educational level, they were more predictive of outcome than all biological risk factors combined.
2. Rutter 1989:23–51.
3. Sameroff 1997.
4. Sameroff and Chandler 1975:119–149.
5. Sameroff 1997.
6. Nelson and Bosquet 2000:37–59.
7. Kolb and Whishaw 1998:43–64.
8. Huttenlocher and Dabholkar 1997:167–178.
9. Rakic, Bourgeouis, and Goldman-Rakic 1994:227–243.
10. Malaspina et al. 2008:71.
11. "Embryo" refers to a human offspring from conception through the first eight weeks of prenatal development, during which the major organs are formed. From the ninth week until birth it is referred to as a fetus.
12. Wen et al. 2008:45.
13. Malaspina et al. 2008.
14. Seckl and Holmes 2007:479–488.
15. Phillips 2007:453–460; Talge and Neal 2007:245–261; Malaspina et al. 2008.
16. Seckl and Holmes 2007; see also Bowman et al. 2004:3778–3787.
17. Catalano et al. 2006:3127–3131.
18. Catalano et al. 2006; Eskenazi et al. 2007:3013–3020.
19. Lynch and Roberts 1982.
20. Bousha and Twentyman 1984:106–114.
21. Sandgrund, Gaines, and Green 1974:327–330.
22. DeWolff and van Izjendoorn 1997:857–865.
23. Main and Solomon 1986:95–124.

24. Suomi 1997:12–15; Suomi 1999a:181–197; Suomi 1999b:189–200; Champoux et al. 2002:1058–1063; Suomi 2008:87–102.
25. Gunnar 1998; Mustard 2000.
26. Brookes et al. 2006:74–81.
27. Kahn et al. 2003:104–110.
28. Wang et al. 2002:195–202.
29. Bohnert and Breslau 2008:1080–1086.
30. Pettitt and Jovanovic 2007:147–149.
31. Caspi and McClay 2002:851–854; Kim-Cohen et al. 2006:903–913.
32. Ducci and Enoch 2008:334–347.
33. Zeanah 2000:230–236.
34. Zeanah 2008.
35. Nelson et al. 2007:1937–1940.
36. Smyke et al. 2007:210–218.
37. Zeanah et al. 2005:1015–1028.
38. Sameroff and Chandler 1975.
39. Olds 2007:205–225; Olds and Kitzman 2007:e832–e845.
40. Bronfenbrenner 1979; Bronfenbrenner 1995:619–647.
41. Mauldon 1992:349–362; McLanahan and Carlson 2002:146–165.
42. Holmberg 2008.
43. Ramey 1990:33–53; Grantham-McGregor 1991:8758; Campbell and Ramey 1994:684–698.
44. Baumrind 2001; Steinberg 2001:1–19.

REFERENCES

Baumrind, Diane. 2001. "Current Patterns of Parental Authority." *Developmental Psychology Monographs* 4(1): Part 2.
Bohnert, K. M. and N. Breslau. 2008. "Stability of Psychiatric Outcomes of Low Birthweight." *Archives General Psychiatry* 65(9):1080–1086.
Bousha, D. M. and C. T. Twentyman. 1984. "Mother-Child Interactional Style in Abuse, Neglect, and Control Groups: Naturalistic Observations in the Home." *Journal of Abnormal Psychology* 93:106–114.
Bowman, R. E., M. J. MacLusky, et al. 2004. "Sexually Dimorphic Effects of Prenatal Stress on Cognition, Hormonal Responses and Central Neurotransmitters." *Endocrinology* 145(8):3778–3787.
Broman, S. H., P. L. Nichols, and W. A. Kennedy. 1975. *Preschool IQ: Prenatal and Early Developmental Correlates.* Hillsdale, NJ: Lawrence Erlbaum.
Bronfenbrenner, Urie. 1979. *The Ecology of Human Development: Experiments by Nature and Design.* Boston: Harvard University.
Bronfenbrenner, Urie. 1995. "Developmental Psychology through Space and Time: A Future Perspective." In *Examining Lives in Context: Perspectives on the Ecology*

of Human Development, ed. P. Moen, G. H. Elder Jr., and K. Luscher, 619–647. Washington, DC: American Psychological Association.

Brookes, K., J. Mill, C. Guindalini, S. Curran, X. Xu, J. Knight, C. K. Chen, Y. S. Huang, V. Sethna, E. Taylor, W. Chen, G. Breen, and P. Asherson. 2006. "A Common Haplotype of the Dopamine Transporter Gene Associated with Attention Deficit/Hyperactivity Disorder Interacting with Maternal Alcohol Use During Pregnancy." *Archives of General Psychiatry* 63(1):74–81.

Campbell, Frances A. and Craig T. Ramey. 1994. "Effects of Early Intervention on Intellectual and Academic Achievement: A Follow-Up Study of Children from Low-Income Families." *Child Development* 65:684–698.

Caspi, A. and J. McClay. 2002. "Role of Genotype in the Cycle of Violence in Mal-treated Children." *Science* 297:851–854.

Catalano, R., T. Bruckner, A. R. Marks, and B. Eskenazi. 2006. "Exogenous Shocks to the Human Sex Ratio: The Case of September 11, 2001 in New York City." *Human Reproduction* 21(12):3127–3131.

Champoux, M. C. Bennett, A. Shannon, J. D. Higley, K. P. Lesch, and S. J. Suomi. 2002. "Serotonin Transporter Gene Polymorphism and Neurobehavioral Development in Rhesus Monkey Neonates." *Molecular Psychiatry* 7(10):1058–1063.

DeWolff, M., and M. van Izjendoorn. 1997. "Sensitivity and Attachment: A Meta-Analysis on Parental Antecedents of Infant Attachment." *Child Development* 52:857–865.

Ducci, F. and M. A. Enoch. 2008. "Interaction Between a Functional MAOA Locus and Childhood Sexual Abuse Predicts Alcoholism and Antisocial Personality Disorder in Adult Women." *Molecular Psychiatry* 13(3):334–347.

Eskenazi, Brenda, Amy R. Marks, Ralph Catalano, Tim Bruckner, and Paolo G. Toniolo. 2007. "Low Birthweight in New York City and Upstate New York Following the Events of September 11th." *Human Reproduction* 22(11):3013–3020.

Grantham-McGregor, Sally. 1991. "Nutritional Supplementation, Psychosocial Stimulation and Mental Development of Stunted Children: The Jamaican Study." *The Lancet* 338:8758.

Gunnar, M. R. 1998. "Stress Physiology, Health and Behavioral Development," in *The Wellbeing of Children and Families: Research and Data Needs*, ed. A. Thornton, Institute for Social Research Report. Ann Arbor, Michigan: University of Michigan.

Holmberg, J. 2008. "Nurse Family Partnership Trials: Cutting Edge Evidence of Successful Child and Mother Adaptation." Field presentation in PowerPoint, Denver, Colorado. August 2008.

Huttenlocher, P. R. and A. S. Dabholkar. 1997. "Regional Differences in Synaptogenesis in Human Visual Cortex." *Journal of Comprehensive Neurology* 387:167–178.

Kahn, R. S., J. Khoury, W. C. Nichols, and B. P. Lanphear. 2003 "Role of Dopamine Transporter Genotype and Maternal Prenatal Smoking in Childhood

Hyperactive-Impulsive, Inattentive, and Oppositional Behaviors." *Journal of Pediatrics* 143(1):104–110.

Kim-Cohen, J., A. Caspi, A. Taylor, B. Williams, R. Newcombe, I. W. Craig, and T. E. Moffitt. 2006. "MAOA, Maltreatment, and Gene-Environment Interaction Predicting Children's Mental Health: New Evidence and a Meta-Analysis." *Molecular Psychiatry* 11:903–913.

Kolb, B. and I.Q. Whishaw. 1998. "Brain Plasticity and Behavior." *Annual Review of Psychology* 49:43–64.

Lynch, M. A. and J. Roberts. 1982. *Consequences of Child Abuse*. New York: Academic.

Main, M. and J. Solomon. 1986. "Discovery of an Insecure-Disorganized Disoriented Attachment Pattern." In *Affective Development in Infancy*, ed. T. B. Brazelton and M. W. Yogman, 95–124. Norwood, NJ: Abler.

Malaspina, D., C. Corcoran, K. R. Kleinhaus, M. C. Perrin, S. Fenni, D. Nahon, Y. Friedlander, and S. Harlap. 2008. "Acute Maternal Stress in Pregnancy and Schizophrenia in Offspring: A Cohort Prospective Study." *BMC Psychiatry* 8:71.

Mauldon, J. 1992. "Children's Risks of Experiencing Divorce and Remarriage: Do Disabled Children Destabilize Marriages?" *Population Studies* 46(2):349–362.

McLanahan, S. and M. Carlson. 2002. "Welfare Reform, Fertility and Father Involvement." *The Future of Children* 12(1):146–165.

Mustard, J. F. 2000. "Learning Early Childhood Development: The Base for Society" Paper presented at HRDC/OECD Meeting, Ottawa, Canada, December 7, 2000.

Nelson, C. A. III and M. Bosquet. 2000. "Neurobiology of Fetal and Infant Development: Implications for Infant Mental Health," in *Handbook of Infant Mental Health*, 2nd ed., ed. C. H. Zeanah, Jr., 37–59. New York: Guilford.

Nelson C. A. III, C. H. Zeanah, N. A. Fox, P. J. Marshall, A. T. Smyke, and D. Guthrie. 2007. "Cognitive Recovery in Socially Deprived Young Children: The Bucharest Early Intervention Project." *Science* 318(5858):1937–1940.

Olds, D. 2007. "Preventing Crime with Prenatal Infancy Support of Parents: The Nurse-Family Partnership." *Victims and Offenders* 2(2):205–225.

Olds, D. and H. Kitzman. 2007. "Effects of Nurse Home Visiting on Maternal and Child Functioning: Age-9 Follow-up of a Randomized Trial." *Pediatrics* 120:e832–e845.

Pettitt, D. and L. Jovanovic. 2007. "Low Birth Weight as a Risk Factor for Gestational Diabetes, Diabetes, and Impaired Glucose Tolerance During Pregnancy." *Diabetes Care* 30:147–149.

Phillips, D. L. 2007. "Programming of the Stress Response: A Fundamental Mechanism Underlying the Long-Term Effects of the Fetal Environment." *Journal of Internal Medicine* 261(5):453–460.

Rakic, P., J. Bourgeouis, and P. S. Goldman-Rakic. 1994. "Synaptic Development of the Cerebral Cortex: Implications for Learning, Memory, and Mental Illness." *Progress in Brain Research* 102:227–243.

Ramey, Craig T. 1990. "Early Intervention for High-Risk Children: The Carolina Early Intervention Program." In *Protecting the Children: Strategies for Optimizing Emotional and Behavioral Health*, ed. R. Lorion, 33–53. Binghamton, NY: Haworth.

Rutter, M. 1989. "Pathways from Childhood to Adulthood." *Journal of Child Psychology and Psychiatry* 30:23–51.

Sameroff, A. and M. Chandler. 1975. "Reproductive Risk and the Continuum of Caretaking Casualty," in *Reviews of Child Development Research*, ed. F. D. Horowitz, M. Hetherington, S. Scarr-Salapatek, and G. Siegel, 119–149. Chicago: University of Chicago.

Sameroff, A. J. 1997. "Understanding the Social Context of Early Psychopathology," in *Handbook of Child and Adolescent Psychiatry*, ed. J. Noshpitz. New York: Basic.

Sandgrund, H., R. Gaines, and A. Green. 1974. "Child Abuse and Mental Retardation: A Problem of Cause and Effect." *American Journal of Mental Deficiency* 79:327–330.

Seckl, J. R. and M. C. Holmes. 2007. "Mechanisms of Disease: Glucocorticoids, Their Placental Metabolism and Fetal Programming of Adult Pathophysiology." *Nature Clinical Practice* 3(6):479–488.

Smyke, A. T., S. F. Koga, D. E. Johnson, N. A. Fox, P. J. Marshall, C. A. Nelson, and C. H. Zeanah. 2007. "The Caregiving Context in Institution-Reared and Family-Reared Infants and Toddlers in Romania." *Journal of Child Psychology and Psychiatry* 48(2):210–218.

Steinberg, Lawrence. 2001. "We Know Some Things: Parent-Adolescent Relationships in Retrospect and Prospect." *Journal of Research on Adolescence* 11(1): 1–19.

Suomi, Stephen. 1997. "Early Determinants of Behavior: Evidence from Primate Studies." *British Medical Bulletin* 53(1):12–15.

Suomi, Stephen J. 1999a. "Attachment in Rhesus Monkeys," in *Handbook of Attachment: Theory, Research, and Clinical Applications*, ed. J. Cassidy and P. R. Shaver, 181–197. New York: Guilford.

Suomi, Stephen J. 1999b. "Developmental Trajectories, Early Experiences, and Community Consequences." In *Developmental Health and the Wealth of Nations: Social Biological and Educational Dynamics*, ed. D. P. Keating and C. Hertzman, 189–200. New York: Guilford.

Suomi, Stephen J. 2008. "How Mother Nurture Helps Mother Nature: Scientific Evidence for the Protective Effect of Good Nurturing on Genetic Propensity Toward Anxiety and Alcohol Abuse." In *Authoritative Communities: The Scientific Case for Nurturing the Whole Child*, ed. Kathleen Kline, 87–102. New York: Springer.

Talge, N. M. and C. Neal. 2007. "Antenatal Maternal Stress and Long-Term Effects on Child Development." *Journal of Child Psychology and Psychiatry and Allied Disciplines* 48(3–4):245–261.

Wang, X., B. Zuckerman, C. Pearson, G. Kaufman, C. Chen, G. Wang, T. Niu, P. H. Wise, H. Bauchner, and X. Xu. 2002. "Maternal Cigarette Smoking, Metabolic Gene Polymorphism, and Infant Birth Weight." *Journal of the American Medical Society* 287(2):195–202.

Wen, Shi Wu et al. 2008. "Folic Acid Supplementation in Early Second Trimester and the Risk of Preeclampsia." *American Journal of Obstetrics and Gynecology* 198(1):45.

Zeanah, C. H. 2000. "Disturbances of Attachment in Young Children Adopted from Institutions." *Journal of Development and Behavioral Pediatrics* 21(3):230–236.

Zeanah, C. H. 2008. "The Importance of Early Experience: Clinical, Research and Policy Perspectives." Paper presented at the Kentucky Center for the Study of Violence Against Children (KCSVAC), Lexington, Kentucky. May 2008.

Zeanah, C. H., A. T. Smyke, S. F. Koga, and E. Carlson. 2005. "Attachment in Institutionalized and Community Children in Romania." *Child Development* 76(5):1015–1028.

8

GENDERED PARENTING'S IMPLICATIONS FOR CHILDREN'S WELL-BEING

Theory and Research in Applied Perspective

Rob Palkovitz

IN THE MOST GENERAL SENSE, worldwide, mothers and fathers share similar parenting goals of survival, protection, teaching, and fostering self-fulfillment in their offspring.[1] Yet, as parents, men and women approach their shared goals through differentiated roles, styles, and levels of behavior. In addition, mothers and fathers may have unique individual aspirations for their children's development. Parents' hopes and dreams, concerns and fears, may be different for sons and daughters. Consequently, mothers and fathers treat sons and daughters differently. These facets of gendered parenting interact to influence developmental competencies and well-being of children in different ways. This chapter reviews theoretical and empirical literature on the relationships between different patterns of gendered parenting and children's well-being.

A broad-based body of theoretical and empirical literature identifies gendered parenting as a key component in a set of influences in shaping children's welfare. The challenge of concisely reviewing the empirical and theoretical literature on the effects of gendered parenting on child outcomes lies in presenting the material in a manner that cogently summarizes trends in parental influence while avoiding reductionistic parent-effects models[2] and appropriately heeding interactive effects of multiple moderating and mediating variables. In order to elucidate variations in the effects of gendered parenting on children's development, it is also essential to consider the contexts of parent-child interaction and development, including the transactional nature of family influence,[3] and cohort changes in culturally grounded gender values.[4]

Recent fluctuations in American culture include a rapidly transforming family landscape characterized by expanded diversity of family forms[5] and shifting balances of role enactments.[6] Demographic indicators reflect prevailing conditions that represent challenges to effectively raising children, such as an increase in the number of single-parent households.[7] At the same time, economic pressures have yielded a growing number of dual earner couples,[8] and an expanding number of hours that parents spend at work each week.[9] These changes have occurred in the context of ideals that espouse egalitarian sharing of family and work responsibilities for men and women.[10] As parents negotiate this complex array of competing circumstances, demands, and values, what are the implications for the development and well-being of their children?

Theoretical understanding of the intricacies of interactive systems in development and in families has far outpaced the limits of empirical capacity. As in all realms of inquiry in human development and family studies where environments contribute significantly to variations in developmental status, the diversity of contexts within which gendered parenting takes place presents daunting challenges to researchers. Approaches that seriously value systems perspectives of development and transactional models of interpersonal relationships and family systems defy the likelihood of single empirical investigations capturing the complexities of influences of gendered parenting on child outcomes. In any given empirical study, it is not feasible to collect data sufficient to control for the interactions of all variables identified by bodies of empirical and theoretical literature as exerting significant influence. Therefore, emerging pictures of the effects of gendered parenting on child well-being must come from meta-analytic syntheses of theoretical and empirical literature that target facets of developmental influence while understanding that full empirical validation of emergent understandings cannot be accomplished in isolated studies.

This chapter will review theoretical and empirical literature regarding the influences of gendered parenting on child development outcomes, with a particular focus on children's cognitive, emotional, and social welfare. There are literally hundreds of studies that link aspects of gendered parenting to child outcomes across diverse developmental domains. To do a comprehensive review of them is clearly beyond the scope of this chapter. Rather, the primary objectives of this chapter are to expand emerging understandings of developmental processes of gendered parenting, to synthesize convergent trends in the empirical findings linking gendered parenting to children's developmental well-being, and to address limitations and applications of the current professional literature.

MECHANISMS AND PROCESSES OF INFLUENCE IN GENDERED PARENTING

Gendered parenting is reflected in the theoretical and empirical literature in a number of interrelated, yet distinct ways: sex differences in behaviors of men and women,[11] differential levels of participation in various categories of involvement in child-rearing,[12] different parental styles of interaction with children,[13] different meanings of the constellations of sex role orientations in men and women,[14] and interactions of these factors within the contexts of parenting and development over time.

The developmental literature identifies multiple factors that are pertinent to our consideration including: parental gender role modeling, parents' differential treatment of girls and boys, direct instruction of children, gendered expectations, opportunities provided, monitoring and management of children's activities, and emotional communication and regulation. These categories of influence are neither exhaustive nor mutually exclusive. We will now turn attention to understanding how these components of gendered parenting affect child welfare.

MODELING AND REWORKING

Modeling entails attempts at replicating the attributes or behaviors of others, while reworking involves efforts to modify one's behavior in order to rectify limitations, shortcomings, or absences observed or experienced.[15] There is widespread agreement that mothers and fathers model different gender roles, engagement patterns, and statuses; thereby shaping children's understanding of what it means to be a man or a woman,[16] or a parent of either sex.[17]

In the developmental literature, modeling is presented as a pervasive and effective means of conveying gender expectations to children. As early as twenty-four months of age, children look longer at adults performing gender inconsistent activities than those engaged in behaviors consistent with gender stereotypes.[18] At the same time, boys and girls are likely to show preference for stereotypically gender appropriate toys.[19] The effects of modeling are not limited to early childhood. As the balance of work and family roles have shifted in contemporary America, corresponding changes have been documented in daughters'[20] and sons'[21] gender attitudes and aspirations.

While gender role modeling is covered in detail in many reviews of the literature, reworking is less frequently discussed. It has been suggested[22] that as people assume parenting roles, a feature of adult development is the reworking of components of the roles and behavioral involvement of their own parents. This process occurs in virtually all adults, even if they perceive their parents to be "good" parents, because as adults engage in parental roles, they come to new understandings of the parenting they received. As they reflect on their parents' decisions and behaviors, they recognize components of parenting that could be improved, and thereby rework their parenting and gender roles.

I would posit that for children, modeling is a more central component of gender attitude formation than reworking, but both have important developmental implications for child outcomes, especially in regard to gender identity and role formation. In comparison to reworking, modeling requires less developmental maturity. Modeling allows one to copy what has been seen or encountered, realms of experience available even to sensorimotor infants. In contrast, reworking requires more advanced cognitive maturity: reflection on or envisioning what was *not* seen or experienced, the creation of alternative models absent from one's experience. Reworking is less sure than modeling because the roles or ideals created, especially if generated during childhood, may not be realistic or practical to implement. While it is possible to assess consequences of modeled behaviors through vicarious reinforcement,[23] creating new, unrealized roles through reworking does not allow observational learning of consequences and it requires more inventiveness and developmental resources than following models who have already successfully forged and modeled a path.

These understandings have profound implications for the gender development of children in single-parent or same-sex parent families. If children are to develop adequate working models of what it means to be a person who is the gender of the absent parent, they will need to emulate and comprehend less frequently available models, such as parent figures or mentors. Alternatively, they can draw on cognitive capacities that develop later in life, reworking available models to create what was lacking in their earlier experience. With contemporary emphasis on the importance of early learning, the implication is that children who experience parental patterns that require significant reworking are at a disadvantage in comparison to children who can model appropriate relationships and roles.

Formulation of working models of heterosexual interaction is only possible in the presence of both sexes. That is, a child can best learn how men and women relate to one another if they have adequate opportunity to observe such interactions. If their parent is unpartnered or partnered with a same-sexed individual, there is less opportunity for the child to form expectations (and evaluative models) of heterosexual relationships.

This discussion also informs understandings of why children suffer developmental delays when they have parents who are present and involved, but who do not engage in developmentally facilitative, positive parenting. The need for these children to rework parental roles may contribute further to the developmental deficits. Fortunate is the child whose proportion of reworking to positive modeling is minimal.

DIFFERENTIAL TREATMENT

It has been suggested that the greatest influence of gendered parenting for children's development is exerted through the differential treatment of sons and daughters.[24] Despite controversies surrounding the size and significance of real sex differences, and ways to operationalize them, differences in behavior can be easily documented in parental involvement with children across time in regard to both amounts of engagement[25] and the nature or style of engagement.[26] These patterns, in turn, can be correlationally, but not causally, linked to child outcome variables.[27] In two-parent households, mothers' enhanced levels of accessibility, engagement, and responsibility may make them more influential than their spouses or partners in shaping child outcomes,[28] though fathers may compensate for their relative absence through increasing the salience of their interactions with their children[29] through rough-and-tumble, exuberant, or unpredictable play styles.[30]

Parental interactions directed toward sons and daughters have been described as having different cognitive, social, and emotional goals. Specifically, exchanges with daughters are characterized as emphasizing compliance and relational synchrony, while interactions with sons are viewed to involve greater emphasis on cognitive stimulation and encouragement for agency.[31] Parents' interactional styles with sons and daughters may foster distinct understandings of the social roles of males and females.[32] Patricia Kerig, Philip Cowan, and Carolyn Cowan note that "these gender differences are not simply pink or blue but are also colored by the emotional quality of the relationships between marital partners and their children."[33]

The roots of differential treatment of boys and girls begin prenatally or while infants are still in the hospital delivery room or nursery.[34] We have each listened as parents interpret the movements of fetuses known to be boys and girls in different ways, using terms that are gender stereotyped.

Differential gender expectations lead to differential interpretations of child behavior and to differential treatment of boys and girls. Early gender stereotyping continues through infancy as parents use gender-biased adjectives to describe the emotions and behaviors of their children.[35]

Differential treatment of children comes from both mothers and fathers, though mothers and fathers manifest different patterns of treatment toward sons and daughters across different developmental realms. As documented elsewhere in this volume,[36] fathers and mothers spend different proportions of their child-involved time in different activities, and with different behavioral styles. Specifically, mothers and fathers treat sons and daughters differently in everyday interactions that discriminate in styles and amounts of language, problem solving, emotional regulation and expression, and play. Fathers are often, though not always, reported to be significantly more involved with sons than daughters and to concentrate more on instrumental aspects of support.[37] In contrast, mothers have a tendency to be more supportive across genders affectively.[38] Parents use different patterns of touch, talking, use of supportive statements, patterns of questioning, comforting of emotions, choice of peers, and activities with boys and girls.[39] Parents are more likely to encourage rough-and-tumble play with sons than daughters[40] and may discourage physical play in daughters.[41]

Mothers more frequently respond to sons' emotional displays than daughters in a contingent manner[42] and are more consistent in responses to sons' than daughters' emotions.[43] Affection is differentially encouraged and tolerated from boys and girls.[44] Fathers may be more cognitively demanding than mothers[45] while mothers frequently show more scaffolding of children's learning than fathers.[46] Fathers tend to reward daughters for positive, compliant behaviors and to reward sons for assertiveness.[47] Both mothers and fathers use fewer directives with sons than daughters, encouraging more active problem solving and independence.[48]

Taken together, these findings establish that mothers and fathers interact differently with sons and daughters, thereby necessitating, at minimum, a two by two (sex of parent by sex of child) matrix to more fully understand the effects of gendered parenting on child development outcomes. As will be established later in this chapter, the number of dimensions and cells in the matrix expands significantly when we consider patterns of interactions in other central variables beyond the sex of the parent and child.

Though both mothers and fathers treat their sons and daughters differently, fathers are more consistently identified as employing different treatment to their children by sex.[49] Even when frequencies of behaviors for mothers and fathers are reported to be similar, the contexts and responses of sons and daughters may be different, so the same parental treatment may affect sons and daughters differently,[50] yielding different developmental outcomes.

We tend to assume that parents initiate gender differentiated treatment, but it may be the case that children's sex differences elicit and discourage different parental behaviors.[51] Child characteristics are known to influence parent behaviors in a transactional manner.[52] "As highlighted in recent reviews, we need to disentangle child and parent effects (as well as interaction) when explaining children's development."[53] Unfortunately, most empirical findings are not assessed in a manner that allows such disentanglement.

PROVISION AND PROHIBITION OF OPPORTUNITIES

Parents are likely to assign household chores that align with gender appropriate stereotypes,[54] and to model traditional divisions of labor in their own household work.[55] Adolescent sons receive more permissive parenting than do daughters.[56] Sons are typically granted permission to go further from home and engage in a broader range of activities with peers[57] with less monitoring than daughters.[58] These factors are likely to foster gendered differences in independence, communality, and instrumentality as well as in gendered approaches to household roles.

PARENTAL SEX AND GENDER DIFFERENCES

In the realm of human development, the term sex differences refers to biologically based physical differences between males and females. In contrast, the term gender differences refers to dissimilarities in patterns of behaviors or traits that define how to act the part of a female or a male in a particular social context or culture. There is general disagreement among social scientists regarding the number and scope of real sex differences in humans.[59] In contrast, there is no doubt that worldwide, there is considerable variation in the magnitude of gender differences observed.[60] Still, the consensus seems to be that there is more similarity than difference in gender expression in humans,[61] but that observed differences may be significant and influential[62] in shaping the behavior and attitudes of subsequent generations. In the grand sense, differences between mothers and fathers are not great: Both parents encourage visual exploration, object manipulation, attention to relations between objects, and cause and effect.[63] However, fathers do so differently from mothers; that is to say that maternal and paternal styles of achieving these larger goals are distinct from one another. Fathers tend to be more unconventional in their toy and object use than mothers and use objects to engage in physical contact with children to a greater degree than mothers.[64] Fathers also destabilize children during play through the use of teasing to a greater extent than mothers.[65]

Daniel Paquette discusses the fact that father's stimulating play styles with children are effective in helping children to develop strong bonds with their fathers even when fathers are less present than the mother.[66] As far as biological sex goes, men tend to be firmer and more nondirective than women as parents, while women tend to be more responsive, structured, and regimented than men.[67] Fathers are more demanding of children in regard to problem solving than mothers[68] and make more action-related demands for accomplishment of tasks.[69]

Parents of either biological sex can be classified into gender categories; masculine, feminine, androgynous, or undifferentiated.[70] Briefly summarized, sex-typed individuals (masculine or feminine) are those who manifest characteristics consistently associated with one sex or another within a culture's role attributions. For example, feminine individuals (either males or females) demonstrate a higher degree of behaviors or attitudes associated with females, and relatively few associated with males. Masculine individuals would have the converse pattern of attributes. Traditionally gender-typed persons are those whose gender roles are consistent with their biological sex. Nontraditionally, or cross-gender-typed persons manifest characteristics of persons of the opposite sex. Androgynous individuals demonstrate role-stereotypic behaviors and attitudes of both men and women simultaneously. Androgenes demonstrate socially desirable qualities of both sexes: greater instrumentality (dominance, agency) and, at the same time, greater expressivity (warmth, communion).[71] In contrast, undifferentiated individuals are not particularly demonstrative of sex stereotyped behaviors or attitudes of either men or women in a given cultural context.

Diana Baumrind published a landmark analysis of parental gender differences and child outcomes in her 1982 article titled "Are Androgynous Individuals More Effective Persons and Parents?" The Baumrind study used nine year olds and was published in the early 1980s—one cohort! The subjects were well-educated, middle class Caucasian individuals in one geographic locale (from 1972 to 1975). Baumrind found that with sex controlled, gender classification adds predictive power, primarily to child-rearing variables assessing responsiveness.[72] Feminine and androgynous parents are highly responsive and undifferentiated and masculine parents are unresponsive. Yet, she summarized her analyses by stating, "parents' gender classifications are not highly discriminative of children's competency ratings."[73] The measures of well-being (by parental gender type) were children's social responsibility, social assertiveness, and cognitive competence as well as optimum competence.

Baumrind went on to explain, however, that where differences are manifested, they tend to support traditional sex role theories. Specifically, sons with masculine fathers tend to be more socially assertive while children of opposite sexed parents with cross-sex gender identity were likely to demonstrate somewhat lower competencies. Baumrind concluded that children of androgynous parents are not more competent than children with parents who are sex-typed or undifferentiated. In speculating about mechanisms behind these patterns of outcomes, she reflected that androgynous parents have a tendency to be child-centered, and that may yield somewhat lower competency than having parents who are moderately more directive. This indicates that parenting style may be more central in influencing child outcomes than parental gender roles, though they are related to one another.

More recently, Daniel Paquette asserted that "while a relative lack of differentiation in parental roles would appear to be more socially desirable, the work of researchers in Toulouse, France, suggests that the family structure that is most favorable to the socioaffective development of young children is one in which both parents are involved from the early stages, but with differentiated fields of activity involving clearly polarized maternal and paternal functions."[74] Such statements may minimize the fact that even in families with egalitarian ideals, parents still have different styles, voices, histories, and connections to their children as well as gendered relationships toward their sons and daughters. Le Camus[75] asserts that children necessarily have different experiences with their mothers and fathers because the psychological and physical differences between the two parents are greater than those between two people of the same sex. Mothers and fathers differ in odor, voice, face, muscle tone, and messages communicated. Thus, children from egalitarian families still have multiple and varied opportunities to develop differential expectations for their parents, and to benefit from discrimination learning in the positive sense, the formulation of and analyses of differences.

Baumrind was astute enough to assess both sex and gender differences as they relate to variables indicative of personal competence in mothers and fathers. She reviewed literature that suggests that in comparison to traditionally-typed and undifferentiated individuals, androgynous people have higher self-esteem and self-confidence, greater individuation, are more intellectually stimulating, more unconventional, less field dependent, and have greater locus of control. Her empirical work with parents and children found that undifferentiated parents have lower self-esteem and androgynous persons have higher self-esteem than sex-typed parents. Androgynous persons also had more internal locus of control than other individuals of the same sex. She reported that on nine of the ten personal variables she assessed there were neither sex nor gender differences.[76] Specifically, there were no variables on which androgynous men differed from masculine men. Androgynous men differed from androgynous women, but not from masculine men by being more nondirective with their children. Yet, gender identity predicted significant differences in certain child-rearing and personal variables, with sex controlled, in particular contrasts involving androgynous men on responsiveness variables. This is consistent with my own research showing that androgynous fathers are more involved with their infants than masculine or feminine fathers.[77] Baumrind contends that "there are no personal variables on which androgynous men vary from masculine men . . . androgynous men vary from androgynous women, but not from masculine men, except that they are less directive."[78]

Baumrind reports that some traditional gender role characteristics in fathers are related to undesirable parental traits. Masculine fathers tend to be less responsive than all other parents and use more coercive power and guilt induction than other fathers. However, on a more positive note, they generally use more positive reinforcement in comparison to other fathers.[79] Feminine mothers generally exhibit traits associated with superior parenting practices. In comparison to other sex and gender combinations, they are the warmest parents, most loving, responsive, and supportive, and the least irascible. To their detriment, however, they are less firm than other parents.[80] Sex-typed couples tend to be very demanding and moderately responsive.

These findings have clear implications for gendered parenting. Several studies have documented that undifferentiated and masculine parents are less responsive than feminine and androgynous parents.[81] These findings suggest that parents with different gender role orientations may manifest different personality types or interaction styles that are associated with different parental styles. Masculine fathers tend to be less responsive than all other fathers and use more coercive power and guilt induction than all other fathers. That is to say, they demonstrate different parenting styles than other parents. Similarly, undifferentiated mothers more often express anger and use punitive parenting styles than other mothers while demonstrating less love/support. Masculine mothers are less responsive than other types of mothers. Masculine fathers and undifferentiated and masculine mothers have outcomes that reflect lower levels of warmth and higher levels of punitiveness than other parents.[82]

As stated earlier, there are correlations between parental gender types and parenting styles. Overall, androgynous couples tend to be more child-centered than authoritative, responsive, but not firm. In comparison, sex-typed parents tend to be very demanding and moderately responsive: authoritative, traditional, and demanding. Traditional couples cover the bases of positive parenting through specialized roles. Traditionally sex-typed mothers and fathers tend to engage in complementary child-rearing roles, with fathers being firm and mothers being outstandingly warm. Sex-typed fathers tend to be firm, demanding, and positively reinforcing. Sex-typed mothers demonstrate loving, responsive, involved styles of child-rearing. Cross-sex-identity mothers are less warm, but cross-sex-identity fathers are not less firm than sex-typed fathers.[83]

Such findings would establish that parents with different gender identity constellations interact with their children differently, which should predict different developmental competencies in their children. However, Baumrind concludes that children's competency ratings are not highly predicted by parents' gender classifications. Where results are statistically significant, they tend to support traditional sex role theories, with sons of traditional fathers showing more social assertion, and children of cross-sex gender identities being associated with lower competence scores for children.[84]

PARENTAL GENDER TYPES INTERACT WITH SEX OF PARENT AND SEX OF CHILD

Theoretical literature indicates that there are often sex by gender interaction effects (seldom considered in research designs and analyses).[85] Masculine fathers tend to be firm, demanding, and positively reinforcing, while leaving the responsibility of daily interaction to their wives or partners.[86] Feminine mothers show tendencies to be loving, responsive, and engaged in directing children's activities.[87] When masculine fathers parent in conjunction with feminine mothers, they tend to display traditional, authoritative, and demanding styles of parenting more frequently than nondirective, permissive, or punitive styles.[88] Daughters from homes of sex-typed couples tend to demonstrate higher levels of competence and assertiveness than daughters from homes characterized by other combinations of parental gender role pairings.[89] Similarly, sons from sex-typed homes typically demonstrate higher levels of competence than sons of androgynous parents.[90]

Goodness of fit for couples' gender identities is sometimes examined (e.g., androgynous-androgynous partners relate to one another differently than masculine-masculine partners). Although researchers often look at goodness of fit for parent-child dyads in regard to social activity and responsiveness or temperament and parenting style, I am unaware of research looking at the goodness of fit for gender identities of parents and children. The literature reviewed earlier would predict that there are "good" fits between some parent-child gender role pairings as well as some less optimal pairings.

UNIQUE PARENTAL EFFECTS

Studies that demonstrate unique developmental contributions of either parent would indicate that there are developmental outcome effects of gendered parenting. In reviewing paternal involvement literature, I have found several studies that point toward the unique contributions of fathers in children's developmental well-being.[91]

Fathers' sensitivity and positive regard during play times have been uniquely linked with two- and three-year-olds' social skills; and the quality of fathers' attachment relationships with their children have been relatively more effective than mother-child attachment types in explaining children's self esteem and pro-social behavior.[92]

Greater positive father involvement with young children tends to be associated with overall life satisfaction, happiness, and psychological well-being when offspring reach early adulthood[93] and fewer behavioral problems for children[94] and adolescents.[95] Similarly, positive father involvement in married parent families is associated with lower psychological distress[96] and fewer depressive symptoms[97] in teens. Father support during adolescence plays a greater role than mothers' in explaining prosocial outcomes for adolescents[98] as well as in adult sons who report good quality relationships with their fathers.[99]

Fathers may play a particularly important role in stimulating children's openness to the world in exciting, surprising, destabilizing, and encouraging them to take risks and to stand up for themselves.[100] Paquette describes paternal roles as comprising an "activation relationship" that is developed primarily through physical play.[101] Bruce Ellis has documented that the presence of a father in a household is associated with a delayed onset of puberty in daughters, suggesting that biochemical links exist between paternal involvement and child outcomes. Similarly, positive paternal involvement is associated with lower risk in children and paternal absence has been cited by multiple scholars as the single greatest risk factor in teen pregnancy for girls.

REALMS OF DEVELOPMENTAL DIFFERENCE ASSOCIATED WITH GENDERED PARENTING

EMOTIONAL EXPRESSION AND REGULATION

Children have been shown to learn about emotional regulation through observational learning and social referencing, parenting practices, and the emotional climate of the family through parenting styles, attachment relationships, family expressiveness, and marital interactions and quality.[102] Fathers' supportiveness and cognitive stimulation have been associated with children's emotional regulation at twenty-four months in both sons and daughters.[103] Parents give daughters more opportunity to practice emotion talk than sons by more frequently discussing emotional experiences and by using more varied emotional references.[104] Parents also vary the types of emotion talk with sons and daughters, using more references to sadness with sons than daughters.[105] From early infancy onward, differential treatment of sons and daughters is contingent on the consistency of children's emotional displays with sex stereotypes. By using different frequencies and ranges of expression around emotional discussion, parents may be teaching boys and girls to think about, express, and control emotions differently.

In studies of emotional expression and regulation in adolescents, multiple research teams have found that children from more emotionally expressive and supportive families demonstrated a greater range of emotions than those associated with traditional stereotypes.[106] These findings have been interpreted to support the notion that better emotional adjustments are associated with androgyny or cross-gendered patterns than those associated with gender role traditionalism.[107]

Male and female respondents in Latino families described differential household activities, socialization of gender-typed behavior, and parental monitoring in parents' relationships with sons versus daughters.[108] Mothers and fathers use different parenting styles for sons and daughters and different combinations of maternal and paternal parenting (e.g., a permissive father parenting with an authoritarian mother) are related to late adolescents' emotional adjustment. Late adolescents who have at least one authoritative parent show better adjustment than those who do not have such a parent.[109] Congruent authoritative parenting is associated with higher emotional adjustment than congruent authoritarian parenting or incongruent parenting.[110]

SOCIAL DEVELOPMENT OUTCOMES

In regard to child outcomes, externalizing behaviors are linked to lack of disciplinary rules and coercive and abusive parenting practices.[111] Paquette argues that the presence of a father and a mother with differentiated roles fosters the development of children who are competent in cooperation and competition.[112] Bourçois has shown that, in dual-parent families, children from households with involved and differentiated parents (with distinct functions such as caregiver and playmate) present a more highly developed sociality (are more interactive, more involved, and more open with playmates) and are better prepared for both competition and cooperation than those with involved but undifferentiated parents.[113] According to Ricaud, as compared to children of differentiated fathers with little involvement in parenting, and children of two involved, undifferentiated parents, children of involved and differentiated parents have fewer conflicts with peers, fewer aggressive interactions, and more affiliative interactions, primarily exercising mutual agreement to resolve conflicts, and employing dissuasive effects of speech rather than physical violence.[114]

EARLY ATTACHMENT RELATIONSHIPS

Parent-child attachments can have different precursors, consequences, and correlates for boys and girls.[115] Attachments appear to be more closely related to emotional maturity in boys than girls.[116] Boys may be more vulnerable to emotional challenges than girls in early childhood.[117] Consequences of insecure attachments are greater for sons than daughters, predicting greater vulnerability to emotional and social difficulties. Sons and daughters are known to become attached to both mothers and fathers, and at approximately the same time in two-parent households.[118] While attached to both mothers and fathers, infants show a slight preference for mothers when distressed.[119] A vast literature links the quality of early attachment to cognitive and social development, indicating that securely attached children experience learning advantages by using their attachment figures as a secure base for exploration and as skilled social partners, who teach turn taking, emotional intelligence, and other skills that translate into more effective peer relationships for securely attached children in comparison to insecurely attached children.[120]

EARLY COGNITIVE DEVELOPMENT

Children form differential expectations for their mothers and fathers as they are treated in a different manner by each parent. Some of those expectations are doubtlessly translated into understandings of the personalities and inter-action styles of their parents as persons, but some are also likely interpreted as scripts for how men and women, fathers and mothers, behave. Such experiences are labeled as discrimination learning, the ability to discern differences, and to form differential expectations and contingencies based on the perceived differences. These are adaptive cognitive skills that translate into social cognition, competence, pragmatics, and nuanced interpersonal interaction abilities.

If a child had two parents who had styles and levels of interaction that were indistinguishable, they would not have the same degree of experience of evaluating and making meaning of differences. Experiencing parental differences affords children the opportunity to develop nuanced understandings of individual differences in personality as well as gender, enhancing social cognition. Two year olds who had highly supportive mothers and fathers were shown to have more advanced cognitive functioning than those who did not.[121]

LANGUAGE DEVELOPMENT

Mothers are often more verbally stimulating than fathers, and more talkative with daughters than with sons.[122] Father supportiveness and cognitive stimulation is related to children's language outcomes at thirty-six months.[123] Intrusive fathers have a small negative effect on language development prior to kindergarten.[124] Sons generally receive more negative reactions to communication attempts than daughters.[125] When sex differences in language ability are reported, girls generally are more advanced than boys.[126]

MODERATING EFFECTS

Many of the associations reported between patterns of gendered parenting and child development outcomes are known to be influenced by contexts of parent-child relationships. Some of the most salient moderating effects are reviewed here.

FAMILY STRUCTURE

Theoretically, all children benefit from having two parents because of the higher probability of being able to model effective behaviors as opposed to reworking ineffective patterns. In addition, children in two-parent families have more opportunity to view different personalities, strengths, and weaknesses, and to model strengths as opposed to reworking weaknesses.

Having two adults in the household also increases the average developmental maturity in comparison to single-parent families. Two-parent families typically enjoy more per capita income, more potential for adult monitoring, availability, and role specialization and efficiency,[127] so that children can potentially have more child-centered time with parents. Studies employing time-use diaries do not strongly support the notion that children in two-parent families experience vastly different amounts of quality time with an adult. Single parents (of both sexes) can be found who are doing heroic jobs of provision, nurturance, and all child-rearing functions in exemplary ways that are beneficial to their children. The functionality of the family appears to be more important than the form. However, on average, in comparison to single-parent families, two-parent families have more opportunity to accomplish higher levels of functioning across an array of important parenting tasks.

MARITAL HARMONY

Emerging research evidence has documented that marital conflict affects the parenting behaviors of fathers and mothers differently, and that maritally discordant mothers and fathers change their behaviors toward sons and daughters in a differential manner.[128] Simply stated, gendered parenting is moderated by marital quality.[129] Growing evidence suggests that marital quality is more influential in altering fathering behavior than mothering,[130] and that father-daughter relationships are particularly susceptible to lower quality with marital discord.[131] Though main effects can be demonstrated for child and parent gender, complex interactions exist between parent sex, gender, and marital quality.[132] Maritally less satisfied fathers are reported to be the most globally negative toward their daughters.[133] There is, in essence, "spillover" of negativity from the marital conflict to the father-daughter relationship to a significantly greater extent than in other dyadic pairings of parents and children. Marital conflict is linked to more overt relational aggression for boys, and maternal coercion in conjunction with less paternal responsiveness has been related to overt relational aggression in a study of Russian children.[134]

METHODOLOGICAL IMPLICATIONS

Findings reviewed earlier indicate that we need to consider the interactions of two sexes of parents by two sexes of children by four parental sex role orientations by four child sex role orientations, yielding sixty-four combinations of parent-child pairings. When combined with the gender roles of an opposite sexed parent that makes for 256 triad types for each mother-father-child set, and that is before considering other important variables (attachment types, hours of interaction, contexts, etc.). This diversity of interactive factors informs the reasons for less than expected robustness of findings in linking specific aspects of gendered parenting to child development outcome variables.

CAUTIONS AND LIMITATIONS

Clearly, gender differences in parenting are one conceptually complex part of a diverse array of variables that exert influence on the welfare of children. Parent-child relationships and developmental outcomes represent transactional processes that are embedded in a complex system of interacting variables that change across time.[135] Therefore, discerning patterns of association between conceptually contested and narrowly operationalized indicators of gendered parenting or child well-being is a tenuous enterprise. Interpretations of the same findings by persons with different theoretical lenses would yield different interpretations.[136]

Most empirical studies are not conducted in a manner that allows controls for a broad array of other centrally influential factors or with large representative samples of parents and children.[137] Age and stage interactions of parents and children are not consistently investigated. In most of the literature on gendered parenting, marital quality is not assessed.

Differential linkages depend on the gender-congruence of particular parental variables,[138] seldom studied in detail in empirical studies. For example, care giving with a young infant may be considered to be a cross-gender behavior for fathers and an on-gender activity for mothers.[139] Further, mother-child and father-child relationships can be conceptualized as differential contexts of development.[140] Different parent-child relationships elicit different behaviors, emotions, and cognitions in the people engaged in the interactions.[141]

Studies often fail to consider differences between dyadic and triadic[142] or larger family systems configurations. It is not just that father-child and mother-child relationships are different, rather, mother-child and father-child dyadic relationships are different than parent-child-parent triadic interactions.[143] Interactions between dyads, triads, and larger groups of people are characterized by differences in parental activity levels, emotional expression, and style. Empirical reports do not generally consider the relative amounts of triadic and dyadic interaction experienced in specific households when examining relationships between gendered parenting and child outcome measures.

The operationalization of sex roles is contested by different researchers and theoreticians.[144] Measures of sex role orientation generally depend on self-report data and, in many studies, categorizations of participants are based on median splits[145] of nonrepresentative samples, so people categorized in particular sex-role orientations may, in a different sample, fall into other categories entirely. The belief-behavior interface is not as predictable as we would like, with low predictive ability from one realm to another.[146] "Whereas self-report tests assess attitudes, self-attributions, or values, they do not assess behavior."[147] The consistency of parental behavior is not measured across time, calling into question major timing, dose, and duration issues.[148] Though there are some reported common patterns of association, the interface of parenting style and sex-role orientation is not clear. It is difficult to find and study true co-parenting families. Parents, even those who highly value sharing child-rearing, vary in amounts and qualities of accessibility, engagement, and responsibility[149] at least in the short term.

Further, it is not just the amount of behavior that a parent engages in that matters. Role competence, satisfaction, and investment are represented in the interaction[150] and influence the overall atmosphere of the exchange. These variables influence the behavior of divorced and nondivorced fathers differently.[151] Parental identity and considerations of whether particular activities or functions are an appropriate part of the parental role may function differently in mothers and fathers. Role investment tasks indicate that there is no relationship between paternal identity and involvement but significant associations between maternal identity and involvement patterns.[152] Thus, parental expectations play a significant role in shaping interactions over time.

Serial position of the child matters as well. For example, the transition to first parenthood is associated with increases in the degree of traditional gender role activity in adults,[153] while later adjustments to the birth of subsequent children may not entail so great of a move toward traditionalization.

Few observational studies have been published that would be capable of addressing process issues. Experimental studies systematically manipulating levels or kinds of gendered parenting and measuring outcomes are nonexistent.

It may be more appropriate to focus greater attention on other factors known to influence parent-child relationships and developmental outcomes, such as parenting style,[154] attachment security,[155] marital conflict,[156] divorce,[157] or poverty.[158] Nonetheless, there is substantial theoretical and empirical support for the aforementioned trends reported. However, it must be emphasized that the patterns noted are best viewed as trends that may or may not weather the tests of changing cohorts across time and more robust methodological controls.

A thorough analysis of the effects of gendered parenting on children's well-being would require the ability to distinguish the unique and additive contributions of fathering and mothering over time and in distinction from other developmental influences (including biological predispositions, potential, and reaction ranges) as well as the influences of other socializing agents (e.g., teachers, mentors, peers, mass media, culture, and cohort effects). In addition, thorough understanding of the relative contributions of fathers and mothers would necessitate an accounting of both direct and indirect influences of both parents. Given the current empirical database, it is not possible to draw more than general understandings.

Quantitative reviews of the empirical evidence can sometimes miss or misinterpret effects that are dependent on child age, parental characteristics, and setting for interaction,[159] or demand characteristics of activities. It is important to consider not only the differential frequencies of behaviors, but the different contexts and meanings of behaviors (or their absence). In fact, comparisons of parent-child interaction across contexts seem to indicate that activity is a better predictor of behavior than either the child's or the parent's gender.[160]

Clearly, gendered parenting exerts differential influence for sons' and daughters' social, emotional, and cognitive development. Some of the effects of gendered parenting may by obscured by personality attributions and recollection of specific events. For example, we may hear a son or a daughter reflect, "I learned assertiveness from my mother (or father) and patience from my father (or mother)." Their perception of learning a particular attribute exclusively or primarily from one parent (and different qualities from the other parent) ignores the contributions of the other parent as well as moderating effects from other family members, peers, teachers, mentors, and media portrayals. Further, if one asserts that they "learned patience" from their father, it is unclear how much of the experience is attributable to the father's sex (male), gender (androgynous), personality attributes (patient), behavioral history over time (modeling patience or the lack thereof, which triggered reworking), or specific, salient events or interactions (e.g., the Christmas Day when Dad overlooked persistently inappropriate comments from his brother).

This chapter has adopted a developmental perspective with a decidedly child-centered focus. What may be beneficial for child development may not be the most satisfying or just division of labor for adults. Baumrind's review[161] makes it clear that there is a need to distinguish between desirability of traits, tendencies, and behaviors, and that roles/functions do matter. However, it is also the case that the ideal spouse may not be the ideal parent or partner. While there may well be significant overlap, there are significant distinctions as well. Integration and differentiation of roles become operative. It becomes crucial to ask what traits are desirable for different roles—and this review focuses on parenting. Those traits that make one an excellent parent may or may not overlap with traits that predispose one for success or failure as a partner, friend, lobster boat captain, or interior decorator. This is important to keep in mind as this review focuses on parental characteristics associated with positive outcomes for children.

CONCLUSIONS

As demonstrated throughout this chapter, parenting is gendered in many ways. Parental gender interacts with sex of parent and child, parenting styles, and personality attributes to shape children's development. Moreover, gendered parenting is embedded in a multifaceted matrix of cultural and contextual conditions that also exert influence in shaping children's well-being. Gender roles are embedded in and confounded with a broad array of other attributes known to influence child outcomes, some of which have been demonstrated to carry greater amounts of variability in child outcome measures, most notably parental warmth and control or demandingness (parenting style).

The applied value of this review can be stated in an answer to the practical question, "what patterns of gendered parenting present developmental benefits and challenges for children?" Clearly, an appropriate response to this question would be, "it depends." This review has demonstrated that it depends on the conceptualization and measurement of gendered parenting and child outcomes. It depends on contexts, meanings, and patterns of interaction within the family over time. It depends on family form, family functioning, and on parental style, competence, warmth, connection, and so on. Baumrind's 1982 study of nine-year-old children used an extensive array of measures and revealed surprisingly few effects for parental gender roles. Significant effects supported positive relationships between traditional parental gender roles and children's well-being and showed neither striking advantages nor disadvantages of androgynous parenting for children's outcome measures. This may be because androgenes demonstrate a high degree of traditional traits as well as socially desirable attributes of the opposite sex. Thus, children with both traditional and androgynous parents experience the functioning of sex-typed norms in the parenting they receive. This pattern of findings may be interpreted as supporting the notion that it is important for children to see traditional gender role characteristics enacted by parents. On the other hand, androgynous parenting may be seen as supportive, validating, and fulfilling by an adult partner. It is possible that the traditional components of androgynous parental roles carry elements of well-being for children while the demonstration of socially desirable traits of the opposite sex contribute positive elements to adult relationships (thereby potentially positively influencing child well-being through indirect pathways).

Are children from androgynous households better off or worse off than children from traditional families? Better or worse off in regard to what? Evidence can be garnered that would support different answers to the questions, depending on one's theoretical and values perspectives.

My read is that children with "good parents" from families with either androgynous or traditional parents fare better than those with parents who are undifferentiated or cross-gendered. All parents are challenged to provide parenting characteristics that always facilitate development: positive affective climate, behavioral style, and relational synchrony.[162] My view of the literature and my experience with diverse families over time have convinced me that many of the factors associated with gendered parenting are secondary to these central characteristics of "good parenting"[163] and positive family functioning. "Children from all parenting types are at risk when they experience parenting that is inadequate in terms of warmth, control, or monitoring."[164]

Nonetheless, I am confident that the literature clearly supports the perspective that children from families that have well functioning males and females consistently engaged in parenting roles are advantaged because they can see how men and women perform a similar task similarly and differently. Children who obtain the most varied resources will be those who adapt best.[165] They are provided with a greater range of possibility for modeling. They are exposed to collaborative sharing with a different level of maturity than others. The difference for children in families with well functioning, role sharing couples in comparison to gender traditional families could be likened to the difference between being immersed in cooperative play versus parallel play.

My advice for parents who grapple with issues of gendered parenting in meeting the various developmental and provisional needs of their families would be to communicate with their partners and to work out balances of role specialization and diversification that bring fulfillment to themselves and their partner.[166] Parents who model engagement and proficiency in a range of roles and behaviors as well as interest in expanding abilities, while demonstrating cooperation and justice in sharing work and enjoyment of family roles establish family environments that benefit all members of the family. Families characterized by these ideals afford children more opportunities to model pro-social attitudes and behaviors and to stimulate thinking and discussions regarding the possibilities for their own role attainment in the future. The literature reviewed in this chapter suggests that it is important for families to encourage and support interactions of both parents with each of their children for regular times of engagement in some one-on-one (dyadic) as well as triadic and full family interactions. The evidence would also suggest that it is developmentally facilitative to purposively engage in a range of activities: some that are child-centered, and some more directive and parent structured.

Parents can increase the developmental impact of their interactions by narrating important features regarding choices and challenges in sharing family roles. It is also facilitative for family functioning to be charitable in pointing out differences in styles and levels of family roles, without devaluing the contributions of others, taking opportunities to narrate the strengths of your partner in parenting, work, relationships, and family roles as well as those of your children in their domains of activity and responsibility.

The primary focus of this chapter has been individual differences in gendered parenting and associated patterns of well-being in children. The literature reviewed has clearly documented that gendered parenting influences family functioning and child well-being. It remains to be seen whether it will prove to be a fruitful intervention to educate parents regarding the relationships between various components of gendered parenting and child outcomes and encourage parents to reflect on and communicate about their gendered roles and values, especially in regard to parenting behaviors as they shape the futures of their children.

NOTES

1. LeVine 1970.
2. Maccoby 2008.
3. Kuczynski and Parkin 2007.
4. Rossi 1984.
5. Cabrera et al. 2002.
6. Rossi 1984; Jacobs and Gerson 2004.
7. Amato et al. 2007.
8. Bianchi, Robinson, and Milkie 2006.
9. Mischel, Bernstein, and Allegretto 2005.
10. Bassett 2005.
11. Rhoads 2005.
12. Pleck and Masciadrelli 2003; Lamb and Lewis 2004.
13. Darling and Steinberg 1993.
14. Maurer, Pleck, and Rane 2001.
15. Snarey 1993; Palkovitz 2002.
16. Bussey and Bandura 1999.
17. Kerig, Cowan, and Cowan 1993.
18. Hill and Flom 2007.
19. Smith and Daglish 1977; Wood, Desmarais, and Gugula 2002.
20. Fulcher, Sutfin, and Patterson 2001.
21. Turner and Gervai 1995; Sabbatini and Leaper 2004.
22. Snarey 1993; Palkovitz 2002:194.
23. Bandura 2006.
24. Leaper 2002.
25. Pleck and Masciadrelli 2003; Lamb and Lewis 2004.
26. Parke 2000; Paquette 2004.
27. Parke 2000.

28. Lamb and Lewis 2004.

29. Palkovitz 2002.

30. Lamb and Lewis 2004.

31. Block 1973; Weitzman, Birns, and Friend 1985; Dunn, Bretherton, and Munn 1987.

32. Block 1973; Tronick and Cohn 1989.

33. Kerig, Cowan, and Cowan 1993.

34. Maccoby 1980.

35. Condry and Condry 1976; Benenson, Philippoussis, and Leeb 1999.

36. Parke 2000.

37. Starrels 1994.

38. Ibid.

39. Leaper 2002.

40. Paquette 2004.

41. Fagot 1978.

42. Malatesta and Haviland 1982; Tronick and Cohn 1985.

43. Biringen et al. 1999.

44. Leaper 2002.

45. Ibid.

46. McLaughlin et al. 1983; Gleason 1987.

47. Kerig, Cowan, and Cowan 1993.

48. Frankel and Rollins 1983; Weitzman, Birns, and Friend 1985.

49. Siegel 1987; Lytton and Romney 1991.

50. Lytton and Romney 1991.

51. Snow, Jacklin, and Maccoby 1983.

52. Kuczynski 2003.

53. Leaper 2002.

54. Burns and Homel 1989; Antill et al. 1996.

55. Hilton and Haldeman 1991.

56. McKinney and Renk 2008.

57. Ibid.

58. Leaper 2002.

59. Rossi 1984; Hyde 2005:590.

60. Hyde 2005.

61. Hyde and Plant 1995:159.

62. Rhoads 2005.

63. Power 1985; Teti, Bond, and Gibbs 1998.

64. Labrell 1997.

65. Labrell 1996.

66. Paquette 2004.

67. Baumrind 1982.

68. Labrell 1992.

69. Marcos 1995.
70. Bem 1981.
71. Baumrind 1982:48.
72. Baumrind 1982:54–55.
73. Baumrind 1982:68.
74. Paquette 2004:203.
75. As cited in Paquette 2004.
76. Baumrind 1982:54–55.
77. Palkovitz 1984.
78. Baumrind 1982:55
79. Baumrind 1982:63–64.
80. Baumrind 1982:64–65.
81. Baumrind 1982; Palkovitz 1984.
82. Baumrind 1982:68.
83. Baumrind 1982:65.
84. Baumrind 1982:68.
85. Baumrind 1982.
86. Ibid.
87. Ibid.
88. Ibid.
89. Ibid.
90. Ibid.
91. I am less familiar with "unique contributions" literature for mothers.
92. Verschueren and Marcoen 1999:183–201.
93. Amato 1994:375–384.
94. Amato and Rivera 1999:1031–1042; Kosterman et al. 2004:762–778.
95. Williams and Kelley 2005:168–196.
96. Flouri and Buchanan 2003:399–406; Carlson 2006:137–154.
97. Cookston and Finlay 2006: 37–158.
98. Stolz, Barber, and Olsen 2005:1076–1092.
99. Barnett, Marshall, and Pleck 1992:505–525.
100. Paquette 2004.
101. Paquette 2004.
102. Morris et al. 2007:361.
103. Cabrera, Shannon, and Tamis-LeMonda 2007:208–215.
104. Eisenberg 1999:267–284.
105. Fivush 1989:675–691.
106. Block 1973; Eccles 1987; Leaper et al. 1989.
107. Leaper 2002.
108. Raffaelli and Ontai 2004:287.
109. McKinney and Renk 2008.
110. Ibid.

111. Greenberg, Speltz, and DeKlyen 1993:191–213; Rubin, Stewart, and Chen 1995.
112. Paquette 2004:210.
113. V. Bourçois (1997) as cited in Paquette 2004.
114. Paquette 2004.
115. Biringen et al. 1999; van IJzendoorn et al. 2000:1086–1098.
116. Lewis et al. 1984:123–136.
117. Leaper 2002.
118. Lamb and Lewis 2004.
119. Lamb 1976:435–443.
120. Sigelman and Rider 2009:419.
121. Ryan, Martin, and Brooks-Gunn 2006.
122. Leaper 2002.
123. Cabrera, Shannon, and Tamis-LeMonda 2007:208–215.
124. Ibid.
125. Fagot and Hagan 1991.
126. Hyde and Linn 1998.
127. Palkovitz 1987.
128. Cox et al. 1989.
129. Kerig, Cowan, and Cowan 1993.
130. Easterbrooks and Emde 1988; Belsky, Rovine, and Fish 1989; Howes and Markman 1989.
131. Goldberg and Easterbrooks 1984; Belsky et al. 1989.
132. Kerig, Cowan, and Cowan 1993.
133. Ibid.
134. Hart et al. 1998.
135. Palkovitz 2002.
136. Baumrind 1982.
137. Parke 2000.
138. Mauer, Pleck, and Rane 2001.
139. Ibid.
140. McBride, Schoppe, and Rane 2002.
141. Morris et al 2007:361.
142. Lindsey and Caldera 2006.
143. Ibid.
144. Baumrind 1982; Spence 1982.
145. Bem 1974.
146. Bem 1968.
147. Baumrind 1982:46.
148. Palkovitz and Daly 2004.
149. Pleck and Masciadrelli 2003.
150. Minton and Pasley 1996.
151. Mauer, Pleck, and Rane 2001.

152. McBride and Rane 1997.
153. Entwistle and Doering 1981; Palkovitz and Copes 1988; Burke and Cast 1997.
154. Baumrind 1982.
155. Lamb and Lewis 2004.
156. Cummings, Goeke-Morey, and Raymond 2004.
157. Amato and Sobolewski 2004.
158. McLanahan and Carlson 2004.
159. Fagot and Hagan 1991.
160. Lewis and Gregory 1987; Caldera, Huston, and O'Brien 1989; Leaper et al. 1995; Leaper 2000.
161. Baumrind 1982.
162. For an expanded discussion of these attributes, see Palkovitz 2007.
163. Palkovitz 2007.
164. Website on Single-Parent Families and Child Well-Being, retrieved June 13, 2011, from http://social.jrank.org/pages/580/Single-Parent-Families-Well-Being-Children-Raised-in-Single-Parent-Homes.html. "Single-Parent Families—The Well-Being of Children Raised in Single-Parent Homes."
165. Paquette 2004:212.
166. Palkovitz 1987.

REFERENCES

Amato, Paul. 1994. "Father-Child Relations, Mother-Child Relations, and Offspring Psychological Well-Being in Early Adulthood." *Journal of Marriage and Family* 56(4):1031–1042.

Amato, Paul. 1999. "Paternal Involvement and Children's Behavior Problems." *Journal of Marriage and Family* 61(2):375–384.

Amato, Paul R., Alan Booth, David Johnson, and Stacy Rogers. 2007. *Alone Together: How Marriage in America is Changing.* Cambridge, MA: Harvard University.

Amato, Paul R. and Julie M. Sobolewski. 2004. "The Effects of Divorce on Fathers and Children: Nonresidential Fathers and Stepfathers." In *The Role of the Father in Child Development,* 4th ed., ed. Michael E. Lamb, 341–367. Hoboken, NJ: John Wiley.

Antill, J. K, J. J. Goodnow, G. Russell, and S. Cotton. 1996. "The Influence of Parents and Family Context on Children's Involvement in Household Tasks." *Sex Roles* 34:215–236;

Bandura, Albert. 2006. "Analysis of Modeling Processes." In *Psychological Modeling: Conflicting Theories,* ed. Albert Bandura, 1–62. New Brunswick, NJ: Transaction.

Barnett, Rosiland C., Nancy L. Marshall, and Joseph Pleck. 1992. "Adult-Son-Parent Relationships and Their Associations with Sons' Psychological Distress." *Journal of Family Issues* 13(4):505–525.

Bassett, Rachel Hile. 2005. *Parenting and Professing: Balancing Family Work with an Academic Career.* Nashville, TN: Vanderbilt University.

Baumrind, Diana. 1982. "Are Androgynous Individuals More Effective Persons and Parents?" *Child Development* 53:44–75.

Belsky, Jay, M. Rovine, and M. Fish. 1989. "The Developing Family System." In *Systems and Development: Minnesota Symposia on Child Psychology*, vol. 22, ed. M. Gunnar and E. Thelen, 119–166. Hillsdale, NJ: Lawrence Erlbaum.

Bem, Daryl J. 1968. "Attitudes as Self Descriptions: Another Look at the Attitude-Behavior Link." In *Psychological Foundations of Attitudes*, ed. A. G. Greenwald, T. C. Brock, and T. M. Ostrum. New York: Academic.

Bem, S. L. 1974. "The Measurement of Psychological Androgyny." *Journal of Consulting and Clinical Psychology* 42:155–162.

Bem, Sandra L. 1981. *Bem Sex-Role Inventory: Professional Manual*. Palo Alto: Consulting Psychologists.

Benenson, J. F., M. Philippoussis, and R. Leeb. 1999. "Sex Differences in Neonates' Cuddliness." *Journal of Genetic Psychology* 160:332–342.

Bianchi, Suzanne M., John P. Robinson, and Melissa A. Milkie. 2006. *Changing Rhythms of American Family Life*. New York, NY: Russell Sage Foundation.

Biringen, Z. R. N. Emde, D. Brown, L. Lowe, S. Myers, and D. Nelson. 1999. "Emotional Availability and Emotion Communication in Naturalistic Mother-Infant Interactions: Evidence for Gender Relations." *Journal of Social Behavior and Personality* 14:463–478.

Block, Jack H. 1973. "Conceptions of Sex Roles: Some Cross-Cultural and Longitudinal Perspectives." *American Psychologist* 28:512–526.

Bourçois, V. 1997. "Modalités de présence du père et développement social de l'enfant d'âge préscolaire." ["Modalities of Father's Presence and Social Development of Preschoolers."] *Enfance* 3:389–399.

Burke, P. J. and A. D. Cast. 1997. "Stability and Change in the Gender Identities of Newly Married Couples." *Social Psychology Quarterly* 60:277–290.

Burns, A. and R. Homel. 1989. "Gender Division of Tasks by Parents and Their Children." *Psychology of Women Quarterly* 13:113–125.

Bussey, K. and Albert Bandura. 1999. "Social Cognitive Theory of Gender Development and Differentiation." *Psychological Review* 106:676–713.

Cabrera, Natasha, J. Brooks-Gunn, K. Moore, J. West, K. Boller, and C.S. Tamis-LeMonda. 2002. "Bridging Research and Policy: Including Fathers of Young Children in National Studies." In *Handbook of Father Involvement: Multidisciplinary Perspectives*, ed. C. S. Tamis-LeMonda and N. Cabrera, 489–524. Mahwah, NJ: Lawrence Erlbaum.

Cabrera, Natasha J., Jacqueline D. Shannon, and Catherine Tamis-LeMonda. 2007. "Fathers' Influence on Their Children's Cognitive and Emotional Development: From Toddlers to Pre-K." *Journal of Applied Developmental Science* 11(4):208–215.

Caldera, Y. M., A. C. Huston and M. O'Brien. 1989. "Social Interactions and Play Patterns of Parents and Toddlers With Feminine, Masculine, and Neutral Toys." *Child Development* 60:70–76.

Carlson, M. J. 2006. "Family Structure, Father Involvement, and Adolescent Behavioral Outcomes." *Journal of Marriage and Family* 68(1):137–154.

Collins, W. A., E. E. Maccoby, L. Steinberg, E. M. Hetherington, and M. H. Bornstein. 2000. "Contemporary Research on Parenting: The Case For Nature and Nurture." *American Psychologist* 55:218–232.

Condry, J. and S. Condry. 1976. "Sex Differences: A Study in the Eye of the Beholder." *Child Development* 47:812–819.

Cookston, Jefrey T. and Andrea K. Finlay. 2006. "Father Involvement and Adolescent Adjustment: Longitudinal Findings From Add Health." *Fathering* 4(2):137–158.

Cox, Martha J, M. T. Owen, Michael J. Lewis, and V. K. Henderson. 1989. "Marriage, Adult Adjustment, and Early Parenting." *Child Development* 60:1015–1024.

Cummings, E. M., M. C. Goeke-Morey, and J. Raymond. 2004. "Fathers in Family Context: Effects of Marital Quality and Marital Conflict." In *The Role of the Father in Child Development*, 4th ed., ed. Michael E. Lamb, 196–221. Hoboken, NJ: John Wiley.

Darling, N. and L. Steinberg. 1993. "Parenting Style as Context: An Integrative Model." *Psychological Bulletin* 113(3):487–496.

Dunn, J., I. Bretherton, and P. Munn. 1987. "Conversations About Feelings Between Mothers and Their Young Children," *Developmental Psychology* 23:132–139.

Easterbrooks, A. M. and Robert N. Emde. 1988. "Marital and Parent-Child Relationships: The Role of Affect in the Family System." In *Relationships Within Families: Mutual Influences*, ed. Robert A. Hinde, 83–103. Oxford, UK: Clarendon.

Eccles, J. S. 1989. "Adolescence: Gateway to Gender-Role Transcendence." In *Current Conceptions of Sex Roles and Sex Typing: Theory and Research*, ed. D.B. Carter, 225–242. New York: Praeger.

Eisenberg, A. R. 1999. "Emotion-Talk Among Mexican-American and Anglo American Mothers and Children from Two Social Classes." *Merrill-Palmer Quarterly* 45:267–284.

Entwistle, D. R. and S. G. Doering. 1981. *The First Birth: A Family Turning Point.* Baltimore, MD: Johns Hopkins.

Fagot, B. I. 1978. "The Influence of Child Sex on Parental Reactions to Toddler Children." *Child Development* 49:459-465.

Fagot, B. I. and R. Hagan. 1991. "Observations of Parent Reactions to Sex-Stereotyped Behaviors: Age and Sex Differences." *Child Development* 62:617–628.

Fivush, R. 1989. "Exploring Sex Differences in the Emotional Content of Mother-Child Conversations About the Past." *Sex Roles* 20:675–691.

Flouri, Eirini and A. Buchanan. 2003. "The Role of Father Involvement and Mother Involvement in Adolescents' Psychological Well-Being." *British Journal of Social Work* 33:399–406.

Frankel, M. T. and H. A. Rollins, Jr. 1983. "Does Mother Know Best? Mothers and Fathers Interacting With Preschool Sons and Daughters." *Developmental Psychology* 19:649–702.

Fulcher, M., E. L. Sutfin, and C. J. Patterson. 2001. "Parental Sexual Orientation, Division of Labor, and Sex-Role Stereotyping in Children's Occupational Choices." Paper presented at the meeting of the Society for Research on Child Development, April 2001, Minneapolis, MN.

Gleason, J. B. 1987. "Sex Differences in Parent-Child Interaction." In *Language, Gender and Sex in Comparative Perspective,*" ed. S. U. Philips, S. Steele, and C. Tanz, 189–199. Cambridge, UK: Cambridge University.

Goldberg, Wendy A. and M. A. Easterbrooks. 1984. "Role of Marital Quality in Toddler Development." *Developmental Psychology* 20:504–514.

Greenberg, Mark T., M. L. Speltz, and M. DeKlyen. 1993. "The Role of Attachment in the Early Development of Disruptive Behavior Problems." *Development and Psychopathology* 5:191–213.

Harris, J. R. 2000. "Socialization, Personality Development, and the Child's Environments: Comment on Vendell (2000)." *Developmental Psychology* 36:711–723.

Hill, S. E. and R. Flom. 2007. "18- and 24-Month-Old's Discrimination of Gender Consistent and Inconsistent Activities," *Infant Behavior and Development* 30:168–173.

Hilton, J. M. and V. A. Haldeman. 1991. "Gender Differences and Performance of Household Tasks by Adults and Children in Single-Parent and Two-Parent, Two-Earner Families," *Journal of Family Issues* 12:114–130.

Howes, P. and H. J. Markman. 1989. "Marital Quality and Child Functioning: A Longitudinal Investigation." *Child Development* 60:1044–1051.

Hyde, Janet Shelby. 2005. "The Gender Similarities Hypothesis." *American Psychologist* 60:581–592.

Hyde, Janet Shelby and Elizabeth Ashley Plant. 1995. "Magnitude of Psychological Gender Differences: Another Side to the Story," *American Psychologist* 50(3):159.

Hyde, J. S. and M. C. Linn. 1998. "Gender Differences in Verbal Ability: A Meta-Analysis." *Psychological Bulletin* 104:53–69.

Jacobs, Jerry A. and Kathleen Gerson. 2004. *The Time Divide: Work, Family, and Gender Inequality*. Cambridge, MA: Harvard University.

Kerig, Patricia K., Philip A. Cowan, and Carolyn Pape Cowan. 1993. "Marital Quality and Gender Differences in Parent-Child Interaction," *Developmental Psychology* 29(6):931–939.

Kosterman, Rick, Kevin P. Haggerty, and Richard Spoth. 2004. "Unique Influence of Mothers and Fathers on Their Children's Antisocial Behavior." *Journal of Marriage and Family* 66(3):762–778.

Kuczynski, L., ed. 2003. *Dynamics in Parent–Child Relations*. Thousand Oaks, CA: Sage.

Kuczynski, Leon and C. M. Parkin. 2007. "Agency and Bidirectionality in Socialization." In *Handbook of Socializaton: Theory and Research*, ed. Joan E. Grusec and P. D. Hastings, 259–283. New York: Guilford.

Labrell, F. 1992. *Contributions paternelles au développement cognitif de l'enfant dans la deuxième année de vie*. [*Paternal Contributions to Cognitive Development of Children in the Second Year of Life*.] Ph.D. thesis, Nouveau Régime, Paris-V.

Labrell, F. 1996. "Paternal Play with Toddlers: Recreation and Creation." *European Journal of Psychology of Education* 11(1):43–54.

Labrell, F. 1997. "L'apport spécifique du père au développement cognitif du jeune enfant." ["The Specific Contribution of the Father of Cognitive Development in Young Children."] *Enfance* 3:361–369.

Lamb, Michael E. 1976. "Effects of Stress and Cohort on Mother- and Father-Infant Interaction." *Developmental Psychology* 12:435–443.

Lamb, Michael E. and Charlie Lewis. 2004. "The Development and Significance of Father-Child Relationships in Two-Parent Families." In *The Role of the Father in Child Development*, 4th ed., ed. Michael E. Lamb, 272–306. Hoboken, NJ: John Wiley.

Leaper, C. 2000. "Gender, Affiliation, Assertion, and the Integrative Context of Parent-Child Play." *Developmental Psychology* 36:381–393.

Leaper, C., S. T. Hauser, A. Kremen, S. I. Powers, A. M. Jacobsen, G. G. Noam, B. Weiss-Perry, and D. Follansbee. 1989. "Parent-Adolescent Interactions in Relation to Adolescents' Gender and Ego Development Pathway: A Longitudinal Study." *Journal of Early Adolescence* 9:335–361.

Leaper, C., L. Leve, T. Strasser, and R. Schwartz. 1995. "Mother-Child Communications Sequences: Play Activity, Child Gender and Marital Status Effects." *Merrill-Palmer Quarterly* 41:307–327.

Leaper, Campbell. 2002. "Parenting Boys and Girls." In *Handbook of Parenting*, vol. 1, 2nd ed., ed. Marc H. Bornstein, 189–225. Mahwah, NJ: Lawrence Erlbaum.

LeVine, R. A. 1970. "Cross-Cultural Study in Child Psychology." In *Charmichael's Manual of Child Psychology*, vol. II, 3rd ed., ed., P. H. Mussen, 559–612. New York: John Wiley.

Lewis, C. and S. Gregory. 1987. "Parents' Talk to Their Infants: The Importance of Context." *First Language* 7:201–216.

Lewis, Michael, C. Feiring, C. McGuffog, and J. Jaskir. 1984. "Predicting Psychopathology in Six-Year-Olds from Early Social Relations." *Child Development* 55:123–136.

Lindsey, Eric W. and Yvonne M. Caldera. 2006. "Mother-Father-Child Triadic Interaction: Gender Differences Within and Between Contexts." *Sex Roles* 55:511.

Lytton, H. and D. M. Romney. 1991. "Parents' Differential Socialization of Boys and Girls: A Meta-Analysis." *Psychological Bulletin* 109:267–296.

Maccoby, E. E. 1980. *Social Development*. New York: Harcourt Brace Janovich.

Maccoby, Eleanor E. 2008. "Historical Overview of Socialization Research and Theory." In *Handbook of Socializaton: Theory and Research*, ed. Joan E. Grusec and P. D. Hastings, 13–41. New York: Guilford.

Malatesta, Carol Z. and Jeanette M. Haviland. 1982. "Learning Display Rules: The Socialization of Emotion Expression in Infancy." *Child Development* 53:991–1003.

Marcos, H. 1995. "Mother-Child and Father-Child Communication in the Second Year: A Functional Approach." *Early Development and Parenting* 2:49–61.

Mauer, Trent W., Joseph H. Pleck, and Thomas R. Rane. 2001. "Parental Identity and Reflected-Apprasals: Measurement and Gender Dynamics." *Journal of Marriage and Family* 63(2):309–321.

McBride, Brent A., Sarah J. Schoppe, and Thomas R. Rane. 2002. "Child Characteristics, Parenting Stress and Parental Involvement: Fathers Versus Mothers." *Journal of Marriage and Family* 64(4):998–1011.

McKinney, Cliff and Kimberly Renk. 2008. "Differential Parenting Between Mothers and Fathers: Implications for Late Adolescents." *Journal of Family Issues* 29(6):806–827.

McLanahan, Sara and Marcia S. Carlson. 2004. "Fathers in Fragile Families" in *The Role of the Father in Child Development*, 4th ed., ed. Michael E. Lamb, 368–396. Hoboken, NJ: John Wiley.

McLaughlin, B., D. White, T. McDevitt, and R. Raskin. 1983. "Mothers' and Fathers' Speech to Their Young Children: Similar or Different?" *Journal of Child Language* 10:245–252.

Minton, C. and K. Pasley. 1996. "Fathers' Parenting Role Identity and Father Involvement: A Comparison of Nondivorced and Divorced, Nonresident Fathers." *Journal of Family Issues* 17:26–45.

Mischel, Lawrence, Jared Bernstein, and Sylvia Allegretto. 2005. *The State of Working America 2004/2005*. Washington DC: Economic Policy Institute.

Morris, Amanda S., Jennifer S. Silk, Laurence Steinberg, Sonya S. Myers, and Lara R. Robinson. 2007. "The Role of Family Context in the Development of Emotion Regulation." *Social Development* 16(2):361.

Palkovitz, R. 2007. "Challenges to Modeling Dynamics in Developing a Developmental Understanding of Father-Child Relationships." *Applied Developmental Science* 11:190–195.

Palkovitz, Rob. 1984. "Parental Attitudes and Fathers' Interactions with Their Five-Month-Old Infants." *Developmental Psychology* 20:1054–1060.

Palkovitz, Rob. 1987. "Consistency and Stability in the Family Microsystem Environment." In *Annual Advances in Applied Developmental Psychology*, vol. II, ed. Donald L. Peters and Susan Kontos, 40–67. New York: Ablex.

Palkovitz, Rob. 2002. *Involved Fathering and Men's Adult Development: Provisional Balances*. Mahwah, NJ: Lawrence Erlbaum.

Palkovitz, Rob and Marcella A. Copes. 1988. "Changes in Attitudes, Beliefs and Expectations Associated With the Transition to Parenthood." *Marriage and Family Review* 12:183–199.

Palkovitz, Rob and Kerry Daly. 2004. "Eyeing the Edges: Theoretical Considerations of Work and Family for Fathers in Midlife Development." *Fathering* 2:215–233.

Paquette, Daniel. 2004. "Theorizing the Father-Child Relationship: Mechanisms and Developmental Outcomes." *Human Development* 47:193–219.

Parke, Ross D. 2000. "Father Involvement: A Developmental Psychological Perspective." *Marriage and Family Review* 29(2/3):43–58.

Pleck, Joseph H. and Brian P. Masciadrelli. 2003. "Paternal Involvement by U.S. Residential Fathers: Levels, Sources, and Consequences." In *The Role of the Father in Child Development*, 4th ed., ed. Michael E. Lamb, 222–271. Hoboken, NJ: John Wiley.

Power, T. G. 1985. "Mother- and Father-Infant Play: A Developmental Analysis." *Child Development* 56:1514–1524.

Raffaelli, Marcella, and Lenna L. Ontai. 2004. "Gender Socialization in Latino/a Families: Results From Two Retrospective Studies." *Sex Roles* 50(5/6):287.

Rhoads, Steven. 2005. *Taking Sex Differences Seriously*. San Francisco, CA: Encounter.

Rossi, Alice S. 1984. "Gender and Parenthood." *American Sociological Review* 49(1):1–19.

Rubin, R. H., S. L. Stewart, and X. Chen. 1995. "Parents of Aggressive and Withdrawn Children." In *Handbook of Parenting*, vol. 1, ed. Marc H. Bornstein, 255–276. Hillsdale, NJ: Lawrence Erlbaum.

Ryan, R. M., A. Martin, and J. Brooks-Gunn. 2006. "Is One Parent Good Enough? Patterns of Mother and Father Parenting and Child Cognitive Outcomes at 24 and 36 Months." *Parenting: Science and Practice* 6(2/3):211–228.

Sabbatini, L. and C. Leaper. 2004. "The Relation Between Mothers' and Fathers' Parenting Styles and Their Division of Labor in the Home: Young Adults' Retrospective Reports." *Sex Roles* 50:217–250.

Siegel, M. 1987. "Are Sons and Daughters Treated More Differently by Fathers Than by Mothers?" *Developmental Review* 7:183–209.

Sigelman, Carol K. and Elizabeth A. Rider. 2009. *Life-Span Human Development*, 6th ed. Belmont, CA: Wadsworth.

"Single-Parent Families—The Well-Being of Children Raised in Single-Parent Homes. Accessed June 13, 2011, http://social.jrank.org/pages/580/Single-Parent-Families-Well-Being-Children-Raised-in-Single-Parent-Homes.html.

Smith, P. K. and L. Daglish. 1977. "Sex Differences in Parent and Infant Behavior in the Home," *Child Development* 48:1250–1254.

Snarey, John. 1993. *How Fathers Care for the Next Generation: A Four-Decade Study*. Cambridge, MA: Harvard University.

Snow, M. E., C. N. Jacklin, and E. E. Maccoby. 1983. "Sex-of-Child Differences in Father-Child Interaction at One Year of Age." *Child Development* 54:227–232.

Spence, Janet T. 1982. "Comments on Baumrind's 'Are Androgynous Individuals More Effective Persons and Parents?'" *Child Development* 53:76–82.

Starrels, Marjorie E. 1994. "Gender Differences in Parent-Child Relations." *Journal of Family Issues* 15(1):148.

Stolz, Heidi E., Brian K. Barber, and Joseph A. Olsen. 2005. "Toward Disentangling Fathering and Mothering: An Assessment of Relative Importance." *Journal of Marriage and Family* 67(4):1076–1092.

Tamis-LeMonda, Catherine, Jacqueline D. Shannon, Natasha J. Cabrera, and Michael E. Lamb. 2004. "Fathers and Mothers at Play with Their 2- and 3-Year-Olds: Contributions to Language and Cognitive Development." *Child Development* 75(6):1806–1820.

Teti, D. M, L. A. Bond, and E. D. Gibbs. 1998. "Mothers, Fathers, and Siblings: A Comparison of Play Styles and Their Influence upon Infant Cognitive Level," *International Journal of Behavioral Development* 11:415–432.

Tronick, E. Z. and J. F. Cohn. 1989. "Infant-Mother Face-To-Face Interaction: Age and Gender Differences in Coordination and the Occurrence of Miscoordination." *Child Development* 60:85–92.

Turner, P. J. and J. Gervai. 1995. "A Multidimensional Study of Gender Typing in Preschool Children and Their Parents: Personality, Attitudes, Preferences, Behavior, and Cultural Differences." *Developmental Psychology* 31:759–772

Van Ijzendoorn, M. H., G. Moran, J. Belsky, D. Pederson, M. J. Bakersman-Kranenberg, and K. Kneppers. 2000. "The Similarity of Siblings' Attachments to Their Mother." *Child Development* 71:1086–1098.

Verschueren, Karine and Alfons Marcoen. 1999. "Representation of Self and Socio-Emotional Competence in Kindergartners: Differential and Combined Effects of Attachment to Mother and Father." *Child Development* 70(1):183–201.

Weitzman, N., B. Birns, and R. Friend. 1985. "Traditional and Nontraditional Mothers' Communication with Their Daughters and Sons." *Child Development* 56:894–898.

Williams, Susan K. and Donald F. Kelley. 2005. "Relationships Among Involvement, Attachment, and Behavioral Problems in Adolescence: Examining Fathers' Influence." *Journal of Early Adolescence* 25(2):168–196.

Wood, E., S. Desmarais, and S. Gugula. 2002. "The Impact of Parenting Experience on Gender Stereotyped Toy Play of Children," *Sex Roles* 47:39–49.

9

DO FATHERS UNIQUELY MATTER FOR ADOLESCENT WELL-BEING?

David J. Eggebeen

THE EVIDENCE IS IN, and it is clear that fathers do matter in the lives of their children. Literally hundreds of studies over the past two decades have consistently demonstrated that fathers have a measureable impact on children (Marsiglio, Amato, Day, and Lamb 2000; Parke 2002; Paquette 2004). Studies show that infants are positively affected by the interactions and care given by their fathers (Pedersen 1980; Yogman 1982). Good studies have found that the quality of parenting exhibited by the father as well as the resources they bring to their family predict children's behavior problems, depression, self-esteem, and life-satisfaction (Marsiglio et al. 2000). The reach of fathers has been shown to extend to adolescents and young adults, as research finds that adolescents function best when their fathers are engaged and involved in their lives (Buehler, Benson, and Gerard 2006). Additional work demonstrates that fathers play an important role in helping their children make the transition to adulthood (Amato 1994). In short, a fairly extensive body of empirical research has established the importance of fathers throughout the life course of children (Parke 2002).

Nevertheless, there remains much we do not know about the nature of fatherhood for the lives of children and youth. In effect, the first stage of work, that of establishing that fathers matter, is well advanced. The next stage, exploring the unique contributions of fathers vis-à-vis mothers or other adults, remains less well developed. Debates about whether fathers are essential to optimal child development have taken place without much anchor in empirical research (see Popenoe 1996; Silverstein and Auerbach 1999; Drexler 2005; Pleck 2007). Assessing the unique effects of fathers on children is important to pursue for several reasons. First, high rates of divorce and nonmarital childbearing mean that about half of children today are likely to experience some of their childhood outside a family of married, biological parents (Bumpass and Raley 1995). This represents a large number of children. As of 2007, 19.2 million children were not living with their fathers, a considerable increase over the 9.7 million children living in fatherless homes in 1970 (U.S. Bureau of the Census 2008). While many nonresident fathers work hard to provide for their children and take parenting seriously, research shows that responsible, involved nonresident fathers remain rare. In a distressingly large number of cases, nonresident fathers are largely absent from the lives of their children (Harris and Ryan 2004; Hawkins, Amato, and King 2006). Given this demographic reality, it remains imperative for family scholars to continue to understand the full cost of fatherlessness for children.

Second, an increasing number of children are growing up in households that differ in important ways from two biological-parent and female-headed households. Certainly the numbers of children in households with adults other than their parents (2.8 million or 3.9 percent), cohabiting couple households (6.7 million or 8.3 percent), and in homes with same-sex partnered adults (416,000, .01 percent) remains small, but the growth of these nontraditional living arrangements where children are exposed to a variety of adults can no longer be ignored (Kreider 2007; U.S. Bureau of the Census 2008). In particular, the social and legal concerns about whether same-sex couples should be allowed to marry have raised questions about the consequences for children of growing up in these types of families. Put another way, do children develop optimally when raised by a father and a mother? Or is it the case that two adults, regardless of their gender, can parent as effectively as a father and a mother?

Finally, there is considerable cultural pressure today for fathers to be involved in the lives of their children. What exactly this involvement means, however, remains unclear. Should fathers be acting like mothers to their children? What does it mean that children might be better off if "there is a man around"? Research on the similarities and differences between mothers and fathers in characteristics, behavior, and parenting may help parents have a greater appreciation for the distinctive contributions of their spouses to the whole parenting enterprise (Wilcox 2008).

To date, research that has attempted to disentangle the effects of mothers and fathers has been comparatively thin. One review of the literature on the effects of fathers on children identified only eight studies out of seventy-two that took into account the relationship between the mother and the child when assessing the effects of father involvement (Marsiglio et al. 2000). A more recent review identified four additional studies of paternal involvement that took into account maternal involvement (Pleck and Masciadrelli 2004). Most of these studies have simply controlled for the effects of mother characteristics in their assessment of whether fathers matter. However, the relationship between mothers' and fathers' characteristics and behavior on a particular outcome can potentially take three possible forms (Cooksten and Finlay 2006). First, fathers' effects may be additive: That is what fathers do has an effect on adolescent outcomes over and above what mothers do. However, it is also possible that fathers' and mothers' involvement or characteristics are redundant. Children benefit from just one parent—either a father or mother—engaging in certain behaviors or possessing certain characteristics. Finally, it is possible that fathers have a unique effect on certain outcomes. That is, fathers—but not mothers—are important for certain outcomes. Little is yet understood about how father effects are distributed across these possibilities.

These issues form the backdrop for this chapter. I begin by sketching out a sociological perspective on fathers' influence. Hypotheses derived from these theoretical ideas are then tested on data drawn from the National Longitudinal Study of Adolescent Health (Add Health). Specifically, I examine whether fathers' human capital and social capital affect adolescent and young adult internalizing and externalizing behavior, and young adult pro-social activities beyond mothers' human and social capital. Finally, in a preliminary fashion, I assess the extent to which a father's and mother's contributions to their adolescent or young adult children are unique, additive, or redundant.

A SOCIOLOGICAL PERSPECTIVE ON FATHERHOOD

When sociologists think about fathers and what effect they might have on children they begin by noting that fathering is more than a set of behaviors within families. Fathers and fathering are embedded in a social and cultural context that guides, shapes, and provides meaning to their experiences. Fatherhood, perhaps much more than motherhood, is a social invention. Thus, a sociological perspective on fatherhood begins with the idea that social forces—be they economic, cultural, or structural—need to be taken into account if we are to fully understand how men think, feel, and act as fathers (Marsiglio and Cohan 2000). Fathering does not happen in a vacuum, but is "nested" within families, communities, cultural milieus, and social and economic conditions.

Second, when sociologists think about what fathers do and how they potentially might make unique contributions to the welfare of their children beyond that of mothers, they focus less on the particulars of how fathers interact with their children (the province of psychologists) and more on what resources they directly or indirectly provide. This has led much of the sociologically oriented research to initially concentrate on using survey data to compare children living in married-couple families with children in mother-headed families. While this approach has been very useful for helping us understand the advantages for children of growing up in a two-parent family, it is not very useful for understanding the precise role fathers play. This is because this approach confounds the absence of a father with being reared by one parent instead of two (Pleck 2007). To better understand the unique role of fathers and mothers, we need to pursue two different research strategies: We need to compare children in two-parent heterosexual families with children in two-parent same-sex families. This is a challenging prospect due to the difficulties with securing sufficiently large, representative samples of children in two-parent same-sex families. However, we could also learn much about the unique contributions of fathers and mothers by carefully comparing them within two-parent heterosexual families—a strategy I pursue in this research.

From a sociological perspective then, what kinds of contributions to children might we expect from fathers? To answer this question, sociologists turn their attention to what kinds of human capital and social capital fathers possess and how these types of capital might uniquely affect children.

HUMAN CAPITAL

How mothers and fathers care for their children is strongly influenced by their human capital—the skills, knowledge, and values that are associated with occupational success in American society. Parents with high levels of human capital, typically indicated by years of education, are more likely to do the kinds of things that enhance their children's cognitive abilities and school performance. They are likely to provide a stimulating home environment by limiting television and encouraging reading. They make it a priority to take their children to museums, libraries, plays, concerts, and other enriching activities. They may choose to live in communities with good schools or sacrifice to send their children to private or parochial schools that have a strong educational mission. Mothers and fathers with high human capital not only encourage high occupational aspirations in their children, they also promote the kinds of behavior in their children that is associated with success in school.

While not all studies show positive effects for both fathers' *and* mothers' education on children's schooling, this is the most consistent finding (Amato 1998; Korrup, Ganzeboom, and Lippe 2002; Marks 2008). Furthermore, most of these studies find that fathers' education affects children independently from mothers' education. Although less studied, fathers' education has also been found in some studies to be positively related to children's self-esteem, life skills, social competence, and cooperativeness (Amato 1998).

Fathers' and mothers' human capital indirectly affect children's well-being by their association with family's financial resources. Although the level of education of each parent is likely to be related to a family's economic circumstances, a father's education is likely to matter more. This is because fathers are more likely to be in the labor force and to work more hours than mothers (U.S. Department of Labor 2008). Also, the economic returns to education are higher for males than females (Crissey 2009).

In short, there is consistent evidence that children benefit from the human capital characteristics of *both* their parents.

SOCIAL CAPITAL

In a classic article in 1988, sociologist James Coleman identified "social capital" as a key resource provided by parents that benefits children. He defined social capital as resources that are embedded in family and community relationships. Sociologists have generally understood social capital as being comprised of several related, but distinct domains. One important element is what Joseph Pleck (2007:198) calls "community social capital," the linkages to the larger world that parents provide children. For example, a father may "know someone" from his work associations that may be able to provide a job to an inexperienced teenager. Social capital is also indicated by how skillfully a mother or a father may deal with the various organizations such as schools, health professionals, sports teams, or summer camps that affect the lives of their children. One implication of this is that each parent potentially can provide not only additional linkages to others, but that mothers and fathers can provide unique ties.

A second component of social capital is the quality of the relationships that exist within a family, what Pleck (2007:198) calls "family social capital." This includes the nature of the marital relationship, but also includes the relationship between each parent and the child. As Paul Amato observes, "parental support and control represent key resources for children. Support is reflected in behaviors such as affection, responsiveness, encouragement, instruction, and everyday assistance. . . . Control is reflected in rule formulation, discipline, monitoring, and supervision" (Amato 1998:245). Studies that have focused on community social capital effects have generally found that they predict adolescent outcomes (Furstenberg and Hughes 1995; Buchel and Duncan 1998; Hango 2007). A careful review of the large number of studies that have investigated associations between paternal supportive behavior and child outcomes found that the overwhelming majority showed significant associations between father support and measures of child well-being. However, only a few studies took into account characteristics of both mothers and fathers, and among those that did, the evidence for father effects was weaker (Amato 1998).

ROLE MODELING

Although this will not be examined in the following empirical analyses, sociologists also emphasize the importance of role modeling. Beyond their resources and relationships, fathers and mothers influence their children by simply who they are and how they act in a variety of circumstances. Children learn much by observation of those around them—and parents are the most visible adults in their world. Children who observe fathers and mothers who treat others with respect, handle conflict in effective ways, and engage in pro-social and appropriate behavior, are likely to emulate these behaviors themselves. On the other hand, children learn quite different lessons about themselves, how to behave, or treat others, when parents treat each other badly, are neglectful or abusive to their children, or engage in inappropriate or illegal behavior. The importance of parental modeling has been shown in a large number of studies, although only a few studies attempted to assess the effects of both mothers and fathers simultaneously. Two recent studies that did account for the role modeling behavior of both mothers and fathers show that *each* parents' psychological health, drinking behavior, availability, as well as the degree of marital conflict are all related to child internalizing and externalizing behavior (Osgood, Wilson, O'Malley, Bachman, and Johnson 1996; Papp, Cummings, and Schermerhorn 2004; Vorrhess, Paunesku, Kuwabara, Basu, Gollan, Hankin, Melkonian, and Reinecke 2008). Clearly, however, the relative importance of mothers and fathers as role models remains poorly understood.

In sum, there are good sociological reasons to expect that fathers can potentially contribute to the lives of their children beyond that of mothers. To test these ideas, I turn to data on families of mothers, fathers, and adolescent children. In part, this is because the bulk of the work done on the unique effects of fathers has been done by psychologists focusing on the differences in parenting behavior on infants or toddlers (Paquette 2004). General studies by developmental psychologists have found that fathers tend to treat their young children differently than mothers and that some of these differences are beneficial for children. For example, fathers engage in more physical play with their preschool children than do mothers; and this rough-and-tumble play has been shown to encourage the development of emotional regulation (Clark-Stewart 1978; Yogman 1982; MacDonald and Parke 1984; Paquette 2004).

The few studies that have focused on the unique contributions of mothers and fathers to adolescent or young adult well-being generally find some evidence that both mothers' and fathers' characteristics or behavior are associated with internalizing or externalizing behavior (Amato 1994, 1998; Buehler, Benson, and Gerard 2006; Cookston and Finlay 2006). With a few exceptions (cf. Amato 1998), studies have not focused explicitly on examining the contributions of each parent's social and human capital for adolescent and young adult well-being and young adult pro-social behavior.

DATA AND METHODS

The data for this study were drawn from the first and third waves of the National Study of Adolescent Health. The Add Health survey is a longitudinal, nationally representative sample of 20,745 middle and high school students first interviewed in 1995–1996. A second wave of interviews was conducted one year later, and a third round of 15,170 persons was interviewed in 2001. Response rates for Waves 1 and 3 were 78.9 percent and 77.4 percent, respectively. Attrition analyses suggest that the effect of nonresponse on representativeness was minimal (Chantala, Kalsbeek, and Andraca 2004). A more detailed description of the data can be found in Harris et al. (2003).

The present analysis is restricted to respondents who were living with both of their biological parents at Wave 1 and participated in the Wave 3 interview ($n = 5494$). Two sets of analyses were performed. The first set focused on the link between mothers and fathers and two adolescent outcomes: Internalizing behavior, indicated by determining the number of symptoms of depression, and externalizing behavior—the extent to which they have participated in violent or delinquent activity in the past year. All these analyses were all weighted using the Wave 1 weights, adjusting the sample to be nationally representative. The second set of analyses were focused on the well-being of these respondents in the Wave 3 interview, which was conducted five years later when these adolescents were mostly out of their parents' homes either at college or living independently. In addition to analyzing the relationship between mothers' and fathers' parenting and young adult internalizing and externalizing behavior, I also explore the extent to which the characteristics of mothers' and fathers' and their parenting influences young adults' participation in pro-social activities. Analyses conducted with these data were weighted using Wave 3 sample weights. Descriptive statistics for the variables used the analyses can be found in table 9.1.

PARENT VARIABLES

SOCIAL CAPITAL   Four variables are used to determine the social capital that mothers and fathers bring to parenting. The first, quality of the relationship, is based on the answers of the adolescent to a series of questions asked about their mother and their father. Respondents were asked whether they strongly agree, agree, neither agree or disagree, disagree, or strongly disagree with four statements about their mother: "Most of the time your mother is warm and loving toward you"; "when you do something wrong that is important, your mother talks about it with you and helps you understand why it is wrong"; "you are satisfied with the way your mother and you communicate with each other"; and "overall, you are satisfied with your relationship with your mother." Responses were averaged across the four questions forming a scale with a range from 1–5, where 5 indicates a high quality relationship ($\alpha = .84$). The quality of the relationship with the father is measured by the adolescent responses to three statements: "Most of the time your father is warm and loving toward you"; "you are satisfied with the way your father and you communicate with each other"; and "overall, you are satisfied with your relationship with your father." Responses were averaged across the three questions, forming a scale ranging from 1–5 ($\alpha = .88$).

The second indicator of parent's social capital is the adolescent's rating of how close they feel toward their mother and their father. Responses could range from 1 (not at all) to 5 (very much).

TABLE 9.1 Descriptive statistics of dependent and parent variables

	MALES				FEMALES			
	MEAN OR PROP.	S.D.	RANGE	*n*	MEAN OR PROP.	S.D.	RANGE	*n*
DEPENDENT VARIABLES								
Adolescent depression	0.556	0.408	0–3	5,087	0.679	0.487	0–3	5,143
Adolescent delinquency	2.80	3.7	0–20	5,055	1.801	2.728	0–20	5,122
Young adult depression	0.437	0.484	0–3	4,092	0.500	0.517	0–3	4,409
Young adult externalizing	0.836	1.730	0–6	4,054	0.286	0.944	0–6	4,397
Young adult pro-soc. act.	1.55	1.26	0–4	4,078	1.653	1.217	0–4	4,406
PARENT VARIABLES								
Social capital								
Quality of relationship								
Fathers	4.156	0.803	1–5	5,487	4.010	0.936	1–5	5,438
Mothers	4.281	0.639	1–5	5,489	4.18	0.788	1–5	5,439
Closeness								
Fathers	4.454	0.833	1–5	5,489	4.177	0.999	1–5	5,441
Mothers	4.601	0.694	1–5	5,490	4.468	0.826	1–5	5,441
Activities								
Fathers	3.073	2.007	0–10	5,484	2.820	1.859	0–10	5,439
Mothers	3.567	1.899	0–10	5,487	4.267	1.926	0–10	5,441
Availability								
Fathers	10.169	2.602	2–15	5,492	9.961	2.693	2–15	5,441
Mothers			2–15	5,492	11.731	2.702	2–15	5,441
Human capital								
Education								
<u>Fathers</u>								
High school dropout	13.67%	—	0–1	4,369	15.56%	—	0–1	4,282
High school grad.	28.14%	—	0–1	4,369	28.16%	—	0–1	4,282
Some college	27.88%	—	0–1	4,369	24.47%	—	0–1	4,282
<u>Mothers</u>								
High school dropout	13.74%	—	0–1	4,628	14.55%	—	0–1	4,562
High school grad.	31.18%	—	0–1	4,628	33.38%	—	0–1	4,562
Some college	28.56%	—	0–1	4,628	25.35%	—	0–1	4,562
Full-time employment								
Fathers	95.41%	—	0–1	4,002	96.07%	—	0–1	3,900
Mothers	54.87%	—	0–1	4,511	55.91%	—	0–1	4,471

The third indicator of parent's social capital measures how involved mothers and fathers are in the lives of their children. This is determined by the adolescent report of which things from a list of ten they had done with their mother in the past month. For example, whether they had gone shopping, played a sport, gone to a religious service or church-related event, talked about someone they dated or party they had gone to, had a talk about a personal problem they were having, had a serious argument about their behavior, talked about schoolwork or grades, worked on a project for school, or talked about other things they were doing in school. Responses were summed to form a scale ranging from 0–10. These ten questions were then repeated for their fathers.

Finally, the availability of each parent was determined from adolescent answers to three questions asked about how often they are at home certain times of the day. For their fathers adolescents were asked: "How often is he at home when you leave for school?" "How often is he at home when you return from school?" and "How often is he at home when you go to bed?" Answers ranged from "always" to "never." Responses were reverse coded and summed, forming a scale with a range from 3–15. These three questions were also asked about the adolescent's mother.

HUMAN CAPITAL   The human capital of mothers and fathers is measured by two variables—education and employment. Fathers' and mothers' level of education was coded into four categories: less than high school, high school graduate, some college, and college degree or more. Employment of each parent was indicated by whether they had worked full-time during the past year.

CONTROL VARIABLES   All the models included respondent's age (measured in years; mean = 15.4, s.d. = 1.87), race (white = 74.3 percent; African-American = 8.4 percent; Hispanic = 7.38 percent; and other = 9.94 percent), marital status of parents (a small proportion of adolescents, 2.11 percent, were living with both biological parents who were cohabiting), and in $1000 units (median =$50.00). Because the distribution of family income was highly skewed, it was logged (mean = $4.37, s.d. = 1.8).

DEPENDENT VARIABLES   Adolescent externalizing behavior is drawn from a series of ten questions asking how often the respondent had engaged in delinquent or violent behavior in the past twelve months. For example, respondents were asked "In the past twelve months, how often did you deliberately damage property that didn't belong to you?"; "take something from a store without paying for it?"; "hurt someone badly enough to need bandages or care from a doctor or nurse?"; "drive a car without the owner's permission?"; "steal something worth more than $50?" Other questions queried adolescents about burglaries committed, petty theft, gang-fighting, and misbehaving in public. Answers for each of the questions ranged from o = never to 3 = five or more times. Answers were summed to form a scale with a range from o–20 (α = .81).

Adolescent internalizing behavior was measured by answers to nine questions designed to assess depression symptoms. For example, respondents were asked, "How often was each of the following true during the past week?: You were bothered by things that usually don't bother you"; "you felt that you could not shake off the blues, even with help from your family and friends"; "you felt that you were just as good as other people." Other questions asked if the respondent felt depressed, had trouble keeping their mind on what they were doing, felt too tired to do things, and so forth. Answers ranged from o = never or rarely to 3 = most of the time. Each item was coded so that high scores represented higher levels of depression. Items were summed and averaged, forming a scale with a range from o–3 (α = .80).

Young adult externalizing behavior was drawn from a series of twelve questions from the Wave 3 data that were mostly similar to those asked in Wave 1, but were designed to pick up delinquent, criminal, or violent activities likely to be committed by young adults such as selling drugs, buying or selling stolen property, writing bad checks, engaging in credit card fraud, using a weapon in a fight, and so on. Answers were summed and averaged, forming a scale with a range from o–6 (α = .75).

Young adult internalizing behavior was measured from respondent answers at Wave 3 to the same nine questions asked in Wave 1 about their current experiences with depression symptoms. A similar scale was constructed with a range from o–3 (α = o.81).

Finally, the degree of participation in pro-social activities in young adulthood was determined from their answers to four questions: whether in the past year they (1) performed voluntary work, (2) donated blood, and (3) were a registered organ donor, and (4) whether they are registered to vote. These yes/no questions were added together forming a simple scale with a range from o–4.

ANALYTIC STRATEGY

For each outcome described earlier, a series of ordinary least squares regression models are estimated separately for boys and girls. For the first series, separate models are estimated for each of the six father variables (see the first column of table 9.2 for the models of male teenage depression). Then a second series of six models are estimated where the parallel mother variable is added (see the second column of table 9.2). This sequence is repeated for each of the five outcomes reported in tables 9.2 and 9.3, for a total of 120 models. All the models include the four control variables and are weighted by the appropriate sample weights.

RESULTS

MOTHERS, FATHERS, AND ADOLESCENT WELL-BEING

Turning to table 9.2, we see that most elements of fathers' social capital and one of the two components of human capital are strong predictors of depression symptoms among adolescent boys and girls. Furthermore, fathers' characteristics and behavior remain statistically significant even when mothers' human and social capital characteristics are taken into account. Specifically the quality of the relationship a father has with his adolescent, the adolescent report of their closeness, the father's level of education, and the number of activities that a father does with the adolescent are significantly related to male and female depression symptoms. Furthermore, father's availability is associated with daughter's depression. All these father effects persisted even after statistically controlling for mother's characteristics.

Fathers also matter a great deal when it comes to delinquent behavior. The higher the father's social capital (quality of father/child relationship and closeness) the less likely are boys and girls to engage in delinquency. In addition, father's education is associated with boy's delinquency and father's availability predicts girl's delinquent behavior. All these relationships exist over and above mother's social and human capital.

DO FATHERS AND MOTHERS MATTER FOR YOUNG ADULTS?

To get some sense of how robust these relationships might be, I took advantage of the longitudinal nature of these data to see whether the human and social capital of mothers and fathers continued to affect the lives of the respondents five years later when they were young adults. Turning to table 9.3, it is clear that, even with the passage out of the household, fathers and mothers remain important in the lives of young adults. The quality of the relationship with both mother and father while a teenager, how close the adolescent felt toward both their mother and father, and the level of education of both parents predict depression symptoms among young adults. For boys, the number of activities in which fathers participated with them as adolescents was significantly related to fewer depression symptoms in young adulthood.

The relationships between fathers' and mothers' social and human capital and externalizing behavior were more complex. The quality of the relationships with fathers significantly predicted delinquent behavior, but this relationship was reduced to insignificance once mothers' relationships were included in the models. This was also true for closeness with daughters. This suggests that it is important for young adults to have had a good relationship and been close to at least one parent while growing up. Unexpectedly, the more activities fathers participated in, the greater the externalizing behavior. Similarly for males, fathers' level of education was positively associated with delinquent behavior, while for females mothers' education appears to predict greater externalizing. I explored several different specifications of the dependent measure and the indicator of activity participation and education. These additional analyses produced similar results. One possible explanation is that father involvement in activities during adolescence is associated with an unmeasured factor that also is predicting externalizing behavior in young adulthood. One might speculate that high levels of father involvement in adolescence may suppress delinquent behavior while the teenager is living at home, but may spark some youth to experiment in externalizing behaviors once they are under less parental supervision as young adults.

Finally mothers' and fathers' human and social capital not only keep adolescents and young adults out of harm's way, but also are associated with positive or pro-social behavior. Fathers' education and the number of activities they were involved in are associated with the likelihood that young adults were themselves involved in volunteer work or other community-minded activities. In addition, for young women, the quality and closeness of their relationship with their father as adolescents was a significant factor in whether they engaged in pro-social activities as young adults.

TABLE 9.2 Effects of fathers and mothers on teenage depression and delinquency

	DEPRESSION				DELINQUENCY			
	MALES		FEMALES		MALES		FEMALES	
	1	2	3	4	5	6	7	8
	SOCIAL CAPITAL							
Quality of relationship								
Father	-.13***	-.09***	-.16***	-.11***	-.75***	-.41***	-.66***	-.43***
Mother	—	-0.9***	—	-.15***	—	-.88***	—	-.63***
Closeness								
Father	-0.11***	-.08***	-.12***	-.09***	-.68***	-.41***	-.63***	-.45***
Mother	—	-.05***	—	-.09***	—	-.63***	—	-.42***
Activities								
Father	-.01*	-.02***	-.03***	-.04***	.05	-.004	-.03	-.05
Mother	—	.02***	—	.01	—	.09*	—	.22
Availability								
Father	-.01	.004	-.01***	-.01**	-.05*	-.04	-.10***	-.09***
Mother	—	.01*	—	-.01*	—	-.07*	—	-.09***

	HUMAN CAPITAL							
Education								
Father								
< High school	.13**	.09***	.16***	.09**	-.67***	-.60*	.08	.18
High school degree	.04*	.02	.08***	.05*	-.15	-.11	.03	.06
Some college	.01	.004	.05**	.03	.09	.08	.15	.14
Mother								
< High school	—	.10***	—	.15***	—	-.11	—	-.18
High school degree	—	.03	—	.06**	—	.03	—	-.07
Some college	—	.03	—	.04*	—	.09	—	.04
Employment								
Father	-.01	-.02	.01	.02	.01	-.01	-.23	-.32
Mother	—	-.01	—	.03	—	-.19	—	.24**

Note: Control variables: race (white, African-American, Hispanic, other), age, marital status, and family income (logged) (*p = .05; **p = .01; ***p = .001).

TABLE 9.3 Effects of fathers and mothers on young adult depression, delinquency, and pro-social activities

| | DEPRESSION | | | | EXTERNALIZING BEHAVIOR | | | | PRO-SOCIAL ACTIVITIES | | | |
| | MALES | | FEMALES | | MALES | | FEMALES | | MALES | | FEMALES | |
	1	2	3	4	5	6	7	8	9	10	11	12
					SOCIAL CAPITAL							
Quality of relationship												
Father	-.07***	-.05***	-.09***	-.06***	-.11***	-.03	-.05***	-.02	.08***	.03	.10***	.07**
Mother	—	-.06***	—	-.06***	—	-.27***	—	-.08***	—	.11**	—	.07**
Closeness												
Father	-.05***	-.04***	-.07***	-.06***	-.16***	-.02*	-.05***	-.01	.04	-.002	.09***	.09***
Mother	—	-.02	—	-.03***	—	-.15***	—	-.10***	—	.09**	—	.001
Activities												
Father	-.01***	-.02***	-.02***	-.000	.03*	.02*	.01	-.01	.07***	.03*	.11***	.08***
Mother	—	.01**	—	-.02***	—	.02	—	.06*	—	.06***	—	.05***
Availability												
Father	.003	-.001	-.01	-.01	.01	0.1	-.01	-.004	-.01	-.01	-.003	-.001
Mother	—	.004	—	-.002	—	-.02	—	-.01	—	-.01	—	-.01

	HUMAN CAPITAL											
Education												
Father												
< High school	.12***	.09***	.15***	.12***	-.34***	-.14*	-.08	-.01	-.67***	-.37***	-.78***	-.43***
High school degree	-.03	-.04	.07***	.06*	-.28***	-.16*	.002	.07	-.55***	-.32***	-.45***	-.18***
Some college	.02	.01	.05*	.04	-.14	-.06	-.002	.03	-.31***	-.17**	-.32***	-.15**
Mother												
< High school	—	.06	—	.06	—	-.38**	—	-.12	—	-.55***	—	-.61***
High school degree	—	.03	—	.02	—	-.24*	—	-.14***	—	-.46***	—	-.52***
Some college	—	.04*	—	.01	—	-.19*	—	-.06	—	-.28***	—	-.30***
Employment												
Father	-.04	-.04	-.02	-.03	.17	.25	.07	.07	.23*	.26**	.15	.19
Mother	—	-.01	—	.01	—	-.01	—	.05	—	-.001	—	.01

Note: Control variables: race (white, African–American, Hispanic, other), age, marital status, and family income (logged) ($^*p$ = .05; $^{**}p$ = .01; $^{***}p$ = .001).

FATHER'S CONTRIBUTION: ADDITIVE, UNIQUE, OR REDUNDANT?

In order to get an approximation of the nature of a father's and mother's effects on their children, I classified each of the estimated sixty relationship patterns into four types: father and mother effects were both significant predictors (additive); either fathers or mothers were significant, but not both (unique); significant father characteristics were reduced to insignificance once mother's characteristics were taken into account (complimentary or redundant); and neither mother's or father's characteristic were significantly related to the outcome (no effect). The most common type of contribution in the sixty relationships analyzed in these data were additive ($n = 25$; 42 percent). That is, fathers typically make additional contributions beyond that which the mother makes to adolescent or young adult well-being. The quality of the relationship and reported closeness to each parent were most likely to be additive in nature. Thirteen relationships, about a fifth, showed evidence of being unique to either mothers or fathers. For example, a father's human capital characteristics, especially his education, were important to the well-being of both boys and girls. In contrast, mothers' availability and closeness uniquely affected boys. In a few isolated instances, mothers' and fathers' contributions showed evidence of being redundant (12 percent). That is, adolescents and young adults benefit from at least one parent engaging in this behavior, but gain no additional benefit from both parents involvement in this. Finally, of the sixty relationships examined, slightly more than a quarter ($n = 16$) showed no significant effect.

DISCUSSION

I was coauthor on a paper with Alan Hawkins in 1991 with the following question for a title: "Are fathers fungible?" (Hawkins and Eggebeen 1991). Our answer at that time was yes. Based on our analysis of data from the National Longitudinal Study of Youth, the effects of father absence for the well-being of preschool-aged children was mitigated by the presence of other adults in the home; that is, fathers were replaceable. These findings are consistent with an argument that is currently making the rounds that says this: while father involvement is a good and worthy thing, we must keep in mind that fathers are not "essential" to optimal child development.

What children need to grow up healthy is good parenting, and good parenting is not anchored in gender (Silverstein and Auerbach 1999; Drexler 2005). The findings reported in this paper stand in stark contrast to my earlier work as well as to the assertions of Drexler, Silverstein, and Auerbach. What these analyses clearly show us is that mothers *and* fathers both make vital contributions to adolescent well-being. Furthermore, the relationships and characteristics of mothers and fathers create an enduring legacy for their children as they transition to adulthood. In most cases, fathers make positive contributions to the well-being of their children that is beyond what mothers are doing. In some instances, fathers and mothers are fungible; however, this appears to be significantly less common than instances where fathers and mothers uniquely influence adolescents and young adults. Fathers appear to especially make unique contributions to the well-being of their children through their human capital while mothers make unique contributions through their availability and closeness to their children.

There are a number of limitations to these conclusions. First, because of data limitations I was only able to tap into one dimension of social capital, the within-family relationship skills of mothers and fathers. I was unable to examine other key aspects of social capital such as the degree to which parents make use of social networks, community resources, and relationships to benefit their children. This is disappointing because some have hypothesized that fathers may have an edge over mothers on this dimension (Pleck 2007; Furstenberg 1998). More work is clearly needed to tease apart the relative contributions of each parent's social capital. Neither was it possible to examine the relative contributions of a mother's and father's income—a crucial component of human capital, and something that in the majority of families, fathers contribute more of. One question I could not answer, for example, is whether gender role complementary on economic provision and childcare has implications for adolescent well-being. There are hints of this in these data, but the lack of income measures by parents prevents a good test of this question. Finally, social theory suggests that fathers and mothers may be unique role models for their children. Unfortunately, I was unable to identify variables in these data that would allow a reasonable test of the reach or impact of gender specific role modeling. At some point, it would be helpful to address questions such as: What might be the modeling effect on children of each parent's involvement in various social activities (good and bad), community organizations, or church or religious groups? What is modeled to the children by each parent's disciplinary style? The few studies that have explored this find that mothers and fathers do vary in their parenting styles, and these variations are linked with child outcomes (Buehler et al. 2006; Roelofs, Meesters, ter Huurne, Bamelis, and Muris 2006; Simons and Conger 2007).

While this research demonstrates that the well-being of adolescents living in biological two-parent families is influenced by both mothers and fathers, significant questions remain. Very little is yet known about how the parenting practices, relationships, and characteristics of the parents or other adults who care for children in cohabiting-couple families, same-sex-couple families, or other nontraditional family arrangements are similar to, or different from, heterosexual married-couple families. Until careful, methodologically rigorous studies based on reasonably heterogeneous or representative samples are conducted, we cannot be confident that these nontraditional arrangements offer the same potential benefits to children as growing up with loving, involved, and resourceful mothers and fathers.

REFERENCES

Amato, P. R. 1994. "Father-Child Relations, Mother-Child Relations, and Offspring Well-Being in Psychological Early Adulthood." *Journal of Marriage and Family* 56:1031–1042.

Amato, P. R. 1998. "More than Money? Men's Contributions to Their Children's Lives." In *Men in Families: When Do They Get Involved? What Difference Does It Make?* ed. A. Booth and A. C. Crouter, 241–278. Mahwah, NJ: Lawrence Earlbaum.

Buchel, F. and G. J. Duncan. 1998. "Do Parents' Social Activities Promote Children's School Attainments? Evidence from the German Socioeconomic Panel." *Journal of Marriage and Family* 60:95–108.

Buehler, C., M. J. Benson, and J. M. Gerard. 2006. "Interparental Hostility and Early Adolescent Problem Behavior: The Mediating Role of Specific Aspects of Parenting." *Journal of Research on Adolescence* 16:265–292.

Chantala, K., W. D. Kalsbeek, and E. Andraca. 2004. "Non-Response in Wave III of the Add Health Study." Unpublished paper. Accessed March 22, 2008. www.cpc.unc.edu/projects/addhealth/files/W3nonres.pdf.

Coleman, J. 1988. "Social Capital in the Creation of Human Capital." *American Journal of Sociology* 94:95–120.

Cookston, J. T. and A. K. Finlay. 2006. "Father Involvement and Adolescent Adjustment: Longitudinal Findings from Add Health." *Fathering* 4:137–158.

Crissey, S. R. 2009. "Educational Attainment in the United States: 2007." *Current Population Reports* P20–P560. Washington, DC: U.S. Bureau of the Census.

Drexler, P. 2005. *How Maverick Mothers Are Creating the Next Generation of Exceptional Men: Raising Boys Without Men.* New York: Rodale.

Furstenberg, F., Jr. 1998. "Social Capital and the Family Role of Fathers in the Family." In *Men in Families: When Do They Get Involved? What Difference Does It Make?* ed. A. Booth and A. C. Crouter, 295–301. Mahwah, NJ: Lawrence Earlbaum.

Harris, K. M. and S. Ryan. 2004. "Father Involvement and the Diversity of Family Context." In *Conceptualizing and Measuring Father Involvement*, ed. R. D. Day and M. E. Lamb, 293–319. Mahwah, NJ: Lawrence Earlbaum.

Harris, K. M., F. Florey, J. Tabor, P. J. Bearman, J. Jones, and J. R. Udry. 2003. "The National Longitudinal Study of Adolescent Health: Research Design." Accessed February 22, 2008. www.cpc.unc.edu/projects/addhealth/design/designfacts.

Hango, D. 2007. "Parental Investment in Childhood and Educational Qualifications: Can Greater Parental Involvement Mediate the Effects of Socioeconomic Disadvantage?" *Social Science Research* 36:1371–1390.

Hawkins, A. J. and D. J. Eggebeen. 1991. "Are Fathers Fungible? Patterns of Coresident Adult Men in Maritally Disrupted Families and Young Children's Well-Being." *Journal of Marriage and Family* 53:958–972.

Korrup, S. E., H. B. G. Ganzeboom, and T. V. D. Lippe. 2002. "Do Mothers Matter? A Comparison of Models of the Influence of Mother's and Father's Education and Occupational Status on Children's Educational Attainment." *Quality and Quantity* 36:17–42.

Kreider, R. M. 2007. "Living Arrangements of Children: 2004." *Current Population Reports* P70–P114. Washington, DC: U.S. Bureau of the Census.

MacDonald, K. and R. D. Parke. 1984. "Bridging the Gap: Parent-Child Play Interactions and Peer Interactive Competence." *Child Development* 55:1265–1277.

Marks, G. N. 2008. "Are Father's or Mother's Socioeconomic Characteristics More Important Influences on Student Performance? Recent International Evidence." *Social Indicators Research* 85:293–309.

Marsiglio, W. and M. Cohan. 2000. "Contextualizing Father Involvement and Paternal Influence: Sociological and Qualitative Themes." *Marriage and Family Review* 29:75–95.

Marsiglio, W., P. Amato, R. D. Day, and M. E. Lamb. 2000. "Scholarship on Fatherhood in the 1990s and Beyond." *Journal of Marriage and Family* 62:1173–1191.

Osgood, D. W., J. K. Wilson, P. M. O'Malley, J. G. Bachman, and L. D. Johnson. 1996. "Routine Activities and Individual Deviant Behavior." *American Sociological Review* 61:635–655.

Papp, L. M, E. M. Cummings, and A. C. Schermerhorn. 2004. "Pathways Among Marital Distress, Parental Symptomatology, and Child Adjustment." *Journal of Marriage and Family* 66:368–384.

Paquette, D. 2004. "Theorizing the Father-Child Relationship: Mechanisms and Developmental Outcomes." *Human Development* 47:193–219.

Pleck, J. H. 2007. "Why Could Father Involvement Benefit Children? Theoretical Perspectives." *Applied Developmental Science* 11:196–202.

Pleck, J. H. and B. Masciadrelli. 2004. "Paternal Involvement by U.S. Residential Fathers: Levels, Sources, and Consequences." In *The Role of the Father in Child Development*, 4th ed., ed. M. E. Lamb, 222–271. New York: John Wiley.

Popenoe, D. 1996. *Life Without Father*. New York: Pressler.

Roelofs, J., C. Meesters, M. ter Huurne, L. Bamelis, and P. Muris. 2006. "On the Links Between Attachment Style, Parental Rearing Behaviors, and Internalizing and Externalizing Problems in Non-Clinical Children." *Journal of Child and Family Studies* 15:331–344.

Silverstein, L. B. and C. F. Auerbach. 1999. "Deconstructing the Essential Father." *American Psychologist* 54:397–407.

Simons, L. G. and R. D. Conger. 2007. "Linking Mother-Father Differences in Parenting to a Typology of Family Parenting Styles and Adolescent Outcomes." *Journal of Family Issues* 28:212–241.

U.S. Bureau of the Census. 2008. Census 2000 PHC-T-30. "Characteristics of Children Under 18 Years of Age, for the United States, Regions, States and Puerto Rico: 2000." Accessed August 28, 2008. www.census.gov/population/www/cen2000/briefs/phc-t30/tables/tab02.pdf.

U.S. Department of Labor. 2008. "Women in the Labor Force: A Databook." U.S. Bureau of Labor Statistics, Report 1011. Accessed January 26, 2009. www.bls.gov/cps/wlf-databook2008.htm.

Vorrhess, B. W., D. Paunesku, S. A. Kuwabara, A. Basu, J. Gollan, B. L. Hankin, S. Melkonian, and M. Reinecke. 2008. "Protective and Vulnerability Factors Predicting New-Onset Depressive Episode in a Representative Sample of U.S. Adolescents." *Journal of Adolescent Health* 605–616.

Wilcox, W. B. 2008. Personal communication. August 20, 2008.

Yogman, M. W. 1982. "Development of the Father-Infant Relationship." In *Theory and Research in Behavioral Pediatrics*, ed. H. Fitzgerald, B. Lester, and M. W. Yogman, 221–229. New York: Plenum.

10

NO ONE BEST WAY

Work-Family Strategies, the Gendered Division of Parenting, and the Contemporary Marriages of Mothers and Fathers

W. Bradford Wilcox and Jeffrey Dew

THE GENDER REVOLUTION of the last half-century has dramatically re-shaped the nature, quality, and stability of marriage and parenthood in the United States. A half-century ago, most married mothers did not work outside the home, and most men and women preferred this arrangement. But over the course of the second half of the twentieth century, mothers streamed into the labor force, fathers devoted more time to childcare and housework, and public opinion largely swung behind these changes, with most Americans expressing normative support for working mothers, as well as for more egalitarian relationships between mothers and fathers in the home (Spain and Bianchi 1996; Bianchi, Robinson, and Milkie 2007).

In the last decade or so, however, there is growing evidence that this gen-der revolution has stalled (Hochschild and Machung 1989). In particular, labor force participation among married mothers has fallen modestly since the late 1990s (Downs 2003; Bradbury and Katz 2005; Percheski 2008),[1] as has normative support for working mothers (Cotter, Hermsen, Kendix, and Vanneman 2006; Taylor, Funk, and Clark 2008); indeed, a large minority of Americans currently believe that it is best for mothers to stay at home when they have infants or young children.[2] Moreover, married mothers remain responsible for the lion's share of child-rearing in the average fam-ily (Sayer 2005; Bianchi, Robinson, and Milkie 2007). In these ways, then, there are more and more signs that the tidal wave of change associated with the gender revolution of the last half-century seems to have reached its high-water mark.

This is not to say that the United States has taken a U-turn, and is now heading in a uniformly gender traditional direction when it comes to parenthood. Among other things, this study acknowledges that both mothers *and* fathers are now investing more of their time in their children than did mothers and fathers fifty years ago, and that fathers are now taking on a larger share of child-rearing than they did in the middle of the twentieth century.

Rather, this study shows that married parents are forging diverse work-family strategies out of the options available to them, with no one strategy guiding a majority of American parents. Currently, a plurality of married parents are relying on an egalitarian arrangement where both parents work full-time (thirty-five or more hours), a minority of married parents are relying on a neotraditional strategy where the father works full-time and the mother works part-time (less than thirty-five hours), a minority of parents are using a traditional strategy where the father is the sole breadwinner, and very small minorities of parents are relying on other arrangements (see also Bianchi et al. 2007). Furthermore, this study reports that a minority of married parents express normative support for each of these three different work-family strategies, though it is interesting to note that the neotraditional strategy is the most popular one among contemporary married parents (see also Amato et al. 2007). To add a further level of complexity to this picture of American parenting, we find that couples' work-family strategies often do not align with their preferences—a reality that is somewhat more true for working-class married parents (see also Amato et al. 2007).

It is in the contemporary context of a seemingly stalled gender revolution where no one set of norms has been institutionalized to guide parents' work-family strategies, where parents are pursuing a range of strategies to combine work and parenting, and where their strategies often do not match their preferences, that we seek to understand how contemporary work-family strategies and preferences shape the quality and stability of married life for American parents. Our chapter explores four important topics. First, we look at how work-family strategies, parental time with children, and attitudes toward maternal labor force participation have changed over the last four decades for married parents. Second, we explore how different work-family strategies, as well as the fit between work-family strategies and work-family preferences, are related to the quality and stability of married life for mothers and fathers. Third, we explore how the gendered division of parenting and the amount of parental time spent with children influences marital quality and stability among parents. Finally, we look at how the relationships between work, parenting, and marital quality and stability vary by class.

WORK-FAMILY STRATEGIES AND THE GENDERED DIVISION OF PARENTING: HAS THE GENDER REVOLUTION REACHED ITS HIGH-WATER MARK?

There is no question that a tidal wave of gender-related change swept over the United States during the course of the second half of the twentieth century—in women's labor force participation, in the absolute and relative time that fathers and mothers devote to their children, and in public attitudes toward the public and private roles of men and women (Hakim 2000; Bradbury and Katz 2005; Bianchi et al. 2007). For instance, many married men and women with children adopted a more egalitarian approach to the division of work and family labor over this period. As figure 10.1 indicates, American couples with children forged work-family strategies that moved in an egalitarian direction for much of the last century.

Specifically, data from the General Social Survey (GSS) show that from 1970s to the 1990s, the percentage of married couples with children aged eighteen and under adopting an egalitarian strategy of juggling work-family responsibilities (both parents work full-time) increased from 24 percent to 43 percent of all married parents; similarly, the percentage of couples adopting a nontraditional strategy (mom works more than the father) rose from less than one percent in the 1970s to three percent in the 1990s. Not surprisingly, the percentage of couples taking a traditional strategy (father works full-time,

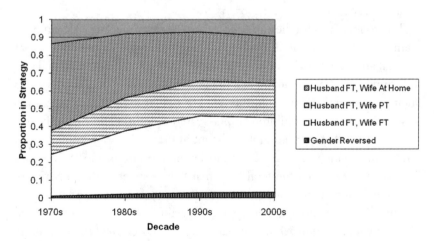

FIGURE 10.1 Married parents' labor force participation strategies.

mother stays at home) fell from 49 percent in the 1970s to 26 percent in the 1990s. Finally, the percentage of couples adopting a neotraditional strategy (father works full-time, mother works part-time) rose from 13 percent in the 1970s to 20 percent in the 1990s. For the most part, then, more egalitarian work-family strategies became much more common during the twentieth century.

But figure 10.1 also suggests that—at least when it comes to maternal labor force participation—the gender revolution reached its high-water mark in the 1990s. Essentially, from the 1990s to the 2000s, all four strategies—the nontraditional, the egalitarian, the neotraditional, and the traditional—to combining work and family held constant. Moreover, the patterns in the GSS are consistent with census data showing that maternal labor force participation stopped its dramatic half-century increase in the late 1990s (Downs 2003; Bradbury and Katz 2005; Percheski 2008). Thus, figure 10.1 provides some evidence that the United States may have reached a new gender regime, where a deeply pluralistic approach is becoming the new pattern, with no one strategy capturing the majority of American parents' approach to juggling work and family responsibilities.

Given the shifts in American work-family strategies—especially increases in maternal labor force participation from the 1950s to the 1990s—some social scientists and family observers suspected that children would be getting less attention from their parents (Coleman 1990; Hewlett 1991). They worried that the time mothers devoted to work would erode the time that they spent with their children. But, surprisingly, this has not happened (Bianchi 2000; Bianchi et al. 2007).

Figure 10.2, which relies on time-dairy data from the Time Use in Economic and Social Accounts study (TUESA); the Family Interaction, Social Capital and Trends in Time Use Survey (FISCT); and the American Time Use Survey (ATUS), indicates that the time that married mothers devote to their children on any given day increased from 1975 to 2003; moreover, married fathers' time with children also increased over this period. Specifically, the total time that married mothers spent in the presence of their children rose from 330 minutes a day in 1975 to 337 minutes in 1998 to 387 minutes in 2003. Furthermore, the total time that fathers spent in the presence of their children more than tripled from 1976 to 1998, from 73 minutes a day to 243 minutes a day in 1998, before largely leveling off such that fathers' total time only increased to 248 minutes in 2003. Moreover, the time that mothers devoted to one-on-one interaction with their children, or primary time, went from 81 minutes in 1975 to 59 minutes in 1998 to 95 minutes in 2003.

Changes in Parent-Child Time

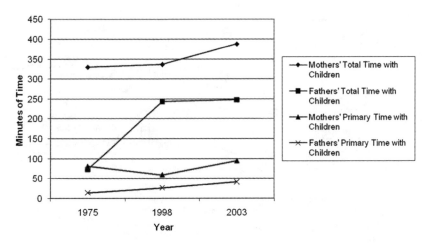

FIGURE 10.2 Changes in parent-child time.

Likewise, the primary time that fathers spent with their children rose from 14 minutes in 1976 to 27 minutes in 1998 to 42 minutes in 2003. So, despite changes in work-family arrangements, the amount of time that American parents are spending with their children has increased over the last four decades (see also Bianchi 2000).

The findings displayed in figure 10.2 beg an important question: Did maternal time with children increase for all married mothers, or just married mothers working part-time or not at all? Figures 10.3 and 10.4, which illustrate time devoted to children by married mothers and fathers during weekdays and also rely on data from the TUESA, the FISCT, and the ATUS, indicate that total time and primary time spent with children increased from 1975 to 2003 among mothers working part-time and full-time, whereas stay-at-home mothers increased their primary time but not their total time during this period. Not surprisingly, figures 10.3 and 10.4 also reveal that stay-at-home mothers spent more total and primary time with their children over the last forty years than did mothers pursuing other work-family strategies. Still, it is striking that working mothers were able to increase their time with children over this time, and that these increases offset the effects of rising maternal labor force participation. Research suggests that working mothers were able to increase the time they spent with their children by cutting back on housework, leisure, and personal time (Bianchi et al. 2007).

Weekday Total Parent-Child Time by Gender/LFP

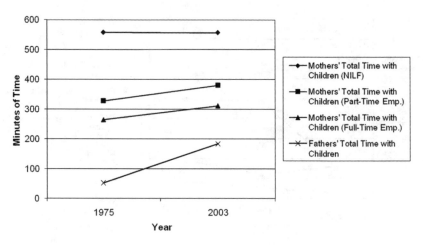

FIGURE 10.3 Weekday total parent-child time by gender/labor force participation.

Overall, then, figures 10.2 through 10.4 suggest that an ethic of "concerted cultivation" (Lareau 2003) has become more common among both mothers *and* fathers. This is an ethic where parents devote more time and resources to cultivating the intellectual, athletic, extracurricular, and emotional lives of their children, both because they are concerned about the immediate welfare of their children and because they want their children to do well

Weekday Primary Childcare by Gender/LFP

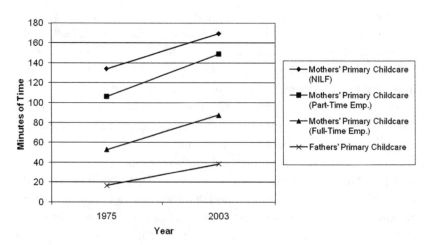

FIGURE 10.4 Weekday primary childcare by gender/labor force participation.

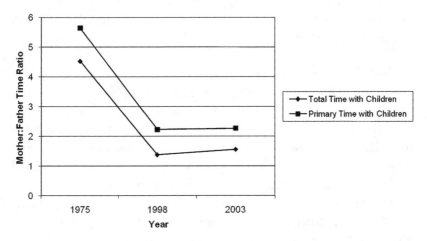

FIGURE 10.5 Changes in parent-child time ratio.

later in life (Lareau 2003). Increases in parental time spent with children are also linked, in all likelihood, to parental desires to protect their children from perceived dangers in the broader culture and in the social environment (Best 1990; Pain 2006). The rise of this ethic of concerted cultivation has undoubtedly been one of the forces pushing parenting in a more egalitarian direction, as both mothers and fathers do more to ensure that their children receive the time and attention that our contemporary society now deems necessary for the welfare of children.

Nevertheless, here as elsewhere, there are limits to the egalitarian trajectory of contemporary family life. A close look at figure 10.2 suggests that increases in paternal time did not keep pace with increases in maternal time from 1998 to 2003. Figure 10.5 provides additional confirmation that the egalitarian trajectory of contemporary parenting flattened out in the late 1990s.

Specifically, figure 10.5 explores the ratio of mother to father time spent with children among married couples with children from 1975 to 2003. From 1975 to 1998, the ratio of mother to father time moved in a dramatically egalitarian direction. Specifically, the ratio of mother to father total time with children fell from 4.5 in 1975 to 1.4 in 1998. Similarly, the ratio of mother to father time spent in primary parent-child interaction with their children fell from 5.6 in 1975 to 2.2 in 1998. But between 1998 and 2003, the maternal to paternal time ratio stopped moving in an egalitarian direction. Specifically, the mother to father ratio of total time rose from 1.4 in 1998 to

1.6 in 2003, and the mother to father ratio of primary time rose from 2.2 in 1998 to 2.3 in 2003. This means that mothers have taken on a slightly larger share of the parenting burden in recent years, and that the gendered division of parenting has become slightly less egalitarian.

Thus, our examination of trends in married parents' workforce strategies and time devoted to parenting reveals that both of these behavioral trends moved in a strongly egalitarian direction during the latter half of the twentieth century. However, at the end of the twentieth century, these two important behavioral indicators of a gender revolution stopped moving in an egalitarian direction. This means that in most American families today fathers still take the lead when it comes to providing for their families and mothers still take the lead when it comes to nurturing. This is the case even though most married couples with children now have more egalitarian work-family and parenting arrangements than did their parents and grandparents, and most mothers and fathers spend more time with their children than did their parents and grandparents. Now, there is also more heterogeneity in how married mothers and fathers juggle work and family, with no one strategy—from traditional to egalitarian to neotraditional to nontraditional—guiding the work-family arrangements of contemporary parents.

The behavioral patterns we document in this chapter may be driven in part by parallel trends in the trajectory of gender and family attitudes and preferences in the larger society, which largely mirror patterns in work-family strategies. Figures 10.6 and 10.7, which draw on GSS data, track gender and family attitudes among married parents in the United States from the 1970s to the 2000s. These figures indicate that these attitudes moved in a markedly egalitarian direction from the 1970s to the 1990s. For instance, figure 10.6 shows that in the 1970s only 50 percent of married parents agreed with the view that a "working mother can establish just as warm and secure a relationship with her children as a mother who does not work." By the 1990s, 69 percent of married parents took this view. Likewise, figure 10.7 shows that 62 percent of married parents thought it "is much better for everyone involved if the man is the achiever outside the home and the woman takes care of the home and family" in the 1970s; by the 1990s, the percent of married parents who took this view had fallen to 33 percent.

But from the 1990s onwards, public support among married parents for more egalitarian family arrangements stalled. Moreover, figures 10.6 and 10.7 provide some modest evidence that attitudes have become more polarized in the last two decades, with more married parents taking extremely egalitarian or traditional positions on gender.

GSS: Working Mother Doesn't Hurt Child (FECHLD)

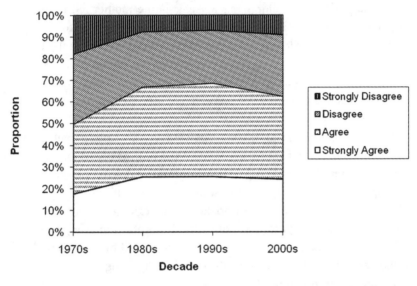

FIGURE 10.6 General Society Survey: working mother does not hurt child (FECHILD).

GSS: Better for Man to Work, Woman Tend Home (FEFAM)

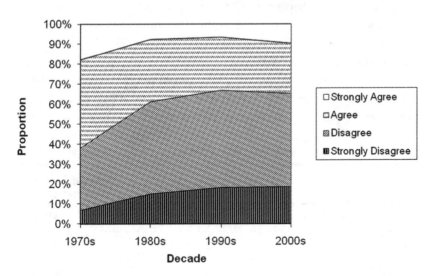

FIGURE 10.7 Better for man to work, woman tend home (FEFAM).

Specifically, figure 10.6 indicates that the percentage of married parents agreeing that a working mother "can establish just as warm and secure a relationship with her children" as a stay-at-home mother fell from 69 to 62 percent, and the percentage taking the opposite view rose from 31 percent to 38 percent. Moreover, the percentage of married parents strongly disagreeing with the notion that working mothers do not hurt their children rose from 7 to 9 percent, which suggests a modest increase in polarization. (Nevertheless, the percentage of married parents strongly agreeing with this notion fell by 1 percent.)

Likewise, figure 10.7 shows that the percentage of married parents endorsing a more traditional family-work strategy rose from 33 percent in the 1990s to 35 percent in the 2000s, just as the percentage endorsing a more egalitarian approach fell from 67 percent in the 1990s to 65 percent in the 2000s. Moreover, parents' attitudes to work-family strategies grew more polarized over this period. The percentage of married parents strongly agreeing with a more traditional approach rose from 6 to 10 percent over this period, just as the percentage of married parents strongly disagreeing with a more traditional approach rose from 18 to 19 percent.

Thus, figures 10.6 and 10.7 both suggest that cultural support for egalitarian work-family arrangements has stopped climbing, that married parents take a range of views about how best to combine work and family, and, indeed, that attitudes toward work and family may be moving in a polarizing direction among married parents.

Table 10.1 moves beyond abstract gender attitudes among married parents to look specifically at married mothers' personal preferences about juggling work and family; this table reveals that those preferences are now also quite pluralistic. Specifically, data from the 2000 Survey of Marriage and Family Life (SMFL) indicate that 18 percent of married mothers prefer to work full-time, that 36 percent prefer to stay at home, and 46 percent prefer to work part-time. Thus, the modal choice for mothers is to work part-time,

TABLE 10.1 Wives' and husbands' preferences for wives' labor force participation

	WIVES REPORT OWN PREFERENCES	HUSBANDS REPORT WIVES' PREFERENCES
Wife stays at home	36.0	45.9
Wife employed part-time	46.3	36.4
Wife employed full-time	17.7	17.7

with significant minorities preferring clearly progressive and traditional positions for their own work-family arrangements (see Taylor, Funk, and Clark [2008] for similar findings from a 2007 Pew Research Center survey).

How can we account for the tidal wave of change in gender and parenting behaviors and attitudes in the latter half of the twentieth century, as well as the leveling off of support for egalitarian family arrangements in the last two decades? At least five factors help account for the gender revolution in the second half of the twentieth century. First, women made tremendous gains in educational attainment over this period, which made it easier for them to find good-paying and interesting work, and increased the opportunity costs for them of staying out of the labor force (Spain and Bianchi 1996; Hakim 2000; Bradbury and Katz 2005). Second, the economy shifted from a strong manufacturing orientation to a strong service orientation; this economic shift led to more white-collar jobs, which are more attractive to women than blue-collar jobs; moreover, these economic shifts were also associated with a decline in the real wages of men, especially working-class men, which increased the pressure on married mothers to work (Hakim 2000; McLanahan 2004; Bradbury and Katz 2005).

Third, the contraceptive revolution of the 1960s reinforced and helped make possible these educational and economic shifts by providing women with reliable and independent control of their own fertility, which allowed them to focus more on work and education, and less on bearing and rearing children (Spain and Bianchi 1996; Hakim 2000; Goldin and Katz 2002). Fourth, the women's movement pushed for cultural and legal changes that opened up virtually all occupations to women, made the public more supportive of women's paid work, and encouraged men to take on a larger role in the domestic sphere so that women could focus more on paid work (Spain and Bianchi 1996; Hakim 2000). Finally, the therapeutic cultural turn of the 1970s increased the importance of personal fulfillment, intimacy, and equality in both the private and public spheres among ordinary Americans; this cultural turn meant that more women sought out fulfilling careers in the public sphere and equality in the domestic sphere (Bell 1976; Hakim 2000). Thus, a range of social and cultural changes during the latter half of the twentieth century pushed American married parents in a more egalitarian direction.

But this chapter suggests that the gender revolution in parenting and the organization of family life among married parents stalled or came to a halt in the late 1990s. At least four factors account for the ceiling in public support for gender egalitarianism. First, a large minority of married parents in the

United States are religious; in fact, the 2000 SMFL indicates that 37 percent of married parents attend church once a week or more. These religious parents are significantly more likely to hold traditional gender beliefs and act upon those beliefs than their nonreligious peers, and they have proven largely resistant to the egalitarian messages of the women's movement (Wilcox 2004; Glass and Jacobs 2005). Second, partly because of the contraceptive revolution, parenting has become more of a voluntary endeavor, with larger numbers of women avoiding parenthood altogether—18 percent, according to one recent estimate (Downs 2003). This means that the women who now decide to become mothers may be more invested in their chosen maternal role, and more likely to prioritize motherhood over work, compared to mothers who came of age in the heyday of second wave feminism (Taylor, Funk, and Clark 2008).

Third, the women's movement has advanced a public message celebrating women's choices when it comes to childbearing, child-rearing, and work—whatever those choices might be. In the last decade, many women—including women who subscribe to feminist or egalitarian beliefs—seem to have taken this message to heart and concluded, especially in light of the rise of the new parental ethos of concerted cultivation, that the best choice for them and their children is to be at home full-time or at least part-time (Hakim 2000; Lareau 2003; Hirshman 2005). Finally, biology also may have played a role. Given the voluntary character of parenthood, feminist and popular support for the idea that women should make their own choices about work and family, and a labor market that is more flexible than most markets in the developed world, the women who are most biologically primed by high levels of estrogen and oxytocin, and low levels of testosterone, toward a nurturing orientation are likely to prefer full-time motherhood, and eschew a work-centered persona—either normatively or practically (Hrdy 1999; Taylor 2002; Rhoads 2004). Thus, in all likelihood, religion, the increasingly voluntary character of childbearing, choice feminism, and biology have all played a role in limiting the appeal of a thoroughgoing gender egalitarianism among contemporary parents.

Finally, it is worth noting that the appeal of the gender revolution also appears to be stratified. College-educated women have benefited most from the gender revolution because they have access to the most intrinsically interesting jobs, and because they are typically married to college-educated men who have not lost financial ground as the economy has shifted toward a service economy (Hakim 2000). These women and their husbands are also more likely to have the financial means to make work-family choices that

TABLE 10.2 Wives' labor force preferences, behavior, and fit

	PREFERENCE	ACTUAL BEHAVIOR	PREFERENCE AND ACTUAL BEHAVIOR MATCH	OVERALL MATCH	PREFER WORKING LESS	PREFER WORKING MORE
No degree						
Stay at home	37.2%	30.9%	50.0%			
Part-time	42.9%	19.2%	48.8%	44.1	39.8	16.1
Full-time	19.9%	49.9%	28.6%			
Degree						
Stay at home	33.9%	25.8%	60.6%			
Part-time	51.8%	26.6%	72.6%	49.4	39.3	11.3
Full-time	14.2%	47.6%	20.2%			

mesh with their preferences. By contrast, women without college degrees have benefited less from the gender revolution. The jobs to which they have access are less intrinsically interesting, and the men in their lives have experienced marked declines in their real wages over the last half-century (Gilbert 2008). Consequently, working-class women and their husbands are less likely to have the financial means to make work-family choices that mesh with their preferences.

Some of these class differences are visible in table 10.2, which explores divergences between preferences and actual work-family strategies by education. Drawing once again on the 2000 SMFL, table 10.2 indicates that married mothers without college degrees are more likely than college-educated married mothers to prefer staying at home or working full-time. By contrast, a majority of college-educated mothers prefer to work part-time, which allows them to keep a foot in the working world even as they focus more than their husbands on family life. But working-class mothers are less likely than college-educated wives to be able to pursue work-family strategies that match their preferences. Specifically, only 44 percent of working-class mothers are engaged in strategies that match their preferences, compared to 49 percent of middle- and upper-class mothers. So, table 10.2 suggests that the gender revolution of the last half-century is more likely to have afforded middle- and upper-class families than working-class families the opportunity to forge work-family strategies that mesh with their ideals about work, parenting, and family life.

WORK-FAMILY STRATEGIES, THE GENDERED DIVISION OF PARENTING, PARENTING INVESTMENTS, AND THE QUALITY AND STABILITY OF MARRIAGE: WHAT IS BEST FOR THE MARRIAGES OF MOTHERS AND FATHERS?

This chapter has shown that married parents in the United States take a pluralistic approach to juggling family and work, with no one strategy dominating the preferences and practices of married parents, that most parents are not pursuing their ideal work-family strategy, that working-class parents are less likely than middle-class parents to be able to match their work-family preferences with their actual strategies, and that mothers still take on the bulk of child-rearing, even though both mothers and fathers have dramatically increased the time they devote to parenting since the 1960s. We turn now to considering how these varied strategies, preferences, and parental investments are related to the quality and stability of marriage among married parents in the United States. We analyze data from the 2000 SMFL and the second wave of the National Survey of Families and Households (NSFH2 [1992–1994]), both datasets that provide us with nationally-representative samples of married parents in the United States.

In analyzing these datasets, we test three different theoretical models of contemporary married life. The first is the companionate model of married life (Burgess, Locke and Thomes 1963; Blumstein and Schwartz 1983; England and Farkas 1986; Amato et al. 2007). This model suggests that married couples enjoy higher-quality marriages when they take an egalitarian approach to married life. Part of the argument is that sharing tasks associated with work and family on a fairly equal basis provides spouses with opportunities to engage in similar activities and experiences, thereby building solidarity. Furthermore, by providing wives with access to income and prestige through work, companionate marriages are supposed to undercut the patriarchal power and authority of husbands, thereby fostering more authentic intimacy between the spouses than in marriages where the husband has more power or authority. Thus, in companionate marriages, spouses are supposed to have more opportunities to build a shared life together, women should feel free to speak their minds, and men should feel a greater kinship with their wives as they take on their fare share of the emotional and practical work associated with family life (Wilcox and Nock 2006). For all these reasons, the companionate model of marriage predicts higher levels of marital quality and stability among couples who organize their work and family lives along egalitarian lines.

By contrast, the gender model of marriage suggests that husbands and wives are happier when they take a gendered approach to marriage, with wives specializing more in nurturing and husbands specializing more in breadwinning (Becker 1991; Rhoads 2004; Wilcox and Nock 2006). This model holds that spouses prefer a gendered approach to marriage and family life because they have been socialized over the life course to think that men excel in breadwinning and women excel in nurturing (Thompson and Walker 1989; Maccoby 1998). But biology is also supposed to play a role here, especially when children enter the picture. The arrival of a child elevates women's levels of the hormone peptide oxytocin, which fosters nurturing behavior (Hrdy 1999; Taylor 2002). This, in turn, is supposed to encourage wives—on average—to be more likely to embrace a nurturing orientation than husbands (Rhoads 2004).

Finally, the gender model holds that specialization is a more efficient way of allocating the labor associated with family and work. Mothers can specialize more in nurturing, and fathers can specialize more in breadwinning, which affords each spouse the opportunity to invest more in their specific domain and to recoup more returns in each of these domains. Specialization also reduces role overload, where spouses get exhausted by trying to combine the demanding roles of full-time work, full-time parenthood, and full-time marriage (Becker 1991; Amato et al. 2007). Moreover, couples who specialize are less likely to argue over the division of family work, including child-rearing; such arguments can be a major source of marital distress (Wilcox and Nock 2006). Accordingly, the gender model of marriage suggests that couples who allow husbands to focus more on breadwinning and wives to focus more on nurturing (even if both spouses contribute to the labor force and to nurturing their children) are more likely to enjoy high-quality and stable marriages.

The preference model of marriage takes a via media between the companionate and gender models of marriage (Hakim 2000). It suggests that women's preferences about the division of work and family life are crucial in determining the quality and stability of married life for couples. If a wife wishes to pursue a work-centered life, she will be happier doing so; the same is true for wives who would like to combine work and family with part-time jobs, as well as for wives who wish to pursue a family-centered life. In keeping with the arguments made here, preference theory further argues that the contraceptive revolution, feminism, better labor force opportunities for women, and increased attention to personal fulfillment on the part of women have made it easier for women to develop distinct preferences regarding their work-family strategies, to realize those preferences, and to attach a high level of importance to those preferences.

Furthermore, for both sociological and biological reasons, the preference model suggests that most married mothers in modern societies prefer an adaptive (combining part-time work with motherhood) or a home-centered (stay-at-home motherhood) work-family strategy, whereas only a minority of mothers, usually about 20 percent, in modern societies prefer a work-centered strategy. (Note that table 10.2 is largely congruent with Hakim's theory in this regard.) Finally, because highly educated women tend to marry highly educated men who earn more than less-educated men, preference theory predicts that college-educated wives (and couples) will have a greater chance of realizing their preferred work-family strategies. (Indeed, table 10.2 indicates that this is currently the case among married mothers in the United States.) So, as against companionate or gendered theories of marriage that suggest a specific work-family strategy will foster higher-quality marriage, preference theory suggests that the success of a given strategy depends on the underlying preferences of the woman in the marriage.

Which of these models is best able to account for contemporary patterns of marital happiness and stability? To answer these questions, we look at two outcomes in the SMFL and the NSFH2. The first is a measure of global marital happiness. Both the SMFL and the NSFH2 asked participants how happy they were with their marriage "overall." Because a plurality of the participants reported being "very happy" and few were in the lowest category, we dichotomized the variables: 1 meant very happy, 0 meant otherwise. Consequently, we used logistic regression to evaluate this outcome. The second outcome was a measure called divorce proneness. Divorce proneness was measured by a series of questions that assessed how far into the process of considering or pursuing a divorce survey participants had ventured. For example, a participant might simply think that his marriage is in trouble. A further step (with many steps in between) might include discussing divorce or separation with one's spouse. The higher the score on the divorce proneness scale, the more steps toward divorce a respondent has taken. The divorce proneness scale has been shown to be a very good predictor of divorce and an important aspect of marital quality (Edwards, Johnson, and Booth 1987;

Amato et al. 2007). Because this was a continuous variable we used ordinary least squares (OLS) regression in the analyses of this outcome.

Model 1 of table 10.3 indicates that no one work-family strategy is linked to higher reports of marital happiness—that is, reporting that one is "very happy" in one's marriage—among married mothers with children under eighteen. For married fathers, the story is somewhat different. For fathers, having a wife who works more than he does dramatically reduces the odds that he is very happy in his marriage; specifically, fathers in nontraditional marriages are 61 percent less likely to report that they are very happy in their marriage, compared to married fathers who have a wife who is a stay-at-home mother.

Model 2 of table 10.3 shows that married mothers' preferences matter for the quality of their marriages. Specifically, wives who are working full-time *or* who are at home in violation of their preferences are, respectively, 46 percent less likely and 39 percent less likely to be very happy in their marriages, compared to stay-at-home wives who prefer to be at home. Likewise, married fathers are also less likely to report that they are very happy in their marriages if their wife is working full-time against her preferences, and they are more likely to report that they are very happy in their marriage if their wife is working full-time in accord with her preferences, compared to fathers who have a stay-at-home-wife who is at home in accord with her preferences. However, Model 2 of table 10.3 also indicates that married fathers who have a wife who works more than they do are less happy in their marriages, regardless of whether or not this work-family strategy is in accord with their wife's preferences. Taken together, Models 1 and 2 provide some support for the preference and gender models of marriage, and no support for the companionate model of marriage.

However, Model 3 of table 10.3 provides some support for the companionate model of marriage. Specifically, wives and husbands are most likely to report that they are very happy in their marriages when they share childcare. (Our measure of relative childcare was anchored at the midpoint by sharing childcare and higher scores meant that the participant did more childcare than their spouse.) By contrast, when wives report that they do more of the childcare (the typical pattern), they are 45 percent less likely to report that they are "very happy" in their marriages, compared to wives who report that they share childcare with their husband. Similarly, when husbands report that either they or their wife does more of the childcare, they are about 30 percent less likely to be "very happy" in their marriage. So, in accord with the companionate model of marriage, Model 3 suggests that wives and husbands are happier when they share childcare.

TABLE 10.3 The relationship between the likelihood of being "very happy" in marriage and wives' labor force participation

	MODEL 1				MODEL 2				MODEL 3			
	WIVES		HUSBANDS		WIVES		HUSBANDS		WIVES		HUSBANDS	
	LOG ODDS	STE	LOG ODDS	STE	LOG ODDS	STB	LOG ODDS	STE	LOG ODDS	STE	LOG ODDS	STE
Wife employed part-time[a]	.96	.22	.88	.27								
Wife employed full-time[a]	.77	.19	.89	.23								
Gender reversed LFP[a]	.79	.39	.39*	.47								
Wife at home, does not match her preferences[b]					.61†	.30	.60	.38	.57†	.30	.57	.39
Wife part-time, matches her preferences[b]					.64	.30	.83	.35	.54*	.31	.82	.36
Wife part-time, does not match her preferences[b]					1.00	.34	.63	.37	.90	.34	.57	.38
Wife full-time, matches her preferences[b]					.94	.33	2.54*	.43	.76	.34	2.27†	.43
Wife full-time, does not match her preferences[b]					.54*	.25	.55*	.28	.43*	.26	.48†	.29
Gender reverse, matches her preferences[b]					.56	.59	.21†	.91	.38	.61	.20†	.94
Gender reverse, does not match her preferences[b]					.68	.51	.38†	.56	.49	.53	.35†	.58
Wife does more childcare[c]									.55*	.18	.68†	.20
Husband does more childcare[c]									.76	.47	.66†	.41
Chi-square of model	11.24		8.85		19.84		32.01*		31.38*		34.92*	

Note: All models control for being African-American or other race/ethnic minority (comparison is non-Hispanic white), number of marriages, marital duration, education, family income (logged), and age of youngest child (†p < .10; *p < .05).

[a]Omitted category is "wife stays at home."

[b]Omitted category is "wife stays at home, matches her preferences."

[c]Omitted category is "share childcare equally."

Table 10.4 explores divorce proneness—again, how far along in the divorce process the participant feels—among married mothers and fathers. Model 1 indicates that the only work-family strategy that is linked to a higher risk of divorce is the nontraditional strategy. Specifically, husbands who are married to wives who work more than they do are more likely to report having progressed toward divorce than husbands with wives who stay at home. Otherwise, no work-family strategy is linked to higher levels of divorce proneness.

Model 2 of table 10.4 indicates that departures from ideal work-family strategies are linked to increased divorce proneness for married mothers but not married fathers. Specifically, wives who are at home, who are working full-time, or who work more than their husbands against their preferences are more likely to report divorce proneness, compared to stay-at-home wives who prefer to be at home. However, to our surprise, we also find that wives who are working full- or part-time in accord with their preferences are more likely to report higher levels of divorce proneness. This may be because women who are considering a divorce often increase their labor force participation in anticipation of establishing their own household (Rogers 1999). Or, consistent with the gender model, these results may reflect the fact that the relative economic independence of working wives makes it easier for them to consider divorce (Becker 1991). Thus, Models 1 and 2 of table 10.4 provide some support for both the preference and gender models of marriage when it comes to the issue of work-family strategies.

However, once again, Model 3 of table 10.4 provides support for the companionate model of marriage. Specifically, when a wife reports she does more childcare than her husband she is more likely to report more divorce proneness, compared to wives who share childcare with their husbands. Likewise, when a husband reports he does more childcare than his wife, he is more likely to report divorce proneness, compared to husbands who share childcare with their wives. Thus, when it comes to the division of parenting responsibilities, more egalitarian arrangements are associated with lower levels of divorce proneness.

Thus, tables 10.3 and 10.4 indicate that married mothers are most likely to enjoy high-quality and stable marriages when they share parenting responsibilities with their husbands, and when they are able to pursue their ideal work-family strategy. Note also that most married mothers prefer a neotraditional or traditional strategy, and that the happiest and least divorce prone wives are stay-at-home mothers who are acting in accord with their preferences. All this suggests that most wives are happiest with a "superdad" arrangement where the husband takes on the primary breadwinning burden

TABLE 10.4 The relationship between divorce proneness and wives' labor force participation

| | MODEL 1 | | | | MODEL 2 | | | | MODEL 3 | | | |
| | WIVES | | HUSBANDS | | WIVES | | HUSBANDS | | WIVES | | HUSBANDS | |
	B	STE	B	STE	B	STB	B	STE	B	STE	B	STE
Intercept	.21	.15	.23	.17	.20	.16	.22	.17	.17	.16	.22	.18
Wife employed part-time[a]	.02	.04	-.01	.05								
Wife employed full-time[a]	.03	.03	.04	.04								
Gender reversed LFP[a]	.10	.07	.15†	.08								
Wife at home, does not match her preferences[b]					.12*	.05	-.02	.06	.13*	.05	.01	.06
Wife part-time, matches her preferences[b]					.10*	.05	-.04	.06	.13*	.05	-.03	.06
Wife part-time, does not match her preferences[b]					.04	.06	.01	.06	.06	.06	.02	.06
Wife full-time, matches her preferences[b]					.11*	.05	-.09	.06	.14*	.06	-.07	.06
Wife full-time, does not match her preferences[b]					.08†	.04	.07	.05	.11*	.04	.09†	.05
Gender reverse, matches her preferences[b]					.11	.10	.13	.15	.16	.11	.04	.15
Gender reverse, does not match her preferences[b]					.19*	.09	.15	.10	.23*	.09	.10	.10
Wife does more childcare[c]									.10*	.03	.03	.03
Husband does more childcare[c]									.13	.08	.25*	.07
R^2	.04*		.04*		.05*		.06*		.07*		.08*	

Note: All models control for being African-American or other race/ethnic minority (comparison is non-Hispanic white), number of marriages, marital duration, education, family income (logged), and age of youngest child ($^†p < .10; ^*p < .05$).

[a] Omitted category is "wife stays at home."

[b] Omitted category is "wife stays at home, matches her preferences."

[c] Omitted category is "share childcare equally."

but also shares childcare (Wilcox and Nock 2006; Smith 2007). Tables 10.3 and 10.4 also indicate that married fathers are happiest and least prone to divorce when their wives do not work more than they do, when their wives' work-family strategies generally fit with their wives' preferences, and when they do not do more childcare than their wives. Thus, for husbands, arrangements that reverse typical gender patterns seem particularly problematic for the health of their marriages.

Do these patterns hold up for both working- and middle-class married parents, or are there class differences in these patterns? Table 10.5a suggests the match between preferences and work-family strategies is especially important in predicting marital happiness for college-educated wives, whereas table 10.5b indicates the match between wives' preferences and work-family strategies is particularly important for husbands without college degrees (and there are no major class differences when it comes to the influence of the gendered division of parenting). Table 6a indicates that the fit between work-family preferences and strategies is especially important in predicting divorce proneness for college-educated wives, and that non-college-educated wives are especially likely to consider divorce if their husbands work less than they do, regardless of their preferences. Similarly, this table indicates that college-educated wives are more divorce prone when they do more childcare, whereas wives without college degrees are more divorce prone when their husbands do more childcare. Table 10.6b indicates that college-educated husbands are more divorce prone when their wives do more childcare, whereas husbands without college degrees are more divorce prone when they do more childcare. This table also indicates that college-educated husbands are more divorce prone when their wives work more than they do.

In general, tables 10.5a through 10.6b suggest that marriage patterns vary by gender *and* class. Marriages among college-educated women are happier and more stable when wives' work-family preferences are met, and when wives do not take on the lion's share of parenting. By contrast, marriages among women without college degrees are more stable when wives do not outwork their husbands, and husbands do not perform more childcare than their wives. In other words, achieving work-family preferences and shared parenting matter more for college-educated wives, whereas avoiding a non-traditional marriage matters more for wives without college degrees (see also Amato et al. 2007). Thus, for women, the preference and companionate models seem more applicable to college-educated wives, and the gender model seems more applicable to wives without college degrees.

TABLE 10.5A The relationship between the likelihood of being "very happy" in marriage and wives' labor force participation by education (wives only)

	MODEL 1				MODEL 2				MODEL 3			
	NO COLLEGE DEGREE		COLLEGE DEGREE		NO COLLEGE DEGREE		COLLEGE DEGREE		NO COLLEGE DEGREE		COLLEGE DEGREE	
	LOG ODDS	STE	LOG ODDS	STE	LOG ODDS	STB	LOG ODDS	STE	LOG ODDS	STE	LOG ODDS	STE
Wife employed part-time[a]	1.20	.30	.76	.35								
Wife employed full-time[a]	.74	.24	.94	.34								
Gender reversed LFP[a]	.46	.53	1.89	.66								
Wife at home, does not match her preferences[b]					.75	.37	.38†	.53	.71	.37	.34*	.54
Wife part-time, matches her preferences[b]					.92	.42	.46†	.46	.86	.42	.35*	49
Wife part-time, does not match her preferences[b]					1.17	.41	.71	.61	1.07	.42	.63	.62
Wife full-time, matches her preferences[b]					.80	.39	2.09	.70	.68	.40	1.44	.74
Wife full-time, does not match her preferences[b]					.60†	.31	.46†	.43	.51*	.32	.38*	.46
Gender reverse, matches her preferences[b]					.39	.96	.76	.83	.27	.30*	.46	.66
Gender reverse, does not match her preferences[b]					.40	.64	3.10	1.20	.34	.66	1.76	
Wife does more childcare[c]									.54*	.23	.54*	.33
Husband does more childcare[c]									.53	.54	1.86	1.25
Chi-square of model	9.35		9.79		11.03		21.23†		17.67		25.35*	

Note: All models control for being African–American or other race/ethnic minority (comparison is non-Hispanic white), number of marriages, marital duration, family income (logged), and age of youngest child (†p < .10; *p < .05).

[a] Omitted category is "wife stays at home."
[b] Omitted category is "wife stays at home, matches her preferences."
[c] Omitted category is "share childcare equally."

TABLE 10.5B The relationship between the likelihood of being "very happy" in marriage and wives' labor force participation by education (husbands only)

	MODEL 1				MODEL 2				MODEL 3			
	NO COLLEGE DEGREE		COLLEGE DEGREE		NO COLLEGE DEGREE		COLLEGE DEGREE		NO COLLEGE DEGREE		COLLEGE DEGREE	
	LOG ODDS	STE	LOG ODDS	STE	LOG ODDS	STE	LOG ODDS	STE	LOG ODDS	STE	LOG ODDS	STE
Wife employed part-time[a]	.57	.36	1.67	.42								
Wife employed full-time[a]	.97	.31	.74	.35								
Gender reversed LFP[a]	.32†	.67	.52	.69								
Wife at home, does not match her preferences[b]					.40†	.54	.99	.61	.34†	.57	.97	.62
Wife part-time, matches her preferences[b]					.38†	.55	1.73	.50	.47†	.57	1.68	.51
Wife part-time, does not match her preferences[b]					.35*	.52	1.62	.65	.42*	.54	1.57	.66
Wife full-time, matches her preferences[b]					2.33	.60	1.97	.66	2.00	.62	1.88	.67
Wife full-time, does not match her preferences[b]					.43*	.44	.63	.39	.30*	.46	.60	.41
Gender reverse, matches her preferences[b]					.19	1.29	.22	1.28	.19	1.32	.22	1.36
Gender reverse, does not match her preferences[b]					.20*	.82	.78	.84	.14*	.84	.86	.88
Wife does more childcare[c]									.59†	.26	.78	.34
Husband does more childcare[c]									.53	.56	.74	.65
Chi-square of model	10.92		7.17		29.90*		11.88		32.80*		12.39	

Note: All models control for being African-American or other race/ethnic minority (comparison is non-Hispanic white), number of marriages, marital duration, family income (logged), and age of youngest child (†$p < .10$; *$p < .05$).

[a]Omitted category is "wife stays at home."

[b]Omitted category is "wife stays at home, matches her preferences."

[c]Omitted category is "share childcare equally."

TABLE 10.6A The relationship between divorce proneness and wives' labor force participation by education (wives only)

	MODEL 1				MODEL 2				MODEL 3			
	NO COLLEGE DEGREE		COLLEGE DEGREE		NO COLLEGE DEGREE		COLLEGE DEGREE		NO COLLEGE DEGREE		COLLEGE DEGREE	
	B	STE	B	STE	B	STB	B	STE	B	STE	B	STE
Intercept	.48*	.24	−.35	.33	.41†	.25	−.57†	.33	.39	.25	−.60†	.32
Wife employed part-time[a]	.02	.05	.02	.06								
Wife employed full-time[a]	.02	.04	.02	.06								
Gender reversed LFP[a]	.25*	.10	−.08	.10								
Wife at home, does not match her preferences[b]					.08	.07	.22*	.09	.09	.07	.22*	.09
Wife part-time, matches her preferences[b]					.11	.08	.12	.11	.12	.08	.17*	.08
Wife part-time, does not match her preferences[b]					.01	.07	.09	.10	.02	.07	.10	.10
Wife full-time, matches her preferences[b]					.13†	.07	−.01	.10	.13†	.07	.09	.10
Wife full-time, does not match her preferences[b]					.03	.06	.13*	.06	.04	.06	.20*	.07
Gender reverse, matches her preferences[b]					.39*	.18	−.06	.14	.43*	.18	.07	.14
Gender reverse, does not match her preferences[b]					.28*	.12	.07	.14	.21†	.12	.21	.15
Wife does more childcare[c]									.04	.04	.16*	.05
Husband does more childcare[c]									.23*	.10	−.21	.16
R^2	.07*		.05		.08*		.08†		.10*		.13*	

Note: All models control for being African–American or other race/ethnic minority (comparison is non-Hispanic white), number of marriages, marital duration, family income (logged), and age of youngest child ($†p < .10$; $*p < .05$).

[a]Omitted category is "wife stays at home."

[b]Omitted category is "wife stays at home, matches her preferences."

[c]Omitted category is "share childcare equally."

TABLE 10.6B The relationship between divorce proneness and wives' labor force participation by education (husbands only)

	MODEL 1				MODEL 2				MODEL 3			
	NO COLLEGE DEGREE		COLLEGE DEGREE		NO COLLEGE DEGREE		COLLEGE DEGREE		NO COLLEGE DEGREE		COLLEGE DEGREE	
	B	STE	B	STE	B	STB	B	STE	B	STE	B	STE
Intercept	.24	.25	.16	.32	.23	.26	.13	.32	.20	.27	.07	.32
Wife employed part-time[a]	-.02	.07	-.02	.07								
Wife employed full-time[a]	.01	.06	.08	.06								
Gender reversed LFP[a]	.05	.12	.24*	.12								
Wife at home, does not match her preferences[b]					-.03	.10	-.05	.10	-.01	.09	-.04	.10
Wife part-time, matches her preferences[b]					-.08	.10	-.04	.08	-.06	.10	-.01	.08
Wife part-time, does not match her preferences[b]					.01	.09	-.04	.10	.01	.09	-.01	.10
Wife full-time, matches her preferences[b]					-.11	.09	-.11	.10	-.11	.09	-.07	.10
Wife full-time, does not match her preferences[b]					.03	.07	.11	.06	.32	.07	.16*	.07
Gender reverse, matches her preferences[b]					-.12	.23	.35	.21	-.21	.22	.41†	.22
Gender reverse, does not match her preferences[b]					.10	.14	.17	.14	.03	.14	.17	.15
Wife does more childcare[c]									-.04	.04	.14*	.05
Husband does more childcare[c]									.33*	.09	.09	.11
R^2	.05		.04		.07		.07		.12*		.11†	

Note: All models control for being African-American or other race/ethnic minority (comparison is non-Hispanic white), number of marriages, marital duration, family income (logged), and age of youngest child (†$p < .10$; *$p < .05$).

[a]Omitted category is "wife stays at home."

[b]Omitted category is "wife stays at home, matches her preferences."

[c]Omitted category is "share childcare equally."

For men, the patterns are not consistent. When it comes to happiness, husbands without college degrees are happier when their wives do not outwork them, when their wives' work-family preferences are met, and when their wives do not take on the lion's share of child-rearing. But when it comes to divorce proneness, husbands with college degrees do better when their wives do not outwork them, and when their wives do not take on the lion's share of parenting. Thus, all three models of marriage have varying degrees of relevance for working-class and middle-class married fathers.

Finally, relying on data from NSFH2, we explore the links between time devoted to parenting and marital happiness for married parents. Despite finding that childcare inequity predicted lower marital satisfaction in the SMFL, table 10.7 indicates that husbands and wives who devote more time to their children both enjoy happier marriages. Table 10.8 also shows that wives and husbands who devote more time to their children have lower levels of divorce proneness. These are important findings because some research suggests time devoted to parenting undercuts the quality of married life (Simon 1995); obviously, our results suggest precisely the opposite conclusion. Indeed, our results suggest that investments made in one's children redound to the benefit of one's marriage.

Parental investments in children probably help marriages in two ways. First, children are typically happier and otherwise better adjusted when their parents are involved (Amato 1998); in turn, parents with happier, healthier children are less likely to experience parenting stress that can undercut the quality and stability of their marriage (Jouriles et al 1988). Second, parental investments are probably interpreted by husbands and wives, and their spouses, as a symbol of their devotion to their families. In all likelihood, such acts of devotion make them feel better about their family life as a whole, including their marriages (Bahr and Bahr 2001).

Using the NSFH2, we also explored the possibility that the link between parental investments and marital quality varies by class. Ancillary analyses indicate that the effect of parental investments on marital quality is particularly important for husbands and wives without college degrees (results available upon request). Perhaps because working-class marriages are more vulnerable to divorce (Martin 2006), the symbolic power of parental investments may be particularly valuable to these couples. Alternatively, because less-educated parents spend less time with their children than do college-educated parents (Lareau 2003), it may be that high levels of parental involvement are more likely to stand out among parents without college degrees, or are a selective group among working-class parents. In any

TABLE 10.7 Likelihood of being "very happy" in marriage and parent-child involvement

| | MODEL 1 | | | | MODEL 2 | | | | MODEL 3 | | | |
| | WIVES | | HUSBANDS | | WIVES | | HUSBANDS | | WIVES | | HUSBANDS | |
	LOG ODDS	STE	LOG ODDS	STE	LOG ODDS	STE	LOG ODDS	STE	LOG ODDS	STE	LOG ODDS	STE
Wife employed part-time[a]	.85	.22	.96	.26	.87	.22	.94	.26	.85	.22	.94	.26
Wife employed full-time[a]	.78	.20	1.08	.23	.84	.20	1.04	.23	.84	.20	1.07	.23
Reversed gender LFP[a]	1.21	.43	.60	.48	127	.43	.58	.48	1.23	.43	.61	.48
Participant's parent-child involvement					1.24*	.09	1.22*	.10	1.20*	.09	1.18[†]	.10
Spouses' parent-child involvement									1.13	.09	1.18	.11
Number of marriages	.98	.20	1.12	.18	1.00	.20	1.16	.19	1.03	.20	1.21	.19
Marital duration	1.00	.02	1.02	.02	1.00	.02	1.03	.02	1.01	.02	1.04[†]	.02
Income	1.03	.12	.78	.16	1.04	.12	.80	.16	1.05	.12	.80	.16
Education	.92*	.04	.95	.04	.91*	.04	.93*	.04	.91*	.04	.92*	.04
Black[b]	.84	.33	.80	.31	.81	.33	.84	.31	.79	.33	.85	.31
Other[b]	.76	.33	1.12	.31	.78	.33	1.08	.31	.78	.33	1.14	.31
Chi-squared model	8.99		10.32		14.83		14.42		16.98		16.98	

Note: [†]p < .10; *p < .05.

[a]Omitted category is wife stays at home.
[b]Omitted category is white, non-Hispanic.

TABLE 10.8 The relationship between parent-child involvement and divorce proneness

	MODEL 1				MODEL 2				MODEL 3			
	WIVES		HUSBANDS		WIVES		HUSBANDS		WIVES		HUSBANDS	
	B	STE	B	STE	B	STE	B	STE	B	STE	B	STE
Intercept	.32	.31	.03	.34	.70*	.35	.26	.36	.75*	.36	.30	.39
Wife employed part-time[a]	.09	.10	-.01	.10	.08	.10	-.01	.10	.08	.10	-.01	.10
Wife employed full-time[a]	.11	.08	-.01	.09	.08	.09	-.01	.09	.08	.09	-.01	.09
Reversed gender LFP[a]	.44*	.19	.05	.17	.42*	.19	.04	.17	.43*	.19	.04	.17
Participant's parent-child involvement					-.08*	.04	-.06†	.04	-.08*	.04	-.06	.04
Spouses' parent-child involvement									-.02	.04	-.01	.05
Number of marriages	-.03	.08	.01	.08	-.04	.08	-.01	.08	-.04	.09	-.01	.08
Marital duration	-.01	.01	-.01	.01	-.01	.01	-.01*	.005	-.02*	.01	-.02*	.005
Income	.09†	.05	.04	.06	.09†	.05	.03	.06	.08†	.05	.03	.06
Education	-.01	.02	.02†	.01	-.01	.02	.03*	.01	-.01	.02	.03*	.01
Black[b]	.08	.14	.50*	.11	.10	.14	.49*	.11	.10	.14	.49*	.11
Other[b]	.01	.14	.12	.13	.01	.14	.14	.13	.01	.14	.13	.13
R^2	.01		.04*		.02†		.04*		.02†		.04*	

Note: †$p < .10$; *$p < .05$.

[a]Omitted category is "wife stays at home."
[b]Omitted category is "white, non-Hispanic."

case, this study suggests that parental involvement is especially beneficial to working-class marriages.

CONCLUSION

Over the last half-century, the United States has witnessed tremendous changes in the nature, quality, and amount of parenting (Stearns, 2003; Bianchi et al. 2007). This study shows that both married mothers *and* fathers are spending more time with their children, and are dividing the responsibilities of parenthood more equally, compared to earlier generations of parents. Moreover, popular support for more egalitarian models of family life has also increased over this period. Clearly, the tidal wave of change associated with the gender revolution has left its mark on the lives of married parents in the United States.

Nevertheless, this study also suggests that—at least when it comes to work-family strategies and the division of parenting labor—the gender revolution has temporarily stalled or come to a close, and that a large minority of parents do not wish to pursue a thoroughgoing egalitarianism as they juggle family and work roles in today's world. Instead, what is clear is that married parents take a pluralistic approach to handling their work and family responsibilities today, with some seeking an egalitarian work-family strategy, others a traditional work-family strategy, a very small minority seeking a nontraditional strategy, and the largest minority aiming for a neotraditional strategy, where the mother works part-time. Furthermore, in looking at the quality and stability of married life, this study finds—consistent with the preference model of marriage—that couples are generally happier when wives are able to pursue the distinctive work-family strategy that they prefer. This seems particularly true for college-educated wives, whose marriages are especially sensitive to the match between their preferences and their work-family strategies.

At the same time, it is also worth pointing out that this study finds that a majority of married parents prefer a traditional or neotraditional work-family strategy where the mother takes the lead in nurturing, and the father takes the lead in providing for the family. And couples that reverse this pattern— that is, nontraditional couples where wives outwork their husbands—are significantly more likely to have husbands who are unhappy and considering a divorce. So, consistent with the gender model of marriage, married parents in the United States enjoy happier marriages when they avoid nontraditional arrangements. This appears to be especially true for working-class husbands, who are significantly less happy when their wives outwork them.

On the other hand, even though women are still responsible for the lion's share of child-rearing in the average couple, this study finds that parents are happier when they share parenting. Perhaps the rise of an ethic of concerted cultivation—what the media has called "helicopter parenting"—among contemporary parents, especially mothers, has made them more interested in husbands who are willing to share the heavy load associated with contemporary parenting (Lareau 2003). Undoubtedly, the popularity of the new "father" ethic—where dads are expected to play a very active and affectionate role in the lives of their children—is also behind this finding (Coltrane 1996). In any case, this study also provides some support to the companionate model of marriage insofar as it shows that parents who share the burden of parenting are more likely to report happy and stable marriages.

What is the cultural and public import of our findings? We draw three conclusions from our findings. First, we want to underline the fact that married parents in the United States have a range of preferences when it comes to the organization of their work and family lives, and that most parents—including most mothers—do not wish to pursue an egalitarian work-family strategy where both parents work full-time. As sociologist Neil Gilbert (2008:107) notes in A Mother's Work, this reality is often ignored by elite academics, journalists, and policymakers who tend to "publicize the presumed universal social and psychological rewards of paid employment (which they themselves do experience), while ignoring the social and psychological benefits of unpaid caring and household work." Accordingly, and in large part because we demonstrate here that marriages are stronger when couples can match their preferences with their work-family strategies, we think that the culture and public policies should respect the full range of choices that contemporary parents seek to make about how to combine work and family. We are particularly supportive of public policies—such as expanding the current federal tax credit for children from $1,000 to $5,000 per child—that would make it easier for working- and middle-class families to realize their preferred work-family strategy (Douthat and Salam 2008).

Second, and on a related note, we think it is time for our society to distinguish more carefully between equity and equality. In particular, academics, journalists, and policymakers should stop promoting an ethic of gender equality where mothers and fathers are expected to do basically the same thing and instead recognize that equity between the sexes will mean, for most couples, a degree of gender specialization when it comes to juggling work and family responsibilities. We reach this conclusion because the gender revolution seems to have stalled *and* because we find that most couples are happy with at least a measure of gender specialization. Here, we agree with Eleanor Maccoby, the distinguished feminist psychologist, who concluded her latest book, *The Two Sexes* (1998:314), by pointing out that "it is probably not realistic to set a fifty-fifty division of labor between fathers and mothers in the day-to-day care of children as the most desirable pattern toward which we should strive as a social goal. We should consider the alternative view: that equity between the sexes does not have to mean exact equality in the sense of the two sexes having exactly the same life-styles and exactly the same allocation of time."

Third, and finally, even though we think that it is legitimate that a majority of married parents will specialize by gender, we also think that the contemporary emphasis on shared parenthood is largely salutary. Given recent research indicating that fathers play an important and unique role in advancing the social, psychological, and economic welfare of their children (see, for instance, Parke 1996; Doherty et al.1998; Eggebeen 2008; Palkovitz 2007), we endorse cultural norms and policy measures that seek to increase the role of fathers in families—including the norm of shared parenthood. We would add, however, that the norm of shared parenthood need not mean that fathers approach parenthood in precisely the same way as do mothers. Rather, recognizing the distinctive parenting styles and contributions that married mothers and fathers often make to the welfare of their children (Parke 1996; Palkovitz 2008), we encourage parents to draw on both their gender-neutral and gender-specific talents as they rear the next generation. Moreover, by sharing in the joys and challenges of parenting, married parents will be serving not only the well-being of their children, but—as this study shows—deepening and enriching the conjugal bond that unites them.

NOTES

1. See also www.census.gov/compendia/statab/tables/08s0580.pdf.
2. CBS News, *New York Times* Poll, July 13–27, 2003.

REFERENCES

Amato, Paul, Alan Booth, David R. Johnson, and Stacy J. Rogers. 2007. *Alone Together: How Marriage in America Is Changing.* Cambridge, MA: Harvard University.

Bahr, Howard M. and Kathleen S. Bahr. 2001. "Families and Self-Sacrifice: Alterna-tive Models and Meanings for Family Theory." *Social Forces* 79:1231–1258.

Bell, Daniel. 1976. *The Cultural Contradictions of Capitalism*. New York: Basic Books.

Best, Joel. 1990. *Threatened Children: Rhetoric and Concern About Child-Victims*. Chicago: University of Chicago.

Bianchi, Suzanne M. 2000. "Maternal Employment and Time with Children: Dra-matic Change or Surprising Continuity." *Demography* 37:401–414.

Bianchi, Suzanne M., John P. Robinson, and Melissa A. Milkie. 2007. *Changing Rhythms of American Family Life*. New York: Russell Sage Foundation.

Blumstein, Philip and Pepper Schwartz. 1983. *American Couples: Money, Work, Sex*. New York: William Morrow.

Bradbury, Katharine and Jane Katz. 2005. "Women's Rise: A Work in Progress." *Regional Review* 14:58–67.

Burgess, Ernest W., Harvey J. Locke, and Mary M. Thomes. 1963. *The Family: From Institution to Companionship*. New York: Prentice-Hall.

Casper, Lynne M. and Suzanne M. Bianchi. 2002. *Continuity and Change in the American Family*. Thousand Oaks, CA: Sage.

Coltrane, Scott. 1996. *Family Man: Fatherhood, Housework, and Gender Equity*. New York: Oxford University.

Doherty, William.J., E. F. Kouneski, and M. F. Erickson 1998. "Responsible Fatherhood: A Review and Conceptual Framework." *Journal of Marriage and Family* 60:277–292.

Douthat, Ross and Reihan Salam. 2008. *Grand New Party: How Republicans Can Win the Working Class and Save the American Dream*. New York: Doubleday.

Downs, Barbara. 2003. "Fertility of American Women: 2002." *Current Population Reports* P20–548. Washington, DC: U.S. Census Bureau.

Edwards, John N., David R. Johnson, and Alan Booth. 1987. "Coming Apart: A Prognostic Instrument of Marital Breakup." *Family Relations* 36:168–170.

England, Paula and George Farkas. 1986. *Households, Employment, and Gender*. Piscataway, NJ: Aldine.

Gilbert, Neil. 2008. *A Mother's Work: How Feminism, the Market, and Policy Shape Family Life*. New Haven, CT: Yale University.

Glass, Jennifer and Jerry A. Jacobs. 2005. "Childhood Religious Conservatism and Adult Attainment Among Black and White Women." *Social Forces* 84:555–579.

Goldin, Claudia and Lawrence F. Katz. 2002. "The Power of the Pill: Oral Con-traceptives and Women's Career and Marriage Decisions." *Journal of Political Economy* 110:730–770.

Hakim, Catherine. 2000. *Work-Lifestyle Choices in the 21st Century: Preference Theory*. New York: Oxford University.

Hirshman, Linda. 2005. "Homeward Bound." *The American Prospect*, November 22, 2005. Accessed August 16, 2011. www.prospect.org/cs/articles?articleId=10646.

Jouriles, Ernest N., Linda J. Pfiffner, and Susan G. O'Leary. 1988. "Marital Conflict, Parenting, and Toddler Conduct Problems." *Journal of Abnormal Child Psychology* 16(2):197–206.

Lareau, Annette. 2003. *Unequal Childhoods: Class, Race, and Family Life.* Berkeley: University of California.

Maccoby, Eleanor. 1998. *The Two Sexes: Growing Up Apart, Coming Together.* Cambridge: Harvard University.

Martin, Steven P. 2006. "Trends in Marital Dissolution by Women's Education in the United States." *Demographic Research* 15:537–560.

McLanahan, Sara. 2004. "Diverging Destinies: How Children Fare Under the Second Demographic Transition." *Demography.* 41(4):607–627.

Pain, Rachel. 2006. "Paranoid Parenting? Rematerializing Risk and Fear for Children." *Social and Cultural Geography* 7:221–243.

Parke, Ross. 1996. *Fatherhood.* Cambridge, MA: Harvard University.

Rhoads, Steven. 2004. *Taking Sex Differences Seriously.* San Francisco: Encounter.

Rogers, Stacey, J. 1999. "Wives Income and Marital Quality: Are There Reciprocal Effects?" *Journal of Marriage and Family* 61:123–132.

Simon, Robin W. 1995. "Gender, Multiple Roles, Role Meaning, and Mental Health." *Journal of Health and Social Behavior* 36:182–194.

Smith, Alison, J. 2007. "Working Fathers in Europe: Earning and Caring?" *Centre for Research on Families and Relationships Briefings 30.* Center for Research on Families and Relationships.

Spain, Daphne and Suzanne Bianchi. 1996. *Balancing Act: Motherhood, Marriage, and Employment Among American Men.* New York: Russell Sage Foundation.

Stearns, Peter M. 2003. *Anxious Parents: A History of Modern Childrearing in America.* New York: New York University.

Taylor, Shelley E. 2002. *The Tending Instinct: Women, Men, and the Biology of Our Relationships.* New York: Times.

Taylor, Paul, Cary Funk, and April Clark. 2008. "From 1997 to 2007: Fewer Mothers Prefer Full-Time Work." *Pew Trends Report.* Washington, DC: Pew Research Center.

Wilcox, W. Bradford. 2004. *Soft Patriarchs, New Men: How Christianity Shapes Fathers and Husbands.* Chicago: University of Chicago.

Wilcox, W. Bradford and Steven L. Nock. 2006. "What's Love Got to Do with It? Equality,Equity, Commitment, and Women's Marital Quality." *Social Forces* 84: 1321–1345.

11

THE EFFECT OF GENDER-BASED PARENTAL INFLUENCES ON RAISING CHILDREN

The Impact on Couples' Relationships

Scott Haltzman

WHILE THE PERCENTAGE OF AMERICAN women conceiving children has declined in the past generation—from 90 percent in 1976 to 82 percent in 2000 (Schodolski 2005)—the vast majority of women has, or wishes to have, children. (Neal, Groat, and Wicks 1989). Most households in which fertile women live will, at one point or another, have a child who will also reside in that household. When women who give birth choose to identify a father of that child, and choose to live with him, together they share the responsibility of raising that child (or children). In contrast, when parents who have a child cannot maintain a healthy marriage, the child's rate of early childhood and teen behavioral problems increases by 250 percent (Amato and Keith 1991).

Bringing together a mother, a child, and a father creates a nuclear family. It differs from the *Murphy Brown*-like version of a dyadic relationship of a mother and child, or from the rarer single father scenario. It also differs from the one-on-one quality of a marriage without children. For when children become a fundamental part of family life that already includes a man and a woman, the roles that men and women play in the raising of the children impact not only the life trajectory of the child, but the direction of the relationship between the two adults who brought the child into the world.

Choosing to form a mother-father-child household provides a socially acceptable framework in which couples can raise children, and it has very practical advantages as well. Choosing to be in a committed lifelong relationship with a partner, especially when such a choice includes marriage, helps secure a shared role in the raising of children, thus reducing the load on any one parent. Attending to a child's physical needs, from feedings to changing diapers, and, later in life, to transportation for recreational or academic activities, can be shared by two individuals who have a biological, emotional, and legal investment in the well-being of the child. Moreover, by pooling resources, couples who live in the same household are better able to handle the financial responsibilities of raising children, by either increasing the amount of revenue by dual contribution to the household income, or by reducing the costs of childcare by arranging for one parent to work, while the other remains home to provide child-oriented supervision and support. Additionally, the overall expenses of combining individuals into one household results in economic advantage for everyday living expenses, such as rents or mortgages, major appliances, and utilities. Moreover, when couples who raise a child live together in matrimony, they tend to save even more money than those who do not marry because "most cohabiting unions are short-lived; live-in lovers hesitate to share expenses to the degree that married people do" (Waite and Gallagher 2000:30).

While the decision of one parent to live together with the other parent of his or her child has many practical advantages, having two individuals involved in the care of a child may also have some potential pitfalls. Each individual, based on his or her own family of origin, personal belief system, and gender may have very specific ideas about how a child should be raised. Adults differ in approaches to parenting and, naturally, parents of the child may not share the ideals, goals, and perspectives of each other. In fact, longitudinal (five-year) studies demonstrated that men and women become more dissatisfied with their marriage when children are in the home (Faulkner, Davey, and Davey 2005).

This chapter addresses the complicated dynamics between man, woman, and child, and seeks to review the literature that establishes whether the gender of a parent affects the raising of a child, and, in turn, whether the differential styles between men and women might lead to either improved cohesion within the family, or might cause an impediment to familial tranquility. These findings will be used as a foundation to set forth some theories on how policymakers, educators, health care providers, and marriage and family therapists might optimize couples' education that would improve the likelihood that couples succeed in maintaining happy and long-lasting relationships. While the extant literature supports the uniquely positive effects of marriage on family dynamics, the data reviewed herein does not pertain strictly to married individuals. However, because this chapter specifically addresses gender differences in families, the material will only include references to heterosexual couples.

BACKGROUND AND LITERATURE REVIEW

Most women who choose to bear and raise a child believe that they bear the brunt of responsibility to be involved in caring for the child (Thompson and Walker 1989; Biernat and Wortman 1991). Current research demonstrates that mothers typically prefer to take the lead in child-rearing (Wilcox 2009). Among single parents living with their children, only 18 percent are men (U.S. Census Bureau 2006). A literature search revealed a predominant presumption that caring for children defaulted to women (except in cases when her employment might render that impractical); men's involvement in raising children was not a default assumption. But when researchers did ask fathers about the role that men should play in the care of children, they found that men very much saw themselves as part of the child-rearing team. A survey of attitudes toward sex, contraception, and child-rearing showed that of 600 men (two-thirds of whom were married), 88 percent believed that they should equally share child-rearing responsibilities with the mothers of their children (Grady et al. 1996).

When a man lives within the same household as his child, there is a much greater likelihood that he will play an active role in its development (Tamis-Lemonda et al. 2004). Data that correlate with fathers residing in the same home as a child include: They were more likely to be their children's biological fathers; they were more likely to be employed; they were more likely to be married to the mothers of the children; were either Caucasian or Latino (this study did not have a significant number of Asians or Native Americans), and they were older and more educated than the nonresident fathers (Tamis-Lemonda et al. 2004).

There are many similarities in the ways the mothers and fathers parent (Parke 2009). Yet, when a father invokes his heartfelt imperative to play an active role in the life of his child, he tends to do it in typically "father-like" ways. Observations of parent-child interaction that have been performed over the last three decades show persistent patterns of parenting styles that are specific to the sex of the parent. Mothers are more verbal and nurturing with their children (Bugen and Humenick 1983), while fathers are more action-oriented, demanding, and logical (MacDonald 1993), and more likely to prohibit certain activities in infants (Brachfield-Child 1986).

As researchers observed parents playing with their infants, they found that moms often contain a baby's movements by holding his or her legs or hips while calming the child down with a soft voice, slow speech, and repeated rhythmic phrases. Fathers, on the other hand, often poke their baby, pedal his or her legs, make loud or abrupt noises, and stimulate the infant to higher pitches of excitement (Moss 1974). Fathers are prone to tease their child, a distinctly non-motherly activity that researchers actually believe helps improve children's ability to handle ambiguity as they grow older (Labrell 1994). A review of the literature demonstrates myriad gender-based stylistic differences; on average, compared to mothers, fathers spend a greater percentage of their time playing with children, and tend to engage in more unconventional and more physical play (Parke 2009). As author John Gottman (1997) describes, "Dads often make up idiosyncratic or unusual games, while moms are more likely to stick to the tried-and-true pursuits. . . . The dads were more able . . . to take their children on an emotional roller coaster, going from activities that commanded minimal attention to those that got the babies quite excited. Mothers, in contrast, kept their play and their babies' emotions on a more even keel" (170).

Parenting styles correlate to biological differences between men and women. Women, compared to men, have higher levels of oxytocin—the hormone responsible for emotional bonding—and oxytocin receptors. Oxytocin serves to calm anxiety, reduce motor activity, and foster an increase in touching. A reciprocal relationship exists between oxytocin and touching—so that the presence of this hormone promotes touching, and the touching increases oxytocin levels (IsHak, Kahloon, and Fakhry 2011). In contrast, testosterone—present in men at levels tenfold higher than women—is correlated to an increase in motor activity in infant boys (Campbell and Eaton 1999) and mammals (Sanderson and Crews 2009), and may be responsible for higher levels of physical activities in men compared to women (Hermann, McDonald, and Bozak 1978).

While biological factors may be at play in some of the differences between mother-play and father-play, there are multiple sociological positive effects of fathers in the household. Among the findings Dr. Gottman (1997) describes:

- "Five-month-old baby boys who have lots of contact with their fathers are more comfortable around strangers" (170).
- "One-year-old babies cried less when left alone with a stranger if they had more contact with their dads" (170).
- "Kids whose fathers showed high levels of physical play were more popular among their peers" (171).
- "While our studies showed that mother-child interactions were also important . . . compared to the father's responses, the quality of the contact

with the mother was not as strong a predictor of the child's later success or failure with school and friends" (172).

While Gottman readily points out the ways in which the father-child bond imbues the young child with strength and confidence, he also reviews data that shows the negative effects on the child of being raised without a father:

- "Research indicates . . . that boys with absent fathers have a harder time finding a balance between masculine assertiveness and self-restraint" (166).
- "Looking at academic achievements . . . boys with absent fathers did the worst, and the boys whose fathers were present and available did the best . . . high involvement by fathers seems to be linked to girls' career and academic achievements as well" (178).

Adolescent well-being also correlates to having a father inside the home. Drawing on data from the National Survey of Adolescent Health, Eggebeen (2012) has demonstrated that fathers make contributions that may exceed that of mothers'. For instance, the number of activities that a father participated in with a son was correlated with a reduction in depressive symptoms in the adolescent male. This finding did not correlate with the mother's frequency of activities with her son. Moreover, while a parent's strategies for dealing with conflict do not seem to affect their sons, a mother's (but not a father's) poor conflict management style predicts social and physical aggression in daughters (Underwood et al. 2008).

Because the default responsibility of raising children lies with the mother, there are no studies that ask whether it is in the child's best interest to be raised by women, only whether and if, it is good for men to be involved in the raising of children. It is clear that the answer to that question is a resounding "yes." Yet, remarkably, despite all the positive impact that fathers have on their children, it is the maternal attitude that frequently acts as a gatekeeper on men's behavior with their children. Many mothers either minimize or marginalize the ways in paternal influence may promote independence or foster improved social functioning in children (Doucet 2008). In cases when women fail to appreciate the positive effect that the child's father may have, or are outwardly critical of his actions, a mother may actually limit a father's involvement against his wishes (Beitel and Park 1998).

Landmark research into the nature of gender tensions is presented in the 1985 paper, "Transitions to Parenthood: His, Hers and Theirs" by Carolyn

Male Pre-Child

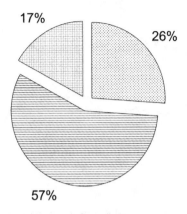

FIGURE 11.1 Male, pre-child: parent, 17 percent, partner, 26 percent; worker, 57 percent.

Cowan and colleagues, in which forty-seven couples from pregnancy to eighteen months postpartum (PP) are compared to fifteen matched control couples who did not have children in that time. Using the self-administered "Who Does What?" questionnaire, the couples were examined along a number of measures. Cowan and colleagues examined changes within three parameters—"Worker," "Partner," and "Parent." Outcome measures did not vary significantly over time in couples without children. In couples with children, however, significant changes in outcome measures occurred during the first 18 months of a child's life. Figures 11.1 and 11.2 compare the distribution of self-identified role in men at baseline and at the end of the study. For obvious reasons, the role of "Parent" increases after the birth of a child, as does the role of the "Partner," but neither of these changes displaces the predominant male identity as "Worker" (Cowan et al. 1985).

The predominance of this principal self-perception is consistent with findings that men work longer hours after the birth of their first child (and longer still, if that child is a boy) (Lundberg and Rose 2002; Aumann, Galinsky, and Matos 2011). Interestingly, men who break with gender stereotypes and "play an equal and active role in household work and childcare" have less developed careers than those who take a more gender "typical" role (Gottman and DeClaire 1997:181). Moreover, in a synthesis of her research of gender roles in parenting, Canadian researcher Andrea Doucet (2008) states: "Each and every stay-at-home father interviewed in my study of fathers as primary caregivers referred in some way to the moral responsibilities he

Male 18 mo. PP

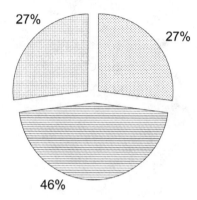

FIGURE 11.2 Male, 18 months postpartum: parent, 27 percent; partner, 27 percent; worker, 46 percent.

felt weighing on him to be a family breadwinner or to earn at least some part of the family wages" (111–112).

In contrast, figures 11.3 and 11.4 show the changes that occur in women during pregnancy and one-and-a-half years postpartum: Relative to other roles, the role of "Parent" has blossomed to consume more than half of her identity, and the role of "Partner" has shrunk by 54 percent. Moreover, there is a reduction in the percentage of her identity assigned to "Worker."

Cowan and colleague's study (1985) demonstrates that within the first six months postpartum, tasks became allocated in a more gender-stereotypic way,

Female Pre-Child

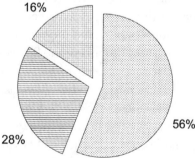

FIGURE 11.3 Female, pre-child: parent, 16 percent, worker, 28 percent; partner, 57 percent.

Female 18 mo. PP

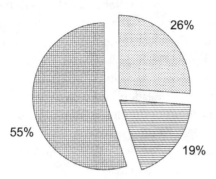

FIGURE 11.4 Female, 18 months postpartum: worker, 19 percent; partner, 26 percent; parent, 55 percent.

and families became much more mother-centered than either parent had predicted prior to the baby's birth. From a researcher's lens, such changes may be viewed as either natural or necessary, but to the actual couples involved in the study, the dramatic shift in the role in the self and in the spouse was not only a surprise, but was often a source of unhappiness. The changes in role allocations between partners from pregnancy to six months accounted for "a significant proportion of change in later marital satisfaction. . . . Partners already vulnerable from lack of sleep and major shifts in their sense of themselves, their roles in the worlds of family and work, and their intimate relationships, find themselves startled by unexpected differences in increased conflict" (Cowan et al. 1985:475–476). Specifically, the authors note that transition to parenthood acts as a stimulus to gender differentiation, which has a negative association with marital satisfaction. One postulated reason for this is the absence of role modeling, since the parents of these couples are likely to have more stereotypical roles than the young couples themselves. Based on their own families of origins, new parents were simply unprepared for the changes.

Another explanation for the increase in marital discontent is that the transition to parenthood creates a diversion of roles, resulting in an increase in conflict, thereby decreasing couple happiness. (Conflict accounted for 42 percent of the variance in men's, and 39 percent of the variance in women's, marital satisfaction [Cowan et al. 1985].) A Canadian study of 320 working individuals concluded that, compared to women, men report more conflict when demands of the family interfere with work, and women report conflict when work demands interfere with the needs of the family (McElwain, Korabik, and Rosin 2005).

Other studies have shown that there is a significantly steeper decline in marital satisfaction for wives than for husbands, with 67 percent of wives becoming unhappier over a 4.5-year period after the birth of a child (Shapiro, Gottman, and Carrere 2000). Ironically, while many women may not understand or appreciate the increased focus on the "Worker" identity of the husband, studies suggest that fathers who provide financially for their families might have better relationships with their partners, and this has a positive effect on the home environment (Tamis-Lemonda et al. 2004). Men are increasingly affected by the work-family divide; in 2008, 49 percent of men reported work-family conflict, compared to only 34 percent in 1977 (Aumann, Galinsky, and Matos 2011).

Work-related issues can be particularly stressful because of how women and men tend to interpret the meaning of work. On a survey of just-married men, "balancing work and family" ranked second (after money) on a list of topics that cause marital disagreement (Chethik 2006). "For many husbands, success at work remains the greatest, and clearest, measure of their worth. And *particularly after they marry* men often feel powerful internal pressure to be financially successful" (63). Because being in the workplace and earning a living often gives a man a sense of connectedness to his family, he may be surprised when his wife complains of feeling disconnected to him after he comes home from a long day at work. As Doucet (2008) observes: "mothers feel pulled toward care and connection while fathers feel pulled toward paid work and autonomy . . . the issue of *responsibility* is the one area where gender differences have stubbornly persisted in mothering and fathering." Because a woman is less likely to identify herself with her job, and more likely to see her prime identity as wife or mother, she may view a husband's commitment to his workplace as abandonment (Haltzman and DiGeronimo 2006). The number of hours a man spends at work is highly correlated with the degree of his wife's (and his own) marital dissatisfaction (Faulkner, Davey, and Davey 2005). Moreover, the husband's marital conflict increased when the wife perceived a lack of fairness (defined as equitable attention to chores, finances, and paid labor) (Faulkner, Davey, and Davey 2005).

While gender differentiation appears to be almost inevitable, not every couple becomes unhappy as a result. Couples with high "marital friendships," who, specifically, demonstrate "expansiveness and awareness of their partner's world," and where husbands express fondness and admiration toward their wives, appear to be protected against the negative impact of the birth of a child (Shapiro, Gottman, and Carrere 2000). It would appear that acceptance of the mates' style (particularly if that "style" represents a gender-specific worldview) leads to a greater likelihood of maintaining family happiness after the birth of a child.

When couples do not have a good mutual support, the distress and discontent also appears to be gender specific. In a study of parents of kindergarten students, marital conflict and relationship insecurity over a two-year period of time correlated to parenting difficulties in men (but not women) (Davies et al. 2009). In an Australian study of 225 first-time parents, 6.2 to 9.1 percent of the men were "distressed" in the first six months after the birth of a child. Compared to the nondistressed men, they were more likely to have been with their partner for less than two years, had a poorer overall quality of relationship with their partner before the birth of a child, and tended to have "a great feeling of being controlled by their partner" (176) in the postnatal period. Men who were distressed had a higher rate of "gender role stress" characterized by fear of physical inadequacy, fear of emotional expression and intellectual inferiority, performance failure, and fear of subordination to women (Buist, Morse, and Durkin 2002). In a related publication based on the same study, mothers were shown to have rates of distress up to 20 percent, and had higher scores on measures of distress; their distress correlated with young age, poor social supports, and negative moods (Morse, Buist, and Durkin 2000).

INTERVENTIONS

Current research demonstrates a high rate of marital distress after the birth of a child, thus opening up the question of what kinds of interventions could minimize or counteract this strain. In *Parenting Stress*, author Kirby Deater-Deckard (2004) reviews modalities associated with reducing parenting stress and maximizing outcomes of child well-being. He points to the effectiveness of problem-focused (cognitive-behavioral) and "approach coping" (positive reappraisal or reframing) strategies, and the relative ineffectiveness of "emotion-focused" or "avoidant coping" techniques. He concludes that effective coping strategies are best practiced within the relationship, particularly when they include empathy-based emotional support by a partner. He also notes that "instrumental support" by others in the family or community (e.g., neighbors who help baby-sit) also correlates with improved relationship stability, and that preemptive coping (learning about parenthood and clarifying expectations of children) also reduces parenting stress. Remarkably, though, his review of current practices fails to point to specific interventions based on preparing couples for gender-based role changes (Deater-Deckard 2004).

In the 1985 Cowan and colleagues study, the issue of gender roles was not ignored. Researchers included one third of the study subjects in a six-month, weekly 2.5-hour group that that began prior to the birth of a child. This group had as its objective to "(1) bridge the transition from before to after the birth of the child and (2) focus not primarily on parenting but on men and women as individuals and as couples. . . . The couples group provided a safe setting in which parents could feel and normalize the changes they were experiencing" (Cowan and Cowan 1988:124). While the group therapy cohort showed a slight decline in marital satisfaction and an increase in conflict between pregnancy and six-months postpartum, their degree of discontent stabilized over the next year. In contrast, nonintervention subjects showed a "steep decline" in marital satisfaction in the same time period, and another "even sharper" decline in the next year. The authors conclude: "The [group] intervention may interfere with the difference-distance-conflict dynamic that translates structural family change into a process that ends with dissatisfaction with the marriage" (143). Of the twenty-four subjects in each group, three from the nonintervention group divorced over the course of the study, but none from the intervention group (Cowan and Cowan 1988). Improved outcomes trickle down to the offspring; the ability to form a closer couple bond and reduced couple conflict can lead to better cognitive and socioeconomic outcome of the children (Cummings, Goeke-Morey, and Raymond 2004).

MOVING FORWARD

Literature supports the beneficial effect of the combined interactions of fathers and mothers on children. The open question, and one which research has not yet answered, is whether the gender specific roles that men and women assume when they become parents help solidify the marriage. At first blush, the answer would be "no," because the differences in child interactions and the differences in role differentiation result in an increase in conflict within the household. A woman who sees her male partner's approach to parenting as "incorrect" (and, in parallel, the male who sees his partner's actions as off the mark) may actually be more prone to stray from the safe territory of "marriage friendship," and will feel a greater incongruence of parental objectives and higher levels of unhappiness. While an increase in conflict is a real risk of shared parenting, studies show that in subtle ways the father influences not only the well-being of their child, but the well-being of the child's mother also.

Since research indicates the profound benefit of a child being raised with both parents, health providers, educators, therapists, and counselors must help couples learn how to function as a team. We know that couples who have a healthy relationship before the birth of the child have a closer postpartum bond to each other (Shapiro, Gottman and Carrere 2000), so one approach is to bolster the couple's friendship, an approach put forth in John and Julie Schwartz Gottman's book, *And Baby Makes Three* (2007). Other modalities to prepare couples for life together with a child include bolstering communication and problem-solving skills between the couple, and discussing specific expectations for the baby-to-be.

Teaching couples the distinct advantages of having both gender approaches to raising children, for all practical purposes, means teaching women the advantages of including male strategies and influences in the child's life. Employment issues, for example, might be a source of great stress for couples who do not recognize that such concerns are typical for new parents, and that many other parents are in the same boat. Educating couples to appreciate the fact that men view work differently than women, and that, on average, women have a strong preference for not working full-time after the birth of a child (Wilcox 2009) will help normalize the kinds of stress that parents feel. Thus, gender differentiation need not be a problem for most couples if they recognize that it is a common response to parenthood and that it fits with the underlying preferences of most married mothers.

GENDER-BASED THERAPEUTIC APPROACHES TO HELPING COUPLES WITH VERBAL COMMUNICATION

Marriage education and relationship-oriented therapy can be effective in helping couples' conflict (Bray and Jouriles 1995), and therapeutic modalities vary from bibliotherapy to psychodynamically oriented exploration into the origins of interpersonal and intrapersonal conflict between and among spouses. Successfully helping a couple with children thrive in their own relationship requires maximizing the strengths of male and female roles within the relationship. For the purposes of this next section, I will refer to couples as "husband" and "wife" and the person (or people) working with couples as the "therapist" recognizing that the couple may not be married, and that the role of service provider could be played by a life coach, marriage educator, spiritual counselor, or any other who is qualified to offer help to improve the relationship of a couple or family.

While there is a great variance within each couple, in general, certain gender specific traits must be recognized and capitalized on by someone who works to improve a couple's understanding and communication.

Problems in interpersonal communications and the perceived discrepancy in the depth of emotional bonds between spouses is a common cause for discord in marriages. Women tend to have a better capacity to appreciate and express emotionally-oriented constructs, and men tend to manifest superior visual-spatial strengths (Baron-Cohen 2004). This may lead to a disconnect in communication, as the man may focus on the content of a discussion, rather than the process and emotions that prompted the discussion. A woman may be frustrated that her husband may want to jump in and "solve" her problems rather than demonstrate good listening skills. Further, the wife may feel a lack of emotional connectivity to the man because his efforts to redirect her away from her verbalizations will feel like he is rejecting her efforts to bond to him. This may result in a pattern of communication in which the wife may seek closeness by talking, and the husband, feeling thwarted by an inability to provide what his wife is looking for, withdraws from the conversation. This approach-avoidance behavioral dyad is a multifactorial phenomenon emerging from brain differences, differences in temperament, and different social training between men and women (Haltzman, Holstein, and Moss 2007).

The first step toward resolving gender-based communication issues is to educate couples about how men and women tend to communicate, and ask them to assess their own communication style and needs for emotional closeness. It is critically important in these days of distorted media messages about the "proper" way for relationships to unfold, that couples understand that real marriages are different than Hollywood versions of relationships. Men will not learn to verbalize their feeling like women do simply because of the presence of love for their spouses. Respecting the differences in styles, and not judging one way of expressing emotions as "right" or "wrong," will help relieve pressures put on individuals attempting to have a successful marriage dynamic. Communication tools can be taught to couples in order to augment their capacity to speak to, and hear, each other.

When men are talking to women, they should be encouraged to minimize extraneous physical activity. While it may be calming to a man to pace about when he talks, it is distracting to women, and will make her feel less connected to him. Likewise, maintaining eye contact is an important indicator of listening. Also, it is important for men to make verbal acknowledgments of their female partners during a conversation. Even though men may listen quite intently while remaining silent, words such as "I see," or "Really!" are interpreted by women as demonstrating interest in what she is talking about.

Because men tend to listen in order to solve problems, they may be tempted to interrupt their wives' descriptions of the day's events in order to offer a solution to her perceived problem. Yet sometimes it is best to listen, acknowledge, and even reflect back upon the content of the discussion without offering to fix things. One useful piece of advice for husbands is to instruct them to clarify what their wives want from the conversation. Simply asking: "How can I be a good listener to you?" will smooth the way for improved communication (Haltzman and DiGeronimo 2009).

Women tend to have excellent verbal skills, but often their style of talking may actually alienate their husbands. If she is using her speech to build a connection, and he is listening in order to extract critical information to solve a problem, neither will find the discourse pleasurable or helpful. When talking to a male partner, women should consider using shorter sentences and try to point out the main objective of the conversation at commencement of the conversation. By telling a man what the purpose of the conversation is, that is to say, differentiating an "I need to blow off some steam" conversation from an "I need some advice" conversation, a wife helps her husband know the best way to be a good listener. If a woman wishes to have a long conversation, and want to keep her husband engaged and attentive, it is often helpful to employ a man's need for psychomotor movement. Talking while taking a walk, going for a drive, or having a meal are good ways to be able to bond through conversation and meet the needs of both the sexes (Haltzman and DiGeronimo 2009). When therapists help men and women understand each other's listening style, and teach them to form stronger communication skills, they improve the couple's ability to work together for the welfare of the child.

BEYOND THE THERAPIST'S OFFICE

It is critical to promote the importance of dual-gendered households when possible, and those who care for the well-being of children should support an improved public health perspective. Approaches toward improving the acceptance of a man's influence in the development of a child might include any of the following interventions:

- Support of public education, beginning in the secondary school system, about the positive attributes of men
- Addition to couples' education courses about gender norms and the unique benefits of both mothers' and fathers' contributions to the raising of children
- Reaching out to educate obstetricians and nurse midwives, who have an opportunity to communicate with mothers-to-be, and providing male-friendly information and literature to distribute to patients
- Integrating information about gender roles in child-rearing to childbirth educators
- Educating pediatricians and child therapists about gender role differences in parenting to help smooth over anticipated areas of gender-mediated conflict
- Helping teachers to understand male and female ways of playing, teaching, and learning, to help perpetuate a message of father involvement in the raising of children
- Informing corporate executives, particularly human resources departments, about gender effects on work and work attitudes once a child is born to a couple
- Educating the court and legal systems about supporting a two-parent home and recognizing the separate gender influences on a child
- Publishing books and articles for the popular press that explain some of the neurobiological and emotional differences between men and women and extol the benefits of male influences in the life of children

Fathers and mothers both matter, particularly if each can parent in a style that reflects their gender role. The evidence suggests that efforts should be made to educate society at large, and parents in particular, that gender differences in parents are real, and, rather than be extinguished or ignored, they should be embraced.

REFERENCES

Amato, Paul R. and Bruce Keith. 1991. "Parental Divorce and the Well-Being of Children: A Meta-analysis." *Psychological Bulletin* 110:26–46.

Aumann, Kirsten, Ellen Galinsky, and Kenneth Matos. 2011. *The New Male Mystique*. New York: Families and Work Institute. Accessed July 9, 2012. familiesandwork.org/site/research/reports/newmalemystique.pdf.

Baron-Cohen, Simon. 2004. *The Essential Difference.* New York: Basic.

Beitel, Ashley H. and Ross D. Parke. 1998. "Paternal Involvement in Infancy: The Role of Maternal and Paternal Attitudes." *Journal of Family Psychology* 12:268–288.

Biernat, Monica and Camille B. Wortman. 1991. "Sharing of Home Responsibilities between Professional Employed Women and Their Husbands." *Journal of Personality and Social Psychology* 60:844–860.

Brachfield-Child, Sheila. 1986. "Parents as Teachers: Comparison of Others' and Fathers' Instructional Interactions with Infants." *Infant Behavior and Development* 9:127–131.

Bray, James and Ernest Jouriles. 1995. "Treatment of Marital Conflict and Prevention of Divorce." *Journal of Marital and Family Therapy* 21(4):461–473.

Bugen, Larry A. and Sharron S. Humenick. 1983. "Instrumentality, Expressiveness, and Gender Effects upon Parent-Infant Interaction," *Basic and Applied Social Psychology* 4:239–251.

Buist, Anne, Carol A. Morse, and Sarah Durkin. 2002. "Men's Adjustment to Fatherhood: Implications for Obstetric Health Care." *Journal of Obstetrics, Gynecologic and Neonatal Nursing* 32(2):172–180.

Campbell, Darren W. and Warren O. Eaton. 1999. "Sex Differences in the Activity Level of Infants." *Infant and Child Development* 8:1–17.

Carlson, Marcia. 2006. "Family Structure, Father Involvement, and Adolescent Behavioral Outcomes." *Journal of Marriage and Family* 68:137–154.

Chethik, Neil. 2006. *VoiceMale: What Husbands Really Think About Their Marriages, Sex, Housework, and Commitment.* New York: Simon and Schuster.

Cowan, Carolyn P., Philip A. Cowan, Gertrude Heming, Ellen Garrett, William S. Doysh, Harriet Curtis-Boles, and Abner J. Boles III. 1985. "Transitions to Parenthood: His, Hers, and Theirs." *Journal of Family Issues* 6:451–481.

Cowan, Philip A. and Carolyn P. Cowan. 1988. "Changes in Marriage During the Transition to Parenthood: Must We Blame the Baby?" In *The Transition to Parenthood: Current Theory and Research*, ed. Gerald Y. Michaels and Wendy A. Goldberg. New York: Cambridge University.

Cummings, E. Mark, Marcie Goeke-Morey, and Jessica Raymond. 2004. "Fathers in Family Context: Effects of Marital Quality and Marital Conflict." In *The Role of the Father in Child Development*, 4th ed., ed. M. E. Lamb, 196–221. Hoboken, NJ: John Wiley.

Davies, Patrick, Melissa L Sturge-Apple, Meredtih Woitach, and Mark E. Cummings. 2009. "A Process Analysis of the Transmission of Distress from Interparental Conflict to Parenting: Adult Relationship Security as an Explanatory Mechanism." *Developmental Psychology* 45(6):1761–1773.

Deater-Deckard, Kirby. 2004. *Parenting Stress.* New Haven, CT: Yale University.

Doucet, Andrea. 2008. "Gender Equality and Gender Differences: Parenting, Habitus, and Embodiment (The 2008 Porter Lecture)." *Canadian Review of Sociology* 46(2):103–121.

Eggebeen, David J. 2013. "Do Fathers Uniquely Matter for Adolescent Well-Being?" In *Gender and Parenthood*, ed. Kathleen Kovner Kline and W. Bradford Wilcox, 249–270. New York: Columbia University.

Faulkner, Rhonda, Maureen Davey, and Adam Davey. 2005. "Gender-Related Predictors of Change in Marital Satisfaction and Marital Conflict." *The American Journal of Family Therapy* 33:61–83.

Gottman, John and Joan DeClaire. 1997. *Raising an Emotionally Intelligent Child: The Heart of Parenting.* New York: Fireside.

Gottman, John and Julie Schwartz Gottman. 2007. *And Baby Makes Three: The Six-Step Plan for Preserving Marital Intimacy and Rekindling Romance After Baby Arrives.* New York: Crown.

Grady, William R., Koray Tanfer, John O. G. Billy, and Jennifer Lincoln-Hanson. 1996. "Men's Perceptions of Their Roles and Responsibilities Regarding Sex, Contraception and Childrearing." *Family Planning Perspectives* 28:221–226.

Haltzman, Scott and Theresa Foy DiGeronimo. 2006. *The Secrets of Happily Married Men: Eight Ways to Win Your Wife's Heart Forever.* San Francisco: Jossey-Bass.

Haltzman, Scott and Theresa Foy DiGeronimo. 2009. *The Secrets of Happy Families: Eight Ways to Building a Lifetime of Connection and Contentment.* San Francisco: Jossey-Bass.

Haltzman, Scott, Ned Holstein, and Sherry B. Moss. 2007. "Men, Marriage and Divorce." In *Textbook of Men's Mental Health*, ed. Jon E. Grant and Marc N. Potenza. Washington, DC: American Psychiatric.

Herrmann, Werner M., Richard J. McDonald, and M. Mahir Bozak. 1978. "The Effects of Hormones on Human Behaviour as Measured by Psychological Tests." *Progress in Neuropsychopharmacology* 2(4):469–478.

IsHak, William Waguih, Maria Kahloon, and Hala Fakhry. 2011. "Oxytocin Role in Enhancing Well Being." *Journal of Affective Disorders* 130(1–2):1–9.

Labrell, Florence. 1994. "A Typical Interaction Behavior Between Fathers and Toddlers: Teasing." *Early Development and Parenting* 3:125–130.

Lundberg, Shelly and Elaina Rose. 2002. "The Effects of Sons and Daughters on Men's Labor Supply and Wages." *The Review of Economics and Statistics* 84(2):251–268.

MacDonald, Kevin, ed. 1993. *Parent-Child Play: Descriptions and Implications.* New York: State University of New York.

McElwain, Allyson K., Karen Korabik, and Hazel Rosin. 2005. "An Examination of Gender Differences in Work-Family Conflict." *Canadian Journal of Behavioural Science* 37:283–298.

Morse, Carol A., Anne Buist, and Sarah Durkin. 2000. "First-Time Parenthood: Influences on Pre- and Postnatal Adjustment in Fathers and Mothers." *Journal of Psychosomatic Obstetrics and Gynecology* 21(2):109–120.

Moss, Howard. 1974. "Early Sex Differences and Mother-Infant Interaction." In *Sex Differences in Behavior*, ed. R. C. Friedman, R. M. Richart and R. L. van De Wiele, 149–163. New York: John Wiley.

Neal, Arthur G., Theodore Groat, and Jerry Wicks. 1989. "Attitudes About Having Children: A Study of 600 Couples in the Early Years of Marriage." *Journal of Marriage and Family* 51:313–328.

Parke, Ross D. 2013. "Gender Differences and Similarities in Parental Behavior." In *Gender and Parenthood*, ed. W. Bradford Wilcox and Kathleen Kovner–Kline, 120–163. New York: Columbia University.

Sanderson, N. S. R. and D. Crews. 2009. "Hormones and Behavior." In *Encyclopedia of Neuroscience*, ed. Larry R. Squire, 1207–1215. Maryland Heights, MO: Academic.

Schodolski, Vincent J. 2005. "Growing Number of Couples Opting Not to Have Children." In *Deseret News*, ed. Mitch Wilkinson. Accessed September 7, 2008 from findarticles.com/p/articles/mi_qn4188/is_20051204/ai_n15904306.

Shapiro, Alyson F., John Gottman and Sybil Carrere. 2000. "The Baby and the Marriage: Identifying Factors That Buffer Against Decline in Marital Satisfaction After the First Baby Arrives." *Journal of Family Psychology* 14:59–70.

Tamis-LeMonda, Catherine S., Jacqueline D. Shannon, Natasha J. Cabrera, and Michael E. Lamb. 2004. "Fathers and Mothers at Play with Their 2- and 3-Year-Olds: Contributions to Language and Cognitive Development." *Child Development* 75(6):1806–1820.

Thompson, Linda and Alexis J. Walker. 1989. "Gender in Families: Women and Men in Marriage, Work, and Parenthood." *Journal of Marriage and Family* 51(4): 845–871.

Underwood, Marion K., Kurt J. Beron, Joanna K. Gentsch, Mikal B. Galperin, and Scott D. Risser. 2008. "Family Correlates of Children's Social and Physical Aggression with Peers: Negative Interparental Conflict Strategies and Parenting Styles." *International Journal of Behavioral Development* 32(6):549–562.

U. S. Census Bureau. 2006. "*Facts for Features.*" CB06-FF.08-2. Last modified June 12, 2006. Accessed September 9, 2008. www.census.gov/PressRelease/www/releases/archives/facts_for_features_special_editions/006794.html.

Waite, Linda and Maggie Gallagher. 2000. *The Case for Marriage: Why Married People Are Happier, Healthier and Better Off Financially.* New York: Doubleday.

Wilcox, W. B. and J. Dew. 2013. "No One Best Way: Work-Family Strategies, the Gendered Division of Parenting, and the Contemporary Marriages of Mothers and Fathers." In *Gender and Parenthood*, ed. W. B Wilcox and K. Kovner Kline, 271–303. New York: Columbia University.

12

SINGLE MOTHERS RAISING CHILDREN WITHOUT FATHERS

Implications for Rearing Children with Male-Positive Attitudes

William Doherty and Shonda Craft

THE HISTORICALLY HIGH NUMBER of children being raised by single mothers without the physical presence of a biological father has been the focus of political, sociological, and psychological scrutiny for well over three decades. Recent data suggest that the scholarly and public debate will not abate any time soon. Dye (2008) explored the fertility trends of American women using data drawn from two surveys conducted by the U.S. Census Bureau in 2006, the American Community Survey and the Current Population Survey. An estimated four million women between the ages of fifteen and fifty years old were reported to have had a live birth during the past twelve months. Of these respondents, 35 percent reported their relationship status as not married (separated, divorced, widowed, or never married). (About 13 percent of these unmarried women reported living with an unmarried partner.) In addition, half of the over one million annual divorces involve couples with children (Anderson, Greene, Walker et al. 2004). In most cases, the mother has primary custody of the children.

This chapter addresses the challenges mothers face when raising children without the active, positive involvement of the biological father, with particular focus on how mothers can raise children with "male-positive" attitudes in the face of the children's loss of an active relationship with their father. We provide a conceptual framework along with strategies for professionals to assist single mothers in the task of parenting with male-positive attitudes.

BACKGROUND AND LITERATURE REVIEW

Single mothers are not a homogenous group, and the pathways to becoming a single mother can differ greatly. Women who are parenting in the absence of a biological father in the home may be doing so because of divorce, marital separation, widowhood, termination of a cohabiting relationship, the breakup of a short-term or long-term noncohabiting relationship, or from sperm donation. When there has been a relationship break up, there are differences in the level of conflict leading to the termination and the quality of the relationship afterwards. Discussions of single mothering and father absence often do not make these important distinctions that can strongly affect the degree of father involvement with the children (Gadsen and Hall 1999). Furthermore, the label single mother can be misleading because it confounds marital status (single) with parental status (one of two parents). A woman may be involved in a new cohabiting union and see herself as coupled (not single) but still single mothering without the involvement of the biological father. These contextual and definitional complexities are not just problems for family researchers; they also may create challenges for women's role definitions in a society so focused on the social category of single mother. We return to these contextual issues when we take up implications for how single mothers can raise children in the absence of involved fathers.

A striking finding of our literature review is the absence of research and other scholarly work on the impact of single mothering on the attitudes of children toward men. Thus we will review related research that bears on this issue.

FATHER-CHILD CLOSENESS

Much of the research regarding father absence and single mothering since the 1980s has focused on the impact of marital disruption on children's academic achievement, school experiences, psychosocial development, criminal behavior, and early parenting. Divorce is often accompanied by poorer economic conditions for women and less contact and involvement with the noncustodial father for children. The complex construct of father involvement has been defined as consisting of three interrelated aspects: engagement, accessibility, and responsibility (Matta and Knudson-Martin 2006). Frequency of contact and physical proximity is often correlated with children's feelings of closeness to their nonresident fathers. However, fewer than 30 percent of nonresident fathers report having weekly contact with their children (Scott, Booth, King, and Johnson 2007). While children of intact and divorced families typically report feeling closer to their mothers, Scott and colleagues not only found that 57 percent children from divorced families experienced a decline in father closeness, but also that 25 percent of children who had a close relationship with their fathers before divorced continued at that level postdivorce.

While parental break up is generally a stressful experience for children, the empirical literature has not always supported a straightforward relationship between nonresident father involvement and children's well-being (McLanahan and Sandefur 1994). In other words, more paternal contact alone is not necessarily good for children. Part of the discrepancy can be resolved by paying attention to the relationship between the mother and father. Dunn and colleagues (2004), for example, found children who reported frequent contact with their nonresident fathers also reported having relationships that were both more positive, and also more conflicted. Moreover "the affection, companionship, and support children reported within their relationship with their nonresident fathers were closely linked to the positivity the children reported in their relationships with their mothers" (562). Thus, the authors concluded children were more likely to have continued contact with their fathers if their mothers maintained positive relationships with their former spouses.

Another answer to the discrepancy of research findings on nonresident father involvement has emerged from studies examining not just the quantity of father contact but also the quality. In a meta-analysis of sixty-three studies on nonresidential father involvement and children's well-being, Amato and Gilbreth (1999) found strong evidence that the benefits accrue to children mainly when the father practices authoritative parenting, that is, nurturing, sensitive parenting combined with limit setting and engagement in the everyday tasks of child-rearing. The implication is that "weekend dads" who indulge children do not necessarily contribute significantly to the child's well-being. The challenge for many fathers, of course, is that traditional custody arrangement and the focus by some mothers on child support but not father involvement can make this kind of active father engagement difficult to achieve in nonresidential situations (Doherty, Kouneski, and Erickson 1998).

Reflecting on these research findings, Matta and Knudson-Martin (2006:20) argue that "the concept of fatherhood emerges at the intersection of meaning and social interaction between men, families, extended families, and larger communities. . . . From a systemic perspective, fathers cannot be understood apart from mothers." Although gender socialization of women imparts a particular imperative to be responsive to and responsible for the needs of their children, they may not perceive the needs of their children for an involved father if the mother's own relationship with the father has ended negatively. As Doherty et al. (1998) conclude from their research review of influences on responsible fathering, fathering is uniquely sensitive to the quality and stability of the relationship with the mother, and any work on father involvement must involve an understanding of the relational triangle of the mother, father, and child. Fathers tend to parent in triads with mothers, and are more apt to exit the lives of their children when the primary relationship with the mother ends. This outcome is apt to have implications for these children's attitudes toward men.

SINGLE MOTHERS' ATTITUDES TOWARD MEN

We could find no research on how single mothers feel about men. But there is indirect evidence in the form of a limited amount of research on how negative experiences with men influence women's attitudes toward men. Stephan and colleagues (2000) found that negative contact with men is associated with less positive attitudes toward men and a perception that men and women have differing value and belief systems. The authors concluded that "[w]omen who perceived large value and belief differences between men and women, who have had many negative experiences with men, and who are anxious about interacting with men, tend to like men less than other women" (71–72). In a similar vein, Maltby and Day (2001) found that women who reported a more positive attitude toward men's roles in marriage and parenting reported significantly less tendencies toward "male-bashing." Interestingly, Maltby and Day also found that women who scored high in femininity and self-esteem also reported less positive attitudes about men's family roles.

When considered in the context of socially constructed gender identities, Matby and Day's findings also provide an indirect and hypothetical explanation of single mother's attitudes toward absent fathers. As Choi, Henshaw, Baker, and Tree (2005) have posited, "marriage and motherhood are central to femininity and are, therefore, a resource for women in constructing feminine identities" (169). It can be hypothesized that regardless of the context of the breakup, women who place high value on being feminine and who perceive that being in an intact relationship (preferably marriage) was the ideal environment for mothering may experience not only feelings of emotional rejection, but also ideological rejection, from the absent father. Moreover, if the previous relationship with their ex-spouse/partner was fraught with conflict or if the union was disrupted unexpectedly, women may internalize a sense of shame and inferiority for not being able to maintain the proper environment for raising children. In this light, our culture often views single mothers from two dominate approaches, the deficit perspective that assumes single mothers' incapacity to manage this challenge, and the idealization perspective that assumes that a "heroic" single mother is all that children need. Women who subscribe to either perspective are drawn into an environment that presumes a certain level of emotional fortitude and parenting prowess. In order for women to regain a sense of control over their lives and their roles as parents, they may focus on the negative aspects of their previous relationship and the negative attributes of their former spouses/partners—both of which can affect their children's attitudes toward their father and toward men in general.

THEORETICAL FRAMEWORK

Two theories have special promise for guiding our thinking about the topic of single mothers raising children with absent fathers. Symbolic interactionism sheds light on the social construction of mothering and fathering in family life (Mead 1967; LaRossa and Reitzes 1993) while family systems theory focuses on family process (Bowen 1976; Minuchin 1974).

A symbolic interactionist perspective on the family begins with the idea that shared meanings about family roles are constructed through every conversation and interaction inside the family and between family members and the outside world. People develop notions of what is normative and counternormative about their families, and respond with satisfaction or dissatisfaction based on these expectations. When there is dissonance between normative expectations and lived reality, family members often do a form of "accounting" to explain or justify the discrepancy and minimize dissatisfaction (LaRossa and Reitzes 1993).

Applied to single mother/father absent families, symbolic interactionism focuses our attention on conversations within the family, especially between mothers and children, about the meaning of the father's absence in light of social norms for father presence. How do mothers explain the unfilled father role in the family in light of the fact that the children know they have a father and expect that he should be around? Do mothers emphasize the value and importance of the fathers even though this particular father is not fulfilling the role? Do they minimize the father role in order to prevent dissonance between expectations and reality in themselves and their children?

How do mothers explain their own role as single mothers without a father present? Do they emphasize the deficits ("I'm just a single mother"), do they swing the other way by indicating that single mothers like them do not need a male partner to raise children, or do they value the father role while stressing that they are capable of doing a good job of raising their children without a father present?

Mother messages not only influence children here and now, but they also socialize children for future roles and relationships. Of course, this socialization does not occur in a social vacuum. Mothers and children are influenced by messages about fathers and mothers in mainstream society and in their own subculture. A mother in a community with many absent fathers may be more likely to believe and communicate a message that de-emphasizes the importance of fathers. For their part, children may have special dissonance between their own hurt and longing for their father on the one hand, and social messages saying that fathers should not be relied on.

Family systems theory illuminates everyday family interactions in single mother/family absent families and, because it is associated with family therapy, has application to what mothers can do to raise children with male-positive attitudes. A particularly useful concept is that of triangles, particularly the mother-father-child triangle (Minuchin 1974; Haley 1976). Even when the father is absent, he is part of this triangle—but he cannot speak for himself and interpret his own behavior. Thus the mother's framing of the father's past and current actions has disproportionate influence on the child's perceptions. However, the child is not just a passive recipient of maternal influence; children have their own internal relationship with the father, often in the form of invisible loyalties (Boszormenyi-Nagy and Spark 1973). Many children feel a loyalty connection to an absent parent; they want to believe that he is a good person and cares for them. Although most children will feel more positive toward a present mother than toward an absent father, these emotional alliances can shift over time as children form a bond with their father.

The family systems concept of boundaries is also important for understanding single mother/father absent families. Boundaries regulate closeness and distance between family members and between subsystems in the family (Minuchin 1974). Enmeshed boundaries lead to lack of autonomy, while disengaged boundaries lead to lack of support. Ideally the mother supports the autonomy of her children in having their own feelings and attitudes about their father, as well as a relationship with him if he re-emerges in their lives. From this perspective, mothers who try to turn their children against their fathers are invading the children's boundaries, harming them and complicating their own maternal relationship with the children. Using different language than that of boundaries, Bowen (1976) stressed differentiation of self in family life, where each member can take an "I" position in complex, emotional family dynamics. The challenge for mothers is to manage their own attitudes and feelings about the father while allowing their children to have their own attitudes and feelings. Of course, this is hard to do when the mother feels deserted and betrayed by her ex-partner, especially if he was abusive.

Finally, family systems theory stresses the importance of adaptability in families: Even in the presence of serious challenges, families can be resilient if they are flexible in adapting their internal roles and external relationships to meet their needs. Thus, single mothers are more apt to succeed in raising healthy children when they adjust to where their children are emotionally vis-à-vis the absent father at different developmental phases, and when they utilize extended family and other social networks to bring loving men into the lives of their children.

Together symbolic interactionism and family systems theory provide a framework for the applied recommendations in the next section, and for future research directions.

WHAT SINGLE MOTHERS CAN DO TO RAISE CHILDREN WITH MALE-POSITIVE ATTITUDES

With the theory and research covered in this chapter as a backdrop, we use our clinical and community-based experiences with father-absent, single mother families to offer specific ideas for how single mothers can raise children with male-positive attitudes. For present purposes, we define male-positive attitudes as generalized beliefs that men are good and trustworthy unless their individual behavior suggests otherwise. The opposite of male-positive attitudes would be a generalized suspicion of the character and intentions of men prior to knowing them and evaluating their individual actions. We divide our proposals into two sections: strategies and messages that mothers can employ directly with their children, and the influence mothers can have through relationships with men in their lives, including romantic partners, friends, and family.

MESSAGES TO CHILDREN

Symbolic interactionism directs our attention to the messages that mothers give their children about their father and about other men. It can be exceedingly difficult for a mother to separate her feelings of anger and resentment toward her ex-partner and the needs of her children for a positive, or at least neutral, attitude toward him. The opportunities for undermining the child's images of the father are especially present when a single mother is stressed by lack of resources, when a son is having behavioral problems that remind her of the father, when the child asks about the father, or when there are new men with whom to compare the father. Following are ways that mothers can manage their feelings and still promote the well-being of their children by promoting male-positive attitudes. We frame the headings as we would in a presentation to mothers.

1. *Say something good about the father for your child to hold onto.* Because children need to have something to admire about their parents, they are apt to cling to anything positive they hear about a missing parent. One adult whose father was missing in her childhood life told us that she cherished the handful of times that her often-critical mother referred to her father as being a charming, socially confident man who drew people to him. A mother who at one time was attracted to a man she had a child with can usually come up with at least one good thing to say about him, and it can mean a lot to a child whose sense of self is intertwined with an image of the father.

2. *Say nothing bad about him.* This is the advice given by every professional working in the divorce field, and the leading message in every self-help book for parents after a break up. It is also very hard to do, especially when the father has behaved irresponsibly, as is often the case when he has chosen to abandon his children or is incarcerated and not able to be with his children. Mothers can try to keep in mind that the children already feel badly about their father's absence. The mother's criticism only makes it harder. We sometimes suggest to mothers that they take the long view that influencing their children's attitudes in this way may rebound someday if the child decides that dad was a good guy after all and that mother had undermined him. It is important to appeal to a mother's self interest in this area: There is nothing to be gained and much to be lost for her as well as her children if she says negative things about her ex and their father.

3. *Acknowledge his absence and the child's feelings.* If the mother avoids criticism and offers something positive about the father, there is an opportunity to have deeper conversations at key moments when the child opens up with feelings of loss, confusion, or anger. It is important that the mother validate the child's feelings. Trying to "cover" for the absent father is likely to backfire: as in "I'm sure your father would be here if he could." (However, this may be true if he is incarcerated and has expressed these feelings to the mother.) The mother can simply say, "I know it's hard to not have your daddy in your life, and it's okay that you get sad and mad some times."

4. *Say you don't know why he's absent.* When a child asks why the father is not involved, and the answer is not factual (like death or incarceration), it is best for the mother to not try to offer an explanation. For one thing, her explanation is likely to be negative and hurtful to the child, as in "He doesn't care. He's irresponsible." No one really knows why a father (or mother) walks away from his children, and no one can speak for him. Thus, the safest route is to just say with compassion, "I just don't know." Not giving a reason also prevents the future scenario when the father reconnects with his children and gives a more benign explanation for his absence, leaving the children wondering if the mother had been sabotaging their relationship with their father.

5. *Emphasize that the absence is not the child's fault.* Feeling responsible for a parent's abandonment is common among young children who want to see their parent as good and therefore see themselves as either driving away the parent or as not lovable enough to keep them in their lives. If a child expresses these beliefs or feelings, nearly every mother knows to say it is not true. (It is important not to follow this up with a put-down of the father, as in, "It's not your fault that your father only cares about himself.") But because these feelings are so shameful for children, they often will not express them directly. Therefore, when the child talks about the father's absence, a mother might broach the issue gently by saying that some children come up with the idea that it is their fault that their daddy is not around—do you ever feel that way? Whether or not the children says yes to this question, the mother can go on to say that when a parent leaves it is not because of what a child has done, and that in fact this particular child is wonderful and lovable.

6. *Tell the relationship story in a way that does not make the father a bad guy.* A group of men whose fathers were absent told us how much they would like to know the story of their parents' relationship. How did they meet?

Where they ever in love? Did they have good times together? Were they happy to be together when I was born? How did they come to break up? Did they both want to end the relationship? These men said it was hard to know who they were without knowing the story of their parents' relationship, good and bad. Clearly, some of these questions are not suitable for children, but it can be valuable for a mother to share with young children something good about the relationship, perhaps in the context of saying something positive about the father. ("He was handsome and fun, and we had really good times together when we were a new couple.") With adolescents and young adults who know something about romantic relationships, the mother can offer a nonblaming perspective on the ending of this pivotal relationship in the lives of their children. There might be lessons to be passed on, such as "We fell in love quickly and had you too young, before we really were grown up."

7. *If the father is minimally or inconsistently involved:*

- Be supportive of his involvement and help the child look forward to it rather than comment on the infrequency or inconsistency. The children will already have painful feelings about this situation without the mother adding commentary. It is a big mistake to punish the inconsistent father by ending his contact with the children. Withholding the children from the father in order to protect them from his inconsistency sets up the mother to be the scapegoat in the future if the father re-enters their lives more responsibly and the children become aware of mother's role in the gap in the relationship.

- Acknowledge all the child's feelings about the father, the good and bad. Children with in-and-out fathers may have more overtly negative feelings than children with absent fathers because they experience emotional whiplash. They need acknowledgment for all of their feelings.

- Acknowledge the father's inconsistency. When it is clear what is going on (dad says he will show up and does not), the mother can simply acknowledge the truth of his behavioral pattern—that dad sometimes promises things he does not follow through on. However, it is important not to use more global labels such as irresponsible or selfish.

- Let children know it is not their fault. Again, even more than with the absent father, children may think that dad did not show up for a particular visit because of how the child acted the last time. Or that he neglected a birthday present this year because the child did not deserve one.

MESSAGES ABOUT OTHER MEN

Socialization of attitudes about men occurs not just through messages about children's own fathers; it occurs through what mothers (and others) say about other men and about men as a group. Some of these messages are ones that mothers deliver directly to children and others the children overhear their mothers say as the children go about their play or eating. Following are strategies mothers might use to ensure that their messages are male-positive:

1. *Look for opportunities to be positive about other men.* This may be especially important when the mother struggles to be positive about the father himself. The men she praises might be in her family or in a faith community or elsewhere in the community—even the news.

2. *Talk about the qualities of good men in general.* There can be times to refer to what good men are like as a group, for example, responsible, caring, hard-working, and respectful toward women. This can even be done in the midst of a criticism of one type of man, for example, those who hurt women: A real man does not hit women; the good men in this world have great respect for women.

3. *Avoid general put-downs of men.* This is the converse of saying good things about men in general. Some of the worst lines that single mothers deliver to their children, with special harm to boys, are ones that disparage the whole class of men: men are pigs, men are like children, men are irresponsible, and men are sexually promiscuous.

4. *Actively contradict negative stereotypes.* There are so many male-negative stereotypes in the lives of children that it is important for mothers to be intentional about counteracting them. She can say that it is a bad thing to speak ill of all men, and that she knows men who do not fit the stereotype. Of course, this has to be authentic: Children will eventually sense that mom is faking it. A mother who cannot break through the stereotypes and say positive things about men needs more exposure to good men. See the following for ideas.

MOTHERS' RELATIONSHIPS WITH MEN

Children learn not just from what mothers say but from what they do, and in particular, how they form and manage relationships with men.

We distinguish between men who are romantic partners and those who are family members and friends.

INTIMATE MEN

1. *Choose men for yourself and your children.* Many adults divide their world into parental relationships and romantic relationships, but it is clear that these two domains overlap. Children are greatly impacted by the men who become romantic partners to their mothers, especially when they men move into the household and become quasi-stepfathers. Many children with absent fathers have no recollection of their parents' relationship; instead, their role models are their mothers' current romantic relationships. The same is true of male image: It is the close-in men who are likely to count. Thus, the mother is choosing men for her children and not just herself.

2. *Choose men who respect and care for you and your children.* A number of men we know feel pain and anger about how the men their mother brought into their lives as children treated the mothers poorly, sometimes abusively, and were negative father figures for the children. As one thirty-five-year-old man told us, "My mom's boyfriends told me to sow my wild oats as a teenager, and I lost my teen years. I can't help but think that my own father, if he had been around, would not have told me to sow my wild oats." A good man, while having faults like anyone else, has fundamental respect and caring for the mother and her children. For example, he will not speak poorly of the children's father because he knows that this will hurt the children.

3. *Choose men willing to share you with the children and who can love women and children at the same time.* Another variation on the theme of this section is that some men are good romantic partners but ignore the children. They are there for the woman, for understandable reasons, and try to pull her away from the children. They may have busy lives with jobs and with involvement with their own children, and they want their romantic partner to themselves. This is a common challenge of stepfamily life: Often even good partners care for the mother but just tolerate her children. Children need to see that a "package deal" is possible in the lives of men: to love the woman and the children.

4. *Tell the children the good reasons why you chose this man.* This is an opportunity to teach children what makes for a good man in a relationship with a woman and her children. By being explicit about his good qualities

as a partner, she is telling her sons how to be in relationships with women and children, and her daughter what to look for in men. Saying "he's hot" or "he treats me fine" is what she might tell her girlfriends, but she would probably not stress this with her children. If a woman cannot "brag" to her children about other qualities in the man she is getting involved with, this may not be the right relationship.

FRIENDS AND FAMILY

1. *Have good men active in your life who are not romantic partners.* A mother cannot choose her family members, but there are probably some men who she would consider responsible men who might become involved with her and her children. She can also deliberately seek out positive relationships with men at a faith community, at work, or in other venues. It is important to show children long-term, positive relationships with men that are not sexual and that do not end in breakups. And it is important to have boys involved with men they can emulate, particularly if their father is not in their lives.

2. *Involve men in family rituals.* One of the ways that men from family and friendship groups can become deeply involved in the lives of children is by being part of central family rituals such as birthdays and holidays, along with children's special school events. An intentional community in Minneapolis called the Extended Family Network (http://extendedfamilynetwork. org) makes special efforts to involve men in the rituals of single mother families. When there are crises with the children, these men already have a relationship and can help.

3. *Give children the message "we are valued by men."* It may not be possible to tell children that they are valued by their father (if his behavior is not saying that), but it is possible, through deep relationships with men in family and community, to let children know that there are men in this world who cherish them and their family. This may be the ultimate male-positive message that mothers can give their children.

CONCLUSION

We are struck with the difficulty of the task that single mothers have in raising children with male-positive attitudes, given how little support there appears to be in most communities and in mainstream culture for this approach. Even professional communities have been mostly silent on the value of raising children with male-positive attitudes, let alone advice for what mothers can actually do about this challenge. Perhaps by breaking the silence and offering specific strategies for mothers to use, we can begin a broader dialogue. The dialogue among researchers can begin with qualitative investigations of how single mothers feel about men in general and how these feelings and beliefs are influenced by the contextual factors discussed in this chapter, especially how a couple's relationship ended and the mother's previous experiences with important men in her life. It would be valuable to know how some women retain male-positive attitudes in the face of injurious male behavior while others become negative toward all men. Subsequent quantitative research could focus on the development of assessment tools to examine single mothers' and children's generalized beliefs about the trustworthiness of men in relationships with women and children, and the application of these tools to representative samples of single mothers and their children.

The dialogue among practitioners could take the form of developing sensitive ways to explore this issue with single mothers and best practices for helping women to unpack, examine, and perhaps modify beliefs that are hurting them or their children. This work would require special sensitivity to the real damage that many single mothers have experienced in their relationships with men. It would also challenge professionals to confront whether male negative attitudes have crept into their own work, especially when working with women who have been abused or abandoned by men.

At the level of cultural change, the dialogue could involve public leaders and everyday citizens examining messages in popular culture about the trustworthiness of men in relationships with women and children. This dialogue will have to go beyond pointing out the deficits of men ("deadbeat" and "runaway" dads) and general exhortations for fathers to be responsible for their children, to also include messages about what fathers are capable of giving to women and children, no matter what has happened in the father's own life history. President Barack Obama has a compelling story to tell here, and may provide the needed leadership. This cultural dialogue must confront problems in male-female relationships, especially in low-income communities across racial and ethnic groups, without which the general message "be a good dad" is likely to be ineffective. An initiative called the Citizen Father Project among single, mostly African-American fathers in Minneapolis has made a start in this direction by honestly confronting past failures of many men and asserting the fundamental goodness and strength of men as partners, husbands, and fathers. After a year of examining the challenge facing unmarried fathers in their community, the group (which Doherty has helped to launch) is doing outreach presentations to fathers in the community, fathers in jail, mothers who are partnered with men in jail, and youth in schools. Perhaps community conversations like these, all of them intense and inspiring, are a good place to begin learning how single mothers can raise children who value and trust men, and how we can raise up a generation of men to become active fathers and committed life partners with women—so that fewer mothers are faced with the extraordinary challenge we have discussed in this chapter.

REFERENCES

Amato, P. R. and J. G. Gilbreth. 1999. "Nonresident Fathers and Children's Well-Being: A Meta-Analysis." *Journal of Marriage and Family* 61:557–573.

Anderson, E. R., S. M. Greene, L. Walker, C. A. Malerba, M. S. Forgatch, and D. S. DeGarmo. 2004. "Ready to Take a Chance Again: Transitions Into Dating Among Divorced Parents." *Journal of Divorce & Remarriage* 40(3/4):61–75.

Boszormenyi-Nagy, I. and G. Spark. 1973. *Invisible Loyalties*. New York: Harper and Row.

Bowen, M. 1976. "Theory in the Practice of Psychotherapy." In *Family Therapy*, ed. P. Guerin. New York: Gardner.

Choi, P., C. Henshaw, S. Baker, and J. Tree. 2005. "Supermum, Superwife, Super-everything: Performing Femininity in the Transition to Motherhood." *Journal of Reproductive and Infant Psychology* 23(2):167–180.

Doherty, W. J., E. F. Kouneski, and M. F. Erickson. 1998. "Responsible Fathering: An Overview and Conceptual Framework." *Journal of Marriage and Family* 60: 277–292.

Dunn, J., H. Cheng, T. G. O'Connor, and L. Bridges. 2004. "Children's Perspectives on Their Relationships with Their Nonresident Fathers: Influences, Outcomes and Implications." *Journal of Child Psychology & Psychiatry* 45(3):553–566.

Dye, J. L. 2008. "Fertility of American Women: 2006." *Current Population Reports* 20–558. U.S. Census Bureau.

Fabricius, W. V. and L. J. Luecken. 2007. "Postdivorce Living Arrangements, Parent Conflict, and Long-Term Physical Health Correlates for Children of Divorce." *Journal of Family Psychology* 21(2):195–205.

Gadsden, V. L. and H. M. Hall. 1999. "Intergenerational Learning: A Review of the Literature." Accessed August 15, 2008. www.ncoff.gse.upenn.edu/litrev/iglr.htm.

Haley. J. 1976. *Problem-Solving Therapy*. San Francisco: Jossey-Bass.

Hetherington, E. M. and M. M. Stanley-Hagan. 1997. "The Effects of Divorce on Fathers and Their Children." In *The Role of the Father in Child Development*, ed. M. E. Lamb, 191–211. New York: John Wiley.

LaRossa, R. and D. Reitzes. 1993. "Symbolic Interactionism." In *Sourcebook of Family Theories and Methods*, ed. P. B. Boss, W. J. Doherty, R. LaRossa, W. R. Scum, and S. K. Steinmetz, 135–163. New York: Plenum.

Maltby, J. and L. Day. 2001. "Psychological Correlates of Attitudes Toward Men." *The Journal of Psychology* 135(3):335–351.

Matta, D. S. and C. Knudson-Martin. 2006. "Father Responsivity: Couple Processes and the Coconstruction of Fatherhood." *Family Process* 45(1):19–37.

McLanahan, S. S. and G. Sandefur. 1994. *Growing Up with a Single Parent*. Cambridge, MA: Harvard University.

Mead, G. H. 1967. *Man, Self, and Society*. Chicago: University of Chicago.

Scott, M. E., A. Booth, V. King, and D. R. Johnson. 2007. "Postdivorce Father-Adolescent Closeness." *Journal of Marriage and Family* 69:1194–1209.

Stephan, C. W., W. G. Stephan, K. M. Demitrakis, A. M. Yamada, and D. L. Clason. 2000. "Women's Attitudes Toward Men: An Integrated Threat Theory Approach." *Psychology of Women Quarterly* 24:63–73.

Wenk, D., C. L. Hardesty, C. S. Morgan, and S. L. Blair. 1994. "The Influence of Parental Involvement on the Well-Being of Sons and Daughters." *Journal of Marriage and Family* 56(1):229–234.

LIST OF CONTRIBUTORS

DAVID F. BJORKLUND is a professor of psychology at Florida Atlantic University.

MARC H. BORNSTEIN is senior investigator and head of child and family research at the Eunice Kennedy Shriver National Institute of Child Health and Human Development.

SHONDA CRAFT is an assistant professor in the Department of Family Social Science at the University of Minnesota.

JEFFREY DEW is an assistant professor of family, consumer, and human development at Utah State University.

WILLIAM DOHERTY is a professor in the Department of Family Social Science and director of the Citizen Professional Center at the University of Minnesota.

DAVID J. EGGEBEEN is an associate professor of human development and sociology at Penn State University.

CATHERINE L. FRANSSEN served as a postdoctoral research fellow at the Randolph-Macon neuroscience laboratory.

SCOTT HALTZMAN, a distinguished fellow of the American Psychiatric Association, is the medical director of NRI Community Services in Woonsocket, Rhode Island.

ASHLEY C. KING is a doctoral student at the University of Arizona, where she studies human development from a life history theoretical perspective, focusing on risky adolescent behavior.

KATHLEEN KOVNER KLINE, a member of the medical school faculty of the University of Pennsylvania, also serves as chief medical officer of the Consortium, a community mental health organization in Philadelphia.

KELLY G. LAMBERT is the Macon and Joan Brock Professor of Psychology at Randolph-Macon College.

ROB PALKOVITZ is a professor of human development and family studies at the University of Delaware.

ROSS D. PARKE is Distinguished Professor (Emeritus) of psychology and the director of the Center for Family Studies at the University of California, Riverside.

CHARLES T. SNOWDON is the Hilldale Professor of Psychology and Zoology at the University of Wisconsin at Madison.

BRIAN STAFFORD is an associate professor of psychiatry at the University of Colorado at Denver.

AYELET TALMI is an assistant professor of psychiatry and associate director of the Irving Harris Program in Child Development and Infant Mental Health at the University of Colorado at Denver.

W. BRADFORD WILCOX is director of the National Marriage Project and an associate professor of sociology at the University of Virginia.

INDEX

absent fathers, effect on children, 308. *See also* single mothers
acculturation, and parenting, 146
adaptability, in family systems theory, 328
adaptation to peers, influence of fathers on, 131–132
Add Health (National Longitudinal Study of Adolescent Health): data and methods, 255–260; overview, 11–12; results, 260–266
additive parental contributions, 11–12, 251, 266
adolescents: emotional expression and regulation, and gendered parenting, 227–228; families with, 175–177; gender development, 101–102, 108; quality of maternal and paternal involvement, 128
—fathers and well-being of: analytic strategy, 260; data and methods, 255–260; discussion, 266–268; overview, 11–12, 249–251, 308; parent variables, 256–259; results, 260–266; sociological perspective on fatherhood, 251–255
affect of fathers, influence on children, 132

African-Americans: impact of presence of parents on adolescents, 176–177; intracultural variation in parenting, 144–145
age: child, and cultural socialization about gender, 105; developmental time and gender development, 107–108; mother and child, and maternal care, 70; of parent, as social determinant of parenting behavior, 137–138
aggression, by cooperatively breeding primates, 51–52
agility, and maternal mammalian brain, 31
Aka pygmies, 76, 99, 144
alcohol abuse: genetic and environmental risk factors, 203–204; by single-parents, 181
alien pups, male California deer mouse responses to, 33–34
Allen, J., 138
Allman, John, 77–78
alloparenting, 33–34, 35. *See also* cooperatively breeding primates; stepfamilies
Amato, P., 130, 254
Amato, P. R., 324